MORE

HTML FOR DUMMIES®

MORE

HTML FOR DUMMIES®

by Ed Tittel and Steve James

IDG Books Worldwide, Inc.
An International Data Group Company

Foster City, CA ♦ Chicago, IL ♦ Indianapolis, IN ♦ Braintree, MA ♦ Southlake, TX

MORE HTML For Dummies®

Published by
IDG Books Worldwide, Inc.
An International Data Group Company
919 E. Hillsdale Blvd.
Suite 400
Foster City, CA 94404

Library of Congress Catalog Card No.: 96-76451

ISBN: 1-56884-996-6

Printed in the United States of America

10 9 8 7 6 5 4 3 2 1

1A/TQ/QV/ZW/IN

Distributed in the United States by IDG Books Worldwide, Inc.

Distributed by Macmillan Canada for Canada; by Computer and Technical Books for the Caribbean Basin; by Contemporanea de Ediciones for Venezuela; by Distribuidora Cuspide for Argentina; by CITEC for Brazil; by Ediciones ZETA S.C.R. Ltda. for Peru; by Editorial Limusa SA for Mexico; by Transworld Publishers Limited in the United Kingdom and Europe; by Al-Maiman Publishers & Distributors for Saudi Arabia; by Simron Pty. Ltd. for South Africa; by IDG Communications (HK) Ltd. for Hong Kong; by Toppan Company Ltd. for Japan; by Addison Wesley Publishing Company for Korea; by Longman Singapore Publishers Ltd. for Singapore, Malaysia, Thailand, and Indonesia; by Unalis Corporation for Taiwan; by WS Computer Publishing Company, Inc. for the Philippines; by WoodsLane Pty. Ltd. for Australia; by WoodsLane Enterprises Ltd. for New Zealand.

For general information on IDG Books Worldwide's books in the U.S., please call our Consumer Customer Service department at 800-762-2974. For reseller information, including discounts and premium sales, please call our Reseller Customer Service department at 800-434-3422.

For information on where to purchase IDG Books Worldwide's books outside the U.S., contact IDG Books Worldwide at 415-655-3021 or fax 415-655-3295.

For information on translations, contact Marc Jeffrey Mikulich, Director, Foreign & Subsidiary Rights, at IDG Books Worldwide, 415-655-3018 or fax 415-655-3295.

For sales inquiries and special prices for bulk quantities, write to the address above or call IDG Books Worldwide at 415-655-3200.

For information on using IDG Books Worldwide's books in the classroom, or ordering examination copies, contact the Education Office at 800-434-2086 or fax 817-251-8174.

For authorization to photocopy items for corporate, personal, or educational use, please contact Copyright Clearance Center, 222 Rosewood Drive, Danvers, MA 01923, or fax 508-750-4470.

 is a trademark under exclusive license to IDG Books Worldwide, Inc., from International Data Group, Inc.

About the Authors

Ed Tittel

Ed Tittel is the coauthor of numerous books about computing and the World Wide Web, including *The Foundations of World Wide Web Programming with HTML and CGI* and *Web Programming Secrets with HTML, CGI, and Perl* (both books' authors also include Mark Gaither, Mike Erwin, and Sebastian Hassinger). These days, Ed's aiming his efforts at Internet programming-related topics, both as a writer and as a member of the NetWorld + Interop program committee.

Ed has been a regular contributor to the trade press since 1987, and has written over 200 articles for a variety of publications, including *Computerworld, InfoWorld, I-Way, NetGuide,* and *Windows NT* magazine. He's a columnist and contributing editor at Windows NT, and works for several online 'zines, including *WebSite, Javaworld,* and *Webster.*

Contact Ed at `etittel@zilker.net`, or visit his Web site at `http://www.lanw.com`.

Steve James

Stephen Nelson James is the coauthor (with Ed Tittel) of the best-selling *HTML For Dummies,* now in its 2nd edition, *ISDN Networking Essentials,* and *Computer Telephony for Home and Small Offices.* He has also authored numerous computer related magazine articles, software user's manuals, and WWW pages.

Steve is a former environmental biologist and ex-president/CEO of FYI, Inc., a software development company. When he's not writing or surfing the Net, you can find him out on the roads in the hills around Austin doing what he really loves to do, riding his bicycle.

Contact Steve at `snjames@wetlands.com`.

Welcome to the world of IDG Books Worldwide.

IDG Books Worldwide, Inc., is a subsidiary of International Data Group, the world's largest publisher of computer-related information and the leading global provider of information services on information technology. IDG was founded more than 25 years ago and now employs more than 7,700 people worldwide. IDG publishes more than 250 computer publications in 67 countries (see listing below). More than 70 million people read one or more IDG publications each month.

Launched in 1990, IDG Books Worldwide is today the #1 publisher of best-selling computer books in the United States. We are proud to have received 8 awards from the Computer Press Association in recognition of editorial excellence and three from Computer Currents' First Annual Readers' Choice Awards, and our best-selling *...For Dummies®* series has more than 19 million copies in print with translations in 28 languages. IDG Books Worldwide, through a joint venture with IDG's Hi-Tech Beijing, became the first U.S. publisher to publish a computer book in the People's Republic of China. In record time, IDG Books Worldwide has become the first choice for millions of readers around the world who want to learn how to better manage their businesses.

Our mission is simple: Every one of our books is designed to bring extra value and skill-building instructions to the reader. Our books are written by experts who understand and care about our readers. The knowledge base of our editorial staff comes from years of experience in publishing, education, and journalism — experience which we use to produce books for the '90s. In short, we care about books, so we attract the best people. We devote special attention to details such as audience, interior design, use of icons, and illustrations. And because we use an efficient process of authoring, editing, and desktop publishing our books electronically, we can spend more time ensuring superior content and spend less time on the technicalities of making books.

You can count on our commitment to deliver high-quality books at competitive prices on topics you want to read about. At IDG Books Worldwide, we continue in the IDG tradition of delivering quality for more than 25 years. You'll find no better book on a subject than one from IDG Books Worldwide.

John J. Kilcullen

John Kilcullen
President and CEO
IDG Books Worldwide, Inc.

Authors' Acknowledgments

Our biggest thanks go to our readers, who helped make the first edition of *HTML For Dummies* such a howling success. Their feedback also helped us figure out what topics we needed to cover in a *MORE* book, and should make this one more useful than if it was based only on our ideas!

Ed Tittel: I'd like to thank my usual helpers in these projects — namely Dawn Rader, my project manager and copy editor extraordinaire, and James Michael Stewart, my Internet ace and bulldog deliverer of all things strange or off the beaten track. I'd also like to thank Charlie Scott, Claire Sanders, and Sebastian Hassinger for their roles in pulling together this book's materials. My special condolences to Charlie and his family for their recent loss. For myself, I'm still incredibly grateful to be working at home, doing what I love to do!

Steve James: First and foremost, a sincere thank-you to Ed Tittel for his continued inspiration and enthusiasm. This is our fifth book together and I'm looking forward to many more successful collaborations with Ed. As always, my eternal gratitude to my wonderful wife Trisha, my daughter Kelly, and my son Chris, for their understanding and support of my writing habit. And finally, a very sincere thank-you to all of you who purchased the first and second editions of *HTML For Dummies,* thereby encouraging IDG to ask us to write this book. Please continue to keep our e-mail filled with your great comments and suggestions.

Together, we want to thank the editorial staff at IDG Books Worldwide, especially Jennifer Ehrlich, who put up with our whining and moaning when we forgot a deadline, Leah Cameron and Susan Christopherson, our copy editors, Dennis Cox, our technical editor, and everybody else who had a hand in this at IDG that we didn't mention here.

Please feel free to contact either of us, care of IDG Books, IDG Books Worldwide, Inc., 919 East Hillsdale Blvd, Suite 400, Foster City, CA, 94404. Ed's e-mail address is etittel@zilker.net; Steve's is snjames@wetlands.com.

Publisher's Acknowledgments

We're proud of this book; send us your comments about it by using the Reader Response Card at the back of the book or by e-mailing us at feedback/dummies@idgbooks.com. Some of the people who helped bring this book to market include:

Acquisitions, Development, & Editorial

Project Editor: Jennifer Ehrlich

Assistant Acquisitions Editor: Gareth Hancock

Product Development Manager: Mary Bednarek

Copy Editors: Leah Cameron, Susan Christopherson

Technical Reviewer: Dennis Cox

Editorial Manager: Mary C. Corder

Editorial Assistant: Chris H. Collins

Special Help

Mary Goodwin

Production

Project Coordinator: Sherry Gomoll

Layout and Graphics: Brett Black, Linda Boyer, J. Tyler Connor, Cheryl Denski, Julie Forey, Todd Klemme, Anne Malani, Jane Martin, Kate Snell, Angela F. Hunckler, Brent Savage

Proofreaders: Arielle Carole Mennelle, Nancy Price, Michael Bolinger, Christine Meloy Beck, Carl Saff, Rob Springer, Karen York

Indexer: Liz Cunningham

General & Administrative

IDG Books Worldwide, Inc.: John Kilcullen, President & CEO; Steven Berkowitz, COO & Publisher

Dummies, Inc.: Milissa Koloski, Executive Vice President & Publisher

Dummies Technology Press & Dummies Editorial: Diane Graves Steele, Associate Publisher; Judith A. Taylor, Brand Manager; Myra Immell, Editorial Director

Dummies Trade Press: Kathleen A. Welton, Vice President & Publisher; Stacy S. Collins, Brand Manager

IDG Books Production for Dummies Press: Beth Jenkins, Production Director; Cindy L. Phipps, Supervisor of Project Coordination; Kathie S. Schnorr, Supervisor of Page Layout; Shelley Lea, Supervisor of Graphics and Design

Dummies Packaging & Book Design: Erin McDermitt, Packaging Coordinator; Kavish+Kavish, Cover Design

◆

The publisher would like to give special thanks to Patrick J. McGovern, without whom this book would not have been possible.

◆

Contents at a Glance

Cartoons at a Glance

By Rich Tennant • Fax: 508-546-7747 • E-mail: the5wave@tiac.net

"...the glitch is in a faulty tag in your page's footer."

page 125

"PUT DOWN 'CAUSES FOOT DAMAGE.'"

page 9

Re·al Pro·gram·mers

Real Programmers curse alot, but only at inanimate objects.

page 329

"Oops, I forgot the closing tag."

page 7

The embarrassment of Laptop Static Cling

page 243

Table of Contents

Introduction

. . . .

*O*nce again, welcome to the wild, wacky, and wonderful possibilities inherent in the World Wide Web. In *MORE HTML For Dummies,* we continue our exploration of the mysteries of the HyperText Markup Language (HTML) used to build Web pages, explore some weird and wonderful Web extensions technologies, and continue your initiation into the wildly burgeoning community of Web authors.

This book expands on the basic coverage of HTML that you find in the original *HTML For Dummies,* 2nd Edition, also from IDG Books Worldwide, Inc. We assume that you've explored the basics of HTML and are reasonably familiar with HTML 2.0, the current official standard version. In this book, we try to extend your knowledge base beyond the basics to include some important emerging HTML standards and proprietary extensions, along with the principles of Web site management. We also cover a number of really cool Web extension technologies that you can use to add considerable spice to your current Web sites and documents.

When we wrote this book, we took a straightforward approach to telling you about authoring documents for the World Wide Web. We tried to keep the amount of technobabble to a minimum and stuck with plain English as much as possible. Besides plain talk about hypertext, HTML, and the Web, we include lots of sample programs and tag-by-tag instructions for building your very own Web pages.

And we packaged all the examples and URLs referenced in the book; the package includes each HTML example in usable form and a number of other interesting widgets for your own documents. You can find these examples, references, and widgets at the *HTML For Dummies* Web site. In addition, you can download the magnificent and bedazzling source materials for the *HTML For Dummies,* 2nd edition, Web pages and a set of pages that we developed specifically for this book. You may find these newly developed pages to be a source of inspiration and raw material for your own uses! All you have to do is point your Web browser at the following URL:

HTML For Dummies, 2nd Edition or *MORE HTML For Dummies*

    http://www.dummies.com

When you browse these sites, check out the Menu pages for download information. Be sure to visit the Navigation instructions to understand how to find your way around these sites, too!

About This Book

Think of this book as a friendly, approachable guide to advanced HTML, Web site management, and extension technologies that you can incorporate into your Web. Although HTML isn't hard to learn, nor the associated technologies hard to use, remembering all the details involved in creating interesting Web pages and keeping track of your Web site can be challenging.

Sample topics you find in this book include the following:

- ✔ Understanding the standards-making process for HTML
- ✔ Designing and managing a small- to medium-sized Web site
- ✔ Using advanced HTML markup on your pages
- ✔ Employing cool Web extensions like Shockwave for Director, VRML, Java, and more
- ✔ Mastering the many aspects of Web publication and management

Although you might think that building Web pages requires years of training and advanced aesthetic capabilities, we hasten to point out that this just ain't so. If you can tell somebody how to drive from their house to yours, you can certainly build a Web document that does what you want it to. The purpose of this book isn't to turn you into a rocket scientist, but to show you all the design and technical elements you need to build a good-looking, readable Web page. We want *MORE HTML For Dummies* to give you the know-how and confidence to extend your Web beyond basic HTML and to explain the tools necessary to manage and maintain the results!

How to Use This Book

This book starts with a discussion of Web site management and maintenance. Then, it tells you about designing and building effective Web documents that exploit a bumper crop of new and emerging advanced markup and Web extensions, if that's what you want to do.

All HTML code appears in monospaced type like this:

```
<HEAD><TITLE>What's in a Title?</TITLE></HEAD>...
```

When you type in HTML tags or other related information, be sure to copy the information exactly as you see it between the angle brackets (< and >) because that's part of the magic that makes HTML work. In fact, we recommend that you download our materials and use them as a point of departure, instead of rekeying everything from scratch. Use the book to find out how to marshal and manage the content that makes your pages special and how to mix the elements of HTML with your own work.

Due to the margins in this book, some long lines of HTML markup or designations of World Wide Web sites (called URLs, for Uniform Resource Locators) may wrap to the next line. On your computer though, you see these wrapped lines as a single line of HTML or as a single URL, so don't insert a hard return when you see a wrapped line. Each instance of wrapped code displays as follows (without the margin note):

Code wraps —
do not insert
hard return
```
http://www.infomagic.austin.com/nexus/plexus/lexus/sexus
            this_is_a_deliberately_long.html
```

HTML doesn't care whether you type tag text in uppercase, lowercase, or both (except for character entities, which must be typed exactly as indicated in Chapter 8 of this book). In order for your own work to look like ours as much as possible, you should enter all HTML tag text in uppercase only.

Assume = Makes an A** Out of U & Me

They say that making assumptions makes a fool out of the person who's making them and the person who's the subject of those assumptions. Nevertheless, we're going to make a few assumptions about you, our gentle reader:

- ✔ You can turn your computer on and off.
- ✔ You know how to use a mouse and a keyboard.
- ✔ You want to build your own Web pages for fun, profit, or because it's part of your job.
- ✔ That you understand the basics of HTML markup in general and are reasonably familiar with HTML 2.0 markup in particular. (If this ain't so, don't fret — just rush right out and buy our companion volume *HTML For Dummies*, 2nd Edition, where you can find everything you need to come up to speed.)

In addition, we assume you already have a working connection to the Internet and one of the many fine Web browsers available by hook, crook, or download from that selfsame Internet. You don't need to be a master logician or a wizard in the arcane arts of programming, nor do you need a Ph.D in computer science. You don't even need a detailed sense of what's going on in the innards of your computer to deal with the material in this book.

If you understand the basic components of an HTML document and can tell a `<BODY>` from a `<HEAD>`, you can build and deploy your own documents on the World Wide Web. If you have an imagination and the ability to communicate what's important to you, you've already mastered the key ingredients necessary to build useful, attractive Web pages. The rest is details, and we help you with those!

How This Book Is Organized

This book contains four major parts. Each part contains three or more chapters, and each chapter contains several modular sections. Any time you need help or information, just pick up the book and start anywhere you feel like or use the Table of Contents and Index to look up specific topics or keywords.

Following is a breakdown of the four parts and the contents of each one:

Part I: Web Site Management

Part I covers the ins and outs of understanding and managing a coherent collection of Web documents and materials that we refer to as a *Web site*. We start off with a tour of a typical site (usually distinguished by its own unique *Uniform Resource Locator*, URL) and its components. And we discuss the virtues of planning and organization. In the five chapters that follow, we cover the basics of administering a Web site, describe a plethora of tools to manage your site and its materials, and document what's involved in managing information via the Web (what we call *the Web publication process*).

We conclude this section with a rumination on where the Web is going, from an administrative perspective, and review some interesting tools and systems to bring Web sites up and keep them running. The information in Part I gives you a good appreciation of the routine elements in managing a Web site and a keen understanding of the tools and techniques you can use to maximize your labors.

Part II: Advanced HTML Markup

HTML mixes ordinary text with special strings of characters, called *markup,* that instruct browsers how to display HTML documents. In this part of the book, you discover new and advanced HTML capabilities that are under development within the standards organizations and within browsers like Netscape Navigator and Microsoft Internet Explorer. We cover HTML tables, frames, math notation, style sheets, and more. The descriptions in Part II help you to appreciate what's going on behind the most interesting pages on the Web and even to build some for yourself!

Part III: Beyond HTML: Cool Web Extensions

Part III examines a number of new technologies available to extend your Web's capabilities well beyond those delivered by vanilla HTML alone. We start out with a discussion of extensions: What they are, how they work, and how best to use them. Next, we cover Macromedia's fascinating Shockwave for Director technology, the Virtual Reality Modeling Language (VRML) that can be used to create three-dimensional *virtual worlds* on the Web, and we introduce Sun Microsystem's incredible Java programming language that promises to revolutionize what we can do with the Web. We conclude with a look at several text display engines available for use on the Web. These engines can deliver precisely formatted documents for viewing or printing, right from your very own browser.

Part IV: Shortcuts and Tips Galore

We use the concluding part of the book to sum up and distill the essence of what we've covered. Part IV helps you review the top do's and don'ts for Web site maintenance, rethink your views on advanced HTML markup, and review major points of Web extension technologies. Our goals for "Shortcuts and Tips Galore" are to revisit the most important ideas covered throughout the book and to give you a condensed and epitomized version to use as a reference at any time.

Icons Used in This Book

 This icon signals technical details that are informative and interesting, but not critical to writing HTML. Skip these if you want (but please, come back and read them later).

 This icon flags useful information that makes HTML markup, Web page design, or other important stuff even less complicated than you feared it might be.

 This icon points out information you shouldn't pass by — don't overlook these gentle reminders (the life you save could be your own).

 Be cautious when you see this icon. It warns you of things you shouldn't do; the bomb is meant to emphasize that the consequences of ignoring these bits of wisdom can be severe.

 The presence of this spiderweb symbol flags a reference to Web-based re-sources that you can go out and investigate further. You can also find all these references on the "Jump Pages" on the diskette that comes with this book!

Where to Go from Here

This is the part where you pick a direction and hit the road! *MORE HTML For Dummies* is a lot like the parable of the seven blind men and the elephant: Regardless of where you start out, you look at lots of different stuff as you prepare yourself to extend your Web pages and get a better grip on your Web site. Who cares if everybody else wonders what you're up to — we know that you're following your bliss onto the Web.

Enjoy!

The 5th Wave   By Rich Tennant

"Oops, I forgot the closing tag."

Part I

Web Site
Management

The 5th Wave   By Rich Tennant

VDT HEALTH HAZARDS
1. Eye strain
2. Headaches

"PUT DOWN 'CAUSES FOOT DAMAGE.'"

In this part . . .

Part I covers various topics related to setting up and catering to a Web site. Chapter 1 examines the anatomy of a typical Web site, pointing out noteworthy elements as it goes. Chapter 2 covers the server side of the equation, from hardware to operating systems and software. Chapter 3 tackles the whole process involved in delivering content via the Web (and living with that content over time). Chapter 4 covers an interesting collection of site management tools and techniques, while Chapter 5 examines the hardest-working programs in the Web business: those tireless crawlers and robots that follow hyperlinks for a living. In Chapter 6, we conclude Part I with a forward look at emerging trends in Web site management and publication technologies.

Chapter 1

What's in Your Web Site?

*Y*ou don't have to build your Web site the way coral polyps build a reef, by adding pieces randomly. You actually do have control over what goes where. Even if you're not running your own Web server software on your own computer, you can work closely with your Web service provider to give you control over what happens at your Web site.

Always remember that there's a difference between the Web server and your Web site. The Web server consists of the computer and software that make placing your HTML documents on the Internet possible, also enabling users to connect to your site to view your fantastic text, images, and other wonderful stuff.

Your Web site consists of all your HTML documents, image files, imagemap files, and custom-made CGI and other program files. If your Internet Service Provider (ISP) provides the Web server hardware and software, and all you do is upload your files to the site, you're paying that ISP to maintain a Web server. This works well for most individuals and small companies.

If you run your own Web server, may you have the brains of an Einstein, the patience of a Job, and the luck of the Irish. It wouldn't hurt to have a UNIX hardware/software technician/programmer chained to the computer, either!

Because this book is named *MORE HTML For Dummies,* not *Web Site Management For Professionals,* Part I discusses only those aspects of Web management that will help you understand what a Web site contains, as well as how to manage it. After you read this book, you will be able to manage the care and feeding of your Web site documents, as well as intelligently discuss higher-level

Web site issues with your service provider. I introduce you to the tools necessary to maintain your Web site, but I'm not going to show you how to set up and run a Web server.

Get to Know Your Web Server Administrator

Your Web server administrator can be your best friend when you need help with your Web site. Get to know him or her, and your life can be much easier. The administrator is the person at your ISP (or in your organization) who's in charge of the care and feeding of the Web server. Frequently, the Web administrator is a network guru who knows "everything" about the Web server's hardware and software. Usually, this person is happy to help you make better use of the resources available for your Web site, if you ask nicely.

Before you start questioning your Web administrator, you need to know some of the jargon and how a Web server fits into the big picture. Chapter 2 provides a slightly more detailed examination of a typical ISP's Web server.

The knowledge you gain from your Web administrator can give you a better understanding of the various platforms available for running Web server software. The following sections detail a few examples of each major kind.

Web server computer platforms

Say that you read this copy in an ad or a vendor's brochure: "You can run the Hype-It Web server on a 386-based PC with DOS 5.0." Some may consider this an old platform; others may consider it ancient. One thing is sure: If you're expecting more than a handful of visits per day or you want to use graphics on your Web pages, you'll need a faster computer!

Without going into the details of document transfer rates and connections per minute, suffice it to say you need at least a 486-based PC running at 66 MHz, or an equivalent Macintosh or UNIX workstation with a 500MB hard drive.

UNIX

More servers and related software tools are available for UNIX than for any other platforms and operating systems around. UNIX is still the best choice for a seriously large or fast Web server. On the other hand, you can run the inexpensive LINUX clone of UNIX on either a 486- or Pentium-based PC, or A/UX on a comparable Macintosh to handle up to 100 connection requests per minute. Thus, UNIX covers the whole spectrum from really cheap (and slow) to really fast (and expensive).

Macintosh

Quarterdeck and Apple have cut a deal to pre-install WebSTAR on Apple's Internet Server Solution, a PowerMac 6150/50 workgroup server. If you want to get up and running as quickly as possible, this is the deal for you. You can have this system up and running within a few minutes, or so they say. In any case, Chuck Shotten's WebSTAR server software on the appropriate Macintosh is probably the easiest solution for setting up your own Macintosh-based Web hardware and software. Don't scoff: The latest reports indicate that up to 10 percent of the Web servers on the Internet run on Macs!

Windows NT

Although not as well suited for heavy multitasking work as UNIX, Windows NT can do a credible job on a fast PC at a lower cost. If you're comfortable using Windows 3.1 or Windows 95, you can get Web server software for one of those systems. The superior performance of Windows NT and its greater number of available Web server packages makes it the system of choice in the Windows world. To get the best performance from a PC running Windows NT Web server, get a PC with the fastest processor, the most RAM, and the fastest hard disk controller and drives that you can afford (in that order).

Web server software

The majority of Web sites currently run on UNIX-based servers. The free servers — NCSA's HTTPd, W3C's HTTPd, and Apache — top the list. Netscape's Commerce and Communications servers round out the top five in the UNIX category, and are also the leaders in the Windows NT world. WebSTAR is far and away the Macintosh leader.

NCSA, W3C/CERN, and Apache

UNIX-based Web servers are highly efficient and the fastest of the lot. However, even though NCSA's HTTPd, W3C's HTTPd, and Apache are all free, they run under UNIX, which requires an administrator who is experienced in UNIX setup, configuration, and maintenance. This expertise can be costly. Sometimes, saving money on software costs you more for human resources (which are always the most expensive kind!).

Windows NT

Netscape's Commerce and Communications servers lead the pack, with Purveyor, WebSite, and WebSTAR NT/95 as the rest of that pack. Purveyor and WebSite are the only two *httpd* servers originally designed for Windows NT. The others were ported from UNIX or the Macintosh. For this reason, Purveyor and WebSite offer easier setup and generally run faster, too.

WebSTAR and MacHTTPd

MacHTTP and WebSTAR Mac are *the* Macintosh Web servers. Both are outstandingly easy to install and use. If you're a Mac fan and want an instant Web
server, you can purchase Apple's Internet Server Solution (a PowerMac 6150/50
server with WebSTAR pre-installed), take it out of the box, power it up, configure WebSTAR in a few minutes, and add your Web pages. It doesn't get any
easier than that!

How your Web site fits into the whole

Your Web site consists of your collection of HTML documents, images, CGI
scripts, and the like that you've copied onto your Web server. The Web server
software makes these documents (and other information) available to the
Internet, and thereby to your users under the aegis of the Hypertext Transfer
Protocol (HTTP), the foundation protocol for the Web.

If your Web site includes a large collection of information, it may be the only
site on your Web server. If your collection is smaller, your site may share that
computer with other sites run by multihosting Web server software. The same
computer may also deliver other Internet services, such as FTP, e-mail, news,
WAIS, or Gopher. Each of these Internet services requires its own server
software.

The software that runs on the various computers at the phone company, on the
Internet, at your ISP, on a Web server, and at a user's workstation all transmit
and receive information for display on a user's screen. All this computer
equipment, cabling, and telephone lines provide only the pipeline through
which the digital information must pass. We tell you more about how this all
works in Chapter 2.

Administrator's jargon and management tools

A Web site administrator must deal with the layout of the documents that make
up the site as they're displayed to the user. The administrator must also handle
the organization of the actual computer files that comprise the site, choose the
appropriate CGI scripts to use (and decide where they reside), and receive and
answer user feedback, among other things.

An administrator also needs to be familiar with a Web site's user access and
error log files and understand their contents. Becoming familiar with terms
such as *cgi-bin* and making decisions such as which directory to use in a
feedback script are part of learning to manage a Web site effectively.

Numerous tools and techniques are available to help you administer a Web site and run and manage a Web server. Chapters 2 through 5 explain what you need to know about Web tools and how to locate them.

Round Up the Usual Suspects!

Before you rush out on the Net and download a Web server package and a bunch of management tools, you really do need to determine what it is that you have to manage. Inventory the resources on your Web server. Find out everything you can about what's there. Answer the following questions: Where's it located? What does it do? Who can use it? How? When? Make sure you know everything about your Web site's files, too.

Inventory Web server resources

Ask your Web server administrator for a list of the back-end service programs available. These can be CGI scripts, actual C or C++ programs that can be called by your HTML documents, e-mail–related programs, hit or click-through counters (little programs that monitor Web page activity), and more. You can't use them if you don't know about them!

The availability of such programs varies with the type of Web server software in use and with your type of Web account. This goes double if you're paying for a Web account from an ISP.

Usually, personal accounts that permit Web pages provide only a few bells and whistles. They usually don't give you access to the `cgi-bin` directory for your CGI scripts, but some do provide access to the `mailto:` program. You probably have to purchase a more expensive business account to gain access to server-side use-counters and other, more complex programs.

Take stock of your Web site

Take inventory of your current Web site. Answer the following comprehensive list of questions:

- How many files are you using? What kind?
- What is your file structure (directories and filenames)? What CGIs are you using?
- Where are your files and programs located?
- Where do their outputs go?

- ✔ How much space do these files consume on the server's hard disk?
- ✔ How much growth space is available to you on the server?
- ✔ How much money will it cost to grow, both in terms of file space and user activity?
- ✔ How much of your time is available for Web administration tasks?
- ✔ How much time do you currently spend on Web administration tasks?

Answer all these questions in writing before you seriously attempt to expand your Web. With these questions answered, you're better prepared to take advantage of those Web management tools and techniques that are available to ease your burden.

Lotsa docs (It's not an M.D.'s convention)

All Web sites contain more documents than you ever thought possible. Just as your desk gathers piles of paper, Web sites gather files. Even a small site may have up to a hundred documents for an administrator to manage and maintain.

Your site inventory shows you what comprises your site, and it may surprise you. Plan to keep track of your files with some type of organized system, not just your memory. Remember, not only must you keep track of those files but you must keep track of their revision dates as well. That way, you can ensure that you always use the appropriate revision for a given file. We give you some tips on this later in the book.

Graphics galore

No matter how many HTML documents you have on your site, you always have lots of graphics around. Some graphics are common elements that occur on many pages; others are more unique or specific. Here's the list of graphics-related questions that you want to answer:

- ✔ What directory structure is used for graphics?
- ✔ Is there a vocabulary of graphical symbols in use?
- ✔ How big is an average icon? image? imagemap?

Remember that many graphic files are quite large, so a few go a long way. Most users still use 9,600 to 14,400 baud modems and don't appreciate encountering 100K images without fair warning (you also run out of hard disk space if you store too many of these). Understanding graphics structure, formats, and usage can greatly enhance your understanding of your Web site.

The supporting cast of applications . . .

Today, any well-equipped Web site includes several back-end service programs such as databases and e-mail and includes peripheral devices. Work closely with your Web server administrator and you, too, can do marvelous things by using only standard tools readily available at your site.

Marvelous miscellany

Imagemaps, map files, indexes, documentation, conversion programs, and all kinds of other interesting things live in Web sites. Look for filenames that don't end in .htm or .html and try to figure out what they're for. Learn to recognize map files, imagemaps, graphics, and CGIs or other programs. Then things get really interesting. Find out what else is around and figure out what those pieces can do. If you can't do it on your own, ask for help!

"Organized Web site" is not an oxymoron

At least *organized Web site* not in the same league as some of the more-often quoted examples of oxymorons. If you take a methodical approach and write everything down, you'll be pleasantly surprised at how easy it is to keep your site under control.

Where does your site live?

What's the URL for your site? If it's something like http://mysite.com, you may be using the same address as the actual Web server. You may be happier in the long run if you name it http://www.mysite.com and establish that as a domain name. Most folks expect the www part anyway — to let them know it's a Web site.

Are all your site's URLs relative, or do your pages use absolute URLs or the <BASE> tag? Either approach has pros and cons. Relative URLs make it easier to move your site, but absolute URLs make it easier for your users to download one of your pages, yet remain able to return to your home page by clicking on a link in the file.

If you use the <BASE> tag, remember to make appropriate changes in your Web pages should you ever move your site. Surrounding this tag with warning comment lines to point it out for future reference (and changes) is also a good idea.

Picture your directory/file structure as a tree

Can't you just see your Web's directory structure up there next to Charlie Brown's kite? No? Well, you're just not using your imagination, so get with it! The easiest way to arrange your files and directories is to make use of your file system's capabilities to organize files into directories or folders.

Keep your directory structure straightforward. Use obvious, self-descriptive directory names that relate to file categories (for example, `graphics`, `images`, `annual_report`, or `quarterly_earnings`). Be careful to copy the right files into the appropriate directories in the future. Keep an annotated list of files (and subdirectories) within each directory. Make sure that this list contains an explanation of the contents of each file, as well as the date and time the file was last revised.

You can't tell the territory without a map

Make a list of the links within each of your HTML documents. Distinguish between local (on-site) and remote (off-site) links. This list provides a map of your site, the way that users view it. The link map is a valuable tool that can help you understand your site's organization and structure. Some of the better Web management tools automatically display such maps for you, as depicted in Figure 1-1 (taken from FrontPage's Explorer).

You can use this kind of management tool, or create your own site map on paper. Whatever you use, keep your site map current!

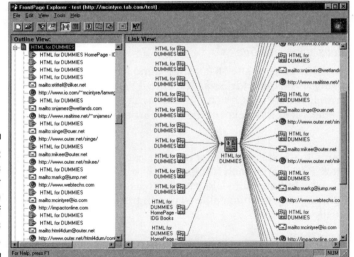

Figure 1-1:
FrontPage's
Explorer
shows two
views of
your site's
links.

Understanding all the pieces and parts

Creating a link map is a valuable exercise in understanding the logical chunks and components of your Web site. The map can help you distinguish content pages from demo pages, download pages from index or navigation pages, and so on. You should know which of these types of pages you have and where you use them.

If this seems a bit like diagramming a sentence in English class or creating an outline for a book, you're getting the idea. The more complex a site becomes, the more you need to visualize and understand its components. Then you're better prepared to combine the components to create the harmonious collection that your users will call a "great Web site."

To make your site better, study those Web sites that you most want to emulate. Examine how they are organized. Look at their source code and figure out how they link among their pages. Imitation is fine, but you don't have to clone their site; just determine their information flow and organization. Then you can create your own site in the same vein, with your own unique text, graphics, and images.

Using remote hyperlinks

Remote links can add value to your site if you select them carefully and keep them up-to-date. Unless you run a specialty collection of hotlists, you should probably limit your remote links to sites that amplify your own content. Hyperlinking to a site that provides more detail on a topic than your site covers is appropriate. Jumping into something totally unrelated is not. Just be sure that external links reach out only to useful sites, or those links won't be worth the time they take to maintain.

When you link to another site, you're opening the door for your users to leave. If you want them to stay at your site, provide as much information at your site as you can, instead of linking to someplace else.

What's the code situation like?

To use CGI scripts or other custom-coded programs, you need to understand several key points:

- ✔ Who controls access to these programs?
- ✔ How can you obtain or create customized versions of code?
- ✔ Who controls test access? production access?

To get the very best from your site, you must obtain the answers to these questions. You must also address all the other issues inherent in using and maintaining code as a part of a Web site.

If you're a programmer, you should already be familiar with the file permissions and other contortions required to manage a large collection of files and programs. If you're not, you need to work closely with your programmer and the Web server administrator to ensure that you have access to (and control over) the code that you need to properly maintain your Web site.

Any imagemaps in the picture?

Understanding your site's imagemap type and format requirements is important. You also want to find out what kinds of tools are available to help you construct and maintain imagemaps. Whether you're in charge of making them or you supervise the person who does, keep in mind that imagemaps can become quite large and are useful only to users with GUI browsers. If imagemaps get too big, they take too long to load and users won't wait for them.

Also, keep in mind that many new users don't understand how to use imagemaps. They don't know that clicking on one section of the picture links them to something related to that section. Using separate images or text for hyperlinks gives users a better idea of what's available and where they're headed. Of course, text doesn't look as nice, but are you trying to win the best imagemap award or help your users navigate?

Strategic Planning for Your Web Site

After you get your site up and running and start maintaining its content, before you can say, "Link Not Found," you need to add new content, update your existing materials, and fix your dead links. If you have made reasonable design and layout choices during your Web site's creation, your job is a lot easier. And if you have a written plan for expanding, updating, and maintaining your site, your job proceeds much more smoothly.

Cliché warning: "If you don't take the time to do it right the first time, you'll be forced to make time to fix it when you least have the time." Or, more concisely, "Fail to plan and you plan to fail!" The more time you put into designing and organizing your Web site, the bigger the payoff will be when the changes start coming thick and fast.

Juggling large document collections

Biologists say that a baboon can count to three. That's himself, his mate, and their latest offspring. So, the baboon number system contains: one, two, three, and one-heck-of-a-lot (the rest of the troop). You'll be using a similar system for your Web pages because, before you realize it, you will have one-heck-of-a-lot of pages. You may have many more files than pages, since each page may contain several images and graphics. The only way to keep track of the whole shebang is to use a hierarchical filing system with carefully planned names and annotation conventions.

This type of system has been widely used for managing computer programming source code libraries on large, multiprogrammer projects. Such systems are available on large computers for large documentation projects, such as the construction of an aircraft carrier.

You don't need anything that extensive or costly, but you do need something similar if your site grows to incorporate hundreds or thousands of documents. We discuss filing systems in a bit more detail in later chapters.

Thinking in terms of functional components, information delivery vehicles, and organizational sets of pages can help you manage your site as a whole, even though it may be constructed of a myriad of small parts. Approach your site in terms of its structures and functions (or systems and subsystems) and you're much better equipped to take care of it in the long run.

Tooling Up for Web Site Management

You're better off focusing on techniques rather than on any specific tool or set of tools for managing your Web, because tools vary widely, depending on what Web server software you use.

However, tools can help you catalog, organize, and update your HTML documents, images, and graphics files. They can do the same for CGI scripts and forms, imagemaps, and whatever else you put into your Web.

But a Web site manager's job is never done. You must also constantly monitor your site's security and your hyperlinks' validity. You really should validate your HTML documents to ensure that they use proper HTML syntax; then you want to check their appearance with your users' favorite browsers. Along the way, you must read, file, and respond to user feedback.

Some of these functions can be automated, some can't. Fortunately, tools are available to help you with most of these tasks, but you still need to maintain a hands-on attitude.

What tools do you really need?

You need any and all tools you can afford to acquire and use, given your time and money constraints. The key to success is found more in planning and carrying out all the necessary site management tasks than in your choice of tools. You can always change tools if you have a good plan! It's a little harder to change plans if you have good tools.

Of course, you need the best HTML editor or Web page construction system you can afford. You also benefit greatly from good graphic creation and image editing programs. Next in line is a link-checking program to keep your links working. This tool may be your most important maintenance tool if your site contains numerous external links. Finally, you want a good log analysis program to keep you informed about who's using your Web and how it's behaving.

Tool search adventures

You can plumb the depths of your favorite search engine site for keywords such as **HTTP** and **management**, or you can visit "The WebMaster's Page" where Bob Allison has assembled an extraordinarily large collection of links to everything a WebMaster might ever need. You find this collection at

```
http://miso.wwa.com/~boba/masters1.html#23
```

Judge what you find

Before you download a program, stop, look, and read — all on the Web, of course. Read the information about the tool on the manufacturer's Web site. Check out any reviews of the tool at the magazine Web sites and search for the tool's name and the word **review**. Ask about the tool on the newsgroups. Leave no stone unturned in your research work — you may turn up a few gems!

How to get 'em when you find 'em

If everything looks good after your evaluation, download the manufacturer's demo or shareware version and give it a try. Also, check out the freeware and shareware Web sites. One good site to try is the C|Net Shareware Library at http://www.shareware.com. Remember to give something back: Let others know what you think of a tool through the relevant newsgroups.

Wheeling and dealing: What's your budget?

The more a tool costs, the more you may want to play *Let's Make a Deal*. Of course, you want to support your local retailer, but direct purchase from the manufacturer or from a large reseller, such as Egghead Software, via the Web, phone, or mail-order may be more cost effective. If you're purchasing a tool for an organization, ask for a discount. Many manufacturers give corporate, nonprofit, and educational discounts, but you have to ask for them.

All in all, the recipe for effective Web site management is two parts knowing what's in your Web, two parts planning, one part using the right tools, three parts organization, and four parts carrying out your plans. Any tools work if you know your Web, make an organized plan, and carry out that plan in an organized way.

As someone on TV keeps saying, "Just do it!" And keep on doing it — that is, your Web maintenance — regularly. Keep adding information that your users want. Keep your Web up-to-date, and you'll have the successful Web you desire.

Now that you have an inkling of what's in store for you, it's time to move on to further details about how you can administer your Web site more easily and maybe even manage your own Web server. That's what we tackle in Chapter 2.

Chapter 2

Web Server Administration — the Easy Way

· ·

In This Chapter

▶ Seeing the truth about Web servers and their administration

▶ Getting to know your Web server hosting options

▶ Fitting the Web server into the Internet whole

▶ Looking at Web server hardware and software options

▶ Surveying Web server management techniques

▶ Following the administrator's information trail

▶ Learning sources for Web administration information

▶ Assessing your Web site's bottom line

· ·

*W*hat is Web server administration? Management, supervision, command, and authority are some of the synonyms for administration — therefore it must mean caring for, feeding, and controlling a Web server. Remember, the Web *server* includes the hardware and software that runs the Web site, not your wonderful HTML documents. Of course, managing all this is just what you had in mind when you thought it would be a great idea to have your own Web site . . . wasn't it? We don't want to paint too dismal a picture of the job, but think of a Web administrator as something like a parent who's expecting one bouncing baby and winds up with quintuplets instead. Ouch!

If your primary goal is to increase your company's profitability through operating your own Web site, you want to minimize the site's — and the server's — administration, both in terms of time and money (Are these redundant?). Several of the best possibilities for how you might actually accomplish this plateau of perfection are discussed in this chapter. Along the way, you also come to appreciate the underlying components — namely, the minimal set of Web server hardware, software, and management tools — to help you work with whomever your Web server administrator happens to be. If we do our jobs well, that won't be you. You'll be educated enough to get someone else to serve the server while you work on accomplishing your primary goal.

Security! How much, and who provides it? Keep this issue in mind throughout the rest of this chapter. Don't say we didn't warn you.

Web Server Hosting Options

So who can you get to administer your Web server? Maybe a better question is, "Who will host your Web site?" Your options are as follows: a hosting service, your ISP (Internet Service Provider), your own organization's LAN server or workstation, or your own computer. In the first two situations, you have access to an experienced person to help you set up and manage your Web site. In the third case, your LAN administrator may be of some potential assistance. In the last case, good luck — remember, we tried to talk you out of it!

Actually, even if you're "doing it yourself," you may go through a local ISP for your link to the Internet, so you may be able to get some help from one of their Web server administrators. The bottom line is that doing it yourself, with only a book or two and some user's manuals, isn't recommended for anyone who's purchased this book, unless you're an experienced UNIX/Internet hacker who likes reading our books for our great insight and humor. Anything less is a ticket to Troublesville.

So, we examine these options in a little more detail in the sections that follow. Notice that "do it yourself" isn't just the last element in this sequence; it's also the last thing we'd recommend to you.

Web server hosting services

Hosting services are relatively newly established companies that have quickly responded to the explosion of the Web. Many ISPs don't really want to host Web servers, especially when it entails connecting your computer directly to their LAN at their office and giving you physical access to it. Web hosting services come in three flavors:

- ✔ A local company that connects your computer to its LAN
- ✔ A Web server space renter
- ✔ A Web Mall operator

No matter what flavor you choose, the organization on the other end of your Web connection provides your Web site's security. Make sure that whoever is providing your security cares about it as much as you do.

Local Web server hosts

A local Web server hosting service is usually a small company with an office, at least one T1 digital telephone link, the appropriate equipment — usually a CSU/DSU, a router, at least one LAN server, and a rack to hold several computers that may or may not be Web servers. A typical small operation probably looks much like the one shown in Figure 2-1.

The company whose operation is depicted in Figure 2-1 is named OuterNET and specializes in setting up, hosting, and managing Web servers. OuterNET currently hosts twelve separate Web servers that belong to its clients. Of these, nine are UNIX based, two are Macintosh based, and one runs Windows NT. All are linked to the same Ethernet LAN that is connected to OuterNET's Ascend 2500 router, through its CSU/DSU, and then to its T1 line.

In addition, OuterNET has its own multihost Web server with several Web sites hosted simultaneously on the same machine. Therefore, if you don't have your own computer for OuterNET to host for you, you can still pay the company to house and administer a Web site on its multihost server on your behalf. If you plan to run a small Web site with less than 100 user connections per day, this might be a good alternative to consider.

Although it has a few modems and ISDN adapters for some of its clients to connect directly with the Web servers, OuterNET primarily relies on its clients and their Web site users to maintain their own Internet accounts. This puts the burden of keeping up hundreds of modems for dial-in connections on other ISPs, and allows OuterNET to concentrate on keeping its Web servers and sites running smoothly. Also, for a small setup charge, OuterNET can order a domain name for you from the InterNIC.

Figure 2-1:
A local
Web server
hosting
location
may look
like this.

Because the company maintains all three types of computer platforms, as well as several types of Web server software on these platforms, OuterNET is well-equipped to handle hardware and software problems and upgrades, quickly and efficiently. OuterNET strives to know what's happening in the Web world and can help you accomplish your primary goal: serving up the best possible Web content.

Companies such as OuterNET usually also provide FTP, WAIS, and Gopher servers, if you need them. They generally don't provide e-mail or news services, owing to the high volume of information involved and the need for more bandwidth and hard disk storage space to accommodate this information (and the corresponding demand from users). These services are generally provided by an ISP with any standard Internet account.

Web server space renters

As covered in the previous section, multihosted Web servers allow companies to place several Web sites on the same computer. This economy of scale decreases costs; if you plan to run a small Web site (with less than 100 modem-attached user connections per day), neither you nor your users are likely to recognize the difference between a multihosted Web site and one that runs on its own computer. As long as the other Web sites in the computer are small and experience the same low levels of usage, no one need ever be the wiser.

Many ISPs provide this type of Web service to individuals via a "personal home page" and to businesses via a "virtual Web presence" account. This service usually includes 5MB of disk space for the personal service, and something like 25MB for a business presence. Details vary, but they generally fall into this ballpark.

For these types of accounts, the level of customer service from an ISP can vary considerably, as can prices. Some ISPs keep their prices low; after they set up your account, you're basically on your own. They answer telephone and e-mail questions, but they aren't really interested in holding your hand (because they don't charge enough to pay for full-time technical support). You're expected to administer your own Web site; for their part, these ISPs keep the Web server running and connected to the Internet.

A local Web server hosting service usually offers a sliding price schedule that depends on the level of Web site administration required. If you administer your own site via FTP, the hosting service keeps the server running and connected to the Internet, and charges only a minimum monthly fee. If you e-mail the service your files and they make the changes to your site's directory structure and generally maintain your site, you pay more, either by the month or on an hourly basis. However, because Web hosting services are primarily concerned with their customers as Web site clients, you probably get much better service than you would from a large ISP.

Web malls

Web malls are services that can host your Web site, along with numerous others, on their own multihost Web servers. Their service offerings generally include assisting you with setting up your Web site, obtaining a domain name for you, and listing that name in their *Mall Directory*. Besides offering you more exposure, mall operators can usually provide secure order taking and credit card transaction processing services, should you wish to sell directly to your users. In other words, it's one-stop shopping for content providers such as you, as well as for the customers who visit such "virtual establishments."

Web malls also advertise their existence — and yours — throughout the WWW to draw more users. Of course, they want to host popular Web sites so that they can get advertisers to pay for mentions on their directory pages. Likewise, they would like to be able to charge you more for hosting your Web site, because of the large number of potential customers that visit their mall and see your directory listing. This is pretty much a standard retail store approach and is priced similarly. Malls offer more services and may be more expensive than the previous Web hosting companies or ISPs we've discussed, but they may be just what an online retail marketing approach needs.

When pondering your decision, your best bet is to check with Web site administrators who use such services, to learn from their experiences before deciding anything. E-mail them and ask for their impressions. You'll be amazed at how open many of them are. Check these newsgroups: `comp.infosystems.www.servers.mac`, `comp.infosystems.www.servers.ms-windows`, `comp.infosystems.www.servers.unix`, and `comp.infosystems.www.servers.misc`. They also provide up-to-the-minute information on who's hot and who's not.

Your friendly neighborhood ISP

Start your search for a home for your Web site at your ISP (assuming that you're happy with their service and pricing, that is). Check their Web site and other ISPs' Web sites for pricing and service options. Competition is fairly intense and pricing seems to be rather reasonable for those ISPs that offer multihosted Web sites. Don't be surprised to find that most ISPs aren't interested in situating your Web server hardware in their offices, attached to their LANs.

Prices for this kind of service, when available, are generally high, unless the ISP has a separate subnet linked to its Internet connection, specifically for hosting Web servers. In that case, it's actually running a Web hosting service, similar to what we described previously.

Remember, these operations provide the security for your Web site. Are they ready for prime time? Are you? Is this starting to sound familiar?

Your organization's LAN

If you work for a company or are in an organization that operates its own local area network (LAN), you may have been asked to set up a Web site at your own location. In this case, you need to work with your LAN administrator to determine which machine should be the Web server. If your organization uses UNIX-based computers, the LAN is probably already running Transmission Control Protocol/Internet Protocol (TCP/IP), which is the primary protocol used on the Internet. Because TCP/IP is already part of UNIX, it's no surprise that most Web servers run on UNIX.

If your LAN is Macintosh- or Windows NT-based, not to worry. Both of these operating systems can also use TCP/IP. In fact, OuterNET's LAN includes all three of these types of computers, where each one uses UNIX, Macintosh, or Windows NT Web server software.

Regardless of which computer platform you use in your organization, your LAN administrator can set up and run a Web server. Of course, numerous other concerns must be addressed when running a Web server on your LAN, especially if the server will be available to the Internet. Your LAN administrator has far fewer worries if you plan to use the Web server only within your organization.

Work closely with your LAN administrator when planning to deploy your Web server (or Web site). In case your LAN administrator is not a Web server expert, you can find several good references listed at the end of this chapter. These references cover the setup and operation of Web server hardware and software; chances are that both you and your administrator may want to consult one or more of these tomes and other resources.

Security for your Web site is your organization's problem now. Doesn't that make you feel more inclined to restrict access purely to internal use?

You!?

Yes, we're talking about, you, our gentle reader (and would-be Web maven). As a Web administrator or designer, ultimately *you* provide the security for your Web site.

If we haven't dissuaded you from setting up and running your own Web server, you need every bit of knowledge you can gain from this book and from *at least one* (or more) of the references listed at the end of this chapter. You probably need to get your Internet feed from an ISP, which can assist you in setting up your hardware and software (especially if you're willing to pay for some help).

However, you must arrange for the phone line from your local telephone service provider, even though you're connected to your ISP's system. Therefore, you need to deal with TPC (The Phone Company). If you're in a residential area and seek to get an ISDN line installed, you may have to pay as much as $500 for installation and wait several weeks for the company to get a magical "round tuit" before you can get a dial tone. If you want a faster leased line, you may have to wait longer (or forever, if it's in a residential area without business services available). If you're in a business district or building, you may be able to get faster service, but don't count on it. There's quite a rush for faster Internet connections, and TPC isn't always up to the task of delivering such lines quickly. If that's the case, look around for an ISP or telecommunication specialist that can handle the job for you, or at least help you with the task!

This bit of information about obtaining phone lines should make you think twice about availing yourself of a Web hosting service or ISP, unless your organization already has excess telephone service installed (or at least, readily available).

But wait! There's just one more thing . . . maybe two: your domain name (and its associated Web server name). You need to order your own domain name instead of instructing your ISP or Web hosting service to obtain one for you. Of course, you want users to find you at `http://www.yourdomain.com` rather than at `http://www.realtime.net:80/~yourname.html`. The cost is $100 to register for the first two years, then $50 per year thereafter. Filling out the form isn't too difficult, but sending it to the InterNIC (the Internet name authority that handles nonmilitary domain names) is sometimes tricky.

And finally, what about you? You're probably one of the folks who ran your own, BBS back in the '80s (or would have, if you'd been into computers at the time). Web sites are the BBSs of the '90s. You obviously enjoy a challenge and the freedom of doing things yourself, your own way. All we can do is wish you "Good luck!" But please, read on . . . you're going to need the knowledge.

You, you, you provide the security for your Web site.

How the Web Server Fits into the Whole

Chapter 1 provided a brief look at Web servers, which we expand in this chapter to just a bit shy of the point where your mind rebels and you start thinking of the sunset over the waves along a seven-mile beach just outside of Georgetown, Grand Cayman (oops, we're doing it already). At least, that's the plan.

Before you start calling Web hosting companies or ISPs, you may find it helpful to understand where and how the Web server fits into the overall picture of the Internet, both from a hardware and a software viewpoint.

The hardware: computer and telephone equipment

Picture your telephone system and the equipment you can see, namely your own phone and the wire that goes into the wall. Now, picture a computer system with an external modem for connecting to the Internet (see Figure 2-2).

Figure 2-2:
Here's a typical phone line/ modem/ computer configuration.

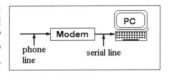

The telephone wire comes out of the wall, plugs into your external modem, which in turn plugs into the serial port on your computer, which is part of the computer's hardware system controlled by its Basic Input/Output System (BIOS) and the computer's operating system. The modem changes the analog telephone signals into digital signals for the serial port. Next, the serial port sends them to the computer's CPU for processing. Of course, this is simplified, but this is the most useful level for you to grasp, okay?

Picture the following: A T1 line comes out of the wall and goes into a Channel Service Unit/Data Service Unit (CSU/DSU), which in turn is connected through a wire to a router, which connects to the LAN through a hub or some other kind of connection. Finally, this connects to your Web server, which is attached to the LAN (see Figure 2-3).

Figure 2-3:
This is a generalized Internet hardware configuration.

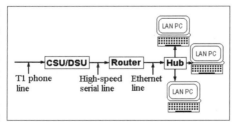

In a way, digital or networked Internet communications are similar to the modem system: Telephone signals arrive over the T1 line, albeit in digital form because that's the way T1 signals are transmitted. The CSU/DSU converts these incoming signals to the proper format for the router. The router controls the flow of Internet information between the CSU/DSU and your LAN, using TCP/IP. The router also converts a high-speed serial data stream from the CSU/DSU into the Ethernet (or other networking) formats used on your LAN. After the signals are in the proper format, your LAN can forward them to the appropriate IP address (that's the *IP* from TCP/IP). Your Web server answers to a specific IP address where all its Web-related packets will be delivered.

If that seems logical to you — it is. Pat yourself on the back; you're catching on quite nicely. In case you're wondering, all of this hardware works in reverse when the information flows out from your Web server to the user. Isn't that clever?

Web server software and (briefly) how it works

The telephone wiring and computer equipment provide only the pipeline through which digital information may pass. It's the software in the various computers at the phone company, on the Internet, at your ISP, in the Web server, and in the user's computer that makes information flow. Incidentally, it's also the software that displays that information in a recognizable form. We hope that you get the idea by now that the software is important stuff. We won't cause your eyes to completely glaze over as we recount all the gory details of the Internet software involved in handling WWW-related transmissions. You really only need to know just a smidgen about how the various pieces of software and the actual Web server software work. Therefore, brace yourself for incoming smidgens!

The basics

Each Internet service is handled by a set of software, be it FTP, e-mail, news, Gopher, or the WWW. In fact, WWW software is commonly called *Web server software*. Actually, it might be called HTTPd (an acronym for Hypertext Transfer Protocol Daemon, a common name for this software in the UNIX world) or something similar. This acronym alludes to Web servers' ubiquitous use of HTTP (Hypertext Transfer Protocol) for communications between Web browsers and Web servers. HTTP is an application level protocol that belongs to the TCP/IP family, or suite, of protocols. Because it provides the foundation for all things Internet, including the Web, TCP/IP is where we pitch the foundation for this discussion, in the very next section.

TCP/IP protocols

The TCP/IP suite includes the intertwined, low-level protocols upon which the Internet depends for its communications. TCP/IP helps to keep each piece of data in the proper sequence and ensures that no errors have crept into the data that gets delivered to its final destination. Internally, TCP/IP uses specific arrangements of groups of 8-bit numbers to represent whatever information you want it to convey. As long as all the software on the Internet uses TCP/IP, that information should be passed along to its proper destination, free of errors — in theory, at least. This depends on a complex combination of factors, the most important parts of which we explain next.

IP addresses

TCP/IP requires each separate computer to have its own unique and permanent IP address. An IP address is a 32-bit number, usually represented by four 8-bit numbers separated by periods (called dots in Internetspeak). A typical IP address is written as follows: 192.15.2.244. As the Internet grows and additional IP addresses are assigned, a new numbering scheme may ultimately replace the current one to make more addresses available for the ever-burgeoning Internet community.

This new system is being designed to be compatible with the existing addressing scheme, but that doesn't prevent this development from sowing consternation among those concerned to keep the Internet working. All we can say is "Don't worry; be happy," because mere mortal users can't do much about addressing, anyway.

Domain names

If you were forced to remember 124.35.223.4 rather than `yourdomain.com` for every domain you used, you would either be pretty irritated or suddenly less able to remember as many phone numbers as you currently do. For this reason, domain names function as more-memorable aliases for the actual numeric addresses to which they correspond.

Domain names reside in the Internet Domain Name System (DNS) under the auspices of the Registration Services maintained by the Internet's Network Information Center (InterNIC). The InterNIC's URL is: `http://rs.internic.net/rs-internic.html`. If you want to find out whether a domain name is available for your use, type the name into the location field in your browser and attempt to link to it. If you succeed, it's already taken. Actually, a more effective approach is to search the InterNIC's DNS database, to find out if the domain name you want is already registered. Unlike the vagaries of the Internet, which may not permit you to access a valid domain name because of accessibility problems, the InterNIC database contains a complete list of such names. You can find it at this URL:

```
http://rs.internic.net/cgi-bin/whois
```

Although you can register your own domain name yourself, you need to have your Web server up and running when you do. Alternatively, if you avail yourself of a Web hosting service, that service can usually register your domain name for you, for a small fee. You are invoiced for a $100.00 fee for name registration (good for two years from date of issue) directly by InterNIC. You are invoiced by your ISP or Web hosting service for whatever additional charges may apply.

Domain names can be *aliased* in your Web server. Instead of assigning your actual server's domain name (domainxyz.com) to your Web server, most Web administrators create an alias for the corresponding Web server that reads like this:

```
www.domainxyz.com.
```

A *www* alias is common for Web sites; this alias also allows you to move your Web site to another physical Web server, as long as you inform the person who runs your local DNS database about this change so that he or she can reassign it to the new address. Remember, each computer has a permanent IP address; your Web server software must reflect its location. That is, you can take your domain name with you, but usually not your IP address.

URLs

Uniform Resource Locators were invented to provide an unambiguous method to tell a Web program where to find a particular item of information; usually, a URL identifies that item's location on the Internet. In common Web usage, a URL defines a Web page address. A typical URL looks like this:

```
http://www.domain.org:80/dir1/dir2/filename.extension
```

Although the Web accommodates a variety of protocols, most URLs begin with http: to tell the browser and server that the HTTP protocol is to be used. The next portion, //www.domain.org, represents the host name where the item resides. Sometimes a port number is given after the host name, as in :80. Frequently, the host name is followed by a path to a specific directory or file, as in /dir1/dir2/filename.extension. If the path indicates a directory, it should end with a slash, as in /directoryname/.

Passing information into and out of the HTTP server

When the user clicks on a bookmark, the browser interprets this action as an instruction to fetch the URL using the HTTP protocol. At this point, the browser connects to the HTTP server indicated by the URL, sends a request for the specific location on the server, receives a reply from the server, and finally displays the contents of the reply on the user's browser screen. The key elements in this communication are the *request* phase and the *response* phase.

The most common *request* methods are

- ✔ **GET:** Returns the specified document's contents
- ✔ **HEAD:** Returns the specified document's header information
- ✔ **POST:** Treats the document as a script and passes information to it

During the *response* phase, the Web server sends various codes to the browser followed by the requested data, if it's available and no problems are encountered. Details of these transactions are useful primarily to script writers and are included here just to give you an idea of what transpires when you click on a link. Got that? *Wake up,* please. . . .

If you remember a little of this, you're way ahead of most folks who want to set up their own Web sites. Your Web server administrator also will appreciate your ability to discuss your server needs more eruditely. And, just in case you're dead set on running your own Web server, next we give you a look at the choices for computer hardware and Web server software.

Web Server Platforms

Can you run your Web server software on any computer with any operating system? Well, you can use quite a few, but not every computer there ever was. You can actually run the Hype-It Web server on a 386-based PC with DOS 5.0. Some may consider that an old platform; others may consider it ancient. If you're expecting any more than a handful of visits per day or you want to use graphics on your Web pages, you need something a little faster. Without going into too many details about document transfer rates and connections per minute, suffice it to say that you need at least a 486 PC running at 66 MHz (or an equivalent Macintosh or UNIX workstation) with at least 500MB of free hard drive space. In case you're really going to dive into the murky waters where the Web server hardware and operating system issues swim, use the guidelines we tell you about next as potential life preservers.

If you're choosing a Web server platform with no other constraints — such as, you already have a Windows NT network or your supervisor hates Apples — determine your anticipated Web usage first and foremost. Next, you must decide which Web server software package best suits that projected usage level. Finally, you must decide which platform is optimal for your chosen software. In the following sections, the three dominant server platforms, based on computer type and operating system, are discussed first; then the server software is presented.

UNIX and the Web

UNIX platforms come in all shapes and sizes based on RAM, processor speed, hard disk capacity, and other factors. For years, UNIX systems were considered the *only* way to run an Internet server. Because the first Web (HTTP) servers were written for UNIX, more servers and related software tools are available for UNIX than for any other platform and operating system. Also, UNIX is still the best choice for the seriously large or fast Web server, because its preemptive multitasking allows it to handle multiple simultaneous requests more quickly than Windows NT or Macintosh OS. And we all know that Computing Rule #1 is: "The only acceptable speed for computer operations is instantaneous." Just ask any user.

You don't need the newest screaming ten-bazillion MHz RISC workstation or server computer running the latest and greatest (read *most expensive*) commercial version of UNIX for your Web server. An inexpensive clone version of UNIX called LINUX runs on a 486 or Pentium-based PC, or an Apple-specific version of UNIX called A/UX runs on a comparable Macintosh. In fact, both of these options do nicely and can handle up to 100 connection requests per minute.

If you plan to run database scripts on your Web server, be cautious in your choice of server platforms. Search times increase dramatically on slower machines as usage increases. Remember Computing Rule #1 (at the end of the first paragraph). To keep your server's performance up, buy as much RAM as you can afford, then get a fast SCSI disk controller with fast, wide SCSI 2 or SCSI 3 hard drives. Anything less can soon become unacceptable, especially as the number of users increases.

Windows (NT and 95) are coming on strong

With the flash flood of Windows NT-based Web server software that's hit the commercial market in the past year, the popularity of NT-based Web servers running on a fast 486 or a Pentium PC has risen sharply. Although not as well suited for heavy multitasking work as UNIX, Windows NT does a credible job on a fast PC at much lower costs. This is especially true if you're not a UNIX hacker and must pay to climb that operating system's often formidable learning curve.

Although the graphical interface of Windows NT consumes large amounts of system resources, that may be worthwhile to obtain its ease of use. If you're already comfortable with Windows 3.1 or Windows 95, you can get Web server software for those operating systems. However, the superior performance of Windows NT and the greater number of Web server packages that it supports makes NT the Web server operating system of choice in the Windows world.

To get the best performance from a Windows NT Web server, buy a PC with the fastest processor, the most RAM, and the fastest hard disk controller and drives that you can afford, in that order.

Although far fewer freeware or shareware Web server tools are available for Windows than for UNIX, a rapidly growing number of commercially available, all-in-one Windows NT-based Web server packages exist. These packages contain virtually all the tools you need to set up, administer, and maintain your Web server. We cover those in more detail later in this chapter and again in Chapter 4.

The Macintosh alternative

MacHTTP is Chuck Shotten's shareware Web server for the Mac, which he turned over to StarNine Technologies (itself now a subsidiary of Quarterdeck Corporation) when he joined them to develop WebSTAR. Although MacHTTP is still available as shareware, and as a low-cost commercial product, Quarterdeck sells WebSTAR as its top-of-the-line Web server product. Several other Macintosh OS-based Web servers are available, but they offer no significant improvements over WebSTAR and MacHTTP.

MacHTTP and WebSTAR are the only options worth considering if you really want to use a Macintosh OS platform for your Web server platform. If budget is more important than performance, use MacHTTP; if performance is more important than budget, use WebSTAR. For a Mac-based Web server, we recommend the biggest, fastest Mac you can afford; certainly nothing less than a Quadra 750, with a Power Macintosh 600 (or better) preferable.

Web Server Software

As you can see from the following lists of Web server software packages, which are grouped by platform, more than enough packages exist for each platform. In addition to the ones mentioned here, it seems that more Web servers are being introduced every week. Each one has more features, runs faster, and makes setting up, running, and maintaining the server easier — or so they all claim. After these product lists, you find discussions of the most popular Web servers. Each product discussion points to excruciatingly detailed, voluminous information available online at its associated URL, so we won't put you to sleep with those details here. Aren't we nice? Actually, we're not that nice — the details change so quickly and so often that we want to point you at a resource that is more up-to-date than anything we could put in this book.

Generally speaking, UNIX-based Web servers are the most efficient and the fastest of the lot. However, even though NCSA's HTTPd, W3C's HTTPd, and Apache are all free and can run on inexpensive computers, they still run under UNIX, which itself requires an administrator experienced in UNIX setup, configuration, and maintenance. In case you've been off the planet for a while, even though the Web server software may be free, UNIX administrators definitely are not!

Several up-and-coming Windows NT-based Web servers have appeared on the market during the past year. The most notable include Netscape Communication's Commerce and Communications servers, Process Software's Purveyor, O'Reilly & Associates' WebSite, and Quarterdeck's WebSTAR NT/95. All of these offer Windows-based, graphical installation, configuration, and administration facilities. However, Purveyor and WebSite are the only two that were designed specifically for Windows NT. The others have been ported, either from UNIX or the Macintosh OS. Therefore, Purveyor and WebSite make better use of the Windows NT or Windows 95 operating system and offer easier usage and better performance.

MacHTTP and WebSTAR Mac are "the" Macintosh Web servers. Both are outstandingly easy to install and use. We're not sure why anyone else tries to compete with these wonderful creations from Chuck Shotten. If you're a Macintosh fan and want an instant Web server, you can purchase Apple's Internet Server Solution: A PowerMac 6150/50 workgroup server with WebSTAR preinstalled. Simply take it out of the box, power it up, start configuring WebSTAR, and add your Web pages. Presto! You're in business. Now that's the *easy* way to set up your own Web server.

In case you don't have the cash or the inclination to get the Apple solution but still want to do it yourself, we give you the lists of Web servers from which you can choose your very own.

Web server software lists

Here, we've grouped your Web server options by platform type. The packages listed in bold are the most popular, according to several recent surveys. A compendium of these surveys is presented after the lists, so you can check to see what's really hot while you're reading this.

UNIX:

Apache	**NCSA**	Spry Web Unix
Boa	**Netscape Commerce**	TEAMate
CERN	**Netscape Communications**	TECWeb
CL-HTTP	OpenMkt Secure WS	thttpd

UNIX: *(continued)*

Cosmos	OpenMktWebServer	WN
GN	Phttpd	Zeus
IBM Connection	SafetyWEB Unix	
NaviServer	Spinner	

Windows NT:

Alibaba	NetPublisher	SuperWeb
Commerce Builder	**Netscape Commerce**	VBServer
Communications Builder	**Netscape Communications**	WebQuest
FolkWeb	**Purveyor**	WebServer
FrontPage	SafetyWEB NT	**WebSite**
HTTPS	SAIC	**WebSTAR NT/95**
NaviServer	Spry Web NT	

Windows 95:

Alibaba	FrontPage	WebQuest
Commerce Builder	**Purveyor**	WebServer
Communications Builder	SAIC	**WebSite**
FolkWeb	VBServer	**WebSTAR NT/95**

Windows 3.1:

FrontPage	VBServer	WebServer
Hype-It		

Macintosh OS:

CL-HTTP	httpd4Mac	**WebSTAR Mac**
FTPd	**MacHTTP**	

Novell NetWare:

NetWare Web Server	SiteBuilder	Webware
IWare Connect		

MS-DOS:

Hype-It

Most popular servers

Several surveys taken during the last quarter of 1995 and the first quarter of 1996 indicated that the following Web servers were used the most. The numbers have been combined for the different platforms for a given server. Actually, more than 80 percent of the more than 75,000 Web servers on the Internet run on UNIX platforms. This table is interesting, because the Macintosh-based WebSTAR and MacHTTP comprise an estimated 4 – 6 percent of the total sites, whereas an estimated 6 – 7 percent of those sites use Windows NT-based Web servers.

The top four packages — Apache, CERN HTTPd, NCSA HTTPd, and Netscape Communications Server — are all available for UNIX. In fact, Apache, CERN HTTPd, and NCSA HTTPd are UNIX-only freeware packages. Netscape's Commerce and Communications servers are commercial packages available in UNIX and Windows NT flavors. They are closely related to the immensely popular Netscape Navigator Web browser. Purveyor and WebSite are the only strictly Windows NT/95 Web servers on the list. Both are relatively new releases and are rapidly increasing in popularity. And since you're wondering, BESTWWWD is a proprietary multihost Web server used by Best Internet Communications, Inc., for its Web site hosting service. As the company's name should suggest, it's hosting a large number of sites.

Free Web servers: W3C/CERN, NCSA, and Apache

Even if the best things in life aren't free, the most popular Web servers are. In the sections that follow, we examine the capabilities of several HTTPd servers. These include offerings from the World Wide Web Consortium (W3C), developed by (and formerly available) at CERN; NCSA HTTPd; and a popular enhancement of the NCSA stuff, known as Apache.

W3C/CERN HTTPd

The CERN HTTPd Web server was created and is maintained at the home of the WWW. Therefore, it is the original Web server. This version is used as the testbed for many new features and, for better or worse, is even more complicated to install and configure than other UNIX Web servers. In fact, this server's configuration is controlled by direct editing of a series of ASCII configuration files, without the benefit of an intermediate interface or any kind of online help. In short, there's no graphical interface to help you here.

CERN HTTPd supports these unique features:

> ✔ It can act as a proxy through a firewall.
>
> ✔ It can cache remote documents locally when acting as a proxy.
>
> ✔ It can also support multiple representations of a single document (in different languages, versions, or layouts).

However, the CERN server does not support either SSL (Secure Sockets Layer) or SHTTP (Secure HTTP) for secure commercial transactions. CERN HTTPd is a good choice for UNIX experts with internal information distribution needs or with free external Internet connections. As public domain software, it's available to the public at no charge.

NCSA HTTPd

The NCSA HTTPd Web server is used at more major Internet Web sites than any other Web server in the world (MacHTTPd may be in use on more home Macintoshes, but many of these aren't actually connected to the Internet). Also known affectionately as *httpd,* the NCSA server provides the basic features offered by the CERN/W3C implementation, plus several interesting features. The most notable of these added features, which probably make sense only to UNIX folks, include

> ✔ The capability to place executable scripts anywhere in the document tree
>
> ✔ The capability to understand and execute "server-side includes" (These allow HTML documents unrestricted access to executable programs anywhere on the Web server.)

Most savvy Web administrators disable this latter feature, because of its inherent security risks, and suggest that HTML authors use submitted and approved CGI scripts instead.

NCSA's HTTPd includes support for secure, encrypted communications. However, using this feature requires considerable expertise and can take a significant amount of time to implement properly. Because it works with only a limited number of browsers, encrypted communication is seldom used in practice.

Apache HTTPd

The Apache HTTPd server is a plug-in replacement for NCSA HTTPd 1.3. Apache release information indicates that it fixes numerous bugs and security holes found in NCSA 1.3 and 1.4. The Apache Group vows to keep the Apache Web server in the public domain, to continue to give it away free of charge, and to allow redistribution according to the GNU free software license terms. The Apache Group also claims that Apache is much faster than NCSA 1.3 and more efficient and faster than either NCSA 1.4 or 1.5. In addition, the Apache Group says that Apache offers better compliance with existing HTTP specs and implements the following user-requested features:

- DBM databases for authentication allow you to set up password-protected pages easily for enormous numbers of authorized users, without bogging down the server.

- Customized responses to errors and problems allow you to set up files, or even CGI scripts, to be returned by the server in response to errors and problems.

- Multiple DirectoryIndex directives allow you to specify statements such as

```
DirectoryIndex index.html index.cgi
```

This instructs the server to either send back the file named index.html or run the program named *index.cgi* when a directory URL is requested, depending on which of these two files it finds in the specified directory.

- Unlimited numbers of Alias and Redirect directives support a rich (and complex) file structure, with good apparent organization.

- Content negotiation — that is, the capability to serve clients of varying sophistication and levels of HTML compliance automatically, with documents that offer the best representation of the information that the client can accept.

- Multihomed servers — a much-requested feature, sometimes known as the APB patches — allow the server to distinguish between requests made to different IP addresses (mapped to the same machine).

The W3C/CERN Web server can be found at the following URL:

```
http://www.w3.org/hypertext/WWW/Daemon/Overview.html
```

The NCSA Web server can be found at the following URL:

```
http://hoohoo.ncsa.uiuc.edu/docs/
```

The Apache Web server can be found at the following URL:

```
http://www.apache.org/
```

A plethora of emerging commercial options

The decline in usage of the free NCSA and W3C/CERN servers can probably be attributed to the rise in usage of several commercial packages. Web administrators are not necessarily switching from the free stuff to commercial software; more new Web servers and sites probably use commercial server software rather than public domain software. The following commercial packages have posted the largest gains in the six months that ended in February of 1996:

- ✔ **UNIX:** Netscape Commerce, Netscape Communications
- ✔ **Windows NT:** Netscape Commerce, Netscape Communications, Purveyor, WebSite, WebSTAR NT/95
- ✔ **Windows 95:** Purveyor, WebSite, WebSTAR NT/95
- ✔ **Macintosh OS:** MacHTTPd, WebSTAR Mac

Even though their usage is growing at terrific rates, commercial Web server software still runs at less than 20 percent of the total number of Web sites in operation.

Netscape's Communications and Commerce Web servers

Netscape's Commerce Web server offers numerous features and relatively easy installation. It's one of only a few Web servers that support Secure Sockets Layer (SSL) secure Web service technology for credit card or other monetary transactions. You can install the server through a simple script and your own Web browser.

Extensive online documentation is available (in addition to a printed version of the documentation that you can order from Netscape) to help you get the server up and running in a few minutes. Add a few configuration variables and your own CGI image maps, and other scripts will run just fine. Netscape's package does not include any CGI utilities, but accepts and runs most available scripts, or those that you've prepared yourself.

Netscape's Commerce Web server is basically a drop-in replacement for any existing NCSA-type Web server. If you already use the NCSA or CERN server, you can simply install the Netscape server and instruct it to use your existing directories for server content and CGI scripts through its configuration interface. Installing the Netscape server from scratch is straightforward but fairly complex, especially if you use the UNIX version. The Windows NT version is a bit easier to install but still not what we'd call plug and play. The NT version provides a strong group of GUI administrative tools that can make your Web work much less onerous, however.

Purveyor

Process Software's Purveyor 1.1a is making a strong showing in the Windows NT Web server market. It combines easy installation, excellent documentation, and a better-than-adequate suite of administration and maintenance utilities into an attractively packaged system.

Like most Windows NT Web servers, Purveyor runs as a service under Windows NT. Its server management features are tightly integrated with NT's Program Manager. Upon installation, Purveyor creates a menu and toolbar buttons to control the server.

Purveyor's outstanding documentation includes a 209-page *User's Guide,* a *Guide to Server Security,* and a *Programmer's Guide.* However, the Web server utility software is so easy to use that this extensive paper documentation may go unused. The server can use standard CERN HTTPd-compatible HTML documents, image maps, and CGI scripts. Server configuration and management can even be performed remotely using Purveyor's Remote System Management (RSM) and your own Web browser.

Purveyor's little sister, Process Personal Web Server for Windows 95, is available for Windows 95 users. It's quite similar to Purveyor and is highly integrated with the Windows 95 operating system to provide easy server installation, configuration, and maintenance.

WebSite

The WebSite Web Server for Windows NT and Windows 95 is the first software product from the well-known technical publisher O'Reilly & Associates. Their server is well constructed, easy to set up and configure, and provides all the features you would expect from a good Web server. WebSite was designed for Windows NT, but runs well on Windows 95. It requires only 12MB of RAM, which is about half as much as many other NT-based Web servers require.

WebSite's 325-page *Building Your Own Web Site* documentation is outstanding, as you'd expect from a publisher. It's professionally written and should make using this software straightforward, even for novice Internet users, providing their heads are screwed on straight and they haven't downed three double espressos in the past hour.

WebSite uses an image-mapping technique that stores actual map coordinates in the registry instead of either internally running an image map applet or using a CGI script. Using the registry improves WebSite's performance. Unfortunately, WebSite doesn't use NCSA-standard .MAP files, thereby making server administrators create and maintain map files manually. WebSite 1.1 promises to include features equal to Purveyor 1.1a; if you're still interested in operating your own Web server, you may want to consider WebSite for your needs.

WebSTAR and MacHTTPd

Quarterdeck and Apple have cut a deal to preinstall WebSTAR on Apple's Internet Server Solution, a PowerMac 6150/50 workgroup server. If you want the fastest setup, this is the deal for you. You can have this server up and running your Web within minutes of taking the computer out of the box. And if you believe that, we have some real choice property for sale on the Gulf coast that's usable most of the time, at low tide. . . . Actually, if you're a knowledgeable Macintosh user, you might be able to get this system up and running with your own Web pages installed in a couple of hours, provided that you already have the telephone line and other necessary hardware installed and working.

You configure the Macintosh server through an administrative utility with a straightforward interface (detailed technical information on configuring your server is available from Quarterdeck's corporate Web site at http://www.qdeck.com).

Installing HTML documents is made easy because you don't need to make any modifications to page links whose sources reside in the same directory. This means that if you have several small Web pages, you can keep their components in the same directory and let the server default to local naming to find them. Numerous third party CGI scripts are available from the sources listed at Quarterdeck's Web site. Or you can write your own CGIs using AppleScript.

MacHTTP, WebSTAR's little brother, is about one-fourth as fast but is cheaper, yet manages to provide much of WebSTAR's functionality. Both are excellent choices for you Macintosh users who want to quickly and easily become Web site overlords.

All-in-one Web site hosting packages

Several companies offer all-in-one systems that are supposed to help you set up and maintain a Web site with as few headaches as possible. The idea behind these systems is to provide you with an authoring toolset in which you don't really have to insert HTML codes to produce Web documents. Typically, they provide an easier interface for managing documents on a Web site as well.

For example, NaviSoft provides software for authoring Web documents and a service to host your Web site (billed monthly). FrontPage takes a different approach: It provides a WYSIWYG Web document creation tool and CGI scripts that semi-automate Web maintenance operations on either a Netscape or Microsoft Web server. These are only two examples of what will undoubtedly become a much larger segment of the industry in the very near future. Read on for more details about each one.

NaviSoft

NaviSoft from AOL offers the NaviPress and NaviServer tools, and a NaviService Web hosting service for Web authoring and publishing. The Navipress HTML authoring system helps beginners get up to speed quickly, yet contains enough features to help experienced users. The NaviService Web hosting service provides small businesses with a professional presence on the Internet. All of this free, in the case of the NaviPress software, or incurs a monthly fee that ranges from about $20 for hosting a personal Web site to about $200 for hosting a small business Web site.

For more information about NaviSoft's products, visit their Web site at

http://www.naviservice.com/index.htm

FrontPage

FrontPage provides users with a fast and easy way to develop and maintain Web sites without programming. In January 1996, Microsoft's acquisition of the company that developed this product, Vermeer Technologies, added this tool to Microsoft's already formidable Internet tool collection.

The FrontPage client-server approach supports authoring, scripting, and Web site management from a desktop PC, whether across a LAN or over the Internet. Its Web authoring and site management features for Windows NT or Windows 95 include

- ✔ An editor to create and modify HTML pages, with WYSIWYG support for many of the latest HTML formatting extensions
- ✔ An Explorer to visualize and manage a complex Web site composed of many documents and images
- ✔ WebBots that implement the most common Web server functionality, such as text searches, feedback forms, and threaded discussion forums, without programming or complex setup requirements
- ✔ Wizards and templates for creating personal and business Web pages in a task-oriented manner
- ✔ A "To Do" list for tracking the status of authoring and management tasks for your site

The server portion of the FrontPage system is called Server Extensions. It runs on Windows NT, Windows 95, and various versions of UNIX. The Server Extensions are designed to function as support scripts for other Internet server products such as Netscape's Communications server or the Microsoft Internet Information Server (IIS). FrontPage includes templates for a Personal Web Server system to help you get started quickly.

You can find information about this excellent product at the following URL:

```
http://www.microsoft.com/msoffice/frontpage/default.htm
```

The Savvy WebMaster's Management Techniques

By careful design and planning, you can avoid the biggest headaches that managing your Web site can sometimes cause. If you take the time to plan its overall structure — that is, to lay out the arrangement of pages within the site, to design its file structures and file handling system logically, and to plan for the inevitable changes that you need to make — you may not need that giant bottle of aspirin after all. If you do these things, you also probably have more time to spend on your primary goal: To make your Web site a boost to your organization and its bottom line.

Laying out your Web space

If you're planning a Web site of more than 30 documents, which we've arbitrarily set as the dividing line between a small- and medium-sized Web site, you probably need to create a sketch of the links between each document. Even if you can mentally picture the links between 30 or more pages, sketching them on paper helps you remember what you were thinking when you're ready to expand your Web a few months down the line. It also helps anyone else in your organization who needs to understand the linking structure. So, whatever structure you choose, commit it to paper. That way, if you ever do get run over by a beer truck, your successor is lucky enough to have a road map to your work.

Of course, we hope that the infamous beer truck is nowhere in your future. But to be on the safe side, we cover more details about site documentation in the next chapter of this book.

Designing and handling the file system

Whether you're operating your own Web server or renting space on a multihost system, you need to plan where your files reside and how to revise or replace them when the time comes. This may not be any more complicated than what you already do on your own computer, if your Web site runs on a similar operating system. But if your Web site is on a UNIX server and you're an inveterate Macintosh or Windows user, you either need to learn a few UNIX commands and how to access the server via telnet, or you need to make arrangements with the server's administrator to set up the directory structure for you. In either case, you must determine where your files will reside, especially in terms of how they fit into the target server's directory structure. Knowing this structure is crucial, because each link that points to a local file must contain the proper URL.

As with your HTML document link layout, sketch the file structure on paper. Plan to place files in directories and subdirectories that remain stable over time so that you won't have to change links in every file just because you need to move a directory. Of special importance is the Web server's *root directory,* and the root directory for your Web site. On many systems these are called the server root and document root, respectively. The *server root* directory contains the Web server software's executable files. The *document root* directory contains the files and subdirectories for files that will be available to visitors to your Web site.

This may not seem important to you, but on UNIX and other secure network systems, file ownership and directory and file access permissions can be a big issue. Placing files in the appropriate directories can simplify the job of assigning and maintaining permissions. If your Web site resides on a Windows NT, Windows 95, or Macintosh system, you need to check security options with the server's administrator.

In any case, a logical arrangement of files with one eye on server and security aspects and the other on easing your administrative tasks — that is, updating the contents of your Web documents, adding new files, and removing stale files — is a must to keep your life reasonably sane. Think about it. Sketch it. Discuss it with your Web administrator. Try your initial designs on your own computer with a few files in each directory. Make a dummy Web site on your own computer and browse it. Try changing, revising, deleting, and otherwise fiddling with the files to see which ones belong where. Make sure that the directory names are appropriate not only for you but for anyone else who may need to use or change the system in the future.

Sometime in the near future, complete Web administration and maintenance systems may become available. These should greatly simplify the task we have just outlined. But for now, if you're the Web site administrator, you either have to do it yourself manually, using whatever tools may be available on your Web server to assist you, or pay the Web server administrator at your hosting service to do it for you. The choice — and associated costs — are yours to bear.

Working with log files

Web server log files can be among your most important administration tools. The NCSA and CERN Web servers use the same log files and formats for their *access* and *error* logs. Each line in the file represents a request by a user for a URL on your Web server. The *access* file format is as follows:

```
host rfc931 username [date/time] request status bytes
```

Here's how to interpret each of these fields:

- ✔ **host:** The DNS name or the IP number of the requesting user's Internet host

- ✔ **rfc931:** The user identification protocol, usually blank or a - (hyphen, dash)

- ✔ **username:** The requesting user's ID. Represented by a dash if no user ID is provided

> ✔ **date/time:** The request's date and time in 24-hour format, based on the requester's local time; the brackets surround this information to mark its beginning and end
>
> ✔ **request:** The type of request issued
>
> ✔ **status:** The status code for your server's response
>
> ✔ **bytes:** The number of bytes transferred to the user; dash if no response sent

Following this format, a typical access file looks like this (the indented material on every other line would actually be on the same line as the preceding one; we don't have enough space to fit everything on one line in this book, however):

```
137.49.10.35 - - [05/Feb/1996:09:49:18 -0600]
    "GET / HTTP/1.0" 200 2752
137.49.10.35 - - [05/Feb/1996:09:49:21 -0600]
    "GET /regimage/tan_sand.gif HTTP/1.0" 200 14820
137.49.10.35 - - [05/Feb/1996:09:49:21 -0600]
    "GET /regimage/wetlogo5.gif HTTP/1.0" 200 10745
137.49.10.35 - - [05/Feb/1996:09:49:50 -0600]
    "GET /regs/t1pge00a.htm HTTP/1.0" 200 1620
```

The error log file's format is even simpler:

```
[date/time]  the error message
```

A typical error file looks like this (here again, we've had to wrap lines that otherwise would show up as individual lines within the log file):

```
[Tue Feb 13 06:37:19 1996] httpd: send timed out for
    193.48.69.2
[Tue Feb 13 06:37:20 1996] httpd: send timed out for
    193.48.69.2
[Tue Feb 13 06:37:38 1996] httpd: send timed out for
    193.48.69.2
```

Most servers allow you to specify which logs to keep active. Some create a new access and error log file for each day. Others just keep adding information to the same two files until they fill up your hard disk or until you archive them and start over. Of course, managing your log files on at least a weekly basis is a good idea if you're receiving numerous hits per day on your site, or if you've been receiving feedback that your site isn't behaving properly.

You need to check the error file to help you determine whether the problem is local to your site or is being caused by something else. You may even want to put your site's usage statistics in an HTML document for display at your site. Whatever you do, you are a better administrator if you set up a regular procedure to summarize and archive your site's log files. Who knows, you may even learn something.

Some newer Web server software even contains tools for log file management and interpretation. You soon find that, without the help of a summarizing tool, obtaining the information you want from the vast amounts of undifferentiated data in a 5MB log file can be an exercise in frustration. Some commercial Web server software companies have therefore added log file manipulation features to their servers. The Macintosh and Windows NT/95-based servers use graphs and other graphical displays for selected mathematical summaries in planned releases (you may find these tools in current versions as you read this book, given the headlong rush to provide new features in this marketplace). To help you deal with the important stuff in log files while ignoring the dross, Chapter 4 covers log file analysis tools in more detail.

Administration and monitoring tools

As discussed in the previous section, an increasing number of commercial Web server software companies have added more sophisticated, easier to use Web administration and monitoring tools to their offerings. We've noticed that the best of these run on Windows NT/95 and the Macintosh. These companies seem to think that UNIX hackers can handle such tasks for themselves, but that Windows and Mac users are more inexperienced and therefore willing to pay for better integrated, simpler administration tools.

Boy, are they ever right about the latter! This is especially true in organizations in which the Windows or Mac guru (probably you) draws the short straw and becomes saddled with getting an organization's Web site up on the Internet and available to the public. All too often, the job must be finished yesterday, because management fears being labeled as *way* behind the times without a Web site of its own. Because you're probably either a Macintosh or Windows person, you may opt for a Web server based on a familiar platform, especially if "they" insist that you run your own Web server in-house.

If "they" allow the recipient of the short straw (that's you, again) to arrange a service to host the Web site, its administration and monitoring tools are determined primarily by the server administrator at the company that provides this service. This is good, because that server administrator can help your organization's Web site administrator (you're everywhere, aren't you?) learn which tools to use and perhaps even provide some instruction or guidance on how to use them.

Even if you do end up running your own server, you will probably obtain your Internet connection from an ISP or hosting service. Chances are good that your ISP employs someone who can assist you in learning about Web management tools. If you're a rugged individualist, or simply don't like asking for help, some of the commercial Web server tools are already quite useful. The descriptions in the next paragraph should give you a pretty good idea about what kinds of tools you can expect from several of the Windows NT/95 packages.

The Purveyor server includes a Log Viewer to manipulate logs in a spreadsheet-like system and a Link Browser that generates a tree diagram of your Web pages (even better, it lets you click on each page graphic to open and edit it). O'Reilly's WebSite server provides a tool named WebView (similar to Link Browser, only better) that lets you view and edit your Web's file tree. O'Reilly also includes another program called WebIndex that lets you index selected files for text searching by the WebFind program (also included in this excellent package). Other tools have other capabilities, but these represent the kinds of tools that Web administrators typically find most useful.

For More about Your Web Options . . .

WebMaster Magazine On-line provides a wealth of information for WebMasters-to-be, and for novice and professional WebMasters. Their WebMaster's Note-book section on Tools and Links, at the `wm_notes.html` URL that follows, is a great list of links to virtually everything you might ever want in the way of Web-oriented information. And if this isn't enough, you can always search Yahoo! or WebCrawler using the search strings "HTTP" or "server" and then follow the hundreds of resulting links.

```
http://www.cio.com/webmaster/
http://www.cio.com/WebMaster/wm_notes.html
http://www.yahoo.com/Computers_and_Internet/Internet/
              World_Wide_Web/HTTP/Servers/
```

Paul E. Hoffman's Web Servers Comparison chart at the following URL contains every Web server known to man, with a comparison chart of specifications for each one and links to each server's home Web site for further information. This is a fantastic resource if you're really interested in the details of a specific Web server package.

```
http://www.proper.com/www/servers-chart.html
```

Okay, now it's time to beat that dead whatever-it-is one more time: If you're going to set up and run your own Web server, several very good books besides this one can help you minimize your headache factor. Why are we telling you about other books? You've already bought this one, so we're happy. And we want to help you every way we can. So, we think that you may find these three most helpful:

- ✔ Blum, Adam, *Building Business Web Sites,* (New York: MIS Press, 1996).

- ✔ Chandler, David M., *Running a Perfect Web Site,* (Indianapolis: Que Corporation, 1996).

- ✔ Coombs, Jason and Ted Coombs, *Setting Up an Internet Site For Dummies,* (Indianapolis: IDG Books Worldwide, Inc., 1996).

- ✔ Hoffman, Paul, *Netscape and the World Wide Web For Dummies,* 2nd Edition, (Indianapolis: IDG Books Worldwide, Inc., 1996).

- ✔ Levine, John and Carol Baroudi, *Internet Secrets,* (Indianapolis: IDG Books Worldwide, Inc., 1995).

- ✔ Morrison, Deborah, *Building a Better Web Site,* (Indianapolis: IDG Books Worldwide, Inc., 1995).

- ✔ Smith, Bud and Arthur Bebak, *Creating Web Pages For Dummies,* (Indianapolis: IDG Books Worldwide, Inc., 1996).

- ✔ Stein, Lincoln D., *How to Set Up and Maintain a World Wide Web Site,* (Reading: Addison-Wesley Publishing Company, 1995).

Weighing Costs against Other Considerations

The cost of running your own Web server is much more than the sum of the costs of the individual parts of the server, plus the cost for the time it takes to administer it. You must also include the costs of the space to house the equipment, the electricity required to run the equipment, the extra heating and cooling needed, and the maintenance, repairs, and replacement of broken or worn-out equipment. That's a lot of costs.

In addition to the time you spend working on the HTML documents for your Web site and babying the Web server hardware and software, you spend time communicating with various people who have trouble connecting to your server or who have problems accessing your Web documents. This looks like, smells like, and sounds like customer support, therefore it must actually be that dreaded job. After all, you *are* the Web Administrator.

And yes, you'll always have those middle-of-the-night power outages, hard disk crashes, network blowups and phone system blackouts. Now do you see why we keep pushing the idea of paying someone else to host your Web site while you concentrate on preparing its contents?

What's your bottom line?

You've probably noticed that we didn't supply any prices on Web server hardware and software in this chapter. Prices change almost daily, so you should check out the Web sites of the Web server manufacturers or call your tried and trusted local computer retailer for the current prices on the parts you think you want.

Before you purchase any equipment, put together a Web site development and management plan that includes phases and cost estimates for Web server hardware, software, procurement, setup, configuration and maintenance; for telephone connection design and acquisition; and for Web site design, setup, and maintenance. From this collection of cost estimates and tasks, you should be able to predict the amount of time you need to get your Web site up and running. You also get a good handle on the associated costs, both in-person hours and out-of-pocket expenses.

Home-grown versus store-bought Web sites

Unless you've already made the decision (or it's been made for you), you benefit from building separate plans for handling your own Web server versus paying a service to host it for you. The bottom line is to make sure that you know your reasons for taking your path to Web site delivery (do-it-yourself, or through a third party), and to predict the effects your choice has on your own bottom line. A better understanding of the overall process of publishing your information on a Web site, which we examine in the next chapter, should help you get to the bottom of this.

Chapter 3

Managing the Web Publication Process

- -

In This Chapter

▶ Deciding what should be in your Web site

▶ Planning for your Web site's future

▶ Updating your Web site

▶ Working as a team to produce your Web site

▶ Converting existing documents to HTML

▶ Reviewing good HTML style

- -

*P*ublishing on the Web is a lot like creating and raising a child. The act of creating it is very enjoyable, but developing it, bringing it into the world, and nurturing it to maturity can become a bit tedious. Also, if you do not care for it properly, you get to watch it rapidly deteriorate and drift into oblivion — you know, just down the coast from incognito.

The act of publishing your fantastic information on the World Wide Web is more than simply hacking together a few HTML documents and putting them on an ISP's Web server. To have a truly successful Web site, you must design your site to accommodate the myriad of changes necessary to keep it fresh and alive. Dead or stale sites don't draw users — or even too many flies.

Nothing kills a Web site's Net appeal quicker than old material or slow deposition of time-sensitive material. You must be keenly aware of your user's needs and desires where your site and its content are concerned. If you don't plan your site to enable you to easily update the content as often as your users demand, you burn out long before your users get tired of your materials. Therefore, managing the publication process for your Web content is perhaps the most important aspect of long-term success for your site.

What's It All About?

Your Web site is about making you happy or, at least, making your employer happy so that he or she doesn't bother you, which, in turn, makes you happy (or at least, not unhappy). You can accomplish this most easily by providing your site's users with the type, amount, and freshness of content that makes them happy. This also keeps them coming back for more, which makes you provide even more, and so on. It's all about giving the customers what they want, when they want it — if not sooner!

What should be hanging in your Web?

Keep in mind that no matter what anyone says, all your customers (users) want everything immediately and for free. Your only possibility of survival is to provide them with a reasonable amount of some small segment of "everything." We don't mean a little of this and a little of that; let the search engine sites provide that. We mean that you should provide an in-depth, up-to-the-minute look at your specific eddy in the information ocean.

Keep just one crucial concept in mind at all times: While users are accessing your Web site, you have their undivided attention. At that time, you can provide as much detail on your service or product as they can assimilate (or download). Unless your real goal is to get people to call you on the phone, put everything the users could possibly want to know about your product(s) or service(s) in your Web site documents. Then their "self-service" experience can be completely satisfying, without requiring you to get involved!

Project the amount of time that you and you staff must spend to keep your site's information up-to-date and alive, while allowing time to add additional areas of coverage. If you're starting a Web site for a new magazine, start with the basics that set the magazine apart from the rest and keep the site simple. Plan to expand it as the magazine's readership increases its usage of your Web site.

If your Web site is primarily a source for internal company information, you can start it with a few of the most time-consuming company programs concerning employee contact (do health care and 401(K) ring any bells?) and then spread out into more static programs. Plan to put your employee newsletter on the site if you can get someone else to prepare its text for you. Or use one of the word-processing-format-to-HTML conversion programs that we discuss later in this chapter.

Remember, you can always expand your Web site as enthusiastic users demand more. Keep it small at first. Do it right from the start. Expand only if you can keep the quality up, along with any increases in quantity. If you overdo it, you may have trouble garnering the right level of attention and respect from users when you're finally really ready for prime time!

Planning for now and the future

With all of the words of wisdom in the previous sections, should you plan your Web publishing? That's easy: You should plan it just like any other publication process, except that you don't have to deal with typesetters, service bureaus, or printers.

By *publication process,* we mean the process from an idea's conception through making that idea available on your Web site. This includes the design of your Web site's format and its layout (both the visible layout and the underlying Web server directory structure), content creation (text and graphics), editing the text, laying out each page's text and graphics, HTML coding and document linking, and finally, uploading your documents to a prefabricated directory structure on the Web server.

If your Web site is meant to be a Web equivalent of an "explore the endless caves" game, by all means, link your Web documents to each other randomly so that nobody can conceptualize its structure. However, if you want to make your Web site easy to navigate, use a standard hierarchical tree or a folder structure metaphor. Sure, both of these metaphors are used everywhere, but for good reason — namely, because everybody can relate to them. You can also very easily add more limbs and leaves to a hierarchy for new products or services.

This idea works equally well for on-screen layout and for a Web server's directory and file structure. To make the process easy on yourself, you may as well make both structures similar. That way, you can visualize the location of the files residing on the hard disk's subdirectory as analogous to the location of the Web pages in the document hierarchy. This approach can also help anyone who works with you (or after you) to upgrade or change the content of those Web pages.

This approach works all the way from the top to the bottom of your Web site, with one notable exception — namely, shared graphical images. You don't want to make multiple copies of the blue dot image file and put a copy in each subdirectory with every HTML document that references it. Instead, create a common graphics subdirectory, and keep only one copy of each shared graphic there. Place this subdirectory immediately beneath the main Web root, set the Web root directory as your <BASE>, and use a relative URL for each graphic every time you use it. Then you can move your site more easily than if you use absolute URLs for such graphics.

If you're careful, you can cross-link a few pages to each other if the content so dictates without turning your site into a completely incomprehensible bowl of spaghetti. You can also differentiate each major limb of your document tree with a unique background or color to give users an immediate cue to its position within your structure. Plan this out, and your users will love you for it. If you just let it happen by accident, however, they may not be so enthusiastic.

If your site deals with large amounts of data that change periodically, you may want to keep the data in a location other than in the "leaves" of your directory structure. Perhaps the data files could reside on a separate hard disk or even another workstation on the network. This approach may be preferable if you want to facilitate any changeovers after completing an update.

You probably don't want to take your Web server offline to make an update. Therefore, plan for a seamless transition by switching from one copy of the data to another (perhaps by reassigning symbolic links) or by replacing files in a preplanned order.

The quickest and safest method for making such a switch is to keep separate subdirectories containing your old and new data files side-by-side on the same hard disk. If you use different names for the subdirectories but identical names for the data files, all you need to do is change a few pointers.

Assume that your Web server accesses a directory named WEBDATA under normal operating conditions, because that is what's used in all your URLs. Further assume that you make updates and changes to your files on other computers on the network and put the updated files in the NEWDATA directory on the same level as WEBDATA. When you're ready for the changeover, rename WEBDATA to OLDDATA and then rename NEWDATA to WEBDATA. It's really a quick and painless process if you plan ahead.

Try this in the wrong order and you wind up with plenty of nothing (for example, two copies of the wrong stuff). Therefore, if you do follow my advice, make sure that you have a backup copy of the old and new materials somewhere else in case you make a mistake. That way, you can get back to where you started (to the old materials) or move on to the updated materials (the new stuff) no matter what happens. And believe me, "no matter what" happens a lot more often than you may think.

Planning for regular updates

As you're designing your Web layout, if it deals with time-sensitive material (for example, newsletters, press releases, or other event-driven or periodical publications), you need to plan appropriate space on your home page. Sometimes, a good idea is to reserve some space on your second-level pages for Hot and New items as well.

But familiarity breeds contempt, even on the Web. If you always place a little "Hot" icon next to the second-line heading, users soon learn to ignore it just as they ignore roadkill along the highway. Shake things up regularly: Prepare and use different icons; rearrange your layout from time to time; keep things visually interesting by changing element placement.

If you plan to use Java applets for animation and to make these elements appropriate to your site's information content, you can really jazz things up. Remember, you're not only trying to attract new users, you're also trying to convert them into regulars who keep coming back for more.

So how should you plan for frequent updates? Determine how often to process updates, based on your users' desires, your own time, and the availability of new information. Providing regular, on-time updates so that your users can expect and receive updated information when promised is essential. In other words, reliability is paramount. How do you react if your morning newspaper is late? How do you react if your morning newspaper doesn't arrive at all? It's not quite as bad as getting up in the morning and finding you're out of coffee, but almost. . . .

Planning for less frequent updates is better than trying to update more often and failing to deliver on time. But if your information changes daily and you can't provide those changes to your users on the same basis, you may want to rethink your Web site objectives. In fact, you may be occupying the wrong niche!

Detailed time-management planning, coupled with automated information processing, may be exactly what you need to convert and transmit your information to your Web site on a timely basis.

Prepare a project schedule for yourself and your staff, preferably using computerized project management or scheduling programs. Prepare a schedule even if you are the only staff member. Doing so helps you determine your limitations by forcing you to list all the tasks necessary to produce an update and then to link them in a critical path with the time required to complete each one.

If you follow this approach, you can see immediately how much information you can update and how often. If you haven't used a project management program, now's a great time to start. Search for one via the Internet; use "project management software" at your favorite search site or on a shareware site; you find many varieties in all price ranges.

Designing documents for multiple uses

You save yourself a great deal of time if you design your original documents for multiple uses. (In hip buzzword terms, this is known as *repurposing;* sounds to us like something you do to an aquatic mammal . . . twice!) That means using your information online as well as in printed form. Depending on the type of information involved, *multiple uses* may also mean deploying your content in video, audio, multimedia, and online multimedia forms.

Fortunately, you have numerous options to convert (or use directly) things such as complex word processor-based documents containing tables and figures for use in your Web site. You may convert such documents into HTML using one of several programs that we discuss later in this chapter, or you may use a special output file format, such as Adobe's PostScript, converted to portable document format (PDF). (That's assuming, of course, that your users have the right plugins or helper applications available to view such files from their browsers.)

Programs that enable most computers to accept video and audio input from almost any source and digitize it into acceptable Web document formats also are available. This is the technical end of the operation and, in many ways, the easiest to accomplish. First, you must design the layout and presentation of your information to make it compatible with multiple formats before you convert it to HTML — or any other format, for that matter — to reach your users effectively, whether online or off.

Although such technology is available in many browsers or in the form of software add-ons, few Web surfers have fast enough Internet connections to enable them to download large multimedia clips quickly. For that reason, many users don't take the time to mess with multimedia. But because most leading-edge browsers can handle Java applets, using a few small animated graphics can be a nice touch. Go easy on the multimedia content, and you're likely to benefit more users than if you concentrate on those who have the links and the equipment to appreciate massive multimedia maneuvers.

Likewise, only a few Web users have audio systems installed in their machines. Sadly, many of those who do have audio ability work in locations (such as offices), where they can't appreciate a "talking" Web site. Of course, sites exist that do enable users to preview audio CDs or listen to radio shows on the Internet. By and large, these are specialty sites that make excellent use of appropriate technology and feed only small, selected audiences.

If your site is geared toward a specialty niche where using one or more of these technologies makes good sense, by all means, plan to use them. But the emphasis is on the world *plan*. You must research your audience to understand how important this content is to your users — in addition to more conventional content delivered in standard text and graphics format.

Working with creation and production staff

If you're not doing everything yourself for your Web site, you need to adjust to working with your information creation and production staff in a way that takes cognizance of the Web's special capabilities and requirements. If you're in charge of getting your organization's Web site up and running by using existing information produced in-house, you're greatly helped in your task if you can get the people who originally created and produced the information to convert it for Web use. Maybe they understand the Web, and maybe they don't. You may need to determine which members of the staff you can expect to know something about the Web and how their creations can be made to work well on the Web.

Enlist the assistance of your supervisor and the supervisors of the creation and production staffs to make sure that you go about the creation of your Web team in a politically correct manner for your organization. Nothing makes your job more difficult than failing to get the support of the appropriate people in the creation and production departments. Mess this up and you find yourself converting every bit of information by yourself or with minimal, grudgingly provided assistance. If you can show some of the information creation folks how well their graphics and nicely formatted text appear on the Web and how easily they can create and produce the information for the Web, they are much more likely to help you. Otherwise, they just resent you for adding extra work to their already busy schedules.

Help the staff members find, acquire, and learn the tools they need to create or convert the information to the required Web formats. Help them to understand that, if they're still thinking paper, they're not prepared to deal with the information age.

Although mastering the transition from paper to the digital landscape may paint a bleak picture for your creation and production staffs, you generally find that they are way ahead of you in their own areas of expertise and are anxious to produce their magic for the Web. In this case, as the Web site administrator, you become their hero for getting them into the process. Work closely with them as you're planning and scheduling your Web projects. Keep them abreast of the latest information, and they happily work with you to make your Web site successful.

Integrating the Web into the overall process

Keep in mind that, in most circumstances, the Web site is only a small part of the big picture in your organization's world presence. Although it's the biggest thing in your life because you're the Web site administrator, it's really only a piece of the puzzle. The site may become a rather large piece of the puzzle in the near future if you do your job well, which may result in your gaining more than a pat on the back for a job well done. However, if you act as if "your" Web site is a divine gift that's going to make your company another Micro-whatever or Global Motors, you may find yourself all alone with your HTML.

Strive to integrate the processes of creation and upkeep of the Web site smoothly into your organization's overall public relations, marketing, advertising, and sales process. To these departments, the Web site is simply another means of placing your organization's information in front of your potential customers, clients, users, or whoever. It's very similar to the television, radio, and printed distribution of your information. So try to find the similarities and help everyone, including yourself, understand that creating and producing information for the Web site isn't really going to be much of an additional burden on them and that the future rewards could be very large.

The Conversion Process Is a Real Time Saver

Converting your current information into Web-ready format saves you a tremendous amount of time. Otherwise, you must re-create that information from scratch. ("Scratch" is the blank word processor screen with the blinking cursor at the top left, with the title "Untitled.doc.") This process is also known as death by boring repetition if you need to insert the HTML codes by hand in numerous, long text documents. Fortunately, you waited long enough that several enterprising companies have begun to market really good conversion programs for many of the most popular word processing and page formatting tools on the market. More about these after you see what you're missing by not doing it by hand.

Doing it by hand

Having manually converted numerous word processor documents into HTML documents ourselves, we know what we're missing . . . and we don't miss it one little bit. You've created HTML documents, so you know at least a little about what we mean. To see the difference, just view a page of text via your browser, and then view the document source. In the latest versions of the most popular browsers (Netscape Navigator and Mosaic), the HTML tags are a different color than the actual text, and the links are still another color. This enables you to see how much HTML code must be added to even the most basic text file to prepare it for use on your Web site.

The more complex your style sheet is, the more work is required to try to duplicate it. It's click, drag, click, drag, drop, click, click, and so on with your HTML editor, provided that it can even handle your big file in the first place. You also must convert your images to either GIF or JPEG and turn your word processor tables into HTML tables. Of course, you must do all this perfectly or you end up with the last half of your ten-page text document formatted in bold, italic, heading 1 font — or worse.

Although the currently available conversion programs are good, they're not perfect, as the following section shows.

The power (and limitations) of automated conversion

The good news: Conversion tools really do work. They actually do a very good job of converting the styles, formatting, tables, and images in your existing files to Web server/browser-compatible files. The bad news: You still must provide the appropriate style, formatting, and layout in your original file, or the Web document produced by the conversion doesn't look good on-screen. Also, conversion tools don't perform complex layout tasks such as creating frames or producing outside links without significant setup on your part. You still need to understand the basics of Web layout and HTML to produce truly high-quality HTML documents and an outstanding Web site.

As we state many times, the layout and flow, both within and between your Web documents, are extremely important to making yours a successful Web site. Conversion programs can't help you with this.

After you design your Web site, using a layout appropriate for your information content and users' needs, you may be able to make use of conversion programs to convert existing text documents for use on parts of your Web site. You still probably need to make adjustments to each document unless the documents are highly standardized forms that never change. If your site presents large numbers of frequently changing text, using a conversion program should prove a great time saver for you. Download a trial version of one to see whether it's worth using for your situation.

Seeking tools

Finding HTML converters is too easy. Just use the Yahoo! search engine (or your favorite search site), searching for **HTML converters,** and you get listings for every type of converter that you ever imagined — and then some. Or you can go directly to the following URLs at the W3C Web site, which contains an extremely comprehensive listing of converters:

```
http://www.w3.org/hypertext/WWW/Tools/Filters.html
http://www.w3.org/hypertext/WWW/Tools/Word_proc_filters.html
```

We discuss a few of the more prominent converters for the major computer platforms and information creation tools in the following sections.

Cyberleaf

Cyberleaf, from Interleaf, converts text, graphics, and tables from Word, RTF, WordPerfect, Interleaf, and FrameMaker formats to HTML and GIF. It has been available on several UNIX platforms since 1995, and the Windows NT version is projected for an early 1996 release. In addition to providing comprehensive conversion capabilities, Cyberleaf contains the following Web document management features:

- ✒ Interactively refines and saves the parameters used to convert your documents and then reapplies the defined styles and hyperlinks to your updated Web site and identifies any broken links that require manual intervention

- ✒ Facilitates browsing by enabling long documents to be outlined based on selected style names such as chapter or section, which creates a table of contents of your Web site

- ✒ Automatically inserts hyperlinks between document outline elements and their corresponding sections in the HTML output file

- ✒ Includes a "Post Web" function that automatically copies completed Web documents to your Web server on demand

```
http://www.ileaf.com/ip.html
```

HTML Transit

HTML Transit for Windows 95 and 3.1, from InfoAccess, uses a template approach to specify how each element of your source document is treated in your Web publication. The HTML Transit template stores everything about your electronic publication, including which input files to translate, which output files to generate, text and graphic treatment, and dynamic link behavior of your document. In Transit, to update your Web site, you revise your source files, reload the template, and click Translate Publication. HTML Transit may be the most comprehensive of the conversion programs available.

As you can see in Figure 3-1, HTML Transit enables you to add both your favorite HTML editor and Web browser by using the lower-right two buttons shown in the figure. It's a bit cumbersome to use because it uses a powerful template method and it doesn't do forms, but if you're administering a large, frequently changing Web site or multiple sites, the program may well be worth the $495 list price.

HTML Transit includes a veritable raft of features and formats, as indicated in the following lists:

Supported input formats

- ✒ ASCII text, RTF, Microsoft Word, WordPerfect, Lotus WordPro (formerly known as AmiPro), FrameMaker, Interleaf

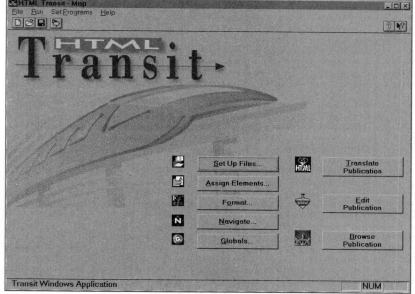

Figure 3-1:
The HTML
Transit main
screen
shows off its
function
buttons.

Supported graphic formats

✔ BMP, CDR, CGM, DIB, DRW, DXF, GEM, GIF, HPGL, JPEG, MSP, PCC, PCX, PIC, TIFF, WMF, WPG

Supported output formats

✔ HTML 2.0 and 3.0 (draft specification)

✔ Netscape Navigator extensions

✔ Microsoft Internet Explorer extensions

✔ Graphics as GIF or JPEG

File controls

✔ Single or multiple source files

✔ Selectable segmentation into smaller, linked files

Automated translation

✔ Automatic generation of HTML tags for body, table of contents, and index

✔ Source document style name recognition

- ✔ Source document attribute/pattern recognition
- ✔ Automatic graphics conversion to GIF or JPEG formats
- ✔ Graphics as full-size or choice of 6 linked thumbnail sizes

Publication formatting

- ✔ Character, paragraph, lists
- ✔ Graphical separators and icons
- ✔ Background colors and patterns
- ✔ Independent formatting for body, table of contents, and index

Navigation buttons

- ✔ TOC, index, next page, previous page, next item, previous item, specified HTML file (home page, Help, and so on)
- ✔ Automatic insertion
- ✔ Control over placement
- ✔ Address/signature e-mail links

You can download a 30-day trial version of HTML Transit from InfoAccess's Web site.

`http://www.infoaccess.com/`

Web Publisher

Web Publisher 1.1 from SkiSoft converts Microsoft Word, WordPerfect, Lotus WordPro (formerly known as AmiPro), RTF, and FrameMaker format files into complete HTML documents, as Figure 3-2 suggests. It's a good conversion program for Windows 95 and 3.1.

Figure 3-2:
The Web Publisher main screen displays its function buttons.

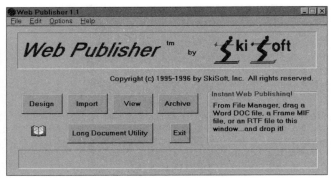

The list price of the standard version of Web Publisher is $495, and the Professional version, which includes the Long Document Utility, is $990 for a single PC. The Long Document Utility splits long HTML files into multiple documents and links them to another HTML file that contains a table of contents. In fact, Web Publisher automatically performs the following tasks:

- Converts images into GIFs
- Builds Netscape 1.1 tables
- Builds tables of contents with links to headings
- Interprets style information to build corresponding headings
- Converts number and bullet lists
- Places signatures, mail-to URLs, and corporate images in your documents
- Converts multiple documents in a single pass according to your templates
- Creates headings and navigation buttons

You can download a trial version of Web Publisher from SkiSoft's Web site but you must e-mail SkiSoft to obtain an activation code before it can run.

    http://www.skisoft.com/

WebWorks

WebWorks Publisher from Quadralay converts FrameMaker files to HTML on Windows, Macintosh, and several UNIX platforms. This program converts graphics, tables, lists, ISO Latin 1, Greek, and equation formats. WebWorks Publisher also supports conversion of RTF, Word, WordPerfect, and Interleaf formats through FrameMaker's file import.

WebWorks contains advanced graphic generation controls to perform the following tasks:

- Generate transparent GIFs
- Generate graphics for viewing in-line, external, or both
- Create graphic thumbnails
- Scale or rotate output graphics
- Adjust colors

    http://www.quadralay.com/Products/WWPub/wwpub.html

Installing and using a conversion tool

We downloaded the trial versions of both HTML Transit and Web Publisher to see how they worked. First, a few comments on the download and installation of each. HTML Transit has a 3.8MB SETUP.EXE file that takes *forever* to download (at least a half hour or so under good conditions) using a 14.4 modem. The Web Publisher's SKISETUP.EXE program is 1.3MB and takes correspondingly less time to download. However, you must e-mail or call SkiSoft to receive an install code to start the trial version. So don't do it on the weekend or you have to wait until Monday to call. We e-mailed them on Saturday morning and received the install code via e-mail late Sunday afternoon.

We tested both programs on a 486, 120 MHz computer with 16MB RAM using Windows 95. Both programs installed quickly, without changing any parameters in any permanent Windows files, and both provide uninstall programs in case you want to remove them. This is a nice touch even though Windows 95 can also uninstall them. Both programs contain extensive Help systems that walk you through their templates. Both programs contain collections of graphics buttons that you can use for navigation in your Web pages, but HTML Transit contains a larger list. (Maybe that's one reason its setup file is so large.) Both programs use similar, template-based approaches to the conversion process.

To use HTML Transit to quickly convert a Word for Windows file, you first click on the Set Up Files button to open the Select Files dialog box, as shown in Figure 3-3.

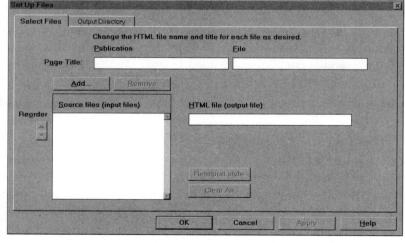

Figure 3-3:
The HTML
Transit
Select Files
window
enables you
to set input
variables.

Click Add and you see the next dialog box, as shown in Figure 3-4, from which you may browse for your input files.

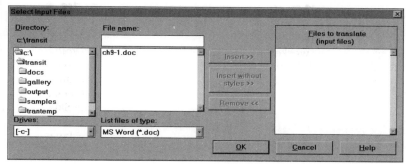

Figure 3-4:
The HTML
Transit
Select Input
Files
window
enables you
to choose
your input
files.

Select the file or files from the left-hand list that you want for input, and click Insert to put them into the right-hand list. Click OK and you're back to the previous window. Click OK in the Select Files window and you see the main screen again. Click the Translate Publication button, and HTML Transit does its thing with your file(s). You see the screen shown in Figure 3-5 while it's working.

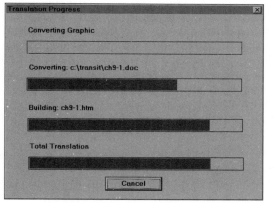

Figure 3-5:
The HTML
Transit
Translation
Progress
screen
shows you
what's
happening.

After the program finishes its translation task, the main screen appears again. You then click the Browse Publication button, and HTML Transit opens your browser with your newly converted HTML document loaded for you to see. This process is actually easier than described here, but it does make you jump through quite a few steps.

On the other hand, Web Publisher performs what some pundits call "Instant Web Publishing." This is a bit of a misnomer because you must run Web Publisher, open Explorer (or File Manager), select the file that you want to convert, drag the file, and drop it onto the Web Publisher Window, which starts the Instant Import facility; then you click OK to convert the file. However, because it takes more time to read the last sentence than it actually takes to do it, it's pretty close to instant. If you don't like Web Publisher's list of templates, you can change just about anything in it or create your own template via the Design button and associated menus. It's a well-designed and smooth-running program.

What should you remember about HTML converters?

When all is said and done, both HTML Transit and Web Publisher are excellent programs for what they are designed to do — convert your existing files into working HTML documents. They don't keep you from needing to know enough about HTML to design and correctly lay out a Web page, but they do help you by automatically performing many of the tedious, repetitive steps.

None of the conversion programs magically convert your existing text, graphics, or data files into fantastic-looking, state-of-the-art Web pages, much less a complete Web site. One way or the other, you and only you must determine which documents to link and in what order, lay out the frames or other HTML 3.0 or browser extension goodies in your Web, size and place the graphics and Java applets, and so on. Some of the conversion programs' templates assist you in accomplishing some of these actions, but you still must picture it in your own mind and either use the conversion program's template maker or manually edit the HTML code to ultimately get the idea across to the Web browser. You are still the key, no matter what tools you decide to use to help you perform your job more efficiently.

Déjà Vu — Elements of Page and Site Design

Yeah, yeah, you already know everything you need to know about Web page and site design, right? Do you know that the only way to get a framitz to link to a gazingleforkee across a 128K ISDN line is to use a skyhook with a frimmer? You do? Well then, why aren't you writing this book?

The next section is more than a review of how to build HTML documents and create a Web site; we hope that it tells you what you need to look out for from the viewpoint of a Web site administrator. You need to stop thinking only about the content and layout of your Web pages and site and add to your outlook the dimensions of user interest, information flow, update cycling, and file management, just to name a few. Mentally step back from the text and GIFs and look at your site from the user's point of view. Don't just look at the pages via your browser. Think about why the user is interested in visiting your site in the first place. Think about what deep psychological need your site can fulfill for the user. Think about what will keep the user coming back for more, over and over. You want your site to be irresistible and addictive but legal.

Now this is a tall order for a site that's going to be providing daily updates of the dilithium futures market trading on Ragnar III. But you can do more than simply dump a load of data into tabular form or several nearly identically formatted Web pages and slap it on the default background. Use your imagination to create at least a little variety that the user's eye and brain can grasp. Maybe you put a new little icon on each page every day. Maybe you put a small box with a daily message in it on the first page. Whatever you do is going to be appreciated by your users if you do it tastefully and don't let it get in the way of the real reason they are visiting your site, whatever that is. (You'd better know what it is, or your site may become the proverbial ghost town virtually overnight.) Always give 'em what they want and a little bit more and do it with a smile.

Give all your pages a title

Every HTML document, not just the first page of your Web, should have a title. Not only is the title displayed in the browser's title bar but it is used by Web search sites (Yahoo!, WebCrawler, Alta Vista, and so on) to index and list your Web pages. And, of course, you want as many of your pages listed as possible. Therefore, take the time to be creative and thorough in creating each document's title.

Text and hypertext links

Text is the prime element in most HTML documents. Although a picture in the right place may be worth a thousand words, it's a rare HTML document that doesn't have some text in it. It's up to you to make maximum use of your text. Keep in mind that you have many ways to enhance the actual content of your text. You have layout, nontext blank space (white space), differently colored fonts, and links to other related pieces of text.

If you're not a very good page layout person, get help from someone who is to ensure that the text of your Web pages is easy to read and pleasing to the user's eyes. Nothing turns Web surfers off quicker than being forced to scroll through screen after screen of tightly packed text to find what they want.

Use tables of contents or icon-based navigation bars with hypertext links to the sections of text documents. Internal links to named locations in your documents not only provide your users with a means of quickly getting to the section they want, but also help other sites to easily address locations on your Web pages other than at the head of a Web document. Remember that an internal link is referenced by a text name, which must be unique among all the anchors defined for each document.

Use graphics for maximum effect

First impressions are critically important to entice a surfer deeper into your Web. Use your most unique, eye-catching images on your front page. But remember, if the image takes forever to load, the surfer may click to another site before the image finishes loading. Small, quickly loaded images are optimal. Save your bigger masterpieces for the internal pages, where you can provide a thumbnail and give the user the option of loading the larger version. A few more tips for using graphics are as follows:

- ✔ Use graphics only if they add value to a page. Don't toss in a few little, annoying graphics just because you like them. Make sure that they perform a function that the user can appreciate.

- ✔ Keep your graphics fresh. Even your corporate logo gets stale over time. Look at the various logos of numerous megacorporations over the past century and you see that they update them as times change. Well, times change very rapidly on the Web, so make sure that your logo represents the message you want to communicate to users. The idea that your organization is cutting-edge can really be emphasized by using improved images and techniques on your Web pages.

- ✔ Use Java applets to animate your images for Java-enabled browsers.

- ✔ Make sure that your GIFs have transparent backgrounds and are interleaved.

- ✔ Compress your JPEGs as much as possible for quick display, while still keeping the resolution acceptable.

- ✔ Keep the graphical elements to a reasonable number per page. If you must use numerous graphical elements on a page, keep them small to minimize transfer time.

The temptation to stick in another image can be very strong. Resist the urge. Ask yourself: "What does this add to my document that my users are going to find irresistible?" Don't fool yourself with your own answer either. Ask someone else's opinion.

Think in 3-D

Although hypertext is new and exciting, the legacy of thousands of years of linear text is hard to overcome. In other words, even though you can do incredible things with linking and hypermedia, your users may not be able to follow your path unless you make it as obvious as the yellow brick road to Oz. Linking adds the third dimension to the Web, but use it wisely and always, always give your users an easy way out to somewhere they can instantly recognize.

Stringing pages together, the book way

If part of your information is a report, it probably should be read linearly. Therefore, you can present it as a single Web document (if it's no more than five screens long) or split it into several HTML documents linked by navigation buttons (next, previous, top, bottom, start, end) at the bottom of each document. Make liberal use of links to other documents, to a glossary, or for cross-referencing to other parts of your document, where appropriate. Just because your primary format is linear doesn't mean that you must force your users to move only linearly. Let 'em jump around if they know where they're going, and always make it easy for them to get back.

Hierarchies are natural

The hierarchical approach to Web document links is universally understood. Because the branched or hierarchical structure is one of the most basic in nature, it is difficult to improve on without adding unintelligible complexity. Unless your intended audience of users is especially good at complex mental gymnastics or your site is designed as a puzzle, stick to the basic structure shown in Figure 3-6, and both you and your users should be much happier.

Multiple tracks for multiple audiences

Building a Web that includes several levels of material to meet the needs of different levels of users within your general audience is somewhat time consuming but may pay off in the long run. Linking your Web's home page with a tutorial, a technical overview, and the detailed reference materials that comprise the bulk of your information is easy. Using this approach, you can design a home page that points beginners at a track that starts them with a tutorial and then leads them through an overview, before assaulting them with the down-and-dirty details of your "real" content.

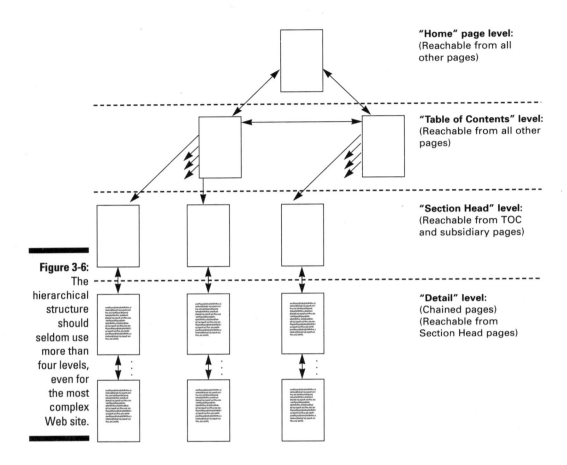

"Home" page level:
(Reachable from all
other pages)

"Table of Contents" level:
(Reachable from all other
pages)

"Section Head" level:
(Reachable from TOC
and subsidiary pages)

Figure 3-6:
The
hierarchical
structure
should
seldom use
more than
four levels,
even for
the most
complex
Web site.

"Detail" level:
(Chained pages)
(Reachable from
Section Head pages)

This kind of organization, as depicted in Figure 3-7, enables you to notify experienced readers on how to access your in-depth content directly, bypassing the introductory and explanatory materials built for novices. Although HTML itself has no limits on the kinds of hierarchies you can build, your readers' ability to handle the added complexity may be limited. For everyone's sake, we suggest keeping the hierarchy as tight and shallow as possible.

This organization combines elements of both a linear and a hierarchical structure in its actual page linkages. The tutorial is typically linear, whereas the reference materials are usually consulted by topic and are best structured in a hierarchy.

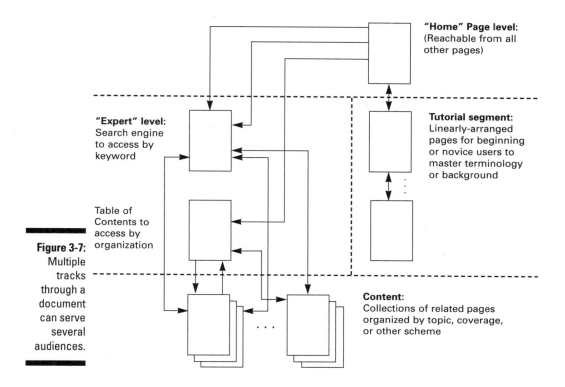

"Home" Page level:
(Reachable from all
other pages)

"Expert" level:
Search engine
to access by
keyword

Tutorial segment:
Linearly-arranged
pages for beginning
or novice users to
master terminology
or background

Table of
Contents to
access by
organization

Figure 3-7:
Multiple
tracks
through a
document
can serve
several
audiences.

Content:
Collections of related pages
organized by topic, coverage,
or other scheme

Extending your Web, a comment at a time

If you really want to encourage feedback, you can use a CGI script to solicit
input from users and append their comments to the end of one of your Web
pages. This creates an open-ended document that grows like a colony of coral
or some other organic life form, more by accretion than by prior design. It is
used also for never-ending story writing and other serial creation sites on the
Web. If you have the hard disk space on your Web server to handle it and the
knowledge of how to program the CGI script to accomplish it, you may want to
explore this approach.

For an example of this kind of living, ongoing document, consult the following
URL:

```
http://bug.village.virginia.edu/
```

WAXWeb is a hypermedia implementation of a feature-length independent film, *WAX or the Discovery of Television Among the Bees* (David Blair, 85 minutes playing time, 1991). WAXWeb is a large hypermedia database available on the Internet that has an authoring interface that enables users to collaborate in adding to the story. It includes thousands of individual elements, ranging from text, to music, to motion videos and video transcriptions of motion picture clips.

The essence of managing Web publishing is implementing a process that provides your users with the fresh, attractive, and timely content that they desire. You must manage the process that gathers the information, creates the HTML documents, and introduces the documents into your Web site in a time frame acceptable to your users, your employer, and you. To accomplish all this, you must carefully plan and execute your procedures and work closely with your Web server administrator to ensure that all of your hard work is made available to your users. Numerous tools to assist you in your tasks are discussed in this chapter, and even more are included in the following chapter, along with more techniques to help you make your Web site a smashing success.

Chapter 4

Web Site Management Tools and Techniques

*W*hatever you put into your Web — text, graphics, CGI scripts, forms, or something truly exotic — must be logically arranged so that you can be sure that you're using the correct version of each element. Constantly monitor your Web's security and frequently inspect your links for freshness and validity. Check your HTML documents for proper syntax to ensure that they work flawlessly with your users' browsers. Read the feedback from your users; then write and file your responses. And most important of all, periodically update your site's content to keep your users happy.

All the work involved in managing your site is up to you and your Web site management team (if you're lucky enough to have one). Without the correct techniques, good rapport with your Web server administrator, and a few handy tools to help you administer your Web site, you and your Web site can always be much more than a day late and a dollar short.

This chapter focuses on site management techniques instead of on specific tools, because such tools vary widely and often depend on the Web server software that you use. Also, the trend is moving toward more comprehensive Web site management systems for Windows 95, Windows NT, and Macintosh platforms. In this new wave of Web servers, each system contains its own proprietary set of management tools and, often, content creation and management tools as well. Nevertheless, you can find plenty of stand-alone Web management tools for all the popular platforms. We've included suggestions later in this chapter about these tools and where to find out about them on the Web.

Managing Multitudes of Documents

Your Web site consists primarily of HTML documents that contain the "content" — your Web site's reason for existence. Whether you have a single, personal home page or minister to a Web site with hundreds of pages of "content," you need to keep track of your documents. The human mind is a wonderful biological computer that is capable of remembering seemingly countless bits of information. However, you still can't remember where you left your reading glasses or when you last changed the oil in your car. Why, then, should you expect to remember when you last revised one of your Web documents or where you left the document on your hard disk?

If you arrange your Web documents' disk files logically and label them correctly, you don't need to remember the details about any specific document. If you follow our suggestions to the letter and keep a *change log* for your Web site, you need to remember only the name of the *change log* file on your hard disk. If you can't remember where the *change log* resides, you can always use the Find feature of your operating system (provided that you can remember the *change log*'s filename).

How big is your Web?

We thought long and hard and then threw a few darts at the board to determine the approximate sizes of Web site categories. For the following discussions, we consider that a small site includes 30 or fewer documents, a medium site includes from 30 to 100 documents, and a large site includes more than 100 documents. A document can be any separate file — whether the file is an HTML document, image file, CGI script, Java applet, or whatever — that you have in your Web site's directories on your Web server.

Because this is a . . .*For Dummies* book, we concentrate our discussion on small- and medium-sized sites. However, the techniques that we cover work for all but the largest sites (those with thousands of documents or more), and even these "monster sites" use fundamentally the same approach that we suggest. Only the tools change drastically: The monster sites use networked document management systems (costing tens of thousands of dollars) to handle the hundreds of thousands of documents that they process every month. You, on the other hand, want to keep your Web site fresh and alive without spending all your time (and money) on its care and feeding.

Organize to untangle your Web

Organize! Organize! Organization is the key to minimizing your Web administration time. Think of organization as the *Vulcan approach* — that is, always logical and precisely arranged. Even though you easily remember more than 100 separate names for people that you know, you probably can't remember 100 disk filenames, nor should you try.

Try this simple file management system. Group your files by common characteristics, name the files with similar, sequential names, and place the files in hierarchical subdirectories. Thirty documents aren't difficult to manage if you separate them into seven subdirectories. Look over the following directory structure with suggested (and frequently used) directory names:

- ✔ **INDEX.HTML:** The primary directory where your Web's home page can reside

- ✔ **GRAPHICS:** A subdirectory for somewhat fixed graphics files such as navigation buttons, logos, and backgrounds

- ✔ **ABOUTUS:** A subdirectory for your organization's information

- ✔ **CONTENT1 and CONTENT2:** Two subdirectories for your Web pages' contents

- ✔ **IMAGE1 and IMAGE2:** Subdirectories of CONTENT1 and CONTENT2, respectively, for unique images pertaining to the content in that directory

Figure 4-1 shows how the hierarchy of this directory structure may look on your hard disk.

Figure 4-1:
A typical hierarchical directory structure.

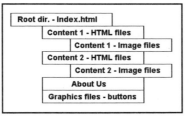

Even if your site has 100 files, you probably need no more than 15 subdirectories. Adding 4 more CONTENT subdirectories, each with its own IMAGE subdirectory, increases the total number to 15. These additions give you 6 content subdirectories where you can put 10 files each and 6 image subdirectories with 6 files each for a total of 96 content-related files. This number of files equates to quite a bit of information; probably 5 to 10MB, depending on your specific information.

You can keep track of this type of arrangement easily. Even if you update your content daily, you can proceed in an orderly fashion through your directory structure.

Keep adequate working and backup copies of the directory structure and files for your Web site. On your own computer's hard disk, make two copies of the directories and files (in the same hierarchical structure) that you have on the Web server. One of the two copies contains your working files; the other contains the most recent copy of each file for your Web site. (The latter is the copy that you upload to your Web server when you update your Web site.) In addition to these two copies, make another backup copy of the directory structure and files on another computer, your LAN server, or other means of directory/file backup.

Document management systems

You may have heard or read about electronic document management systems that enable you to store computer files in a database just like the files' paper equivalents would be placed in a filing cabinet. Some systems even manage images and help you attach keywords to the image files before storing the files in a database. In turn, the keywords help you easily search for the images.

This concept looks great on paper, and many document management systems cost less than $500. The best products support full-text and customizable keyword indexes that use fuzzy-logic, Boolean, and template-based searching. They also include OCR-based, full-text indexing if you have a scanner and your information isn't available in electronic form. (You live in the middle of the Sahara desert maybe?)

So why don't you rush right out and buy a document management system? The following ideas and examples may help you decide whether you need to do that:

- ✔ If you handle numerous paper documents each day, a document management system may help you. A main useful feature of these systems is their capability to scan and store the images of documents and have these images quickly available for viewing by searching the database. For example, someone who processes insurance claims for a small company may need such a feature.

Combine the output from a document management system with an HTML conversion program for the text and an image converter to make GIF or JPEG format files from the images prior to placing them on your Web site. Because these formats are native to most Web browsers, users can therefore view your graphics without going through unnecessary contortions.

- ✔ If the primary thrust of your Web site is to provide your readers with a searchable database of large amounts of electronically available data, you can definitely benefit from any of several available software systems. If you're going to charge for your database service, you may be interested in the Basis Document Manager system from Information Dimensions, Inc.

The Basis Document Manager is an integrated server component built on BasisPlus, a proprietary extended-relational database, also from Information Dimensions. This software provides document management library services, full text retrieval, document control, document delivery, security, and authentication. The Basis Document Manager is integrated with Netscape's Communications Web Server and Commerce Web Server software and is scaleable from small implementations up to thousands of users. Starting at $7,500, the Basis Document Manager provides a relatively low-cost tool for posting corporate information on the Web.

✔ If you're running a one-person Web administration department on a limited budget and you process several but not hundreds of pieces of electronic information a day, your needs are pretty modest. You can concentrate on a simple, straightforward system for receiving, processing, storing, and placing your incoming information on your Web site. You don't need to bring out the heavy artillery.

We hope you get the picture. If you don't think that an electronic document management system is for you, don't despair — other Web management alternatives may better suit your needs, time, and budget. We discuss some of these alternatives in the following section.

Examining the Alternatives

Commercially available Web management tools haven't proliferated as rapidly as Web browsers and servers. The reason for this situation may be that most Web servers are UNIX based, and the UNIX crowd creates its own utilities (which only they can use). Do you get the idea that Web management has been a somewhat programmer-oriented culture until recently? With the unveiling of several Windows 95-, Windows NT-, and Macintosh-based Web servers, the game has opened up considerably.

Of course, Windows and Mac users aren't going to use command-line utilities — as UNIX folks do — because their entire outlook on life is GUI based. You can't just kludge together a GUI-based Web management tool in the same way that UNIX users created their tools in the past. As a result, you can find only a few shareware tools for Windows or Macintosh Web administrators. We discuss the more promising tools briefly in the following sections to give you some ideas about where to start your quest for the perfect tool set.

Augment these discussions by checking your favorite search engine sites and checking out the very good compendium of information and links at the webreference.com site.

`http://webreference.com/`

Web site managers

A new class of tool is emerging to help Web administrators manage their sites. Some tools consist of a collection of utilities, and some take more of an all-in-one system approach. We discuss examples of each kind in the following sections.

SITEMAN

SITEMAN is a set of utilities that checks internal references, lists all files that contain a call or a link to a file, and identifies *orphan* files (those files that are not hyperlinked to any other files in the directory). The utilities run under Windows 3.1 or Windows 95 and present the user with the following processes that help with managing their Web site's files.

File integrity check

The file integrity check routine reviews each internal link from each file to ensure that the link connects to another file in the directory. The routine does not check external, extra-directory, and same-page links. The resulting output lists all links that are not connected to a valid file and all files that are referenced but do not exist in their indicated directories.

Reference list

For each file or set of files selected, the reference list routine lists all occurrences of references to other files found in `<A HREF="...">..</A>`, `<IMG .. SRC="..">` or `<BODY...BACKGROUND="...">` tags. The resulting list contains all such references, including those that are not tested by the file integrity check.

Global filename change

The global filename change is available in SITEMAN 2, which is due for release early in 1996. By using this function, you can select a file, modify its name, and have all references to that file (in all HTML files in the site) changed automatically to the new name. We like this concept, and we hope that the global change function works as well as it sounds like it should!

Individual filename linkages

The individual filename linkage function lists all files in the site that link to the file you select. Use this function to find file dependencies within your site.

Orphan file search

This routine lists orphan files — that is, those files in a selected directory that aren't connected by links to any other files in the directory.

Find more information about SITEMAN at the following URL:

```
http://www.morning.asn.au/siteman/index.html
```

LivePAGE WebMaster

LivePAGE WebMaster, a collection of Web management tools for Windows 3.*x*, Windows 95, and Windows NT, is currently a 16-bit application that doesn't support HTML 3.0 or Java. The LivePAGE WebMaster includes the complete LivePAGE Local Developer Kit, LivePAGE Browser, and LivePAGE Updater.

When this package becomes available as a 32-bit application with HTML 3.0, Java, and additional support, it may live up to its potential. At this time, LivePAGE WebMaster offers basic features that do the following:

- ✔ Manages your Web site as a single document
- ✔ Publishes your site document for the Web at the press of a button
- ✔ Resolves links
- ✔ Generates navigation buttons and dynamic tables of contents automatically
- ✔ Ensures valid HTML 2.0 syntax with some Netscape extensions
- ✔ Works with existing HTML editors
- ✔ Requires no special Web Server software

Inforium provides an extensive look at the multiple functions of its LivePAGE WebMaster package at the following URL:

```
http://www.inforium.com/inforium/webmastr.html
```

SiteMill

Adobe Systems, Inc., offers SiteMill for Macintosh and Power Macintosh. SiteMill includes the functionality of Adobe's outstanding PageMill software, which you can use to create HTML documents. SiteMill includes WYSIWYG Web page editing, integrated image manipulation, and format conversion.

Link management

Adobe SiteMill enables you to easily maintain correct links for your entire Web site, including links to external sites, because SiteMill automatically repairs links that break after you rename pages or files or change the location of files (move them into subfolders, for example). The program displays a view of your Web site that shows your page structure, along with pop-up menus of the links to and from each file.

One-step error correction

SiteMill finds and summarizes any errors present in your Web site. You can then correct them with a simple, one-step, drag-and-drop procedure. From then on, under the watchful eye of SiteMill, your site remains error-free. Adobe SiteMill can also read existing Web sites and automatically find and summarize the errors present in them, too.

Creating new links

The SiteMill software integrates the *Site view* (the display of your Web site's structure and resources) and the *Page Editing view* (the layout of your Web page document), enabling you to create new links by simply dragging a file or an image icon from the Site view into the Page view. You don't need to know about the uniform resource locator (URL) link addressing scheme or the page path name syntax, and you don't need to type any filenames. SiteMill automatically creates the correct links.

Summary of SiteMill features

The following list summarizes SiteMill's features:

- ✔ Shows all resources, page titles, and folders in the Site view
- ✔ Shows warnings for unreachable or unused resources
- ✔ Automatically fixes all links throughout the site after files or folders are renamed, moved between folders, or deleted
- ✔ Enables link creation by simply dropping a resource from the Site view into a page
- ✔ Shows all bad links and enables one-step correction from the Error view
- ✔ Shows all references to external Web sites and enables easy global renaming of files through the External References view

Additional information on SiteMill is available at the Adobe Systems, Inc., URL:

```
http://w1000.mv.us.adobe.com/Apps/SiteMill/
```

FrontPage

With its purchase of Vermeer Technologies, Microsoft has garnered FrontPage, perhaps the top Web management all-in-one system available today. If Microsoft continues to develop this system and opens it up for use with other Web servers, FrontPage may become a major player in the Web management game. The system already contains extensive online tutorial and context-sensitive Help to assist you in understanding its many features and functions. The FrontPage graphical interface is a big attraction for Windows users; see Figure 4-2 for a look at this interface.

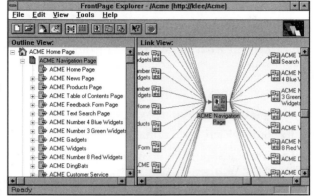

Figure 4-2:
FrontPage's
Explorer
displays two
separate
Web views.

The FrontPage client/server architecture enables you to develop Web content locally, across a LAN, or over the Internet on a Windows PC or a Macintosh. At the same time, your Web server can reside on Windows NT, Windows 95, or UNIX platforms. In addition, you can copy Web sites between platforms and Web servers while preserving all programming, access controls, and clickable image maps. FrontPage integrates into a seamless environment all the functions typically required to develop and administer a Web site. FrontPage features include the following:

✔ WYSIWYG editing of HTML pages, including text, headings, inline images, and most HTML extensions (page background images, custom text colors, font point sizes, and so on)

✔ WYSIWYG editing of HTML forms, including text input fields, scrolling text boxes, check boxes, radio buttons, drop-down pick lists, and push buttons

✔ Link, Outline, and Summary views of all the hyperlinks, documents, and multimedia files comprising the Web site as a whole

✔ Drag-and-drop adding of hyperlinks between pages or from pages to any other file type (sound, video, PDF, and so on)

✔ WebBots™, which quickly add sophisticated interactive functions (such as threaded discussion groups, full-text search, Web registration, and form-driven surveys) to the Web without programming

✔ Wizards and templates to easily create complete Webs and individual pages

✔ Clickable image maps created by using the mouse to indicate hotspot boundaries

✔ Remote, collaborative authoring support that enables multiple users, who are geographically dispersed, to develop against the same Web simultaneously

✔ Multi-user To Do List, which tracks the tasks remaining to complete a Web site

Also, with FrontPage you can perform the following tasks:

- Set permissions for end-users, authors, and administrators of a Web site
- Copy an entire Web site from one Web server to another including documents, clickable image maps, programming (via WebBots), and permissions. FrontPage can copy between Web servers from different vendors that run on different hardware and software platforms
- Verify that all hyperlinks to external Webs are still valid
- Automatically convert Rich Text Format (RTF) and plain text files to HTML
- Autoatically convert most popular image formats into GIF or JPEG, the native formats of the Web
- Automatically create transparent GIF images
- Browse (and, potentially, import) any page on the global Web from directly within the FrontPage Editor by specifying a URL or by Ctrl+clicking any hyperlink

Learn more about FrontPage from Microsoft at the following URL:

```
http://www.microsoft.com/msoffice/frontpage/default.htm
```

Let someone else manage your Web

Cookware runs the ClubWeb site to help you with your Web needs for just a little bit every month . . . that is, for just a few dollars, son, dollars. Check out this site's various offerings if you really need to put up your Web page in a hurry and if you want to conserve up-front costs. Cookware offers numerous options for Web authors and administrators:

- **IShop:** Virtual shopping carts for commercial sales over the Web.
- **Forms4U:** The advanced Forms4U form handler enables you (for a fee) to use HTML forms in your WWW documents without a server.
- **Find4Me:** Database searching for your pages. Find4Me enables you to search data by clicking a hyperlink, by submitting a form, or by bringing up a page.
- **MembersOnly:** Membership and security for your pages. The MembersOnly system enables you to have pages that are accessible only by users with passwords and membership names.
- **Sticky Pages:** Fantastic marketing capabilities. Sticky pages enable you to have your logo, buttons, or advertising stay with the user as they surf the Web, even after they leave your site.

▶ **RandomLink:** Add fun to your pages! RandomLink changes the graphics and text each time a page is displayed.

▶ **Demographics:** For a small monthly fee, the Web site demographics service provides you with an analysis of your Web's hits that it drops off in your home directory every night.

Access ClubWeb at the following URL; make sure that you check out Cookware's other offerings:

```
http://www.cookware.com/
```

Cool Management Tools

You can find several really cool, stand-alone management tools directly via the Internet. Certain management tools enable you to check up on your Web site and its pages from your own Web browser. "How does this work?" you ask. You simply supply the management tool's site with the URL of your Web page; the management tool software does the rest. After the stand-alone tool finishes the check-up, it sends a report back to your browser.

Doesn't this convenience beat running a UNIX command line utility? Yes and no. Using these tools is better if you're not into UNIX and don't run your own Web server. But using the management tools is not better if you want an automated system, because you must enter the URL for each of your HTML pages individually. And you receive reports for one page at a time. If you have a small Web site, tools such as these may be all you need. If so, give them a try.

Dr. HTML

Dr. HTML retrieves your specified Web page and performs several tests to see whether your document conforms to applicable standards. This management tool offers a selectable set of tests on its main page. You enter the URL for the page you want examined; then wait while Dr. HTML performs these tests:

▶ Checks the document for spelling errors, so you don't look like a dummy!

▶ Performs an analysis of the images, so you know how much bandwidth is consumed when the image is downloaded, as well as estimated download times.

▶ Tests the document structure to easily find unclosed HTML codes that may cause problems on some browsers.

✔ Looks at image command syntax, so you don't have absent image commands. These tags are important for quick image loading and page formatting, as well as providing information for browsers lacking images.

✔ Examines the table structure to make sure that you don't have any unclosed TR, TH, and TD tags inside a correctly defined table (that is, one with both an open and close table tag). It also reports on TR, TH, and TD tags that appear outside of any correctly defined table, because these may cause formatting errors on some browsers.

✔ Verifies that all the hyperlinks are valid (to avoid frustrating your users).

✔ Examines the form structure. This feature is handy for checking input types and variable names. Currently, it looks only at INPUT commands and does not test SELECT or TEXTAREA commands.

✔ Shows the command hierarchy. This task presents the HTML commands that are found in the document.

Give Dr. HTML a look at your Web pages by contacting the following URL:

```
http://imagiware.com/RxHTML.cgi
```

Weblint

Weblint checks the HTML code in your Web pages to ensure that the code conforms to your chosen HTML specifications. As with Dr. HTML, you simply supply the URL for a page anywhere on the Web. Alternatively, you can paste or type HTML code that you want checked directly into a window. Weblint currently performs the following tests, in a very precise manner:

✔ Checks the basic HTML structure for completeness

✔ Lists unknown elements and element attributes

✔ Performs context checks (where a tag must appear within a certain element)

✔ Lists overlapped element

✔ Expects to see a TITLE in the HEAD element

✔ Lists IMG elements that do not have ALT text

✔ Shows illegally nested elements

✔ Alerts you to mismatched tags (such as <H1> ... </H2>)

✔ Displays unclosed elements (for example, <H1> ...)

✔ Catches elements that should appear only once

- ✔ Flags obsolete elements

- ✔ Checks for an odd number of quotes in a tag

- ✔ Checks the order of headings

- ✔ Lists potentially unclosed tags

- ✔ Flags markup embedded in comments, which can confuse some browsers

- ✔ Whines if you use `here` as anchor text

- ✔ Checks tags where attributes are expected (for example, anchors)

- ✔ Checks the existence of local anchor targets

- ✔ Flags the case of tags

- ✔ Alerts you to leading and trailing whitespace in certain container elements

- ✔ Flags unclosed comments (comments should be `<!-- . . . -->`)

- ✔ Supports the format formerly known as HTML 3.0 — elements such as `TABLES`, `MATH`, `FIGURES`, and the rest

The output from a Weblint check looks as follows:

```
Weblint Results
Please keep in mind that Weblint is a lint and can be picky.
Weblint Warning Messages
    line 23: illegal value for WIDTH attribute of IMG (100%)
    line 23: IMG does not have ALT text defined.
    line 41: illegal value for WIDTH attribute of TD (25%)
    line 43: illegal value for WIDTH attribute of TD (25%)
    line 125: IMG does not have ALT text defined.
    line 147: IMG does not have ALT text defined.
    line 169: illegal value for WIDTH attribute of IMG (100%)
    line 169: IMG does not have ALT text defined.
    line 175: empty container element <A>.
The HTML Source Listing
    1.<HTML>
    2.<HEAD>....
```

(The rest of the HTML source listing was omitted to protect the guilty.)

Weblint really gives your HTML code a thorough going-over. You may choose to ignore some of its suggestions, but you should run your pages through this or another similar program to learn. Access the Weblint program at the following URL:

```
http://www.unipress.com/weblint/
```

WebTechs's HTML Validation Service

WebTechs's HTML Validation Service checks your HTML files to make sure that they comply with your chosen level of HTML (2.0, 3.0, Netscape, or SoftQuad extensions). WebTechs's validation service works the same way as Weblint. The WebTechs's site also has some CGI scripting utilities available for UNIX users. Give the service and the utilities a try at the following URL:

```
http://www.webtechs.com/html-val-svc/
```

If you run your own Web server, you can use other Web site management tools. When you're ready to acquire a set of these tools, the following sections can assist you in finding the right ones for your site.

Acquiring the Perfect Tool Set

You can find Web site management tools to help you with various aspects of your Web site or to perform certain Web site functions for you. To find the latest versions of available tools, use the terms from Table 4-1 in several of your favorite search engines and follow the links. In the following sections, we discuss just a few of the more useful tools for your perfect tool set.

Table 4-1	Web Site Management Aspects and Functions	
Converters	Data Base Access	Diagnostic Tools
Firewalls	Forms	Gateways
Image maps	Indexing tools	Information Retrieval Tools
Messengers	Real Audio	Robots
Searching tools	Security	Scripts
Sound Players	Spiders	Statistics/tracking tools
Verifiers	Viewers	VRML

Web site usage tools and services

If you're running your own Web site, you want to find out who's visiting the site. Web site usage tools and services can give you a better picture of who's visiting your site and for how long and, if used correctly, can even tell you something about why. The following list was extracted from the list at the Webreference.com site. Please use this URL to access the links that this site provides to each of the listed packages:

`http://webreference.com/usage.html`

- **Access Watch:** Shareware statistics analyzer with graphical output. (Access Watch was created by Dave Maher.)

- **Analog:** A freeware log analysis program. (Analog was created by Stephen Turner.)

- **The Internet Audit Bureau:** A free Web site auditing service. Tracks unique page hits; it is better able to distinguish the number of actual users, as opposed to the number of hits. Just join, place a few lines of HTML in the pages you want to track, and you're done.

- **Interse Market Focus:** A commercial site usage analysis tool that uses inference-based algorithms to reconstruct the actual visits, stay duration, and organizations that interact with a Web site.

- **Netcount:** Monitors traffic both within a Web site and between specified Web sites.

- **I/Count:** I/COUNT enables for the tracking and analysis of usage of a specific Internet site. Web site owners use the tracking results to understand aspects of site usage, such as total number of users, time spent per page, sections read within each document, and the geographic and organization origin of users." From I/PRO: Internet Profiles Corporation.

- **SiteTrack:** A powerful drop-in user tracking tool that enables WebMasters to monitor entire sessions inside your site and monitor where users go after they leave your site. SiteTrack also enables you to customize your Web site for each user's preferences. This tool includes a shopping basket and real-time page creation.

- **Statbot:** A shareware log analyzer, statistics generator, and database program. Statbot works by *snooping* log files and creating a database that contains information about the WWW server. This database is then used to create a statistics page and IF charts. Because it snoops the log files, Statbot does not require CGI-bin access and can be run from a user's home directory. (Statbot was created by David Tubbs.)

- **Web Audit:** A shareware site statistics generator. Similar to The Internet Audit Bureau, Web Audit uses an external graphic that counts *impressions* (the actual number of users, not hits). You can use Web Audit to monitor 10 Web pages free of charge; shareware fees apply if you want to monitor more than 10 pages. Web Audit also contains Web Guest, a shareware guestbook program.

- **WebTrac:** A site analysis tool from Logical Design Solutions. WebTrac is Windows-based donation-ware, but it supports any platform's log files.

Log file analysis tools

If you're using a UNIX-based Web server that produces NCSA compatible log files, you can use one of the stand-alone log file analysis programs such as WWWStat, GWStat, or Wusage. You can combine the HTML output from WWWStat with the GWStat program to produce usage charts and graphs — in color even.

Although it may be less complete than other tools, Wusage is easy to use and produces reports and graphs that can be automatically installed on your Web site simply by setting the location. Be aware that these programs aren't designed for use by the UNIX-challenged (nonprogrammer types), because the programs need to be customized for your specific Web site, and in some cases, they must be compiled.

WWWStat can be found at the following URL:

```
http://www.ics.uci.edu/WebSoft/wwwstat/
```

GWStat can be found at the following URL:

```
http://dis.cs.umass.edu/stats/gwstat.html
```

Wusage can be found at the following URL:

```
http://www.boutell.com/wusage/
```

You can get at least the following types of information from most good log file analysis tools:

```
Daily Transmission Statistics
%Reqs %Byte  Bytes Sent  Requests   Date
_____ _____  _____|  _____   ____
 0.35  0.38     695752        161  | Jan  9 1996
 0.55  0.92    1692956        254  | Jan  8 1996
 0.48  1.21    2230875        220  | Jan  7 1996
 0.30  0.33     606164        137  | Jan  6 1996
```

```
Hourly Transmission Statistics
Total Transfers by Client Domain
Total Transfers by Reversed Subdomain
Total Transfers from each Archive Section
%Reqs %Byte   Bytes Sent  Requests  Archive Section
_____ _____   _____|  _____  _____
 0.07  0.33      604700         34  | /coe/87manapc.htm
 0.04  0.07      126641         17  | /coe/87manapd.htm
 0.03  0.05       94061         16  | /coe/87manbib.htm
```

Some of the tools produce nice graphic representations of usage. Look for Windows 95 and NT, as well as Macintosh log file analysis tools, through your favorite Web search engine. We expect more and more of these tools to arrive on the scene in the near future.

The details of Web site management techniques change with the availability of new and improved management tools. However, the basics stay the same. No matter what types of tools you use, your primary objective is to provide unique, original, fresh content to your target audience in an engaging, easy-to-navigate, timely manner. To reach this form of "Nerd-vana," you must establish a Web management routine.

Your Web Management Routine

Plan for change! After your Web is up and running, your primary concerns are maintenance and improvement. Your Web management routine should be a process that evolves with changes in your personal situation, with changes in your site's content, hardware, and software, with changes in the Internet, and with changes in your users' needs, desires, and expectations.

Make your management routine workable so that it doesn't drive you screaming from your office just before an update deadline. To create a workable Web management routine, you need a plan based on your own (and your staff's) available time; the volume, availability, and timing of your site's content; and the following sound principles of Web site maintenance.

The principles of Web site maintenance

The primary principles of Web maintenance are appropriateness, timeliness, and thoroughness. Use feedback from your readers to find good reasons for changing only appropriate portions of your site. Provide timely updates and renovation of your content and Web pages. Be thorough in your search for new content and in your quest to provide your users with a perfect Web site.

Analyze the following areas for your Web site maintenance process:

- **Content:** Are you updating your site frequently and thoroughly enough? Are you adding new content in your niche?

- **Graphics:** Have you given your users a change of eye-catching graphics recently?

- **Links:** Are the URLs all still available? Have you added any new links to enhance your site?

- ✔ **Web walker:** Is your site in the top 10 listings of the major search engine sites? Why not?

- ✔ **Usage:** Is your hit counter working? What does your log file analysis tell you?

- ✔ **Feedback:** Are you reading user feedback and responding to it in a timely fashion?

- ✔ **Server:** Have you installed the most recent updates or fixes to your Web server software?

- ✔ **Browser:** Are you keeping abreast of updates in browsers that enable you to update your Web's look and feel (frames, Java, and so on)? Do you test your pages with new versions of popular browsers to ensure that they're still compatible?

- ✔ **CGI scripts:** Do your CGI scripts still work? Do they need updating?

To ensure that your maintenance is complete, make a checklist of these areas and fill in the date and time whenever you perform any maintenance task. Recording your maintenance activity should be a part of your overall Web management plan.

Creating your Web management plan

The details of your Web management plan vary depending on whether you administer your own personal Web or manage a Web management team for an organization. However, the basic steps to follow remain the same. Use these steps to create and revise your Web management plan:

1. **Determine your Web site's basic management needs on a daily, weekly, and monthly basis.**

2. **Type the determined needs into a file.**

3. **Prioritize the Web site management needs.**

4. **Describe the work and tools necessary to fulfill each need (task).**

5. **Guestimate the amount of time necessary to accomplish each task; enter your guestimate into the file.**

6. **Determine how often you want to perform each task.**

7. **Determine who should perform each task.**

8. **Create a critical path chart or sketch a time line on a sheet of paper.**

9. **Revise the Management Plan until the plan looks feasible.**

10. Try your plan on a small scale with a dummy Web site on your own computer.

11. Revise the plan.

12. Try your plan again on a small scale and revise until it works smoothly.

13. Use the plan on your Web site.

14. Record how long each task takes to accomplish.

15. Revise the tasks that take too long or get better tools (or both).

16. Continually look for new tools and techniques to improve your management routine.

Your Web management plan can be as detailed as you or your organization demands. But whatever you decide, formalize the plan into an electronic or hard copy form. Using a checklist to record the time, date, and the name of whoever performed each task is a good way to ensure that you get all the tasks done. Make this checklist a part of your Web site management log. You'll be pleasantly surprised at what you can learn over time from this log. It may save you considerable time in the future by providing you with information about your site that you can't get any other way.

The virtues of regular attention

All humans appreciate consistency in their daily lives, up to the point of boredom. We all habitualize mundane tasks so that we don't have to pay too much serious attention to them. This fact is the primary reason that Windows and Macintosh user interfaces have become so popular: They've simplified and standardized many tasks into oblivion. Now we can concentrate on reaching our objectives by *using* software instead of spending time trying to figure out *how* to use different applications.

The common navigation buttons and layouts used throughout your Web site should work the same way. Follow this path of consistency to its logical conclusion by providing your users with regular updates, feedback replies, and other types of attention to their needs, wants, and desires.

Regular attention to your Web site, and thereby to your users, shows them that you really do care. A basic human desire is to be cared for, so use it to your advantage. But be aware that regularity is a two-edged sword: If you promise your users that you'll provide them with daily, weekly, or other regular updates, you'd better produce on time. They'll turn on you faster than a starving Tasmanian devil if you're late with their update. Remember the morning paper?

On a different tack, scheduling time for attention to your Web site — whether you perform maintenance, add new content, or update the look of your pages — helps ensure that you actually perform the Web management function that you intended. If you know you're scheduled to run the link-checking spider every Monday morning at 8 a.m., you're more likely to get it done. Schedule each task at regular intervals and set aside a specific time in your schedule to accomplish it. You and your users will be happy that you did.

It's a (part/full-time) job: Here's the description!

Web site administration can range from a part-time job a few hours a week to a seven-day-a-week, on-call at night full-time-plus job. Check out this list for an idea of the various hats you may be called upon to wear as a Web site administrator:

- ✔ Artist
- ✔ Author
- ✔ Customer service specialist
- ✔ Director
- ✔ Editor
- ✔ Evangelist
- ✔ HTML programmer
- ✔ Planner

- ✔ Salesperson
- ✔ Server engineer
- ✔ Visionary
- ✔ Web guru
- ✔ Web layout architect
- ✔ Web link finder
- ✔ Web manager
- ✔ Writer

You should now see why many larger organizations assign entire teams to share the job of WebMaster. Can you imagine how many people work to administer the Netscape site with its several million hits per day?

You probably don't need to concern yourself with the problems of a such a large site tomorrow. However, starting out on the right foot and continuing along the path toward a perfectly administered Web site is an admirable goal. When the number of hats you wear each day outnumbers the hours you work, you should consider finding an assistant, providing your budget permits. Otherwise, your Web site could become an albatross around your neck instead of the eagle that carries you to your dreams.

Chapter 5
Denizens of the Web

- -

- -

*T*here be dragons out there. Spiders, Robots, Wanderers, Agents, Worms, and Viruses are all loose on the World Wide Web. These are all names for programs that automatically travel around the Web. Most are more than merely benign — they're downright useful. But some are malicious. Many go about their jobs efficiently, without bothering anyone.

Many Internet users love these critters. Some Web administrators hate them. Bots in the Web are similar to bees on the earth that produce honey but sting us when we try to get some. We've accepted their good and bad aspects and learned to live with them. This chapter gives you an inside look at the creatures of the Web and how you can make them work to your benefit.

Of Spiders, Robots, Worms, and Other Agents

Web bots come in all types and sizes. They've been (somewhat artificially) classified by some Web pundits into these four categories:

- Robots, wanderers, and spiders
- Commerce agents
- MUD agents and chatterbots
- Worms and viruses

Robots, wanderers, and *spiders* are programs that follow hyperlinks in HTML documents to see where they lead. They collect the URLs for those links and report them to their owners. Then they usually index them into a searchable database for your use, probably in connection with some kind of search engine.

Do the names Lycos, WebCrawler, Excite, and Yahoo! ring a bell? They all use Web spiders to find new Web sites to add to their collections. Some spiders, such as MOMspider (Multi-Owner Maintenance spider), are great for helping you maintain your Web by locating inactive links within your Web pages.

Commerce agents are just emerging onto the Web. They help you find bargains and do your shopping on the Web. Some of these agents have recently begun to act as brokers or traders to assist in completing commerce-based transactions on the Web. Look for commerce agents to greatly increase their presence on the Web in the near future.

MUD agents and *chatterbots* are programs from the Multi-User Dimensions, better known as Multi-User Dungeons, of the Internet. These programs answer questions, provide directions, and chat with game players. Whereas MUD agents are limited to their MUD environments, chatterbots are frequently found plying their trade on the Web, much to the delight of humans who chat with them.

The last group, *worms* and *viruses,* are malignant inhabitants from the dark side of the Web. These self-replicating programs slime their way around the Internet infecting unsuspecting and unprotected computers. Some of these are relatively innocuous and even humorous in their effects on your system. But infection from other worms and viruses can produce disastrous consequences. Run the latest version of your antivirus software frequently on your computer to ensure that you won't be the next victim.

Because they are the most prevalent type of useful robots on the Web, the rest of this chapter concentrates primarily on hyperlink-finding spiders and how you can use them on your own Web site.

The past and future of Web agents

As long ago as 1970, Nicholas Negroponte (director of the Media Lab at MIT) recognized and wrote about the ultimate value of delegating a program to move around within a network and perform tasks on your behalf. In 1984, Alan Kay expanded upon this idea in an article in *Scientific American.* Now that the Internet is used by millions around the world to access an uncounted number of Web sites, the idea of agents is no longer just an interesting concept, it's a necessity.

In 1994, General Magic introduced its *Telescript* agent programming language. Telescript is specifically designed to produce personal agents to send out on the Internet to accomplish specific tasks. Obvious uses of such agents include finding the best route and ticket price for your trip to Tahiti, making a reservation for you at your favorite restaurant, finding out all about XQP company, and locating a hubcap for your 1964 Stingray. Although widespread personal use of such agents has yet to occur, considerable work is underway to develop personal agents that can deliver on their enormous potential.

The goal of most agent visionaries is to produce an easily customizable computer program that "knows" your preferred working patterns and information desires, and operates on your behalf to accomplish whatever you direct it to do. Such agents would keep you informed of their progress, and may even ask for clarification of instructions after finding and assimilating partial information while completing their tasks.

Intelligent agents not only go out on the Net to find sources of information but they also filter incoming information (e-mail and newsgroups) to index and prioritize that information for you. They can apply regular queries to known databases for information in specified interest groups, and look for new databases that match your interests. They can even present all this information in a nicely formatted layout of your own design (or one designed by another smart bot).

One of the handiest agents is the *ComBot*. Instead of sending standard, static e-mail and waiting for a reply, or playing phone tag with George, you can instruct your ComBot to deliver your message to George ASAP (or *stat* if you're into medical terminology) and to confirm its receipt. Your ComBot can contact George's ComBot and the two can work together to deliver your message to George. Your ComBot can then tell you when George received it. If you want to meet with George in person (or via video-conference), your ConfBot can schedule a time with George's ConfBot.

ConfBots work with the ComBots to communicate and gather the appropriate information from your and George's schedules. Of course, your schedule calendar is private; your ConfBot knows what areas to protect and which are open for scheduling. Thus, it acts as your gatekeeper as well as your schedule manager.

These examples of next-generation agents may seem unrelated to the Web. However, the role of the Web is rapidly changing. Today we tend to think of e-mail, newsgroups, and the Web as three separate sections of the Internet, possibly on three separate servers, accessed by users using three separate programs (probably an e-mail reader, a newsreader, and a Web browser).

But numerous Web browsers, such as Netscape Navigator and Microsoft's Internet Explorer, already have integrated these access functions into a single program. The idea is to provide a single tool and interface, through which you can access anything on the Internet. This interface blurs the distinction between these information sources, and makes a single agent focus make sense.

In the future, Web information will become much more dynamic, and both e-mail and newsgroup messages will undoubtedly gain sound and video capabilities. Web browsers may evolve into personal site managers where any communication will be facilitated by agents. With such an agent, you could place information on your computer that your library agent could provide to someone else's search agent. You could even require that agents pass your security requirements before surrendering any information. But for the time being, you'll have to content yourself with using one or more of the readily available Web spiders to help you manage your Web.

Agents in search engines and other WWW environments

According to Fah-Chun Cheong (*Internet Agents, Spiders, Wanderers, Brokers & Bots,* New Riders, 1996), the first known use of a Web robot was when Matthew Gray deployed his World Wide Web Wanderer robot in 1993 to discover and count the total number of Web servers on the Internet. His objective — to discover existing Web sites — is still one of the two primary uses of Web robots. The other is to maintain your own Web links by finding *unresolved links* — that is, the ones that no longer reach their referenced Web sites.

In addition to these uses, robots are also used to mirror popular Web and FTP sites on other servers to spread the usage load. Using a robot such as HTMLGobble, Tarspider, or Webcopy, you can place a complete copy of a Web site on another server, but the internal HTML links must still be updated manually to reflect that new site's base address. Undoubtedly, more sophisticated Web-mirroring robots will be developed in the near future.

Perhaps The ForeFront Group will automate Web Whacker to be used in this capacity. It's not automated, but you can use it to copy entire Web sites. And it does convert relative hyperlinks to reflect the new server's address. To find out more about Web Whacker, visit the following URL:

```
http://www.ffg.com/whacker.html
```

Robots that follow hyperlinks around the Web and return the URLs of each Web document they encounter are the basis for search engine sites such as Alta Vista, Excite, Lycos, WebCrawler, and Yahoo!, to name just a few. These sites send their robots onto the Internet to search for new or changed Web sites. Their robots keep track of every URL they visit, and report back information about each URL. All of them are basically designed to gather the most important information from each HTML document they encounter, and to transmit that information back to their owners' sites.

Some robots are programmed to capture the first paragraph or a certain number of lines of text from each document. Others index the HTML document's text and create a keyword set that they transmit back to their owners for inclusion in the search engine's database. For example, Lycos's search robot extracts a document's title, its headings and subheadings, the first 20 lines of text, the 100 most important words, the total number of words, and the size of each document (in bytes).

Most discovery robots contain sophisticated algorithms that determine what to do when they access a Web site. These boundaries are extremely important, as the next section explains.

Building search boundaries

Web search robots are self-contained programs that are too closely related to the much-maligned viruses and worms to be released into the Web without restraints. These restraints usually take the form of carefully set boundaries. Although a search robot won't intentionally damage a Web site, it has the potential to greatly disrupt a site's operation if the robot fails to behave itself.

Martijn Koster's (1994) *Guidelines for Robot Writers* and Dave Eichmann's (1995) *Ethical Web Agents* offer outstanding insights into the proper use of robots on the Web. You can access these documents at the following URLs:

```
http://info.Webcrawler.com/mak/projects/robots
          /guidelines.html
http://www.ncsa.uiuc.edu/SDG/IT94/Proceedings
          /Agents/eichmann.ethical/eichmann.html
```

Next, we hit the highlights of these two papers to tell you how to run an ethical robot. This should also help you to understand what it takes to run any robot, ethical or otherwise.

Need

Be absolutely certain that you really need to employ a robot. A single robot is so fast at accessing Web sites and is capable of transmitting such a large volume of information, that it uses more resources than any single user. Robots actually strain portions of the Web enough to slow transmission times for everyone. Be sure that your purpose is valid and that you can't obtain the information through other means (such as a questionnaire). Also, be certain that you're ready to process the amount of information your robot retrieves.

Accountability

Identify your robot with HTTP's USER-AGENT field; also, identify yourself with your e-mail address in the FROM field. Announce that you're planning to run a robot in the comp.infosystems.www.providers newsgroup before turning one loose. Use the HTTP REFERRER field to tell administrators at your target sites why you're accessing theirs. Only run your robot when you can be present to "talk" with anyone who requests your input.

Test first

Test your robot on your own server first. Fix any and all problems. Next, test it on a friend's server before inflicting it on any other Web sites.

Conserve resources

Instruct your robot to run slowly. Although it can probably retrieve hundreds of documents per minute, you'll consume all of the transmission and computing resources of many Web servers if you attempt to do so. You'll also probably incur the wrath of Kahn, along with that of every Web server administrator your robot visits, if you don't rein it in. Keep your accesses to no more than one every five minutes at any given site.

Ask and ye shall receive

Ask for what you want, but ask only for what you really need. Retrieve each page only once. Use the HTTP ACCEPT field to specify the kinds of data your robot can handle. This allows clever servers to refrain from sending data the robot can't handle. Whenever possible, instruct the robot not to visit nonproductive sites by including the URLs for those sites in an exclusion list.

Check discovered URLs for validity

Because some Web sites don't require the trailing slash (/) at the end of a URL for a directory, you can get some really strange names by concatenating sub-URL names.

Check results

Immediately check what your robot sends you. When a server refuses to send several documents in a row, that server may be refusing to let you have anything because you're using a robot. Yes, discrimination is alive on the Web.

Don't revisit the same site too quickly

Instruct your robot to maintain a list of visited sites and pages, to avoid revisiting them unnecessarily.

Search only at appropriate times

Check with the system administrators at those sites that you want to frequent. Find out when their servers are least used, and instruct your robot to access them during these low-traffic periods.

Run your robot as infrequently as possible

Run your robot only as often as is absolutely necessary to accomplish your objectives. Use your previous data to avoid the sites of unhappy WebMasters.

Don't try queries

Instruct your robot to ignore searchable pages (ISINDEX) or forms. Otherwise, the robot will provoke Web documents that require user interaction; since a robot is not really a user, it can't interact with them. Worst case, its interaction with searchable pages will tie up a connection to the Web server until the robot times out and moves on to the next site. Because this is a complete waste of resources, it's better to avoid it in the first place.

Monitor your robots' progress

Either watch your robot's activities, or make sure beyond a shadow of a doubt that your robot is extremely well behaved. Knowing what your robot is doing is imperative, as is keeping it under tight control.

In any event, instruct your robot to construct an extensive log to document its activities. Make sure that you can guide your robot interactively and that you can respond quickly to any requests from WebMasters to cease and desist any "attacks" on their sites.

Give something back

After you run your robot and collect your information, remember those whose sites you "invaded" and let them know that you appreciate their patience and understanding. Acknowledge that they're running a Web site worthy of your attention by publishing your findings on the Web. How you share your results is entirely up to you, but do it.

Also, report any problems you experience with a site to that site's administrator, who will really appreciate your feedback. Remember, without these sites, your robot would have no place to go!

What works globally also sometimes works locally

If robots work well on the Web, just think how useful they might be at your own Web site. You think your site is too small to benefit from a spider's help? Well, just how can you ensure that all your outside links remain valid? How will you know when the WebMaster at your favorite link decides to shuffle the site's pages, or move it to another server? How can you make sure that all of your internal hyperlinks remain valid when you change your own pages?

You can either do this by hand, one link at a time until you go screaming bonkers, or you can get MOMspider (or its "lite" version, WebWalker) or some other robot to check your links for you.

Here's how using robots on your own Web site works: You can instruct MOMspider and other maintenance robots to traverse your Web site to check for dead links. These robots can even prepare a list of dead links for your perusal, and can save hours of pain and suffering if you take the time to get to know them. But before you do that, look at some of the secret agents available for your use on the Web in the following section.

The Best of Bots

Get your spiders and bots here! To give you an idea of the more than 40 different Web robots and their uses, we extracted the following list from the `Webreference.com` site. Please use the URL that follows the list to access `Webreference.com` and the links shown in bold.

- ✔ *Aaron's Daily WWW Newspaper* — A customized daily newspaper based on the findings of an intelligent spider.

- ✔ *Agent Info* — People, research, papers, agents, and a list of other related sites. By Andy Wood.

- ✔ *Agents, Inc.* — A spin-off from the MIT Media Lab, the same folks who did HOMR now bring you *Firefly,* your own personal music agent.

- ✔ *Freeloader* — An on- or off-line automatic surfer that can download entire Web sites for speedier surfing. It automatically notifies you when selected pages are updated, and can check sites at specified intervals and depths.

- ✔ *Grab-a-Site* — A Windows-based Web site downloader for off-line viewing. You can filter downloaded pages by domain, time, number, and depth.

- ✔ *Intelligent Agents Home Page* — A collection of the products and research that IBM is conducting, along with related links.

- ✔ ***Intelligent Software Agents*** — A collection of agent resources from UMBC's Tim Finn.

- ✔ ***Milktruck Delivery*** — A browser enhancement that automatically downloads Web sites for later surfing. Like Freeloader, it also notifies you when selected pages are changed.

- ✔ ***MIT's Autonomous Agents Group*** — Research into intelligent software agents from the MIT Media Lab, run by Professor Pattie Maes, founder of Agents, Inc.

- ✔ ***NetWatch Top 10*** — Top ten list of Intelligent Agents.

- ✔ ***Newshound*** — Mercury Center's news agent automatically scans a number of national newspapers and returns the results.

- ✔ ***Telescript*** — General Magic's server-side scripting tool that can be used to create Web agents.

- ✔ ***The @gency*** — A large collection of agent-related resources by Serge Stinckwich.

- ✔ ***Web Whacker*** — This program allows off-line viewing of Web pages by capturing them onto your hard disk and relinking them locally. This is useful for demos when a connection is not available. Available for both the Mac and Windows. From the ForeFront Group, Inc.

- ✔ ***Webcompass*** — An intelligent searching agent, reportedly the first of its kind. Input your areas of interest and this program automatically finds sites that most closely match your criteria at up to 70 search engine sites from Quarterdeck. Currently runs on Windows only.

- ✔ ***Webwatch*** — Windows users can give this utility a list of their favorite sites, and Webwatch returns a list of only those URLs that are new or modified. Saves precious surfing time. An ingenious utility from Specter, Inc.

The Webreference.com listing — and much more — can be accessed at the following URL:

```
http://www.Webreference.com/agents.html
```

The following URLs are great sites to start your search for Web robots, wanderers, and spiders. The first URL contains a comprehensive, annotated list of about 40 different robots and links to their sites. The second is the front page for the World Wide Web Robots, Wanderers, and Spiders site.

```
http://info.Webcrawler.com/mak/projects/robots/active.html
http://info.Webcrawler.com/mak/projects/robots/robots.html
```

MOMspider

MOMspider (Multi-Owner Maintenance spider) was developed by Roy Fielding as part of the Arcadia project at the University of California at Irvine. MOMspider is a Web-roaming robot that specializes in helping you maintain the hyperlinks on your Web.

The program is written in Perl for UNIX systems using version 4.036. MOMspider requires that Perl4 (Version 4.036) and *libwww-perl* (Version 0.30 or later) be installed on your system. MOMspider contains powerful user input and report customization sections. In addition, as its name suggests, it spreads the computing load over multiple users simultaneously. MOMspider can help you maintain Web sites of any size, from minuscule to monstrous.

MOMspider isn't for beginning Web server administrators, unless they're well versed in UNIX and Perl.

The free MOMspider is available as a gzipped *tar* file or as a compressed tar file from the following URLs:

```
http://www.ics.uci.edu/WebSoft/MOMspider/
ftp://liege.ics.uci.edu/pub/arcadia/MOMspider
```

WebWalker

WebWalker is an 1,800-line Perl script (compared to the 4,000-line MOMspider) written by Fah-Chun Cheong (the author of *Internet Agents, Spiders, Wanderers, Brokers & Bots,* New Riders, 1996). It uses Roy Fielding's *libwww-perl* library package from his MOMspider robot.

WebWalker does not contain all of MOMspider's user input and reporting features, but it checks your hyperlinks more quickly, and is easier to set up. WebWalker doesn't share its processing load across multiple servers as MOMspider can (from whence the Multi-Owner part of MOMspider's name arose).

WebWalker is designed for use within a local network or for light maintenance of small- to medium-sized Web sites. If you're into running Perl scripts on a UNIX server, this is the one to try first.

WebWalker uses a task file to specify its global and task directives and boundaries. A typical task file for your own Web site (yoursite) might look like this:

```
ReplyTo              Webmaster@yoursite.com
MaxDepth             1
<
  Name               Yoursite
  TopURL             http://www.yoursite.com
  BoundURL           http://www.yoursite.com
  ChangeWindow       1
  ExpireWindow       1
  Exclude            http://www.yoursite.com/cgi-bin/
>
```

The following is typical output from a WebWalker search:

```
WebWalker/1.00 starting at Wed, 13 Mar 1996  09:00:49
Checking for http://www.yoursite.com:80/robots.txt ... 200 OK
Traversing http://www.yoursite.com/ ... 200 OK
Testing http://www.yoursite.com/images/logo.gif ... 200 OK
Testing http://www.yoursite.com/products/ ... 200 OK
Testing http://www.yoursite.com/products/new/ ... 200 OK
Reusing test of http://www.yoursite.com/products/ ...
Testing http://www.yoursite.com/orgstuff/ ... 200 OK
Testing http://www.yoursite.com/disclaimer/ ... 200 OK
Done Traversing http://www.yoursite.com/ ...
... at Wed, 13 Mar 1996  09:05:21 — 0 remaining on queue

Broken Links:
      http://www.yoursite.com/newdir1/     (603 Timed Out)
Changed Links:
      http://www.yoursite.com/newdir2/stuff1/     (200 OK)
Last-modified:
      http://www.yoursite.com/newdir2/stuff2/     (200 OK)
Last-modified:
      http://www.yoursite.com/newdir2/stuff3/     (200 OK)
Last-modified:

Summary of Results:
```

	References		Unique URLs		Local URLs	
	number	pct	number	pct	number	pct
Traversed	1	5.00	1	2.26	0	0.00
Tested	9	86.24	10	0.00	0	0 00
Reused	1	06.12	0	0.00	0	0 00

(continued)

(continued)

```
Avoided     |   0   86.24  |  0    0.00  |   0     0 00  |
Untestable  |   0   86.24  |  0    0.00  |   0     0 00  |
            |-------+------+----+--------+-----+-------|
Broken      |   1   86.24  |  1    1.00  |   0     0 00  |
Redirected  |   0   00.00  |  0    0.00  |   0     0 00  |
Changed  1  |   3   86.24  |  3    5.58  |   0     0 00  |
Expired  1  |   0   00.00  |  0    0.00  |   0     0 00  |
            |-------+------+----|--------+-----+-------|
Local       |   0    0.00  |  0    0.00  |   0   100 00  |
Remote      |  10   86.24  |  8  100.00  |   0     0 00  |
            |-------+------+----|--------+-----+-------|
Totals      |  10  100.00  |  8   92.24  |   0     0.00  |
            |--------------|-------------|---------------|
```

Finished Infostructure [Yoursite] at Wed, 13 Mar 1996
        09:25:30

WebWalker/1.00 finished at Wed, 13 Mar 1996 09:25:30

As you can see, WebWalker provides a considerable amount of information about your site's links. Give it a try if you're running a UNIX server.

WebWalker is a free Perl script file available at the following URL:

```
http://www.mcp.com/softlib/Internet/WebWalker
```

Checkbot

Checkbot, created by Hans de Graaff, is a stand-alone Perl 5 tool that can verify links on your HTML documents. Checkbot can check a set of documents on a single server or on a set of servers (for example, all the servers within a domain). Checkbot creates a report that summarizes all links that caused an error or warning. It uses two categories of links: *internal* (to other URLs matching a given string) and *external*. All internal links are checked first, and then Checkbot examines external links using the HEAD method.

Checkbot does not currently adhere to the "robot standard" of first examining the robots.txt file (but it should by the next update). After progressively longer intervals, Checkbot writes its current results to a file. This results file contains a list of pages (sorted by server and by page name) that contains links that generated HTTP error codes, along with these codes, and various statistics that include the number of links processed.

Hans seems to be serious about providing a quality tool for UNIX Web administrators. You'll find it at this URL:

```
http://dutifp.twi.tudelft.nl:8000/checkbot/
```

Harvest

The *Harvest Information Discovery and Access System* is an integrated set of UNIX-based tools designed to gather, extract, organize, search, cache, and replicate relevant Web information across the Internet. Harvest's claim to fame is its capability to index topic-specific collections, instead of merely locating and indexing all the HTML documents that it finds.

You control Harvest with stop lists, and depth and count limits. Therefore, Harvest provides a much more controlled method for indexing the Web than typical discovery robots. Harvest also claims to make far better use of network traffic, remote servers, and disk space than conventional robots.

The Harvest system is part of the Harvest Project at the University of Colorado. For more information about this unique and powerful robot system, visit this URL:

```
http://harvest.cs.colorado.edu/
```

Surfbot 2.0

Surfbot 2.0 is a Web-searching robot from Surflogic LLC (Specter Communications). It works on Windows 95 and Windows NT. Originally developed as WebWatch by Specter Communications, the commercial release of Surfbot 2.0 (list price $40) provides Mosaic and Netscape users with intelligent bookmark monitoring, automated agent delivery, advanced searching, off-line browsing, and easy-to-use Wizards.

Surfbot 2.0 monitors sites that you select (your bookmarks or other links, such as those on your own Web site) and retrieves whatever you request. You can schedule Surfbot to deliver your favorite newspapers, stock quotes, Web sites, and updated bookmarks overnight. Thus, each morning you'll have a customized, personal report based on any combination of Internet information sources.

Surfbot installs preconfigured agents that monitor your bookmarks and Windows Favorites and deliver the Reuters newsfeed. In addition, you can build and publish your own agents with Surfbot's easy-to-use Wizards. Surfbot also prepares standard HTML reports that you can load into any browser.

Surfbot's agents reside on your PC and connect to the Internet to look for updated information using your standard connection (whether dial-up or direct). Surfbot works with any Web site and requires no server-side modifications or proprietary HTML markup. However, it does use the date information from the HTTP document headers, which your Web server should be providing to check the freshness of each HTML document.

Get the free test version of Surfbot 2.0 and more information from the following URL. You can even register and pay the $40 registration fee online or via your CompuServe account. These folks really seem to be on to something here for Windows 95 and Windows NT users.

```
http://www.surflogic.com/home.html
```

CyberPilot Pro with WebMap Engine

The *NetCarta WebMap Engine,* included in NetCarta's CyberPilot Pro product for Windows 95 and Windows NT, is a personal agent that can visually map and copy WebMap sites. The Web mapping product uses its robot to search a site, and creates its WebMaps from that information. You can use WebMaps to display the structure and content of Web sites, to analyze and verify their links, to track additions and deletions, and to copy entire Web sites quickly and easily.

You can launch the NetCarta robot from multiple domains but it is intended to focus on a particular site; therefore, each robot issues only one request at a time to a site. The robot's user-agent field contains a coded ID that identifies the instance of a spider. This provides a means to block specific users based on the ID in the `robots.txt` exclusion file.

NetCarta's WebMaps work with your browser to let you see your Web in context. They can also help you to find what you seek, without requiring you to click on a whole series of hyperlinks. A NetCarta WebMap is a compact information base that includes a catalog of Web objects, including the following elements: HTML pages, hypertext links, Internet services and gateways, graphics, audio, video, Java, PDF, Microsoft Word, program files, and any other files used by valid helper applications or Netscape plugins.

It also includes information about Web objects such as: creation/modification date, owner, location within a site, URL, alternate string name, file size, page transmission size, MIME type, all headings, links, broken/active link status, and any annotations that you might care to add by hand.

NetCarta's package is a good deal for Web administrators or anyone who's seriously interested in using the Web for research. Its list price should be around $100 when the final version is released. Get more information about this product at NetCarta's Web site:

`http://www.netcarta.com/`

From these brief descriptions of the agents available today, it's clear that they can help to save maintenance and update time for any serious Web site administrator. We suggest that UNIX-aware Web server administrators investigate any of the many UNIX-based Perl script robots available. The rest of you may benefit from running one or more of the Windows 95 (or NT) and browser-based agents from your own computers, using your our own Web sites as your targets.

For Macintosh users, no really good agent packages are currently available. However, a few Macintosh-based agent packages are under development, but we have no firm information on them. Keep looking at the URLs previously listed for their arrival, or ask on your favorite Macintosh WWW newsgroup, such as `Comp.infosystems.www.servers.mac`.

Benefiting from Robot Labor

No matter how good the agent, it's only as good as its users. If you use your agents intelligently and regularly as part of your overall program of Web maintenance, you'll be able to obtain the maximum benefits from its capabilities. You must be prepared to accept, store, process, analyze, summarize, and report your agent's information with the proper hardware and software to support its activities and house its results.

The key is to turn gigabytes of retrieved data into concise information to guide your decisions. Beginning with first things first, you must activate your agents, situate your spiders, build your bots, or otherwise get your creatures into your computer and prepare them for action!

Introducing a spider into your Web

Installing MOMspider or WebWalker on a UNIX Web server is not difficult for anyone who works with UNIX systems and Perl scripts regularly. However, it's not something that we can describe adequately in a few paragraphs, or even a few pages.

We suggest that you UNIX folks give it a go. The rest of us will make do with other packages, or get our Web server administrator to install a UNIX-based agent on our behalf.

However, installing and running one of the Windows 95/NT-based agents is a quark of another color. You can do this yourselves. These agents install just like any other Windows 95/NT applications, with nice, graphical interfaces and lots of help when you need it. Each is slightly different, but all are similar. But hey, isn't that what Windows is all about, familiarity with the interface? Go for it!

Scheduling regular robot activities

When using a robot to check the links on your own Web, don't forget to take your users into consideration. You might think of it as your Web site, but actually, it's not — it's your users' Web site. You put it there for them. So, when you let your robot loose, don't unleash it during the busiest times of the day. Following the cardinal rule of maintenance ("Stay out of your users' way!"), you should schedule robot exercises at slack times. If in doubt, analyze your server's log files to determine when is a slow time — and therefore a good time — to run your robot.

It's best if you schedule maintenance on a regular basis, such as once a week, at the least active time of day or night. Let your users know when regularly scheduled maintenance occurs so that they will understand why your Web site may react sluggishly at times.

Remember, keep your users informed and pay close attention to their feedback. They'll be much happier, and so will you!

Dealing with the aftermath: refreshing stale links

Once your robot has identified all your unresponsive links, it's up to you to do something about them. If they're internal links, determine why they don't connect. You may have moved a page, or misspelled an anchor name when you updated a page. Check all the possibilities. Be patient and you'll find the cause of your problem.

External links must be browsed and each problem identified before it can be rectified. Maybe the Web server was down when your robot called. If so, you'll see the error as a time-out or other nonconnection. When you try the link with your browser, it may work. Do nothing in this case, except to note the problem in your Web site maintenance log file. That way, you will be able to tell whether the offending site has an unusually large amount of down time. If you find that a page has moved, simply copy its new URL and insert it into your own HTML documents; then upload them to your Web server. Of course, you should test them to make sure they work.

Keeping a Web up-to-date and minimizing unresolved links are time-consuming, no matter how you do it. But a robot friend can handle most of the drudgery, if you run it regularly.

Robot exclusion

If you don't want robots wandering around your Web site, you must place a robot exclusion file, named `robots.txt`, in the same directory as your `index.html` file (usually known as the *Web server root* or *Web root* directory). This file can contain several commands to exclude robots from all or parts of your Web. Not all robots conform to the standards for robot exclusion proposed by Martijn Koster. But more and more do adhere to them, because most robot makers and users understand that politeness and common courtesy — especially in robots — is one of the keys to keeping the Web healthy and thriving.

If you don't want any robots roaming your site, your `robots.txt` file should contain the following lines:

```
# No bots allowed here.
User-agent: *
Disallow: /
```

All text following the pound (#) symbol is ignored as a comment. The asterisk (*) symbol denotes *anything* or *everyone,* so the second line excludes all User-agents. The slash (/) in the Disallow: field keeps it from being empty, therefore it means *everywhere,* that is: "Disallow all robots everywhere."

To exclude all robots except a specific model, place the following lines in the `robots.txt` file after the two previous lines that disallow all robots:

```
User-agent: nicebot
Disallow:
```

This lets the User-agent named `nicebot` go everywhere, because `Disallow:` is empty, meaning disallowed nowhere. Of course, because some spiders fail to conform to the proposed standards, they may ignore your `robots.txt` file. They will go about their merry searching, and there's not much you can do about it at the time. However, you're not completely without recourse, as the next section shows.

You can find the complete text of Koster's standards for robot exclusion at the following URL:

```
http://Web.nexor.co.uk/mak/doc/robots/norobots.html.
```

They're baaaack!!

What to do when your Web is invaded by an ill-mannered bot, despite your best efforts? Again, our secret agent man, Martijn Koster, has given the problem serious thought. He suggests several possible steps; his suggestions may be found at:

```
http://Web.nexor.co.uk/mak/doc/robots/against.html
```

We have hit only the highlights from Koster's list of suggestions here. The bottom line is that you can't really do anything to stop a robot while it's rummaging around your Web, unless you want to burn down the barn to get rid of the rat (that is, pull the plug on the server or disconnect the phone line). First of all, remember that it's just a dumb program taking up more of your precious resources than you like, for a small amount of time. Don't waste more of your time by retaliating. Ignore it until it happens again.

After two or three times, check your logs to find out as much as you can about the robot and its owner. Contact the owner directly if you can and ask that the robot be stopped. If you can't find the owner, post a message about the invasion on comp.infosystems.www.providers to see whether any other Webs have experienced the same problem. Help others to help you so that you all can stop the problem. As the man said: "You can run but you can't hide." It's not possible for a person to operate a robot on the Web indefinitely without someone finding out who's responsible.

Keep this in mind when you're using a robot on any Web site other than your own. Run your robot responsibly and on a short leash. You'll get your results without irritating everyone else. If you think that having agents work for you on the Web is the greatest thing since the invention of the double mocha latte, you'll love what's in store for you on the Web of the future. Keep on reading to catch the emerging trends in the next chapter. There, you'll get the opportunity to hang your toes over the leading edge of the Web as you gaze into the vastness of the Internet and the future.

Chapter 6

Management Means Looking Forward, Too!

● ●

In This Chapter

▶ Looking through the all-in-one Web site managers

▶ Checking up on integrated publishing systems

▶ Understanding the uses of SGML

▶ Viewing through the crystal ball

● ●

Web site management means more than getting your site up and running smoothly. It means keeping it up-to-date and making it better, both in terms of your management and your content. Keep your eyes and your mind open for new techniques and tools to help you attain Web greatness.

The best way to keep up is by taking a three-pronged approach:

1. **Read one or more of the magazines aimed at Internet and Web administrators.**

2. **Search the Web frequently for changes in Web sites that will provide you with new ideas for your site.**

3. **Actively participate in one or more Web-specific newsgroups, such as**

```
comp.infosystems.www
comp.infosystems.www.announce
comp.infosystems.www.authoring.html
comp.infosystems.www.browsers.misc
comp.infosystems.www.browsers.ms-windows
comp.infosystems.www.misc
comp.infosystems.www.servers.mac
comp.infosystems.www.servers.misc
comp.infosystems.www.servers.ms-windows
comp.infosystems.www.servers.unix
cern.www.talk
```

In addition to the previously mentioned resources, Bob Allison's WebMasters site is an excellent one-stop resource for all your management Web needs. Check it out at the following URL:

```
http://miso.wwa.com/~boba/masters1.html
```

In the rest of this chapter, we introduce a few of the most recent innovations in Web publishing. We also let you share the view of my own crystal ball as we tempt fate and make a few prognostications!

Emerging Web Site Trends

Several companies already offer total Web service packages in which you create HTML documents and supporting materials, upload them to their server, and leave the rest to them; well, almost the rest. Some even perform periodic site maintenance.

Following this approach, you still need to update your content when necessary. But some companies even offer HTML creation services, so you simply need to provide them with text and graphics, or ideas for the graphics for them to create. For those of you who want a business presence on the Web but don't want to do much other than pay for it, these services may be the way for you to go.

Other companies offer complete Web publishing systems, such as ShockWave for Director, that enable production of complete multimedia presentations for your Web site. When coupled with any compatible Web server, these systems can help you build professional-looking Web pages with little or no HTML document creation. Many advertising and marketing companies are already using such services.

Turnkey systems and environments

Several of the (more or less) complete Web systems that have recently become available are worth a quick look here. More are under development, so stay tuned for their announcements in your favorite Internet spots.

NaviService

NaviService, from America Online, is a one-stop solution for building and maintaining your Web site. NaviService features the NaviPress HTML authoring system with one-button instant publishing to their NaviServer Web host. The NaviService hosting facility provides users with high-speed Internet connections with quick response times 24 hours a day.

The NaviService Commercial Service is aimed at busy, small- to medium-sized business Web sites. This service includes full administration access, database access, and scripting facilities using the NaviServer Tcl programming interface. Enhanced server access includes a dynamic table and forms builder to help you to create custom Web applications, such as a catalog, on the fly.

The Commercial Service includes

- ✔ NaviPress Software with User Guide
- ✔ Disk space: 100MB
- ✔ Transfer allowances: 3000MB per month

The Commercial Service costs

- ✔ $249 — One-time startup fee
- ✔ $100 — Initial InterNIC domain registration (2-year registration)
- ✔ $199 — Per month
- ✔ $548 — Total launch costs

NaviService also offers a Personal Hosting Service, which includes the NaviPress Software with User Guide, 20MB of disk space, and a 500MB-per-month transfer allowance for a startup cost of $99.00 and $19.95 per month. (You don't get your own domain name with this level of service, however.)

The NaviPress HTML creation software is available for $99 for Motif (SunOS), Windows 3.1/3.11/95/NT, and Macintosh. The Windows version is 16-bit, but it runs under both Windows 95 and Windows NT. To order NaviService, call 800–879–6882. You'll find more information at

```
http://www.naviservice.com
```

ClubWeb

Cookware runs the ClubWeb site to help you with your Web needs for a low monthly cost. It's worth checking out this site's offerings if you really need to put your Web page up in a hurry and you want to conserve up-front costs. Cookware offers numerous options for Web authors and administrators, including

- ✔ Ishop — Virtual shopping carts for commercial sales via the Web.
- ✔ Forms4U — Their advanced Forms4U form handler allows you to start using HTML forms in your WWW documents without a server, for a fee.
- ✔ Find4Me — Database searching for your pages.

- ✔ MembersOnly — Membership and security for your pages.
- ✔ Sticky Pages — fantastic marketing capabilities.
- ✔ RandomLink — Add fun to your pages!
- ✔ Web Site Demographics service — Provides an analysis of your Web Site, dropped off in your home directory every night, for a small monthly fee.

For hosting your site, ClubWeb charges $50 per month minimum with throughput charged at 50 cents per megabyte; therefore, the $50 covers 100MB of throughput per month. You get 10MB of storage free of charge. Storage beyond 10MB is $1 per megabyte per month. Throughput or storage over the $50 minimum is added to your monthly bill.

Access ClubWeb at the following URL to see Cookware's other offerings:

```
http://www.cookware.com/
```

Fully integrated publishing systems

Several applications have recently been introduced that are basically HTML authoring systems with extensive additional features that enable you to publish your existing information on the Web. To call these *converters* would be like calling Microsoft Word a word processing file converter simply because it will import numerous file formats and output them in other formats.

These systems import many formats, provide editing capabilities without using HTML directly, and output HTML documents or complete Web sites. Most of these systems are presently associated with their own Web server software, but most of their developers are working to broaden their server's compatibility.

FrontPage

With its purchase of Vermeer Technologies, Microsoft has garnered perhaps the top Web management publishing system available today. By using a client-server architecture, the FrontPage system supports authoring, scripting, and Web-site management from your desktop to your corporate LAN, or over the Internet.

The client portion of FrontPage includes the following features:

- ✔ FrontPage Editor for creating and editing HTML pages, with WYSIWYG support for many HTML formatting extensions.
- ✔ FrontPage Explorer for graphically visualizing and managing a complex Web site.

✔ WebBots that implement text searches, feedback forms, and threaded discussion forums, without programming.

✔ Wizards and templates for easily creating personal and business Web pages using a task menu system.

✔ To Do List for tracking the status of authoring and management tasks.

The server portion of the product, known as Server Extensions, is implemented using the open industry standard Common Gateway Interface (CGI) and can run on Windows 95, NT, and popular versions of UNIX. These extensions support Netscape's Web servers and Microsoft's Internet Information Server. The FrontPage system includes an easy-to-set-up Personal Web Server to get you up and running right out of the box.

You'll find information about FrontPage from Microsoft at

`http://www.microsoft.com/msoffice/frontpage/default.htm`

Adobe PageMill and Adobe SiteMill

Adobe's PageMill for HTML document creation and SiteMill for Web site management combine to provide a total Web publication and site management solution for Macintosh and Power Macintosh users. Adobe PageMill Web page authoring software is a well-integrated package in which you write your pages in what looks and feels like a word processor — except that your pages are displayed as they will appear in your Web browser.

You apply styles, place and resize images, and drag and drop parts of your document in other locations. Creating links is easy, and PageMill ensures that links remain valid as you copy and paste them throughout your Web pages.

Adobe SiteMill makes Web site management easy by helping you maintain correct links for your entire Web site, including links to external sites. SiteMill automatically repairs links that break when pages or files are renamed, or are moved into subfolders. SiteMill uses icons and a view that shows your page structure with pop-up menus of the links to and from each file to help you manage your entire Web site.

You create new links by simply dragging a file or an image icon from the Site view window into the Page view window. SiteMill automatically creates the correct links. It even shows all references to external Web sites and allows you to globally rename them.

Although the suggested retail price of Adobe SiteMill (including PageMill) is $595, you can order and pay for it via secure credit card transaction online from Adobe for $399. Check it out at Adobe's Web site:

`http://www.adobe.com/Apps/SiteMill/`

These aren't the only two publishing systems on the market. A few others are available but they aren't as comprehensive as these two. If you need more than Web publishing and want to get the most out of your existing information, you might be interested in a more generalized approach, as discussed in the next section.

SGML-Based Publishing Systems

Standard Generalized Markup Language (SGML) has been around for several years. So, why haven't you heard more about it? It has been used primarily by governmental and educational institutions and larger corporations for information to be published in many different forms. Using SGML to mark up a document with a standardized Document Type Definition (DTD) allows many different programs to convert documents into their own formats.

Remember, the browser converts the HTML documents on your Web into a nicely formatted display. It uses the HTML markup in your document to tell it which parts to format in certain ways, according to its settings, which you control.

If your crystal ball view of the future shows that you need to publish information on a variety of platforms in several different formats, SGML may be the way to go.

Generalized markup covers many sins

The active part of SGML is the generalized markup that you insert into your text file. This added information separates logical elements within the document and specifies the types of processing (usually formatting) that you want to apply to the elements (for example, font, color, size, position).

To mark up the text, SGML uses tags similar to HTML. This shouldn't come as a surprise, because HTML was originally derived from SGML. Like HTML, SGML's utility comes from the use of standardized DTDs, which ensure that everyone is working from the same definition of any given format.

DTDs describe formal documents abstractly

DTDs describe the elements in a document without explicitly stating how the elements will be presented. If you have a particular format that you want to standardize for your own use, you can produce your own DTD. Although this capability can lead to the proliferation of DTDs, it allows standardization within each published DTD. Providing a DTD and applying its SGML to a document allows the reading program to separate the description from the structure of the document. This separation allows the reader to format the document according to its own built-in rules.

Many industries have defined their own DTDs for their particular documentation needs. DTDs are available for software reference manuals, semiconductor data sheets, newspaper articles, aircraft maintenance manuals, and many other areas.

Output DTDs can drive print, Web, CD-ROM, and other delivery forms

The most common use of multiple DTDs is to output a document in multiple formats. By inserting the SGML tags for specific output DTDs in a document, you can run a program to produce completely customized output for a CD-ROM, paper printing, and Web use from the same document. Unless you've conjured up a completely new output type, you'll undoubtedly be able to find a DTD for whatever you need.

To find more information on SGML, search your favorite site (Yahoo!, WebCrawler, and so on) using the keyword **SGML.** You can also check out the discussions on the `comp.text.sgml` newsgroup.

Off the Edge

Like the cartoon character who has run off the cliff and is afraid to look down, we're off the edge of known technology and wading into uncharted waters. Managing your Web site in the midst of the rapidly changing computer world doesn't have to be a nightmare. You don't have to perpetually float three steps off the cliff, afraid to look down. Keep your feet firmly on virtual Web ground with tried and proven tools and techniques. But if you're wondering what may pop up in the near future, even if just for your amazement and amusement you should read the prognostications that follow!

Applets bear fruit

It won't be long until most Web pages use frames. And in those frames, you'll find all kinds of really great Java applets to provide you with currently unimaginable interactivity. Like water over the falls, the masses are rushing to get the newest and best browsers. They are adding Shockwave and other plugins and helper applications to their browsers. They want animation, in living color, with 3-D stereo sound. Those who preach text only, and Lynx compatibility are a decreasing minority. Text-only and Lynx are as retro as a 12-inch green monochrome monitor screen!

Text will always be around

Of course, text-only Web sites will abound for years until sufficient bandwidth becomes available for transmitting HDTV-quality information. This may be sooner rather than later, if the cable modem backers have their way. Otherwise, it may take a few years for the telephone companies to replace their copper wires with fiber-optic cables to every home and business.

Even then, an enormous amount of textual information will remain in that form until there's an economic reason to convert entirely to multimedia. This is especially true of educational, legal, and regulatory materials in government repositories. That text will probably stay unchanged until it fossilizes.

Commercialization of the Web

Commerce will take over the Web as we know it. Access still won't cost anything, but you'll see advertisements on most Web sites. At the same time, you may be asked to pay a small amount to access databases that contain valuable information.

By a *small amount,* we mean less than one cent. The ability to conduct nanocommerce is just over the horizon. Following on the heels of MasterCard's and Visa's recent agreement on a security system for credit card transactions online, it won't be long before you can purchase anything on the Net. So, why not pay a mill or two (10 mills equal 1 cent) per page to read the latest article from your favorite magazine online? You might help to save a tree. . . .

Large companies are making strategic alliances to provide Internet hardware and software to cable TV and regional phone companies. Rupert Murdoch's News Corp. has joined with Oracle to produce an Internet news service called Interworld. Microsoft has allied with Motorola, MCI, Sprint, and six of the seven Baby Bells to provide Integrated Services Digital Network (ISDN) high-speed digital Internet service for its Windows 95 users.

All these commercial initiatives will push more users onto the Internet and into the Web. There, advertisers will ply their wares in an ever-upward spiral of "advertise, buy," "advertise, buy."

Your future Web site

In the near future, your Web site may be on your own computer or on a commercial Web hosting site or your company's Web server. With AT&T's decision to offer direct dial-up Internet access, the doors are wide open for anyone with a computer to access the Web. Whether AT&T will host Web sites is still undecided.

In the near term (the next year or so), software to create and run your Web site will be integrated and bundled even better than FrontPage. It will probably take the form of GUI applications that you'll use to create, edit, and upload information to your Web site in a few easy steps. Already, Microsoft seeks to produce add-ons for MS Word for Windows for this very purpose. They just haven't gotten their act completely together . . . yet.

Slightly further down the road, your Web browsers and servers may evolve into a combined package that includes e-mail, voice-mail, computer telephony applications, and video capabilities. Newsgroup software may be included to handle images and maybe even high-quality audio and video at your site. Thus, the Web may become a complete communication conduit in the 21st century.

Or maybe the Web will evolve into something unimaginable to us today. (Only time will tell.) But whatever direction the Web takes, you'll be able to watch it happen and be a part of it.

Part II

Advanced HTML Markup

"... the glitch is in a faulty tag in your page's footer."

In this part . . .

Part II covers a whole slew of draft standard HTML, plus a number of interesting proprietary tags and extended attributes. In Chapter 7, we begin with a general description of how HTML markup is developed and standardized (and we look at the forces in the marketplace that keep things moving). In the remaining chapters of Part II, we cover families of tags for building tables (Chapter 8), constructing subwindows called *frames* within the browser display (Chapter 9), and dealing with mathematics notation (Chapter 10). These discussions are followed by coverage of recent advances in defining style sheets for HTML documents (Chapter 11). Then in Chapter 12, we discuss the `<EMBED>` tag that is used to invoke plugins and extensions, and we conclude Part II with a grab bag of miscellaneous markup and attribute additions in Chapter 13.

Chapter 7
Understanding How HTML Happens

- -

In This Chapter

▶ Discussing how standards are made

▶ Tracking down and using the prevailing HTML DTDs

▶ Keeping your eye on HTML

▶ Elevating the table tag in proprietary browsers

▶ Polishing your own custom tables

- -

*H*ave you ever wondered who's responsible for deciding what HTML features become officially accepted? Would you like to know who can be thanked (or blamed) for creating renegade extensions such as <BLINK>? Or, perhaps you would like to know who determines what exciting tags an up-and-coming HTML standard should contain? If so, read on and be enlightened.

The "Official" Channels, Organizations, and Approaches

For an Internet protocol to become a standard, it must pass a hard-core series of development stages from the Internet Engineering Task Force (IETF), the Internet's protocol engineering and development arm. The IETF's mission is to coordinate the technical developments of new protocols, and it possesses the power to decide what becomes standard within the Internet protocol suite. Although anyone can join the IETF, most of its members are network designers, operators, marketplace representatives, and researchers.

The IETF's history is heavily connected to the government, as is the Internet's. Created in 1986, the IETF was intended to coordinate technical developments for contractors working on U.S. defense projects (so it's obvious why they control the standards for today's blisteringly-paced Web developments, right?).

The IETF sees its mission like this:

- ✔ To identify operational and technical problems in the Internet and propose corresponding solutions
- ✔ To specify the usage and development of protocols and the near-term architecture
- ✔ To facilitate technology transfer from the Internet Research Task Force (IRTF) to the Internet community at large
- ✔ To provide a forum for the exchange of information between Internet researchers, users, vendors, network managers, and agency contractors

Nine topical areas exist in which working groups address technical activity on specific Internet topics. Each group has a director (or two) who assumes responsibility for the group's area of activity, and together these directors form the Internet Engineering Steering Group. These nine areas include

- ✔ Applications
- ✔ Internet
- ✔ IP, Next Generation (IPnG)
- ✔ Network Management
- ✔ Operational Requirements
- ✔ Routing
- ✔ Security
- ✔ Transport
- ✔ User Services

These groups aren't permanent; after their mission is accomplished, they can disband (many persist, but others come and go).

Although these groups hold meetings three times a year, most of the debate and decision making occurs through electronic mailing lists. No formal votes are taken; instead, most ideas are discussed and demonstrated among a group's members until a rough consensus is reached.

If you're interested in more information about these groups, sign on to the IETF announcement list by sending a request to

```
ietf-announce-request@cnri.reston.va.us
```

Before you descend upon an IETF meeting, it's also a good idea to read *The Tao of the IETF,* written specifically for the hordes of IETF newcomers. You can find it at this address:

```
http://www.ietf.cnri.reston.va.us/tao.html
```

How a Proposal Becomes a Standard

The Internet has many proposed protocols but few of them actually make it through the long, arduous process of becoming an Internet standard. The IETF puts all protocols through a series of rigorous development stages, beginning with an informal experimental stage. If a protocol passes this stage, it must possess the following characteristics to continue rising through the standards hierarchy.

Proposed standard

- Demonstrated utility
- Credible and complete specification

The proposed standard stage lasts for a minimum of six months and a maximum of two years. After this period, the protocol is either elevated, depreciated, or recycled (a protocol can reenter the standards track at a later date if appropriate).

Draft standard

- Must work well in limited operational experience
- Must have independent, multiple, interoperable implementations

The draft standard lasts a minimum of four months and a maximum of two years. The protocol can then be elevated, depreciated, recycled, or sent back to the proposed stage.

Standard

- Must have a demonstrated operational stability
- Must have been successfully implemented at least twice during the draft period

After a protocol becomes standard, it can be classified in any of these categories:

- **Required:** It must be included in any TCP/IP implementation.

- **Elective:** It's an optional standard and can be used as the developer desires.

- **Recommended:** This status is used for standards that aren't required but are highly recommended, usually because they are widely used or demanded.

- **Information or historic:** These categories are used only occasionally. *Information* is used to describe a part of the standards process, whereas *historic* is employed for standards that are no longer in use.

A Brief Review of HTML Standards to the Present

HTML standards are currently numbered zero through three, which is something of a misnomer, as you find out a little later. But this is terminology that you encounter frequently, so read on for the real details.

HTML 0.0

HTML 0.0, the original HTML language, was a text-only markup language developed at CERN by Tim Berners-Lee. It was used at CERN as a prototypical language while CERN was developing Web browsers. HTML 0.0's capability to handle text, although ground-breaking at the time, is rudimentary by current standards. For that reason, it's never used today — you run across it as an archaic artifact only.

HTML 1.0

Dan Connolly began developing HTML level 1 in March 1992 and released it to the Web community in July of that year. Tim Berners-Lee wrote an Internet draft RFC (Request for Comment, an official IETF standards document format) for level 1 HTML in 1993, which resulted in its release to the general public.

In addition to the text control that HTML 0.0 offers, HTML 1 also lets you reference graphical elements. Browsers still exist (such as Cello and Lynx) that operate at level 1 HTML — but don't count on finding any cutting-edge Web pages written at this level.

HTML 2.0

HTML 2.0 is HTML's current implementation, so it defines a standard HTML document type. Dan Connolly and Tim Berners-Lee began working on level 2 as soon as level 1 HTML was released. Level 2 HTML can handle text in a more advanced manner than its predecessors; it provides tags for interactive forms and image maps, which both contributed to the Web's increase in popularity.

Although still incorporating all of level 1 HTML's beneficial markup elements, HTML 2.0 ameliorates many of level 1's elements and eliminates several elements that had become obsolete (such as <XMP> and <LISTING>). Unlike level 1 HTML, level 2 supports a fill-in form interface. We expected that the IETF will accept HTML 2.0 during 1996.

HTML+

HTML+ never made it to the standard level, and it never will. That's a factual statement rather than a pessimistic one — HTML+ has basically been recast as HTML 3.0. Because Dave Raggett, the creator of HTML+, is involved in the development of HTML 3.0, the two are being smoothly integrated. Many of the same ideas were proposed in HTML+ as are proposed for HTML 3.0, such as math equations and table definitions.

If you're curious about HTML+, you can read its proposal at

```
http://www.mcis.duke.edu/duke/html3.0/htmlPlus.html#2
```

HTML 3.0

Even though the collection of standards once known as HTML 3.0 has been scrapped, you still see lots of references to this term, even at the W3C's own Web site. Dan Connolly, Dave Raggett, and Tim Berners-Lee of the World Wide Web Consortium originally led this effort.

Even though its components are important, still under development, and making their way through the standards process, HTML 3.0 has been killed as a standards designation. That's because it took almost two years to get HTML 2.0 approved, and the powers that be — that is, the IETF and the W3C — decided that they didn't want to take another two years to shepherd another monolithic group of standards through the same process again.

That's why the individual standards that used to be collectively referred to as HTML 3.0 are still underway. But they're being worked through the process individually, rather than en masse. This means that some may be finished sooner than others.

In fact, as you read the following chapters in this part of the book, you find that we have tried to fill you in on the standards status of some of the most important members of "the collection of standards formerly known as HTML 3.0." (You know, like a certain rock star who has changed his name to an unpronounceable character, who's often called "the performer formerly known as. . . .") Anyway, Table 7-1 shows you what you can find in Chapters 8 through 13.

Table 7-1:	Meet Some Members of the Former HTML 3.0 Family of Standards.
Chapter	*Topic(s) Covered*
Chapter 8	HTML tables
Chapter 9	HTML frames
Chapter 10	HTML <MATH> notation
Chapter 11	HTML Style Sheets
Chapter 12	The HTML <EMBED> tag
Chapter 13	HTML Miscellany

Although the IETF's stringent testing process makes it hard to say exactly what features may be included in each individual standard's final release, you can expect to see more support for style sheets, mathematical notation, frames, and tables, among other fascinating things (more on those in the last part of this chapter). These elements build not only on HTML 1.0 and 2.0, but also on HTML+, which was developed after HTML 2.0.

The HTML 3.0 collection was defined as an application of the International Standard ISO8879:1986 Standard Generalized Markup Language (SGML). This specification has been proposed as an Internet Media Type (RFC 1590) as well as MIME Content Type (RFC 1521) and is still called `text/html; version=3.0`, despite the formal demise of HTML 3.0 in November, 1995.

The process of HTML standards development is ongoing and is open to suggestions from Netizens. If you'd like to become involved in the discussion, you can find a discussion list called `www-html`, whose archives are available at

```
http://www.eit.com/goodies/lists/www.lists/
```

You can also investigate Arena, the World Wide Web Consortium's HTML 3.0 browser, at this site:

```
http://www.w3.org/pub/www/arena/tour/math1.html
```

Pressure from the Marketplace

The time required for a protocol to pass through the labyrinthine process of becoming an IETF standard is often too leisurely for the speed of 20th century capitalism. By the time the IETF accepts an HTML standard, its elements are often old hat (or simply accepted as standards *de facto,* if not *de jure*) because they have been available through commercial Internet implementations for many months.

Cognizant of the fact that the hottest technology often attracts the most customers, companies such as Netscape and Microsoft have jumped at the opportunity to profit by creating new HTML tags and extensions. The Netscape `BACKGROUND` tag and its extensions such as `FONT`, `BLINK`, and `CENTER` are all examples of proprietary developments that it has created in an attempt to influence future HTML standards and woo customers. However, the IETF's final jurisdiction still holds some clout — Netscape has said that it will conform to the final set of standards "formerly known as HTML 3.0."

The Web's user base also influences the development of new HTML standards. Netscape might have pioneered frames and tables, but it did so because the Web community demanded them — and because it was clear that the lethargic IETF process wouldn't produce such technology quickly enough.

Proprietary Extensions versus Standards of Many Kinds

When the IETF was founded in 1986, its founders clearly had no idea how forcefully market forces would challenge their standards-making process. Although the IETF would like to think that its standards are the most influential, the fact is that the extensions and tags created by private industry incite a lot more excitement among the Web community.

The IETF's standards are still considered important — after all, they are "The Standard," which means that those standards are always safe to use and have at least a modicum of enduring value. But because the Web's free-for-all structure enables companies such as Netscape and Microsoft to ignore the standards-making process and create their own HTML versions, they frequently exercise the "proprietary option."

By taking such a rebellious route, vendors can push functionality into users' hands quickly. This gives them a (possibly ephemeral) competitive edge, builds a stronger customer base, and diminishes the degree of control that standards bodies like ISO, IAB, IEEE, and others can exert. But, unfortunately, this rebellion also diminishes the truly global reach of the Internet (and the Web) and may ultimately lead to its balkanization, fragmenting a single global community into ever more mutually incompatible communities of interest (or groups of users of particular kinds of software, as the case appears to be).

Netscape 2.0 Extensions

Netscape isn't trying only to create exclusive extensions but is hoping that, by proving the undeniable value of their extension technologies, those technologies (and their related HTML markup) may appear in some HTML standard or another. When this inclusion occurs, we see a powerful example of collaboration between commercial interests and standards bodies. When these groups diverge, the result is often an exercise in frustration.

The Fountain of All (Netscape) Wisdom . . .

Too many Netscape extensions exist to cover in detail here in the small space allowed. You can find them fully outlined and explained in our companion volume, *HTML For Dummies,* 2nd Edition (on the diskette), or you can discover them for yourself at

```
http://home.netscape.com/assist/net_sites
            /html_extensions.html
```

Netscape and standard HTML incompatibilities

Certain elements supported in NHTML (Netscape HTML) aren't compatible with the emerging HTML standards formerly known as HTML 3.0. Although the following attributes appear in both HTML3 and NHTML tags, their values are interpreted differently. The "real" standard will eventually emerge from the IETF/W3C collaboration, so employing the draft standard markup rather than NHTML is best when such conflicts occur, if you want to reach the broadest audience. However, be aware that Netscape's dominance of the user base also means that you may have to recognize that browser's capabilities to keep up with other, less fussy Web authors.

For example, following are some incompatibilities that you're likely to encounter:

- **The** <HR> **tag's** WIDTH **attribute.** The NHTML version supports pixel count, percentages, and a "wild card," whereas the standard version supports only percentages of the display (and wild cards).

- **The** <OL> **tag's** TYPE **attribute.** Although the HTML version is more flexible, it uses values of complete words, not single letters, as does NHTML.

Our final watchword here is *be careful.* You may end up being forced to use Netscape extensions just to offer features and functions that your users expect. Don't be too alarmed if you have to change that markup at some point in the future, because the Netscape version fails to show up unaltered in an official standard. Don't be dismayed: This kind of thing happens all the time!

Internet Explorer 2.0 Extensions

In case you were speculating about how long it would be before Microsoft Corporation sought to dominate Web development, wonder no more: Microsoft has endowed its Internet Explorer 2.0 with unique extensions that create inline video, marquee effects, and background sounds. Internet Explorer also features support for Internet shopping applications and delivers Secure Socket Layer (SSL) support. Extensions to the HTTP protocol keep the channels open between the server and the client to speed up communications.

<FONT FACE> and <FONT COLOR> are two of Internet Explorer's new extensions. They let you specify what color and typeface you want to use for text and give you more control over your document without requiring cumbersome bitmap files.

<MARQUEE> is another new Internet Explorer extension. It lets you select a portion of text to use as a moving marquee on a page. Used in moderation, this tag can be an effective way to convey information. Used too freely, it has the potential to be even more irritating than the <BLINK> tag!

Microsoft has taken steps to ensure that Internet Explorer can handle future HTML standards. Like Netscape 2.0, Explorer 2.0 already supports popular emerging HTML standards such as centered and aligned text, tables, and graphics. For the latest information about the Internet Explorer Extensions, please visit this URL:

```
http://www.microsoft.com/windows/ie/IE20HTML.htm
```

Extending HTML's Representational Abilities

HTML's representational abilities are getting better and better, and will only continue to improve. The FRAMESET tag and the TABLE tag have contributed significantly to this process because their strides in formatting let you showcase your page's data in a whole new way.

For example, frames let you display important but static information such as copyright, title bars, and control graphics in an individual frame. This information holds its form even while surrounding content is being redrawn. Frames also allow interesting new formats, such as side-by-side question-and-answer frames.

This site contains a listing of companies using frames:

```
http://home.mcom.com/comprod/products/navigator
           /version_2.0/frames/frame_users.html
```

The end of this chapter talks briefly about these two emerging extensions, and Chapters 8 and 9, respectively, cover them in excruciating detail.

The buzz over tables and frames, though, is soon to be eclipsed by style sheets. Read on for some coming attractions from Chapter 11.

Style Sheets

The advent of style sheets takes HTML into a whole new arena. Content creators and Web users alike have been champing at the bit for the arrival of the kind of fabulous control offered by these babies. When your Web site is armed with a style sheet, your creative control increases dramatically because you can specify how you want the design elements and layout to appear in terms of fonts, colors, and indentation depths.

With the constantly growing variety of Web browsers, style sheets are a welcome addition to cyberspace — no longer is a document's appearance completely at the mercy of the browser! Check out Chapter 11 for an in-depth discussion of style sheets' beauty.

Finding, Understanding, and Using HTML DTDs

Understanding HTML DTDs is easier if you understand a little about SGML. SGML is a metalanguage that defines structured document types and the markup languages that represent any instances of those types. The primaryu example is HTML, which is a markup language that was originally created using an SGML DTD. In other words, because HTML is built upon SGML, whenever a conflict occurs between the two, SGML overrules HTML.

The nature of an SGML document

Every SGML document is divided into three parts, whose descriptions follow.

SGML declaration

The SGML declaration attaches SGML syntax token names and processing quantities to specific values. In the HTML DTD, the SGML declaration specifies that </ opens an end tag and no name can be more than 72 characters.

Prologue

The prologue includes one or more DTDs, which are responsible for specifying the element relationships, element types, and attributes. The HTML 3.0 DTD tells you specifically what syntax is allowed in HTML documents that incorporate its current markup tags and capabilities.

References

References can be represented by markup. They contain a document's data and markup of the document. In order to represent instances of that data type, HTML refers to the document type, as well as the markup language.

For more information about SGML, check out the "Gentle Introduction to SGML" at this site:

```
http://info.ox.ac.uk/~archive/teip3sg/
```

Or "A little bit of SGML" at this site:

```
http://www.ozemail.com.au/~dkgsoft/html/sgml.html
```

About DTDs . . .

DTD stands for Document Type Definition. A DTD is a formal description of how a particular class of documents is structured in SGML. The DTD is the file that's responsible for specifying how the various parts of an SGML document relate to each other. It declares what all the document's elements are, specifying the name and data content model of each element. DTDs are generally used to

- ✔ Formalize the document's markup conventions so that other applications can parse conforming documents
- ✔ Let parsing tools perform document validation and deviation reports
- ✔ Define what a document's "official" structure is
- ✔ Declare names for a document's external data (such as sound or graphics files) and their notations

What does a DTD contain?

Any HTML DTD tells you the specifics of what's legal for every element. Most elements in a DTD are specified so that they contain other elements, although elements can also contain parsable character data (#PCDATA).

You can tell how frequently an element occurs by the symbol that's attached to the element name. You encounter these three occurrence indicators in an SGML DTD:

✔ ? means zero or one occurrence.

✔ * means zero or more occurrences.

✔ + means one or more occurrences.

When you don't see an occurrence indicator in a content data model, that means that the element occurs only once. When this is the case, the element's presence is mandatory, and it can't be repeated.

Within a DTD, you can use three "connectors" between elements:

✔ | indicates that one of the elements in the list must occur.

✔ , indicates that both elements have to occur in a specific order.

✔ & indicates that both elements must occur, but in any order.

A DTD also includes elements used to define specific content data models, called entities, which are described by these special words:

✔ **RCDATA** means that the entity references are recognized but no content is permitted.

✔ **CDATA** means that any markup except </ within a tag is ignored.

✔ **EMPTY** means that the element can't ever have content or an end tag.

A DTD's elements are allowed to have mixed content models, so you can create a combination of subelements with character data. However, be cautious when you're mixing content data models, because the resulting ambiguity may be confusing.

Where the DTDs live

The following document is the DTD for HTML 2.0:

```
http://www.ics.uci.edu/pub/ietf/html/rfc1866.txt
```

You can view the HTML 3.0 DTD at

```
http://www.webtechs.com/sgml/html-3.0/DTD-HOME.html
http://www.w3.org/hypertext/WWW/MarkUp/html3
         /Contents.html
```

Although it's tempting to follow the HTML 3.0 DTD to the letter, remember that it became obsolete in November 1995. You want to locate and read the DTDs for the individual markup elements (frames, tables, math notation, style sheets, and so on) to get the ultimate level of detail. A bit of judicious investigation at the WebTechs or W3C's Web sites helps you find these in a hurry.

Deciding Which Flavor of HTML to Use

As the IETF's approval of new HTML standards draws nearer, many developers are choosing to create content using those standards. Netscape Navigator and Microsoft's Internet Explorer offer their own types of HTML as well, and some of their proprietary extensions have a seductive appeal.

The safest choice is always the "official" standard (currently HTML 2.0) because it's guaranteed to work with just about any browser. Consider these next questions if you're having difficulty choosing an HTML specification.

Who will be viewing the document that you create?

If you write a document using extensions that are viewable only with the Internet Explorer browser, and the majority of your viewing audience doesn't use Explorer, your hard work has gone to waste. And some WWW tools, such as HotMetaL, load only valid HTML 2.0 documents. By using an unapproved HTML DTD, you also run the risk of alienating your users, because even if they want to see what you're doing with your fancy extensions, they can't. They may consequently seek out a site that's more compatible with their browsers.

How long will your content be around?

If you think that your creation's life is only a few months, worrying about standards is not crucial. However, if you want your content to endure, you're much better off using an established standard.

Are you concerned about automatic Web document construction?

If so, it's much more preferable to have a stable DTD to work with. May we recommend the HTML 2.0 DTD for now?

How much work could creating content in a new or unstable DTD create in the long run?

If the DTD that you use isn't going to be around in a few months, you'll have to sink time into retyping and restructuring. Depending on how long you take to finish your project, you might want to adopt an emerging DTD rather than a diminishing (or soon-to-be-depreciated) one.

The advantages of using valid HTML

Any number of HTML checking and validation services are available on the Internet today. These tools check your documents and flag any deviations from the DTDs that you choose to govern them. Using such services is definitely the best way to make sure that your pages are "legal," and it offers a range of other benefits as well:

- The increased portability it offers means that your valid HTML document can be moved to another WWW server and used there with only minor adjustments.

- The compliance with a known DTD legitimizes the document's content and structure.

- A valid HTML document's information has greater fidelity, which improves its capability of communicating.

- Valid HTML can be parsed successfully by an SGML parser (such as sgmls), so you don't have to rely on a human to inspect your site.

- It's easier for an indexing agent (sometimes called a robot or WebCrawler) to catalog your site if it follows standard HTML style, which translates into greater exposure for your site.

The disadvantages of using valid HTML

Although it's hard to believe that "crimes against the standard" might be beneficial, you'd be surprised how many authors proceed along this course. Just for the record, we list some of the reasons why many authors choose to violate the standards in the face of opprobrium:

- By the time an HTML level becomes a standard, it's no longer on the cusp of the cutting-edge.

- Creating valid HTML requires you to have the necessary tools and the process. Although you can find HTML validation checks to run, that still requires some human involvement.

- The valid standards are very rigid and you don't have the option of playing around with their structure.

Some New HTML Worth Watching

With all the efforts to extend HTML that are underway, both standard and proprietary, you can easily get lost in the sheer number of options and capabilities under development. To help steer you through this swamp, we want to tell you our choices for the contenders for future HTML immortality.

Tables

The <TABLE> tag extends HTML to support tables. Users have been waiting impatiently for the TABLE's formatting options — it unleashes an entirely new realm of formatting possibilities, because you can place almost any other HTML tag into a table cell. Because Netscape has already implemented tables successfully, one of the standard's major goals is to catch up with the marketplace and provide backward compatibility with Netscape's widely deployed implementation. Earlier table models from HTML+ and early drafts of HTML 3.0 are extended in response to these requests:

- Alignment on designated characters such as "." and ":" (for example, aligning a column of numbers on the decimal point)

- Greater flexibility for specifying table frames and rules

- The capability to support scrollable tables with fixed headers, as well as improved support for breaking tables across pages for printing

- Incremental display for large tables as data is received

- Optional column-based defaults for alignment properties

The HTML Table Model (DTD) Working Draft and miscellaneous information are available at (look for the highest number where the question marks appear; that is the most current version):

```
ftp://ds.internic.net/internet-drafts
          /draft-ietf-html-tables-??.txt
http://www.hpl.hp.co.uk/people/dsr/html3/CoverPage.html
http://www.hpl.hp.co.uk/people/dsr/html3/tables.html
```

Netscape Navigator, NCSA Mosaic, and Microsoft Internet Explorer have all incorporated the <TABLE> tag into their browsers. For more information about the details of these implementations, head to Chapter 8 — it contains the juicy specifics, as well as the URL for each browser's home page.

Frames

Why would you use the <FRAMESET> tag? Because it brings a powerful flexibility to the surfing experience. Although tables may let you format information onto the browser screen, they don't have the capability to be dynamic the way frames do: You can't scroll within frames when you're using tables, but you can when you're using frames.

FRAMESET lets you create HTML documents that enable information to move within and between the frames, which means that you can keep information on the browser display while you're simultaneously scrolling through dynamic content or large amounts of text. This extension is a great boon to Webheads whose attention span has been diminished through hours of surfing.

Netscape created the <FRAMESET> tag, and Navigator 2.0 is the only browser that currently supports frames. Netscape has submitted its implementation of this tag to the IETF and is hoping that the tag makes it into an upcoming DTD. Chapter 9 contains extensive information about frames and their markup.

Style sheets

Using the STYLE tag lets you extend the properties associated with edges and interiors of cells (or groups of cells). You can format the line style; for example, you can make dotted, double, thin/thick, and so on. Similarly, you can adjust the interior's color/pattern fill the edgelines, as well as cell margins and font info. Style sheets can also let you control font selection, heading level appearances, margins, indentation, and more, giving you a new level of control over how you want your Web documents to appear.

The following code is an example of how a single STYLE element, included in the document head, lets you include style rules within your HTML creation:

```
<HEAD>
<TITLE>Title</TITLE>
<STYLE TYPE="text/css">
H1 { color: green }
P { color: blue }
</STYLE>
</HEAD>
```

The STYLE element is formally defined by

```
<!ELEMENT style - O (#PCDATA)>
<!ATTLIST style
type     CDATA    #REQUIRED —
    Internet media type for style
title    CDATA    #IMPLIED —
    advisory title for this style —>
```

You can find all the cool details about style sheets, including pointers to a brand-new draft specification, in Chapter 11.

Mathematics notation

The <MATH> element is used to include math expressions in the current line. HTML math has the capacity to describe the range of math expressions you create in common word processing packages. In addition, it's suitable for rendering to speech equations and other mathematical forms of expression. You find all the inside scoop on HTML and mathematics in Chapter 10.

Miscellaneous standard goodies

You find a whole grab bag of other emerging HTML elements covered in Chapter 13, which we called "Marvelous HTML Miscellany." Read on for a preview of that chapter's many attractions.

FIG

You can use <FIG> for inline figures — it lets you handle hotzones at the client end while catering to nongraphical browsers as well. <FIG> makes your text flow around a figure, allowing you to determine where you want the flow to break for a new element. When browsers support <FIG>, it should be used instead of <IMG>, because it has more powerful representational capabilities in terms of graphics, captions, and overlays.

LINK

You can use the <LINK> element to provide standard toolbar/menu items for navigation, such as Previous and Next buttons. It promises to improve Web page interfaces across the board.

NOTE

Employ the <NOTE> element when you want to endow your page with footnotes, cautions or warnings, or just plain notes. It should help scholars reproduce their writings and materials more effectively on the Web.

BANNER

Use the <BANNER> element for navigation aids, disclaimers, corporate logos — basically, any information that shouldn't scroll with the rest of the document. <BANNER> gives you an alternative to using the <LINK> element in the document head when you want to reference an externally defined banner.

Promising proprietary phenomena

Microsoft's release of Internet Explorer's DTD has brought some excitement to the market. You can take a glance at what it contains at the Internet Explorer page:

```
http://www.microsoft.com/ie/news/ieguide.htm
```

Netscape has done some excellent work on frames, which they've now handed over to the W3C. Look at what Netscape has to say about frames:

```
http://home.mcom.com/assist/net_sites/frame_syntax.html
```

There are various proprietary extensions that Netscape is submitting for consideration in emerging HTML standards. For more information on Netscape extensions, see this site:

```
http://home.netscape.com/assist/net_sites
            /html_extensions.html
```

Following are four of the extensions that Netscape would most like to see in some new HTML standard.

Font color

This is a very cool feature — it lets you specify the color that you would like to use for a selected range of text. It looks like this:

```
<FONT COLOR=####>
```

Targeted windows

Targeted windows let you have names associated with browser windows. With a TARGET attribute, any window can feature links referring to another window by name. Clicking on the link causes the requested document to materialize in the named window. If you don't already have the window open, Netscape opens and names one for you.

The syntax for the targeted windows is

```
<A HREF="url.html" TARGET="window_name">
Click here and open a New Window
</A>
```

The <BASE> tag now supports a TARGET attribute as well, which lets you pick a default named target window for document links that otherwise lack an explicit TARGET attribute.

This is its format:

```
<BASE TARGET="default_target">
```

Forms enhancements

The WRAP attribute in the <TEXTAREA> tag gives you control over how you would like the word-wrapping to be handled in the text input areas of forms.

If you use this default setting, wrapping won't happen — the words are sent exactly as they are typed:

```
<TEXTAREA WRAP=OFF>
```

If you use this setting, the display is word wrapped, but long lines are sent as single lines, without new lines:

```
<TEXTAREA WRAP=VIRTUAL>
```

If you want your display to wordwrap, with the text being transmitted at all wrap points, use this:

```
<TEXTAREA WRAP=PHYSICAL>
```

Embedded objects

The <EMBED> tag describes plugins in HTML pages much like the <IMG> tag describes images. It lets you embed different kinds of documents of varying data types into an HTML document. When a capable browser (such as Netscape 2.0) encounters the tag, it knows that the material requires a plugin and loads whatever plugin is indicated by the file's extension and corresponding MIME type.

These attributes are defined on <EMBED>:

- ✔ **SRC,** which is required, specifies the source URL.
- ✔ **HEIGHT** makes the object's image scaled to fit the specified height.
- ✔ **WIDTH** makes the object's image scale to fit the specified width.

See Chapter 12 for a more extensive discussion of <EMBED>. There, you see how it can be used (and for what), along with the details required to make it sing!

The proliferation of new tags and extensions, of both the standard and proprietary variety, brings exciting new possibilities to HTML markup. The battle between proprietary extensions and standard ones is one that merits watching, so keep an eye out. Even the best-informed industry insiders have a difficult time predicting accurately what the Web may look like in a few years — but it's sure to have a different, more powerful look than it does now. The material covered in this chapter helps explain why that's true.

A parting word of wisdom: If it's absolutely, positively necessary for your Web page to endure through the ages, use the standard DTD for creation. The next chapter begins an investigation of the details and tackles tables on their own home ground.

Chapter 8

HTML Tables Can Hold Up the World!

· ·

In This Chapter

▶ Gazing over the table landscape

▶ Deciding to table or not to table

▶ Tabling your HTML

▶ Elevating the table tag in proprietary browsers

▶ Polishing your own custom tables

▶ Evaluating some interesting table examples

· ·

*T*ables are marvelous things: they hold our food off the floor, let us stall a vote, and can even help us format information. In HTML, tables are quite handy for arranging everything from numbers to images on your Web pages. Although only a few browsers support tables today, these few are the browsers used by the vast majority of Web surfers. Thus, even though tables are still kind of experimental (as HTML goes), you're pretty safe in using them on your Web pages.

Each major browser — and we mean Netscape Navigator, NCSA Mosaic, and Microsoft Internet Explorer — keeps extensive discussions about its implementation of the <TABLE> tag at its Web site. For this reason, the chapter emphasizes how to get the most out of the <TABLE> tag and its related attributes, instead of describing the differences between the browser's implementations. Also, the HTML DTD for <TABLE> is still changing, so nobody knows the eventual outcome for the <TABLE> tag. But because you have to start somewhere, this chapter takes you on a tour of this tag's basic capabilities and syntax.

More information on the latest innovations in tables is readily available at the following WWW sites:

Netscape Navigator 2.0

```
http://home.mcom.com/assist/net_sites/tables.html
http://home.mcom.com/assist/net_sites/table_sample.html
```

NCSA Mosaic 2.0

```
http://www.ncsa.uiuc.edu/SDG/Software/Mosaic/Tables/
           tutorial.html
```

Microsoft Internet Explorer

```
http://www.microsoft.com/windows/ie/ie20html.htm
```

HTML3 Table Model (DTD) Working Draft (1-Feb-96) and miscellaneous information

```
ftp://ds.internic.net/internet-drafts/draft-ietf-html-tables-
           06.txt
http://www.hpl.hp.co.uk/people/dsr/html3/CoverPage.html
http://www.hpl.hp.co.uk/people/dsr/html3/tables.html
```

Do you really need to use the <TABLE> tag? You can use a list, an image, preformatted text, or a frame instead of a table. Each of these structures has its own good and bad points:

- **Lists:** Lists are relatively simple to implement but don't give the formatting capabilities of tables, especially for images.

- **Images:** You can make an image in tabular form with borders and colors, but the image then becomes relatively static and difficult to change.

- **Preformatted text:** Browsers generally display preformatted text in a non-proportional font that looks terrible.

- **Frames:** Netscape is the only browser that currently recognizes frames. But if you're willing to be Netscape-dependent in your HTML documents, frames may offer an additional dimension instead of a replacement for tables.

The preceding caveats notwithstanding, we believe that tables are great for many uses, from tabulating financial results to organizing lists of related elements (like dates and birthdays, for example).

HTML <TABLE> *Overview*

The <TABLE> tag has been one of the most anxiously awaited features since HTML's inception. This tag provides a formatting method that was sorely missing until its introduction. Because you can put almost any other HTML tag into a table cell, the formatting possibilities afforded by tables are virtually unlimited.

As is frequently the case in the personal computer business, the software development companies didn't wait around for the standards committees to finalize their specifications for the <TABLE> tag. They took the bit between their teeth and ran off headlong into the hills, implementing those table functions they wanted to implement. Netscape stuck fairly closely to the HTML3 Table draft DTD but added the WIDTH and HEIGHT attributes, Microsoft decided to add colors to tables, and NCSA Mosaic provided only the basics. All three developers are moving rapidly to add other table attributes that they believe can cause you to switch to their browsers.

By using specific attributes recognized by one (as opposed to another) browser of choice, you can have the fun of trying different approaches to using tables. You also have the option of sticking to the basics so that all browsers can recognize and display your tables. Because no "standard" for tables is likely to appear in the near future, you can happily use the currently available table attributes of your choice and add new ones to your Web pages as browser vendors implement them. Regardless of the table attributes you choose, you should always combine your creativity with your content to use the table structure that best communicates your message.

We strongly recommend that you stick with the basic table elements in your tables, unless you're developing documents for a private Web server where you know that your audience is using a particular browser. Sticking to the common denominator (the common table elements) is the best way to ensure the widest audience for your tables.

In fact, if your readership includes members who may be print-handicapped or otherwise visually impaired, we strongly recommend that you provide an alternative form for your table data. Many browsers that produce Braille or convert text to speech aren't yet able to handle the HTML <TABLE> tag. As a result, many Web sites offer text-only implementations of their tables as an alternative to tabular information. And you should consider doing the same, if an alternative is appropriate for your audience.

HTML Table Markup

Dave Raggett did a great job of editing the HTML3 Table Model (DTD) Working Draft (1-Feb-96), but this document isn't going to teach you how to use the table tags and their attributes. Do read it, though, if you want to see all the great features that may be implemented someday via tables. The rest of this chapter shows you the basics and some nifty uses of tables. We even show you how to use some of the proprietary extensions that we believe may soon become available in most browsers.

Remember, you can put any HTML body element into the cell of a table. You can even nest multiple tables in a single table cell. And you can use Netscape formatting tags, such as <CENTER>, on an entire table to position the table on your screen. So if you think that some particular formatting might work for your table, give it a try. Your idea might work better than you think, or it might not work at all — the only way to be sure is to experiment!

The parts of a table

The basic parts of a table are the <TABLE> and </TABLE> tags that surround an entire table, the <TR> and </TR> (table row) tags that define each row of a table, and the <TD> and </TD> (table data) tags that define each cell of a table. Optional tags include <CAPTION> and </CAPTION>, which place the contained text above or below your table, and <TH> and </TH> (table header), which you can use to describe columns and/or rows in your table. The following simple table illustrates all these tags in the most boring way we could imagine. Hey, we can't jump all the way to the jazzy stuff just yet, ya know!

```
<TABLE><CAPTION>This is the default caption placement.
   </CAPTION>
   <TR>
   <TH> Header: row 1, column 1</TH><TH> Header: row 1,
   column 2 </TH></TR>
   <TR>
   <TD> Cell: row 2, column 1</TD><TD> Cell: row 2, column
   2</TD></TR>
</TABLE>
```

If you put the preceding table code in your Web page, you'll have a table, but it won't excite your users much. That is, your users won't be excited because the table looks like the one depicted in Figure 8-1 when you view it in your browser. Pretty bland, eh?

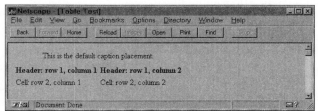

Right, you can do only so much with plain text. But hang in there, pardner: We get to the good stuff soon enough. Now that you see how you can easily use the table tags to construct a basic table, you need to know a little about each of these tags. Because Netscape is far and away the most widely used browser today, the following explanations include the Netscape implementation of the table tags (which the other browser developers will no doubt quickly emulate). The explanations of the table tag attributes follow shortly, so don't get all stirred up when you don't see immediate explanations in the quick overview materials that follow.

<TABLE> . . . </TABLE>

The <TABLE> . . . </TABLE> tags provide the container for all other table tags. Browsers ignore the other table tags if they aren't contained inside the <TABLE> . . . </TABLE> tags. The only attribute of the table tag that is widely implemented by browsers is the BORDER attribute. Netscape also responds to the WIDTH and HEIGHT attributes for the table tag.

<TR> . . . </TR>

The table row tags contain the information for all cells within each row of the table. Each set of table row tags represents a single row in the table, regardless of the number of cells in the row. The table row tag can contain both the ALIGN and VALIGN attributes, which if specified, become the default alignments for all cells in the row.

<TD> . . . </TD>

Each cell in the table is defined by the table data tags (<TD> . . . </TD>), which must be nested within table row tags. The following are good tidbits to know about table data tags and how they work:

✔ You don't have to worry about making each row contain the same number of cells because short rows are padded with blank cells on the right.

✔ A cell can contain any HTML tag normally used within the body of an HTML document.

✔ The default alignment of table data is ALIGN="left" and VALIGN= "middle", which you can override by any alignments that you specify in the table row (<TR>) tag. Similarly, you can override the alignment of the <TR> tag by any ALIGN or VALIGN attributes that you explicitly specify in a cell's table data tag (<TD>).

✔ Lines of text within a cell automatically word wrap to fit the overall cell width unless the NOWRAP attribute is included within the table data tags.

<TH> . . . </TH>

Table header tags (<TH> . . . </TH>) display text in BOLD with the default of ALIGN="center". Otherwise, they are identical to table data tags.

<CAPTION> . . . </CAPTION>

Place the <CAPTION> tags inside the <TABLE> tags, but not inside table rows or cells. The default is ALIGN="top", but a browser responds to ALIGN= "bottom" by placing the caption beneath the table. Like table cells, any document body HTML can appear in a caption. Captions are horizontally centered with respect to the table, and their lines are wrapped to fit within the width of the table.

The basic table attributes

You can use several attributes with the table tags. Innovative use of these attributes is the key to making your tables truly outstanding or, at least, visually interesting. Following is a quick overview of these basic attributes; then we show you how to use them.

BORDER

The BORDER attribute is used in the TABLE tag to instruct the browser to display borders around the table and all table cells; see the table shown in Figure 8-2. Space is left for borders around tables so the table width does not change when a border is added.

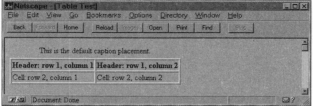

Figure 8-2:
Borders
create
interesting
edges
around
tables.

ALIGN

When you use the ALIGN attribute with the <CAPTION> tag, specify
ALIGN="top" or ALIGN="bottom" to control whether the caption appears
above or below the table. The default alignment for the caption is "top."

When used inside of a <TR>, <TH>, or <TD> tag, ALIGN accepts values of left,
center, or right to control the horizontal placement of text within the cells. See
Figure 8-3 for examples of text placed in different locations within a table cell.

```
<TABLE BORDER WIDTH="90%" HEIGHT="90%">
<CAPTION>ALIGN=left, center, right can be applied to
   individual cells or an entire row</CAPTION>
  <TR>
  <TH>Head Col 1</TH>
  <TH>Head Col 2</TH>
  </TR>
  <TR ALIGN="right">
     <TD>Right</TD>
     <TD>Right</TD>
  </TR>
  <TR>
     <TD ALIGN="center">Center</TD>
     <TD>Default left</TD>
  </TR>
</TABLE>
```

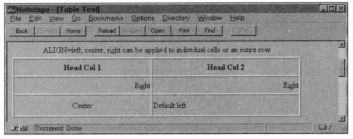

Figure 8-3:
Horizontal
alignment
controls the
right-to-left
placement
of data
within a cell.

VALIGN

The VALIGN (vertical alignment) attribute is used inside a <TR>, <TH>, or <TD>
tag to control the placement of the cell's contents at the top, middle, or bottom
of the cell. Figure 8-4 shows table text with various vertical cell alignments.

```
<TABLE BORDER WIDTH="90%" HEIGHT="90%">
<CAPTION>VALIGN=top, middle, bottom can be applied to
   individual cells or an entire row</CAPTION>
  <TR>
  <TH>Head Col 1</TH>
  <TH>Head Col 2</TH>
  </TR>
  <TR VALIGN="top">
     <TD>This row's cell's text aligned to top</TD>
     <TD>Cell row 1, col 2</TD>
  </TR>
  <TR>
     <TD VALIGN="bottom">This cell's text aligned
     bottom</TD>
     <TD>Cell's text default aligned middle</TD>
  </TR>
</TABLE>
```

NOWRAP

When used in a table cell (<TH> or <TD>), the NOWRAP attribute makes the
browser display all the text for that particular cell on the same line. Using this
attribute can cause very wide cells, so be careful.

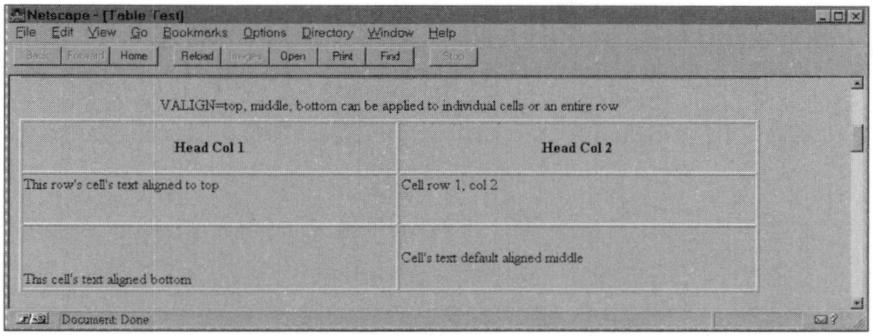

Figure 8-4:
Vertical
alignment
controls the
up-and-
down
placement
of an
element
within a cell.

COLSPAN

Use COLSPAN in any table cell (<TH> or <TD>) to specify how many columns of
the table the cell should span, if you want it to span more than the default of
one cell. This feature works great for multi-column headings (see Figure 8-5).

```
<TABLE BORDER WIDTH="90%" HEIGHT="90%">
  <CAPTION> Multiple Column Span Example</CAPTION>
  <TR><TH colspan=3>3 column span</TH></TR>
  <TR><TH colspan=2>2 column span</TH><TH>default</TH></TR>
  <TR ALIGN=center><TH>Row 1 Header</TH><TD>100</
          TD><TD>1000</TD>
</TR>
  <TR ALIGN=center><TH>Row 2 Header</TH><TD>200</
          TD><TD>2000</TD>
</TR>
  <TR ALIGN=center><TH>Row 3 Header</TH><TD>300</
          TD><TD>3000</TD>
</TR>
</TABLE>
```

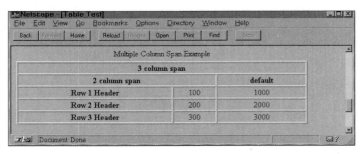

Figure 8-5:
Column
spanning is
often a
useful
technique
for table
headings.

ROWSPAN

Use ROWSPAN in any table cell (<TH> or <TD>) to specify how many rows of the table the cell should span, if you want it to span more than the default of one cell. This feature works great for multi-row vertical headings (see Figure 8-6). A span is truncated if it extends into rows that were not specified with a table row tag (<TR>).

```
<TABLE BORDER WIDTH="90%" HEIGHT="90%">
   <CAPTION> Multiple Row Span Example</CAPTION>
   <TR ALIGN="center"><TH ROWSPAN="3">Rows 1-3 Header</
        TH><TD>100</TD><TD>1000</TD></TR>
   <TR ALIGN="center"><TD>200</TD><TD>2000</TD></TR>
   <TR ALIGN="center"><TD>300</TD><TD>3000</TD></TR>
   <TR ALIGN="center"><TH ROWSPAN="2">Rows 4-5 Header<TD>400</
        TD><TD>4000</TD></TR>
   <TR ALIGN="center>"<TD>400</TD><TD>5000</TD></TR>
</TABLE>
```

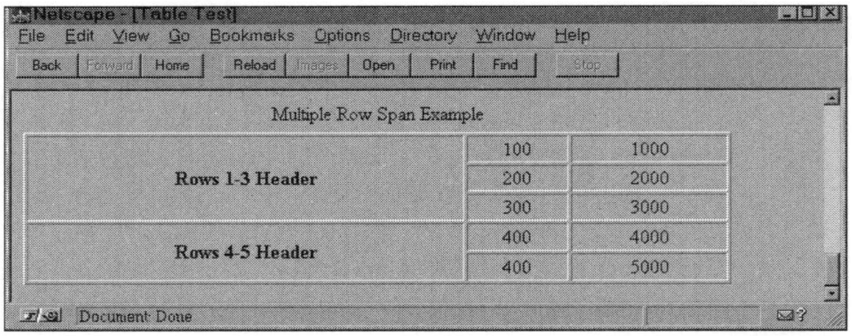

Figure 8-6: Row spanning is great for vertical headings.

Proprietary <TABLE> *Extensions*

The previous sections cover the common elements of HTML tables; in this section, we discuss the <TABLE> markup that's unique for the leading browsers. Other vendors may ultimately support these extensions, but for the time being, we can't recommend that you use them unless

- ✔ You warn your audience that you rely on these features.
- ✔ You can safely assume that your audience is properly equipped to handle the features.

Netscape 2.0

The latest version of Netscape includes some interesting extensions to the draft standard definitions for table markup. In the sections that follow, you see exactly what we mean by *interesting!*

BORDER="<value>"

Netscape responds to several values after the BORDER attribute. BORDER= "<value>", where <value> is a number, causes Netscape to display the border that number of pixels wide. By setting the border value to zero, the space originally reserved for borders between cells is eliminated, thereby allowing very compact tables. The following example (depicted in Figure 8-7) shows the use of nested tables (or "tables within tables") to group three other tables of varying border sizes horizontally across the screen. The outermost table has no border.

```
<TABLE><CAPTION>Table Border Sizes - No Border on Master
    Table</CAPTION>
<TR>
<TD><TABLE BORDER><CAPTION>Standard Border </CAPTION>
  <TR><TD>Element 1</TD> <TD> Element 2</TD></TR>
  <TR><TD>Element 3</TD> <TD>Element 4</TD> </TR></TABLE>
</TD>
<TD><TABLE BORDER="5"><CAPTION>Border=5 (pixels) </CAPTION>
  <TR><TD>Element 1</TD> <TD> Element 2</TD></TR>
  <TR><TD>Element 3</TD> <TD>Element 4</TD> </TR></TABLE>
</TD>
<TD><TABLE BORDER="10"><CAPTION>Border=10 (pixels) </CAPTION>
  <TR><TD>Element 1</TD> <TD> Element 2</TD></TR>
  <TR><TD>Element 3</TD> <TD>Element 4</TD> </TR></TABLE>
</TD>
</TR>
</TABLE>
```

Figure 8-7:
Netscape
supports
extensions
to control
BORDER
size.

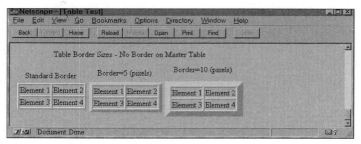

VALIGN

VALIGN (vertical alignment) is used inside a <TR>, <TH>, or <TD>tag to control the placement of the cell's contents at the top, middle, or bottom of the cell. Netscape accepts the value VALIGN="baseline" to vertically align the contents of all cells in the row to the same location.

CELLSPACING=<value>

CELLSPACING is a Netscape attribute used within the <TABLE> tag. The value represents the amount of space inserted between individual cells in a table. Netscape uses a default space of of two pixels between cells. Couple this with the following attribute (CELLPADDING), and you can really make interesting-looking tables. Figure 8-8 shows tables with different cell spacing applied.

```
<TABLE><CAPTION>Cell Spacing Examples</CAPTION>
<TR><TD>
<TABLE BORDER><CAPTION>Default Cell Spacing</CAPTION>
  <TR><TD>Element 1</TD> <TD> Element 2</TD>
  </TR>
  <TR><TD>Element 3</TD> <TD>Element 4</TD>
  </TR>
</TABLE></TD>
<TD>
<TABLE BORDER CELLSPACING="10"><CAPTION>Cell Spacing 10
   pixels</CAPTION>
  <TR><TD>Element 1</TD> <TD> Element 2</TD>
  </TR>
  <TR><TD>Element 3</TD> <TD>Element 4</TD>
  </TR>
</TABLE></TD>
</TR>
</TABLE>
```

Figure 8-8:
Cell spacing
in Netscape
provides
additional
layout
controls.

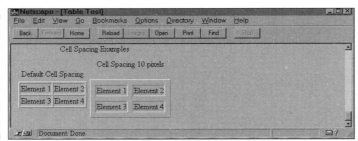

CELLPADDING=<value>

When used within the <TABLE> tag, the CELLPADDING value indicates the amount of space between the border of a cell and the contents of the cell. Netscape's default value is one pixel. Setting the cell padding to zero on a table with borders would cause the text to touch the border, but using the following line results in a very compact arrangement:

```
<TABLE BORDER="0" CELLSPACING="0" CELLPADDING="0">.
```

Padding cells can help you greatly enhance the visual impact of your tables (see the examples in Figure 8-9), especially when you couple the padding with cell spacing and border sizing.

```
<TABLE><CAPTION>Cell Padding Examples</CAPTION>
<TR><TD>
<TABLE BORDER><CAPTION>Default Cell Padding</CAPTION>
  <TR><TD>Element 1</TD> <TD> Element 2</TD>
  </TR>
  <TR><TD>Element 3</TD> <TD>Element 4</TD>
  </TR>
</TABLE></TD>
<TD>
<TABLE BORDER CELLPADDING="10"><CAPTION>Cell Padding 10
  pixels</CAPTION>
  <TR><TD>Element 1</TD> <TD> Element 2</TD>
  </TR>
  <TR><TD>Element 3</TD> <TD>Element 4</TD>
  </TR>
</TABLE></TD>
</TR>
</TABLE>
```

Figure 8-9:
Cell padding
in Netscape
also
provides
more
sophisticated
layout
controls.

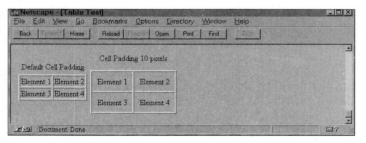

WIDTH="<value_or_percent>"

In Netscape, use the WIDTH attribute inside the <TABLE> tag to set the width of the table as an absolute width in pixels or as a percentage of the Web page width. If all cells can't fit in the table display at the width you specify, Netscape gets as close as possible to the desired width while displaying all the cells.

When you use the WIDTH attribute in the <TH> or <TD> tag, you set the width of the cell either as an absolute width in pixels or as a percentage of the table width. Again, Netscape gets as close as possible to your specified cell width while displaying all cells. Figures 8-5 and 8-6 illustrate the use of the WIDTH attribute.

HEIGHT="<value_or_percent>"

In Netscape, use the HEIGHT attribute inside the <TABLE> tag to set the height of the table either as an absolute width in pixels or as a percentage of the Web page height. If all cells can't fit in the table display at the specified height, Netscape gets as close as possible to the desired height while displaying all of the cells.

When you use this attribute in the <TH> or <TD> tag, you set the height of the cell either as an absolute width in pixels or as a percentage of the table height. Again, Netscape gets as close as possible to your desired height while displaying all cells. Figures 8-5 and 8-6 illustrate the use of the HEIGHT attribute.

Check out Netscape's examples of its proprietary table attributes at the following URL:

    http://home.mcom.com/assist/net_sites/table_sample.html

MS Internet Explorer 2.0

Microsoft's Internet Explorer 2.0 browser responds to several color-related <TABLE> tag attributes:

- ✔ BGCOLOR="#rrggbb or colorname" sets the background color.
- ✔ BORDERCOLOR="#rrggbb or colorname" sets the border color when used with the BORDER attribute.
- ✔ BORDERCOLORLIGHT="#rrggbb or colorname" sets one of two colors that make a 3-D border.
- ✔ BORDERCOLORDARK="#rrggbb or colorname" sets the other of two colors that make a 3-D border.

Check out the following URL for information on Microsoft Internet Explorer's usage of these attributes:

```
http://www.microsoft.com/windows/ie/ie20html.htm
```

Building Your Own Tables

Building tables by hand is time consuming, repetitious work, so be sure that your content really is enhanced by displaying it in tabular form. No doubt, someone will introduce a fast-and-easy table converter for mass conversions of spreadsheet data into HTML tables right after you finish doing yours by hand. Such is life.

However, you can simplify your work by carefully planning the layout of your tabular data and making use of search, replace, copy, and paste functions in your HTML editor. These functions can help you insert a table's tags and attributes. If your table holds numeric values, consider which option is better: making an HTML table template and typing in the values or converting your numeric data into text and surrounding the data with HTML tags.

Laying out tabular data for easy display

First of all, make a sketch of how you want your table to look. Then make a small HTML table with only a few rows of data to test your methodology and to see whether the table looks the way you want. If you're using multicolumn-and multirow-spanning heads, you may need to make some adjustments to get them properly spaced to fit your data. Finally, you may want to test your tables with several browsers to see how they look. As we said at the start of this chapter, no standards for tables exist, so each browser displays them differently.

A slick trick for the upper-left problem

Using empty cells with COLSPAN and ROWSPAN is a nifty formatting trick to help you with that pesky upper-left corner problem in your table. Check out the next example and its display in Figure 8-10.

```
<TABLE BORDER><CAPTION>Blank Upper Left Corner</CAPTION>
  <TR><TH ROWSPAN="2"></TH><TH COLSPAN="2">COLUMN
  HEADING</TH>
    </TR>
  <TR><TH>Subhead 1</TH><TH>Subhead 2</TH></TR>
  <TR><TH ROWSPAN="3">ROW<BR>HEADING</TH><TD>Element
  1</TD>
    <TD>Element 2</TD></TR>
  <TR><TD>Element 3</TD> <TD>Element 4</TD></TR>
  <TR><TD>Element 5</TD> <TD>Element 6</TD></TR>
</TABLE>
```

Figure 8-10:
A table with
a blank
upper-left
corner is a
common
layout.

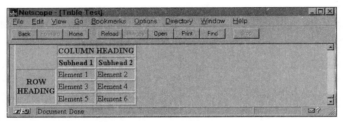

In English and many other languages, people read from left to right and top to bottom. So, isn't it strange that the upper-left corner of so many tables is blank? I guess we leave the corner blank because we don't know what to do with it. Anyway, now you know how! You can also start building your own tables by using these tags. All you need to do is mix and match the elements to get what you want. You may need to experiment a bit, but you'll have fun finding out how various combinations of table tags and attributes result in interesting presentations.

Just remember, you must build your tables by rows. If you use ROWSPAN="3" in one table row (<TR>), you must account for the extra two rows in the next <TR> (as shown in the preceding example).

Mixing graphics and tables makes for interesting pages

Tables are an effective way to present text or numbers in a visually pleasing and well-ordered manner, so that your readers won't be frightened off by a screen-full of dense and impenetrable text. Something about a long, unbroken list of bare numbers quickly drives away all but the truly masochistic. However, putting those numbers into an attractive table (or better yet, several tables interspersed with a few well-chosen images) can do wonders for your Web site's attractiveness.

Figure 8-11 shows how you can use a table format to display a relatively large amount of text in a small space attractively without its looking squeezed. Notice how the simple use of the colored ball images adds visual interest and attracts your eye to the different sections of the table. This simple use of the table format shows that you don't have to put each element into its own cell to make effective use of a table. Take a look at the actual URL to get the full color effect.

http://www.swimtex.com/

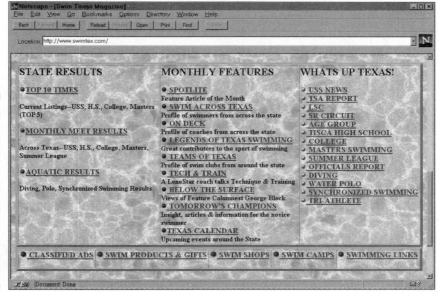

Figure 8-11: Strategic use of graphics and text can turn an imposing collection of data into an enjoyable reading experience.

Some Stunning Table Examples

These examples may not be the best in the world, but all we said was that they're *stunning*. Figure 8-12 shows the use of multiple nested tables to arrange text and graphics in an interesting manner on a personal Web page.

The HTML code for Figure 8-12 is rather extensive; but if you review it, you can see most of the table tags and attributes in use, along with the old familiar HTML links and other tags.

```
<center><table cellspacing="10" border="2" ><tr>
<td align="middle" valign="top">
<h3>Click the button to see some of the funniest web
    pages I've encountered.</h3>
<a href="/~snjames/chris/funny.htm"><img align="top"
    src="/~snjames/chris/here.jpg" alt="HERE"border="0">
    </a></td>
```

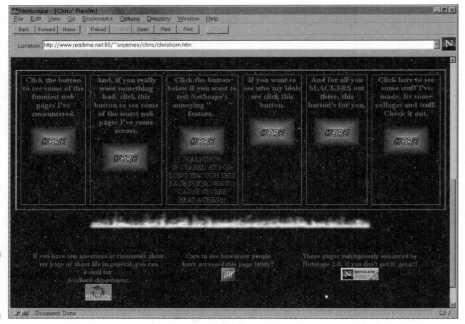

Figure 8-12:
CSJ's Home
Page.

```
<td align="middle" valign="top">
<h3>And, if you really want something bad, click this
   button to see some of the worst web pages I've come
   across.</h3>
<a href="/~snjames/chris/dumb.htm"><img align="top"
src="/~snjames/chris/here.jpg"alt="HERE"border="0"></a>
   </td>

<td align="middle" valign="top">
<h3>Click the button below if you want to test NetScape's
   annoying "<BLINK>blink</BLINK>" feature. </h3>
<a href="/~snjames/chris/blink.htm"><img align="top"
src="/~snjames/chris/here.jpg"alt="HERE"border="0"></a>
<br>WARNING!!<br> IF STARED AT FOR LONG ENOUGH, THIS PAGE
   IS KNOWN TO CAUSE SEVERE HEADACHES!!!</td>

<td align="middle" valign="top">
<h3>If you want to see who my idols are click this
   button.</h3>
<a href="/~snjames/chris/idols.htm"><img align="top"
src="/~snjames/chris/here.jpg" alt="HERE" border="0"></a></
            td>

<td align="middle" valign="top">
<h3>And for all you SLACKERS out there, this button's for
   you.</h3>
<a href="/~snjames/chris/slacker.htm"><img align="top"
   src="/~snjames/chris/here.jpg" alt="HERE" border="0">
   </a><p></td>
<td align="middle" valign="top">
<h3>Click here to see some stuff I've made. It's some
   collages and stuff. Check it out.</h3>
<a href="/~snjames/chris/byme.htm"><img align="top"
   src="/~snjames/chris/here.jpg" alt="HERE" border="0">
   </a><p>
</td></tr></table></center>
<center><IMG ALIGN="BOTTOM"
   SRC="/~snjames/chris/flame.jpg"></center>
<center><table cellspacing="30"><tr>
```

(continued)

(continued)

```
<td align="middle" valign="top">
<h4>If you have any questions or comments about my page
    or about life in general, you can e-mail my
    <br><i>feedback department</i>.<br>
<a href="mailto:73146.2223@compuserve.com">
    <img align="middle" src="feedback.jpg"
    alt="Feedback Department" border="0"></a>
</h4></td>

<td align="middle" valign="top">
<h4>Care to see how many people have accessed this page
    lately?<br>
<A HREF="http://www.internet-audit.com"></A>
<A HREF="http://stats.internet-audit.com/cgi-bin/stats.exe
            /0015687">
    <IMG ISMAP BORDER=0
    SRC="http://two.internet-audit.com/act/ZQ0015687.gif"
    ALT="Make your visit count, load this image."></A>
</center>
</h4></td>

<td align="middle" valign="top">
<h4>These pages outrageously enhanced by Netscape 2.0.
    If you don't got it, get it!!<br>
<a href="http://www.netscape.com"><img align="middle"
    src="netscape.gif"alt="Netscape.com"
    border="0"></a></h4></td></tr></table></center>
```

So now you know all about the latest and greatest feature of HTML, the <TABLE>. (We'll just pretend that Java, VRML, and other more outrageous extensions don't exist for now, okay?) Hey, you're smart. You bought this book, didn't you? Now you know how to make use of the table tags and attributes to make your Web site all the more inviting to potential users. In the next chapter, we tackle the topic of frames, which allow you to break your user's browser window into separate, scrolling display areas.

Chapter 9
HTML Frames Enhance Page Controls!

*F*rames keep pictures from falling off the wall and houses from crashing down. Frames delineate, outline, and give structure to HTML documents while providing for movement of information within and between the frames. In this chapter, we discuss the Netscape implementation of frames and show you, step-by-step, how you can use frames to enhance your own Web pages.

More information on the latest innovations in frames is readily available at the following WWW sites:

```
http://home.mcom.com/assist/net_sites/frames.html
http://home.mcom.com/assist/net_sites/frame_syntax.html
http://home.mcom.com/assist/net_sites/target.html
```

HTML Frames Overview

Do you really need to use the <FRAMESET> tag? You can use a table to format the information into areas, complete with borders, on the browser screen. But remember: Although r^2 and cornbread are round, tables are static, and frames can be dynamic. For the mathematically challenged, this concept means that you can scroll information within frames.

Each frame is similar to a separate browser screen. Depending on the attributes you give it, a frame can act just like a standard browser screen, or it can be frozen into Elliot Ness untouchability. A frozen frame is great for displaying your company's logo at the top of the browser screen without actually placing it first on every one of your Web site HTML documents. What a time saver, eh? Oops! We're jumping the gun a bit. We know many more nifty uses for frames, and we discuss them later in this chapter (in the section on framing your Web site). But first, a word (actually, a wealth of words) of caution about using frames.

Only Netscape Navigator 2.0 supports frames. The Netscape folks have submitted their implementation of the <FRAMESET> and associated tags to the IETF (Internet Engineering Task Force) working group for inclusion in a future HTML DTD (Document Type Definition). Although only Netscape supports frames, an estimated 80 percent of Web users use the Netscape browsers. Thus, even though frames are still "experimental," as HTML goes, you're still going to reach the vast majority of the Web surfers if you include frames on your Web pages. You can always provide your current set of pages in addition to your new set of *framed* pages so that you can reach even more Web users.

According to Netscape's documentation

- Frames divide Web pages into multiple, scrollable regions.
- You can give a frame a URL so that the frame can load information independently from other frames and documents.
- You can name a frame and target it from other URLs.
- Frames can be dynamically resized if the user changes the browser's window size.
- The user can manually resize a frame if you set up the frame to enable resizing.

These features bring to mind a few interesting possibilities for using frames such as

- A Web page with a fixed logo at the top and a scrolling main bottom section.
- A page with a fixed top logo, a bottom navigation bar and copyright notice, and a scrolling middle section for displaying page content.
- A Web page with side-by-side frames containing a table of contents on the left and a scrolling text frame on the right.
- A left frame filled with icons linked to different parts of your Web site: The particular part displayed in the right frame is based on a selection from the left frame.
- A combination of any or all of the above.

In short, frames are flexible. They enable you to keep constant chunks of information on the browser display, while permitting users to scroll through large amounts of text or dynamic content. You find out how to set up the structures we just described a bit later in the chapter. But first, you need to understand the HTML markup tags that make frames possible.

HTML Frame Markup

The HTML tags for frames are listed in the following subsections, along with discussions of their correct syntax and use. Using these tags isn't particularly taxing, and it's certainly not a sin. Frames have good uses and better uses, which we know that you'll grasp quickly, just so you can hang some nice frames around your own Web site! We begin with a discussion of the structure of a document that includes frames and then look at the tags that you use to make the frames. Frameward ho!

The Frame Document structure

A Frame Document can simply be a normal HTML document in which the `<BODY. . .>` container is replaced by a `<FRAMESET. . .>` container that characterizes the HTML sub-documents — frames — that constitute the Web page. The basic Frame Document starts within the following overall HTML framework. (Dontcha just love/hate puns?)

```
<HTML>
  <HEAD>
  </HEAD>
  <FRAMESET>
  Your frame information goes here.
  </FRAMESET>
</HTML>
```

If you're a nice person and want to provide something for frame-challenged browsers to display, you can use the `<NOFRAMES>` tag to include your existing, nonframed HTML document in the following structure:

```
<HTML>
  <HEAD>
  </HEAD>
  <FRAMESET>
  Your frame information goes here.
  </FRAMESET>
<NOFRAMES>
  <BODY>
```

(continued)

(continued)

```
    The non-framed HTML code for your page goes here.
    </BODY>
 </NOFRAMES>
 </HTML>
```

Frame syntax

Frame syntax is quite similar to the syntax used within HTML tables. In fact, you can think of frames as movable and dynamically updateable tables. We discuss the syntax of the various frame-related tags in the following sections. After you start using frame-related markup in your own Web pages, you find the syntax to be pretty straightforward stuff.

<FRAMESET>

<FRAMESET> is the main container for a frame. This tag has two attributes, ROWS and COLS. Because a frame document uses <FRAMESET> instead of <BODY>, the <FRAMESET> tag should immediately follow the </HEAD> tag. If any <BODY> tags appear before the <FRAMESET> tag pair, the <FRAMESET> tag is ignored. Between the outermost <FRAMESET> . . . <FRAMESET> tags, you can use only nested <FRAMESET> tags, <FRAME> tags, or <NOFRAMES> tags. We talk specifically about *nesting* in a later section of this chapter, so all you birds and squirrels pay attention!

ROWS="row_height_value_list"

The ROWS attribute determines two things: the number of frames to be displayed vertically (stacked on top of each other) in the browser window and the height of each of these frames. The ROWS attribute uses a comma-separated list of values. These values can be pixels, percentages between 1 and 100, or relative scaling values (as described a little later in this chapter).

The number of elements in the ROWS value list determines the number of frames that appear vertically up and down the screen. Yes, this seems backward to us, too. But if you think of the ROWS value as the number of screen rows used by each frame or the number of frames that can fit in the *n* rows available on your browser screen, you may not get too confused.

Because the total height of all the simultaneously displayed frames must equal the height of the browser window, the browser may adjust the ROWS height values to make them all fit. Omitting the ROWS attribute results in a single stack of frames sized vertically to fit the browser window and extending horizontally from one side of the browser window to the other. ROWS values can be any valid mixture of the following elements:

- ✔ **Value:** Any number is regarded as a number of pixels. Take care if using this type of value because the size of the viewer's window can vary substantially. If you use a fixed pixel value, using one or more of the relative size values (described below) is a good idea, too. Otherwise, the user's browser may override your specified pixel value to ensure that the total height and width of all the frames equals 100 percent of the user's window. Remember, the browser is going to display all defined frames, even if it must squeeze them into very small areas.

- ✔ **Value%:** This value is a percentage between 1 and 100. If the total for all frames is greater than 100 percent, all percentages are scaled down to fit the browser window. If the values total less than 100 percent, extra space is allocated to any relative-sized frames that may be present (see Value* below).

- ✔ **Value*:** A single asterisk (*) character designates a *relative-sized* frame. Browsers give the * frame all remaining space left over after other allocations are satisfied. If you use multiple relative-sized frames without values before the *, the remaining space is divided evenly among them.

    If you place a value in front of the *, the frame gets that much more relative space. For example, an entry such as 3*, * allocates three times as much space to the first frame (3/4 of the total) and the remaining portion (1/4) to the second frame.

You don't have to be a mathematics expert to use these different types of values, but you should test your work carefully to make sure that you're getting the results you want. Be especially careful to test if you mix value types. The following are a couple of examples to get you started:

Example 1: Two Vertically Stacked Frames

This example shows HTML code for two frames vertically stacked on the screen. The first gets 20 percent of the available space and the last gets 80 percent:

```
<FRAMESET ROWS="20%,80%">
<FRAMESET ROWS="20%,*">
```

Example 2: Three vertical frames

This example shows HTML code for three vertical frames. The first frame, which appears at the top of the screen, is a fixed height of 100 pixels. The last gets 20 percent of the space available and is displayed at the bottom of the screen. The second, or middle, frame gets whatever vertical space remains after the sum of 100 pixels, plus 20 percent of the total is subtracted from the total vertical screen space.

```
<FRAMESET ROWS="100,*,20%">
```

COLS="column_width_list"

The COLS attribute functions in the same manner as the ROWS attribute, except that it governs the number of frames displayed horizontally across the browser's screen and the horizontal width of each frame. Yeah, we know that columns go up and down, but just think of COLS as telling you how many column widths each frame occupies.

A quick example of the HTML code to display two frames across the screen with the first one (on the left) getting 20 percent of the available space and the second (on the right) getting the rest, looks like this:

```
<FRAMESET COLS="20%,*">
```

This format is a good way to display the contents of your Web site vertically on the left side of the screen (in the 20 percent frame), with the information scrolling on the right in the rest-of-the-screen sized frame.

<FRAME>

Each separate frame in your Web site must be defined by a separate <FRAME> tag. You can modify the <FRAME> tag by using the following six attributes: SRC, NAME, MARGINWIDTH, MARGINHEIGHT, SCROLLING, and NORESIZE. Any or all of these attributes and their corresponding values must be inserted between the word FRAME and the ending bracket (>) of the tag. The <FRAME> tag has no associated end tag.

Generally, you use a standard HTML file, an image file, or a URL for display in each frame. You can display these elements as you would display them in a standard browser window by themselves without frames. The main difference is that the frame designates the amount and shape of the on-screen space available for any framed element's display. Following is an example of the syntax for a <FRAME> tag:

```
<FRAME SRC="yourstuf.htm" NAME="Your Frame"
    SCROLLING="yes">
```

SRC="url"

The URL for the SRC (source) attribute points to the source material to be displayed in the frame. The source material may be a link, an image, an HTML file, or any other legal URL. If you omit the SRC attribute, the frame appears as a blank space of the appropriate size.

NAME="window_name"

The NAME attribute assigns a name to a frame so that you can target the frame as the recipient of information. You do this targeting (by using the new TARGET attribute, discussed later in this chapter) by placing links to the frame in other documents. This linking method is how you tell the table of contents (TOC) in the TOC frame to display a selected file in the TEXT frame. The NAME attribute is optional, and all NAME values must begin with an alphanumeric character.

MARGINWIDTH="value"

The MARGINWIDTH attribute accepts a value of one or more pixels to determine the exact width of the left and right side margins of a frame. Margins must be one or more pixels wide to ensure that objects do not touch a frame's edges. You cannot specify margins so that no space exists for a document's contents. The MARGINWIDTH attribute is optional; omitting this attribute enables the browser to set its own margin widths.

MARGINHEIGHT="value"

The MARGINHEIGHT attribute works just like MARGINWIDTH, except that it controls the upper and lower margins of frames instead of the left and right margins.

SCROLLING="yes\no\auto"

The SCROLLING attribute forces a frame to display a scrollbar. A value of yes forces the browser to display the scrollbars on that frame at all times. A no value keeps scrollbars from being visible at any time. The SCROLLING attribute is optional. The default value is auto, which instructs the browser to decide whether the frame requires vertical, horizontal, or both scrollbars and then to place the scrollbars wherever they're necessary.

Because auto is the default, specifying the SCROLLING attribute at all is unnecessary. Take the easy way out — simply omit the SCROLLING attribute whenever you want scrollbars to appear automatically.

NORESIZE

The NORESIZE attribute indicates that a frame may not be resized by the user. By default, users can resize frames by dragging a frame edge to a new position. If any frame adjacent to the edge of another frame isn't resizable, that entire edge cannot move. This unmovable edge affects the resizing of any adjacent frames. The NORESIZE attribute is optional and quite useful for keeping viewers from removing your logo or advertising space from their view. However, we don't recommended using the NORESIZE attribute as a general technique for content display frames because the restriction limits users' abilities to resize your handcrafted display settings to fit their screens.

<NOFRAMES> . . . </NOFRAMES>

The <NOFRAMES> tag enables you to create alternative content that is viewable by frame-challenged browsers. Any frame-cognizant browser ignores all tags and data between starting and ending <NOFRAMES> tags.

Targeting frames

The `TARGET` attribute gives you control over where the linked data appears after a user clicks a link in your documents. You can use the `TARGET` attribute in the `<A>`, `<BASE>`, `<AREA>`, and `<FORM>` tags, but the attribute is most beneficial if used in the `<A>` (anchor) tag in conjunction with the frames feature. So how exactly does targeting work?

Normally, after a user clicks a link, the browser displays the new document in a full browser window. *Targeting* enables you to assign names to specific frames and to target certain documents to always appear in the frame bearing the targeted name. In an earlier section of this chapter, we tell how to use the `NAME` attribute to name a frame. Using the `TARGET` attribute to target the frame is equally easy.

Adding the `TARGET` attribute to the `<A>` tag in conjunction with the frames feature is as simple as inserting the attribute and its value (the frame name) in the `<A>` tag. In the following example, the name of the targeted frame is *frame name:*

```
<A HREF="url" TARGET="frame name">Targeted Anchor</A>
```

Allowed and special `TARGET` *names*

A valid frame name specified by a `TARGET` attribute must begin with an alphanumeric character, with the exception of a few special-purpose target names that begin with the underscore character. Any targeted frame name (other than a special-purpose name) that begins with an underscore or a nonalphanumeric character is ignored.

- ✔ `TARGET="_self"`: Specifying the `_self` target always causes the linked document to load in the frame where the user selects the anchor. Use this attribute to override a globally assigned `BASE` target.

- ✔ `TARGET="_parent"`: Specifying the `_parent` target makes the linked document load in the immediate `FRAMESET` parent of the document. If the current document where the `_parent` target appears has no parent, this attribute behaves like the `_self` value.

- ✔ `TARGET="_top"`: Specifying the `_top` target makes the linked document load in the full body of the window. The `_top` target name acts like `_self` if the current document is already at the top of the document hierarchy. Use this attribute to escape from a deeply-nested `FRAME`.

Framing Your Own Web Site

Your Web pages may be like pictures waiting to be framed. Even if you primarily provide text for your users, you can still make great use of frames to help them navigate within your site. Remember, perhaps the most important feature of frames is that they enable you to keep important information constantly on-screen, while other portions of the screen change to reflect new content information.

If you skim the next few pages, you see a few screen shots and great heaping stacks of HTML code. As they say in Jamaica, "No problem, Mon." Look at each screen shot and the HTML code that drives it as a unit. The explanation of each small HTML document appears beneath the screen where it's displayed. As you can see, working with frames causes you to create more (but generally smaller) HTML documents, because each frame requires its own HTML document. Ahh, such is the price you must pay to provide your users with the best possible Web site. Don't say we didn't warn you!

The first thing you must do to use frames successfully is to visualize your Web page in its framed incarnation. Sketch it on a napkin, the back of an envelope, or whatever's handy in the trash can. Next, you must understand that you need one HTML document to define your sketched-out frame page and a separate HTML document for each frame in the sketch.

If you sketched a simple page with a small frame at the top and a large frame at the bottom, you need three HTML documents just to get started. What a *co-inkydink!* (That's *coincidence* for those of you who are jargon challenged. Jargons? Aren't they cousins of the Klingons?) Anyway, we just happen to have such an example, and (surprise, surprise) we put it next!

The basic, two-frame Web page

The HTML code that follows describes the Web page shown in Figure 9-1. This code is short and to the point; it sets up the top frame as 20 percent of the screen and names it Top Frame. Notice that the top frame is set for no scroll-ing and no resizing. The HTML code sets the bottom frame as the rest of the screen by using the * value and names the bottom frame Your Stuff. The bottom frame is set to SCROLLING so that both scrollbars show at all times, regardless of whether enough text is present to require scrolling. We set up the code this way just to show you how these scrollbars look.

If you omit the SCROLLING attribute, the browser automatically displays the appropriate scrollbars, horizontal and/or vertical, if the frame contains enough information to require them. Why not let the browser do its thing and not worry about scrollbars? The following code shows everything you need to create the basic structure for a Web page that contains two frames.

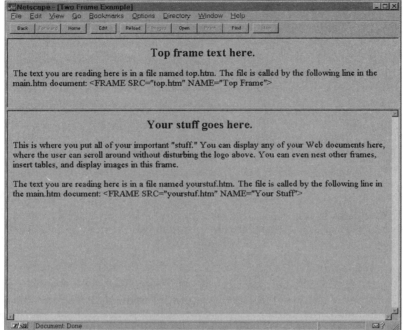

Figure 9-1:
A basic,
two-frame
Web page
requires
three
underlying
HTML
documents.

```
<HTML>
<HEAD>
<TITLE>Two Frame Example</TITLE>
</HEAD>
<FRAMESET ROWS="20%,*">
<FRAME SRC="top.htm" NAME="Top Frame"
    SCROLLING="no" NORESIZE>
<FRAME SRC="yourstuf.htm" NAME="Your Stuff"
    SCROLLING="yes">
</FRAMESET>
</HTML>
```

Next is the HTML code for the Top Frame shown in Figure 9-1. This document is simply a standard HTML document in a file named top.htm, which is used as the source for the Top Frame in the preceding Web page code. In case you're wondering, the < and > in the body of the code make the browser display the angle brackets (< and >, respectively) and keep the browser from interpreting the line as HTML code, because all we want to do is display the line for you.

```
<HTML>
<HEAD>
<TITLE>
Top Frame
</TITLE>
</HEAD>
<BODY>
<CENTER><H2>Top frame text here.</H2></CENTER>
<FONT SIZE="+1">The text you are reading here is in a
  file named top.htm. The file is called by the following
  line in the main.htm document: &#60;FRAME SRC="top.htm"
  NAME="Top Frame"&#62;
</FONT>
</BODY>
</HTML>
```

Finally, the next set of HTML code is for the Your Stuff frame shown in Figure 9-1. Again, this is a standard HTML document. Keep reading. It gets more interesting RSN (real soon now).

```
<HTML>
<HEAD>
<TITLE>
Your Stuff Frame
</TITLE>
</HEAD>
<BODY>
<CENTER><H2>Your stuff goes here.</H2></CENTER>
<FONT SIZE="+1">
This is where you put all of your important "stuff." You
  can display any of your Web documents here, where the
  user can scroll around without disturbing the logo
  above. You can even nest other frames, insert tables,
  and display images in this frame.<P>
The text you are reading here is in a file named
  yourstuf.htm. The file is called by the following line
  in the main.htm document:
&#60;FRAME SRC="yourstuf.htm" NAME="Your Stuff"&#62;
</FONT>
</BODY>
</HTML>
```

A basic, three-frame Web page

The following HTML code, for the Web page document shown in Figure 9-2, sets up a top frame 150 pixels high and a bottom frame 100 pixels high. Both frames are nonscrolling, and the bottom frame is not resizable. The middle frame is set to scrolling to illustrate the scrollbars. This type of setup is quite versatile and accommodates many different uses. Next is the HTML for the structure of the three-frame page:

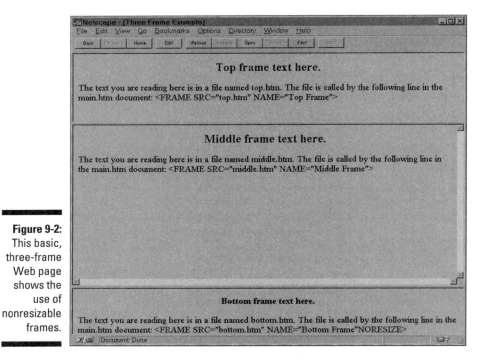

```
<HTML>
<HEAD>
<TITLE>Three Frame Example</TITLE>
</HEAD>
<FRAMESET ROWS="150,*,100">
<FRAME SRC="top.htm" NAME="Top Frame" SCROLLING="no">
<FRAME SRC="middle.htm" NAME="Middle Frame"
    SCROLLING="yes">
<FRAME SRC="bottom.htm" NAME="Bottom Frame"
    SCROLLING="no" NORESIZE>
</FRAMESET>
</HTML>
```

Next is the HTML code for the Top frame shown in Figure 9-2. The document is the same as the one shown for the previous figure. Hey, it worked there, didn't it? Why mess with a good thing?

```
<HTML>
<HEAD>
<TITLE>
Top Frame
</TITLE>
</HEAD>
<BODY>
```

```
<CENTER><H2>Top frame text here.</H2></CENTER>
<FONT SIZE="+1">The text you are reading here is in a
 file named top.htm. The file is called by the following
 line in the main.htm document:
 &#60;FRAME SRC="top.htm" NAME="Top Frame"&#62;
</FONT>
</BODY>
</HTML>
```

The following is the HTML code for the `Middle Frame` shown in Figure 9-2. Once again, this code shows a standard HTML document where you can place any legal HTML tags and other information (preferably, some content that's a bit more useful than what we show).

```
<HTML>
<HEAD>
<TITLE>
Middle Frame
</TITLE>
</HEAD>
<BODY>
<center>
<center><H2>Middle frame text here.</H2></center>
</center>
<FONT SIZE="+1">The text you are reading here is in a
 file named middle.htm. The file is called by the
 following line in the main.htm document:
 &#60;FRAME SRC="middle.htm" NAME="Middle Frame"&#62;
</FONT>
</BODY>
</HTML>
```

Finally, the following listing shows the HTML code for the `Bottom frame` shown in Figure 9-2. This listing is another standard HTML document, but remember, the document is displayed within a fixed-height (100-pixel) frame that can't be resized.

 Your job, as a Web page author, is to make sure that the information is compact or short enough to fit the specified frame space, even if users resize their entire browser screens. If you can't make the information fit the frame, use relative values for the frame height and allow resizing instead.

```
<HTML>
<HEAD>
<TITLE>
Bottom Frame
</TITLE>
</HEAD>
```

(continued)

(continued)

```
<BODY>
<center><H3>Bottom frame text here.</H3></center>
<FONT SIZE="+1">The text you are reading here is in a
  file named bottom.htm. The file is called by the
  following line in the main.htm document:
  &#60;FRAME SRC="bottom.htm" NAME="Bottom Frame"
  NORESIZE&#62;
</FONT>
</BODY>
</HTML>
```

Fancy that: a three-frame page with logo, text, and navigation bar

The following listing shows the HTML code for the Web page document depicted in Figure 9-3. The document illustrates a common usage of the three-frame page with a logo area on top, text in the middle, and a fixed navigation bar at the bottom. The HTML source code also shows typical usage of the <NOFRAMES> tags. In this example, users with browsers that can't interpret frames see a link to an alternative set of pages, with the gentle suggestion that they might want to download a frame-capable browser at the URL shown.

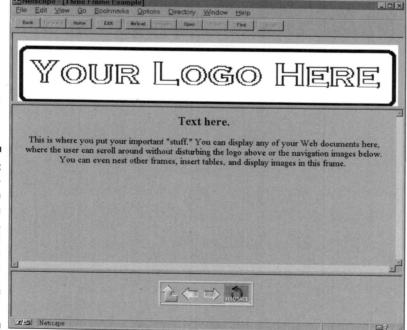

Figure 9-3:
A three-frame Web page with logo, text, and navigation bar shows a typical, real-world use of frames.

```
<HTML>
<HEAD>
<TITLE>Three Frame Example</TITLE>
</HEAD>
<FRAMESET ROWS="150,*,100">
<FRAME SRC="logo.htm" NAME="Logo" SCROLLING="no">
<FRAME SRC="text.htm" NAME="Text" SCROLLING="yes">
<FRAME SRC="navbar.htm" NAME="Navigation" SCROLLING="no"
   NORESIZE>
</FRAMESET>

<NOFRAMES>
<CENTER><STRONG><H1>FRAME ALERT!</STRONG><P>
<B>This document uses Netscape's FRAME function. If you
 are seeing this message, you are using a <I>frame
 challenged</I> browser. You can see this page without
 frames <A HREF="regular.htm"> here.</A><P>
You can get your own free copy of Netscape Navigator 2.0
 <A HREF="http://home.netscape.com/"> at:
<IMG ALIGN="middle"
 SRC="netscape.gif"ALT="http://home.netscape.com/"
 BORDER="0"></A>
</CENTER>
</NOFRAMES>
</HTML>
```

Next is the HTML code for the Logo frame shown in Figure 9-3. Please notice that the markup not only displays the logo.gif file in the frame, but uses the WIDTH=100% and HEIGHT=100% in the <IMG> tag to cause the 3K logo.gif to be automatically resized. That is, the browser automatically resizes the logo to fill the frame regardless of the frame's size after the user resizes the browser screen. If your logo or image resizes well (without losing too much resolution), using these attributes is a good way to make sure that your image always fits the user-specified frame size.

Using a fixed logo frame means that you must include the frame only once in your documents. You don't need to repeat the frame on every HTML document across your entire Web site. We think that this convenience makes the structure worthwhile.

```
<HTML>
<HEAD>
<TITLE>
Logo Frame
</TITLE>
</HEAD>
<BODY>
<CENTER>
<IMG BORDER="0" WIDTH="100%" HEIGHT="100%" ALIGN="middle"
   SRC="logo.gif" ALT="Your Logo here">
</CENTER>
```

(continued)

(continued)

```
</BODY>
</HTML>
```

Next comes the HTML code for the Text frame (in the middle) shown in Figure 9-3. Once again, this is a standard HTML document that can contain whatever content you want to display.

```
<HTML>
<HEAD>
<TITLE>
Text Frame
</TITLE>
</HEAD>
<BODY>
<CENTER>
<CENTER><H2>Text here.</H2></CENTER>
<FONT SIZE="+1">
This is where you put your important "stuff." You can
  display any of your Web documents here, where the user
  can scroll around without disturbing the logo above or
  the navigation images below. You can even nest other
  frames, insert tables, and display images in this frame.
</FONT>
</BODY>
</HTML>
```

Next, you find the HTML code for the Navigation bar (bottom) frame shown in Figure 9-3. This example shows how you can fix your navigation icons in a nice-looking bar that is continually available to your users. Notice the use of a table structure to format the various navigation icon images. Also, check out the use of the TARGET attribute to point the output into the middle Text frame.

Remember, TARGET="Text" in the following code refers back to the NAME="Text" attribute in the main page <FRAMESET> structure document.

```
<HTML>
<HEAD>
<TITLE>
Navigation Bar
</TITLE>
</HEAD>
<BODY>
<center>
<TABLE BORDER="1" ALIGN="middle">
<TR>
<TD>
```

```
<A HREF="text.htm" TARGET="Text"><IMG ALIGN="middle"
   SRC="B_arrow.gif" ALT="Homepage" BORDER="0"></A>
<A HREF="prepage.htm" TARGET="Text"><IMG ALIGN="middle"
   SRC="larrow.gif" ALT="Previous" BORDER="0"></A>
<A HREF="nextpage.htm" TARGET="Text"><IMG ALIGN="middle"
   SRC="rarrow.gif" ALT="Next" BORDER="0"></A>
<A HREF = "mail.html" TARGET="Text"><IMG ALIGN=middle
   BORDER="0" width="50" height="40"
   SRC="feedback.jpg"></A>
</TD>
</TR>
</TABLE>
</CENTER>
</BODY>
</HTML>
```

What's next? A four-frame basic page

Now we want to tackle a four-frame page. What follows next is the HTML code for the Web page document shown in Figure 9-4. This document illustrates the nesting of `<FRAMESET>` tags to achieve a four-frame structure. The `<FRAMESET ROWS="120,*"` tag sets up two frames stacked on top of one another, where the top frame is 120 pixels in height and the bottom frame occupies the rest of the screen's vertical space.

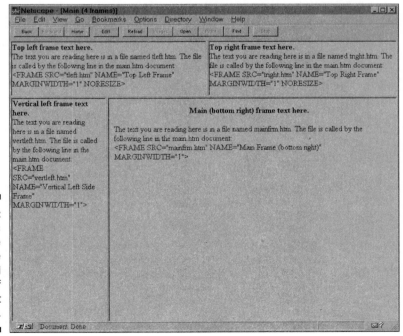

Figure 9-4: A basic four-frame Web Page provides all kinds of layout options.

Then the <FRAMESET COLS="400,*" SCROLLING="no"> tag sets up two frames side-by-side, where the leftmost frame is 400 pixels wide and the rightmost frame occupies the rest of the screen's width. These frames appear in the code as the Top Left Frame and Top Right Frame in the two <FRAME> tags immediately following the <FRAMESET> tag. Are you still with us? Good!

The next <FRAMESET COLS="200,*"> tag sets up two frames where the leftmost frame is 200 pixels wide and the rightmost frame occupies the rest of the screen's width. Because these frames are still within the original <FRAMESET> container, both have vertical heights equal to the rest of the available screen height. The frames are named Vertical Left Side Frame and Main frames, respectively. These sets of tags cause the browser to display the four frames shown in Figure 9-4.

Whether you set the scrolling, margins, or resizing as we specified them in the HTML source code is your choice, and your settings depend on the type of information you present in your frames. We hope you see that using these features is not really as complicated as it sounded a few pages back. The biggest trick (when setting up frames) is keeping the up/down and right/left distinctions and controls straight, both in your head and in your HTML code. Whew!

```
<HTML>
<HEAD>
<TITLE>Main 4 Frame Example</TITLE>

<FRAMESET ROWS="120,*">

<FRAMESET COLS="400,*" SCROLLING="no">
<FRAME SRC="tleft.htm" NAME="Top Left Frame"
   SCROLLING="no" MARGINHEIGHT="0" NORESIZE>
<FRAME SRC="tright.htm" NAME="Top Right Frame"
   SCROLLING="no" MARGINHEIGHT="0" NORESIZE>
</FRAMESET>

<FRAMESET COLS="200,*">
<FRAME SRC="vertleft.htm" NAME="Vertical Left Side Frame"
   MARGINWIDTH="1" NORESIZE>
<FRAME SRC="mainfrm.htm" NAME="Main">
</FRAMESET>

</FRAMESET>

</HTML>
```

Following is the HTML code for the Top Left frame shown in Figure 9-4. You've seen this baby more than once with different names. Nothing special is going on in this code, except that the document all must fit in the fixed-frame size that's been specified — namely, 120 pixels high and 400 pixels wide.

```
<HTML>
<HEAD>
<TITLE>
Tleft
</TITLE>
</HEAD>
<BODY>
<b>Top left frame text here.</b><br>
The text you are reading here is in a file named
  tleft.htm. The file is called by the following line in
  the main.htm document: <br>
&#60;FRAME SRC="tleft.htm" NAME="Top Left Frame"
   MARGINWIDTH="1" NORESIZE&#62;
</BODY>
</HTML>
```

Following is the HTML code for the Top Right frame shown in Figure 9-4. The Top Right frame is quite similar to the Top Left, but it has 120 pixels of height and the rest of the width to display its contents.

```
<HTML>
<HEAD>
<TITLE>
Tright
</TITLE>
</HEAD>
<BODY>
<b>Top right frame text here.</b><br>
The text you are reading here is in a file named
  tright.htm. The file is called by the following line in
  the main.htm document: <br>
&#60;FRAME SRC="tright.htm" NAME="Top Right Frame"
   MARGINWIDTH="1" NORESIZE&#62;
</BODY>
</HTML>
```

Next, you find the HTML code for the Vertical Left frame shown in Figure 9-4. This frame is the nifty one where you can put all sorts of cool images or your TOC.

```
<HTML>
<HEAD>
<TITLE>
vertleft
</TITLE>
</HEAD>
<BODY>
<b>Vertical left frame text here.</b> <br>
```

(continued)

(continued)

```
The text you are reading here is in a file named
  vertleft.htm. The file is called by the following line
  in the main.htm document: <br>
&#60;FRAME SRC="vertleft.htm" NAME="Vertical Left Side
  Frame" MARGINWIDTH="1"&#62;
</BODY>
</HTML>
```

Finally, we show the following listing of the HTML for the Main (bottom right) frame shown in Figure 9-4. As usual, anything goes in this document, as long as you specify legal HTML code. With no SCROLLING attribute specified, the browser automatically displays any needed scrollbars and enables your users to see all your fantastic stuff.

```
<HTML>
<HEAD>
<TITLE>
Mainfrm
</TITLE>
</HEAD>
<BODY>
<center>
<b>Main (bottom right) frame text here.</b><br>
</center>
The text you are reading here is in a file named
  mainfrm.htm. The file is called by the following line in
  the main.htm document: <br>
&#60;FRAME SRC="mainfrm.htm" NAME="Main Frame (bottom
right)" MARGINWIDTH="1"&#62;
</BODY>
</HTML>
```

Wow! Four frames with icons, graphics, logos, and scrolling text

You've waited long enough for this example, or did you jump straight here, you little imp? Anyway, following is the HTML code for the Web page document shown in Figure 9-5. As the figure plainly shows, the document uses the basic, four-frame structure, like that in Figure 9-4, but with some more interesting information inside its frames. Remember, you can set the frame sizes to suit your information. When you're matching frame sizes to information, a little experimentation and testing goes a long way!

As you can see, the images fit nicely inside each frame. When you look at the

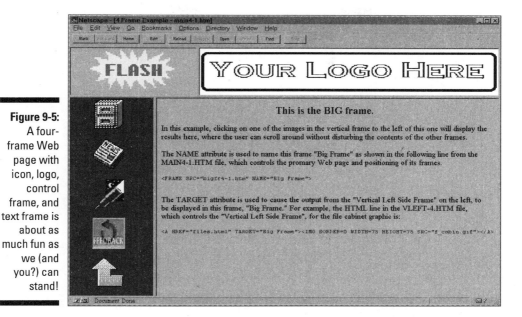

Figure 9-5:
A four-frame Web page with icon, logo, control frame, and text frame is about as much fun as we (and you?) can stand!

HTML documents for each frame in the following code examples, notice these elements:

- ✔ The Flash image is a fixed size (WIDTH="200" HEIGHT="100") because its frame is a fixed size (120 pixels x 300 pixels).

- ✔ The Flash image is frozen in place with the NORESIZE attribute.

- ✔ The Logo image is instructed to be 100 percent of that frame's size (WIDTH="100%" HEIGHT="100%") because the frame width is relative (*) and because we don't want a small logo in a big frame or only part of the logo in a small frame if users resize their browser screens.

```
<HTML>
<HEAD>
<TITLE>4 Frame Example - main4-1.htm</TITLE>
<FRAMESET ROWS="120,*">
<FRAMESET COLS="300,*" SCROLLING="no">
<FRAME SRC="flash.htm" NAME="Top Left Frame"
   SCROLLING="no" MARGINHEIGHT="0" NORESIZE>
<FRAME SRC="logo.htm" NAME="Top Right Frame"
   SCROLLING="no" MARGINHEIGHT="0" NORESIZE>
</FRAMESET>
```

(continued)

(continued)

```
<FRAMESET COLS="200,*">
<FRAME SRC="vleft-4.htm" NAME="Vertical Left Side Frame"
    MARGINWIDTH="1" NORESIZE>
<FRAME SRC="bigfr4-1.htm" NAME="Big Frame">
</FRAMESET>
</FRAMESET>
<NOFRAMES>
</HEAD>
<BODY>
It's a nice touch to put in a normal Web page here for
  the users whose browsers don't recognize frames. Just
  use a standard page format or a table to simulate the
  frames if you wish. Only the users with "frame
  challenged" browsers will see this section.
</BODY>
</NOFRAMES>
</HTML>
code last
```

The following is the HTML code for the Top Left Frame — Flash Frame — shown in Figure 9-5. The code uses a fixed size for the image because the frame is a fixed size.

```
<HTML>
<HEAD>
<TITLE>
Flash Frame
</TITLE>
</HEAD>
<BODY>
<CENTER>
<IMG ALIGN=BOTTOM BORDER="0" WIDTH="200" HEIGHT="100"
    SRC="flash.gif" ALT="Your Icon Here">
</CENTER>
</BODY>
</HTML>
```

This next listing is the HTML code for the Top Right Frame — Logo Frame — shown in Figure 9-5. The code uses the WIDTH and HEIGHT attributes to ensure that the logo fills the frame.

```
<HTML>
<HEAD>
<TITLE>
Logo Frame
</TITLE>
</HEAD>
<BODY>
```

```
<CENTER>
<IMG BORDER="0" WIDTH="100%" HEIGHT="100%" ALIGN="middle"
   SRC="logo.gif" ALT="Your Logo Here">
</CENTER>
</BODY>
</HTML>
```

Next, you see the HTML code for the Vertical Left Side Frame — the frame with the images — shown in Figure 9-5. Ahhh! This is the fun frame: The images are sized to fit and aligned by simply using the <P> tag. If the user resizes the browser so that the last image isn't completely visible, the browser automatically displays a vertical scrollbar. Each of these images uses the TARGET attribute to point its output to the Big Frame that appears to the right.

```
<HTML>
<HEAD>
<TITLE>4 Frame Example - VLEFT-4.HTM</TITLE>
</HEAD>
<BODY BGCOLOR="#530059" TEXT="#FFFFFF" LINK="#9F0F9F"
 ALINK="#FF0000" VLINK="#FF0000">
<CENTER>
<A HREF="files.html" TARGET="Big Frame">
<IMG border="0" width="75" height="75"
   SRC="f_cabin.gif"></A><p>
<A HREF = "news.html" TARGET="Big Frame">
<IMG border="0" width="75" height="75"
   SRC="newspap.gif"></A><p>
<A HREF = "stars.html" TARGET="Big Frame">
<IMG border="0" width="75" height="75"
   SRC="telescop.gif"></A><p>
<A HREF = "mailto.htm" TARGET="Big Frame">
<IMG border="0" width="75" height="75"
   SRC="feedback.jpg"></A><p>
<A HREF = "bigfr4-1.htm" TARGET="Big Frame">
<IMG border="0" width="75" height="75"
   SRC="b_arrow.gif"></A>
</CENTER>
</BODY>
</HTML>
```

Finally, we conclude with the HTML for the Big Frame that is shown at the bottom right in Figure 9-5. Because this frame is the designated recipient for all the information from the images in the frame to its left, the frame scrolls automatically. Although it doesn't have the NORESIZE attribute set, the frame can't be resized anyway because all the other frames aren't resizable. Therefore, the Big Frame doesn't have anyplace to go; it just sits there and happily displays whatever it receives.

```
<HTML>
<HEAD>
<TITLE>
Main of 4-1 (mfrm4-1.htm)
</TITLE>
</HEAD>
<BODY>
<CENTER><H2>This is the BIG frame.</H2></CENTER>
<FONT SIZE="+1">
In this example, clicking on one of the images in the
  vertical frame to the left of this one will display the
  results here, where the user can scroll around without
  disturbing the contents of the other frames. <P>
The NAME attribute is used to name this frame "Big Frame"
  as shown in the following line from the MAIN4-1.HTM
  file, which controls the primary Web page and
  positioning of its frames.<P>
</FONT>
<PRE>
&#60;FRAME SRC="bigfr4-1.htm" NAME="Big Frame"&#62;<P>
</PRE>
<FONT SIZE="+1">
The TARGET attribute is used to cause the output from the
  "Vertical Left Side Frame" on the left, to be displayed
  in this frame, "Big Frame." For example, the HTML line
  in the VLEFT-4.HTM file, which controls the "Vertical
  Left Side Frame", for the file cabinet graphic is:<P>
</FONT>
<PRE>
&#60;A HREF="files.html" TARGET="Big Frame"&#62;&#60;IMG
BORDER="0" WIDTH="75" HEIGHT="75"
       SRC="f_cabin.gif"&#62;&#60;/A&#62;<P>
</PRE>
</BODY>
</HTML>
```

Now you know just about everything about frames. Weeeell, at least you know what frames are, their HTML syntax, and have a good idea how you can use them to enhance your own Web sites. To get a few more ideas, you may want to check out other Web sites that are successfully using frames. That's what we cover next!

Stunningly Framed Web Sites

More and more Web site administrators are adding frames to their Web sites. A picture on a sheet of paper doesn't do justice to the innovative ways that these administrators use frames to help their users navigate their Webs. Start at the URLs that we mention next and take a look for yourself. You'll be amazed — and sometimes amused — by what you see.

Netscape's Web site lists numerous other WWW sites using frames:

```
http://home.mcom.com/assist/net_sites/frame_users.html
```

The most stunning use of frames we've ever seen is located at the Shockwave Productions Web site. Their use of the seamlessly painted images in the vertical frame to the left of the page and the Java animated applet in the top right frame fit very well with their company name and the other information in the other two frames. This Web site really shows you what the pros can do with frames.

```
http://www.swave.com/html/htmlwel.html
```

With frames to help you help your users easily navigate through the maze of your Web site, how can you go wrong? If you take your time and carefully consider your Web site's content as you set up your frame structure, you can enhance your site immensely. However, if you try to stuff large amounts of hexagonal content into small square frames, you'll probably feel like you've been unjustly framed.

Just take frames one <FRAMESET> at a time, and you can make all your information look as good as the *Mona Lisa*. You know that she's just smiling because of the great frame she's in, don't you? In the following chapter, we leave frames behind and spend some time with the "Queen of the Sciences" as we take the royal tour of HTML's newly minted <MATH> notation!

Chapter 10
HTML Gets Fully Mathematical!

*M*athematics, often called "the Queen of the sciences," deals extensively with measurements, properties, and relationships among quantities expressed in numbers and symbols.

If the preceding sentence flies straight over your head, so will the rest of this chapter. Do yourself a favor: If you're not mathematically inclined, skip to the next chapter. This goes double if you're mathophobic. But if you want to learn a bit about the state of mathematics within HTML and the Web, read on!

A Math Made in Heaven?

The original HTML 3.0 Specification draft introduced the first true math-related HTML tags in March 1995. Even though HTML 3.0 is an idea that has come and gone (which is why we refer to post-2.0 HTML as "the specifications formerly known as HTML 3.0"), the mathematical coverage from this document is still useful.

For more information on this initial effort, visit this URL:

```
http://www.w3.org/hypertext/WWW/MarkUp/
```

Because the focus and direction of the HTML standards committee has changed in the interim, math and several other "new" HTML elements may appear to be in limbo. What's actually happened is that each of these standards is being pursued independently, none more vigorously than the mathematical notation specification, currently in draft status.

Given its current uncertain status — because it's not a "real" standard yet — it's fair to ask: "What will happen to the <MATH> tags?" Difficult to say; we have a few good ideas. Because we love to speculate, and because mathematics notation is in high demand in the Web community (it was originally developed for a bunch of high-energy physicists, remember?), we'll tell you what we think.

The W3C standards team is currently working on style sheets (see Chapter 11), tables (see Chapter 8), and frames (see Chapter 9). In addition, other areas are appearing on the HTML buffet faster than they can be properly dealt with, so some items may get overlooked along the way.

But far from fading into obscurity, the <MATH> tags should be among the next major set of HTML tags to advance their standards status to an official, recognized HTML standard. In case you can't wait until the third or fourth quarter of 1996 to use <MATH> notation in your pages, we cover some alternatives to using these tags later in this chapter.

If you feel compelled to use HTML <MATH> notation, you need to download the Arena browser for X11/UNIX environments; it's the only one we know of that can display this stuff. For the record, you can find it at this URL:

```
http://www.w3.org/hypertext/WWW/Arena/
```

If you're in the mood for a surfeit of mathematical data, especially as it pertains to the Web, visit the QED site at:

```
http://www.mcs.anl.gov/qed/index.html.
```

The QED Project seeks to "build a single, distributed, computerized repository that rigorously represents all important, established mathematical knowledge." This makes it a pretty heavy hitter in our book.

More important, Dan Connolly, one of the chief HTML architects at the W3C, thinks that QED will have a solid influence on future HTML math implementations. If you visit his math-related page at

```
http://www.w3.org/hypertext/WWW/MarkUp/Math/
```

you'll probably agree with this assessment. And if this is the kind of thing that really turns you on, I'll just stand back and let you enjoy yourself!

A Quick <MATH> Review

The proposed HTML <MATH> tags were designed around LaTeX's math mode. LaTeX is a high-quality typesetting system with features designed for the production of technical and scientific documentation. The system is based on the work of Donald Knuth, the dean of computer science. He took a seven-year hiatus from his seven-volume *Encyclopedia of Computer Science* to invent the TeX computerized typesetting system because his publisher couldn't handle mathematical typesetting to his satisfaction.

For more information, please visit

```
http://www.cl.cam.ac.uk/CTAN/latex/
http://jasper.ora.com/texhelp/LaTeX.html
```

LaTeX uses reserved characters, however, and a few cryptic syntax constructs that were removed and simplified in the HTML math tags. HTML math tags were designed to construct a wide range of math expressions and to be easily rendered into speech.

For the expired draft of the math tag set, please visit Mark Gaither's HTML archives at

```
http://www.webtechs.com/html/
```

Then select the "HTML 3.0 Specification" hyperlink and then the "math" hyperlink. The exact URL for this page follows:

```
http://www.hpl.hp.co.uk/people/dsr/html3/maths.html
```

Meet the <MATH> markup team

The HTML 3.0 Specification draft defined 22 new math tags. These tags are listed and described for you in Table 10-1.

Table 10-1	Proposed HTML `<MATH>` Tags	
Tag	**Tag Name**	**What It Does**
`<ABOVE>`...`</ABOVE>`	Math Line Above	Draws a line or symbol above the enclosed text.
`<ARRAY>`...`</ARRAY>`	Math Array	Defines a math array. The syntax is similar to tables and uses the `<ROW>` and `<ITEM>` tags.
`<ATOP>`	Math Box Atop	Places the section of text to the left of this tag above the section to the right within a `<BOX>`.
`<BAR>`...`</BAR>`	Math Vector: Bar	Draws a bar above the enclosed text.
`<BELOW>`...`</BELOW>`	Math Line Below	Draws a line or symbol below the enclosed text.
`<BOX>`...`</BOX>`	Math Box	Defines a math box and uses the `<LEFT>`, `<RIGHT>`, `<OVER>`, `<ATOP>`, and `<CHOOSE>` tags.
`<CHOOSE>`...`</CHOOSE>`	Math Box Choose	Similar to `<ATOP>`, places one expression over another, encloses both in brackets within a `<BOX>`.
`<DDOT>`...`</DDOT>`	Math Vector: Double Dot	Draws a double dot or umlaut (¨) above the enclosed text.
`<DOT>`...`</DOT>`	Math Vector: Dot	Draws a single dot above the enclosed text.
`<HAT>`...`</HAT>`	Math Vector: Hat/Caret	Draws a hat, or caret (^), above the enclosed text.
`<ITEM>`	Math Array Item	Defines an item in an array.
`<LEFT>`	Math Box Left	Defines the delimiter that appears on a `<BOX>` expression's left side.
`<MATH>`...`</MATH>`	Mathematics	Defines math expressions and allows for special math-related rendering elements.
`<OF>`	Math Root Of	Separates the radix from the radicand in a root expression.
`<OVER>`	Math Box Over	Places one section above another within a `<BOX>`.
`<RIGHT>`	Math Box Right	Defines the delimiter which appears on a `<BOX>` expression's right side.
`<ROOT>`...`</ROOT>`	Math Root	Defines a root expression, uses the `<OF>` tag.

Tag	Tag Name	What It Does
<ROW>...</ROW>	Math Array Row	Defines a row of an array, acts similar to the <TR> table tag.
<SQRT>...</SQRT>	Math Square Root	Draws a square root symbol (√) around the enclosed text.
<TEXT>...</TEXT>	Math Text	Identifies inserted text or comments within a math expression.
<TILDE>...</TILDE>	Math Vector: Tilde	Draws a tilde (~) above the enclosed text.
<VEC>...</VEC>	Math Vector: Right Arrow	Draws a right arrow (>) above the enclosed text.

This list of tags represents only the proposed tags. Other tags may be added; those tags that survive the standards process may be altered, changed, or removed as well. In other words, double-check everything, because nothing is set in stone where this markup is concerned!

The ultimate <MATH> authority

The tags proposed use and functionality are defined at length in the draft specification and the Webified DTD that you find at

```
http://www.webtechs.com/html/
```

under the "HTML 3.0 Documents" section. To learn how to use them (before they're approved, standardized, and supported), go online and get mathematical!

Complex Equations, Anyone?

We thought you might like to see what properly rendered HTML 3.0 math expressions look like, so we went out of our way to capture these screen shots just for you. Below each of the images shown in Figures 10-1 through 10-3, we present the math tags that created their associated expressions.

Figure 10-1: Example of a math equation.

```
y=sum_i=1_^n^{1<over>1+x_i }
```

Yielding:

$$y = \sum_{i=1} \frac{1}{1+x_i}$$

and on a dumb terminal:

$$y = \sum_{i=1}^{n} \frac{1}{1+x_i}$$

Figure 10-1 was created by using the following <MATH> tag markup:

```
<title>A Quick Review of HTML 3.0</title>
<h1>An introduction to HTML Math</h1>
<hr><br>
<h3><img src="ball.red.gif">  Why TeX isn't the
    answer!</h3>
<h3><img src="ball.red.gif">  Simple to enter,
    and inspired by TeX</h3>
<h3><img src="ball.red.gif">  Designed to allow
    wysiwyg editing</h3>
<h3><img src="ball.red.gif">  Rendering on Dumb
    terminals</h3>
<h3><img src="ball.red.gif">  Rendering to Braille,
    Speech, ...</h3>
<HR><BR>e
<h3>An example with SHORTREFs:</h3>
<PRE>          <B>y=sum_i=1_^n^{1&lt;over&gt;1+x_i_}</B></PRE>
<table>
<tr>
<td><td><td>
<td align=left nowrap rowspan=3>
<tt>
      n<br>
     
-     1<br>
y =  >     
--<br>
     
-        i<br>
    i = 1  
1 + x<br>
</tt>
<tr>
<td nowrap align=left>Yielding:
<td nowrap align=left>
<math>y=sum_i=1_^n^{1<over>1+x_i_}</math>
<td nowrap align=left>and on a dumb terminal:
<tr><td><td><td>
</table>
<HR><address><a href="math2.html">
Next Slide</a> </address>
```

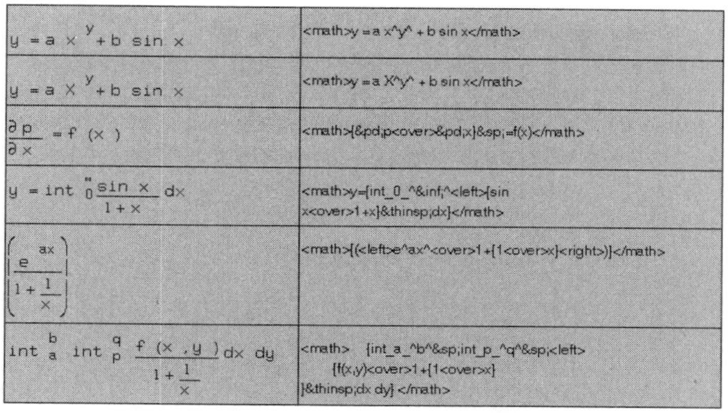

Figure 10-2:
Example of
a math
equation.

Figure 10-2 was created using the following `<MATH>` tag markup:

```
<h2>Some more examples:</h2>
<table border>
<tr>
<td><math>y = a x^y^ + b sin x</math>
<td>&lt;math&gt;y = a x^y^ + b sin x&lt;/math&gt;
<tr>
<td><math>y = a X^y^ + b sin x</math>
<td>&lt;math&gt;y = a X^y^ + b sin x&lt;/math&gt;
<tr>
<td><math>{&pd;p<over>&pd;x}&sp;=f(x)</math>
<td>&lt;math&gt;{&amp;pd;p&lt;over&gt;&amp;pd;x}
&amp;sp;=f(x)&lt;/math&gt;
<tr>
<td><math>y={int_0_^&inf;^<left>
{sin x<over>1+x} dx}</math>
<td>&lt;math&gt;y={int_0_^&amp;inf;^&lt;left&gt;
{sin x&lt;over&gt;1+x}&amp;thinsp;dx}&lt;/math&gt;
<tr>
<td><math>{(<left>e^ax^<over>1+{1<over>x}<right>)}</math>
<td>&lt;math&gt;{(&lt;left&gt;e^ax^&lt;over&gt;
1+{1&lt;over&gt;x}&lt;right&gt;)}&lt;/math&gt;
<tr>
<td><math>{int_a_^b^&sp;int_p_^q^&sp;<left>{f(x,y)<over>1
+{1<over>x}} dx dy}</math>
<td>&lt;math&gt;<img src="blank.xpm">
{int_a_^b^&amp;sp;int_p_^q^&amp;sp;&lt;left&gt;<br>
<img src="blank.xpm"><img src="blank.xpm">
```

(continued)

(continued)

```
{f(x,y)&lt;over&gt;1+{1&lt;over&gt;x}<br>
}&amp;thinsp;dx  dy} &lt;/math&gt;
</table>
<address><a href="symbols.html">Next Slide</a></address>
```

Greek symbols

Entity name	Appearance	Entity name	Appearance	Entity name	Appearance
&alpha;	α	&beta;	β	&gamma;	γ
&delta;	δ	&epsi;	ε	&zeta;	ζ
&eta;	η	&theta;	theta	&thetav;	ϑ
&iota;	ι	&kappa;	κ	&lambda;	λ
&mu;	μ	&nu;	ν	&xi;	ξ
&pi;	π	&piv;	ϖ	&rho;	ρ
&sigma;	σ	&sigmav;	ς	&tau;	τ
&upsi;	υ	&phi;	phi	&phiv;	φ
&chi;	χ	&psi;	ψ	&omega;	ω
&Gamma;	Γ	&Delta;	Δ	&Theta;	Θ
&Lambda;	Λ	&Xi;	Ξ	&Pi;	Π
&Sigma;	Σ	&Upsi;	Υ	&Phi;	Φ
&Psi;	Ψ	&Omega;	Ω		

Mathematical operators

Entity name	Appearance	Entity name	Appearance	Entity name	Appearance
&perp;	⊥	&plusmn;	±	&or;	∨
&and;	∧	&le;	≤	&ge;	≥
&equiv;	≡	&ap;	≈	&ne;	≠
&sub;	⊂	&sube;	⊆	&sup;	⊃
&supe;	⊇	&isin;	∈	&larr;	←
&rarr;	→	&uarr;	↑	&darr;	↓
&harr;	↔	&lArr;	⇐	&rArr;	⇒
&uArr;	⇑	&dArr;	⇓	&iff;	⇔
&forall;	∀	&exist;	∃	&inf;	∞

Figure 10-3:
Tables of
math
symbols.

Figure 10-3 was created using the following `<MATH>` tag markup:

```
<html>
<head>
<title>Symbol support in Arena mathematics</title>
<!- Changed by: , 30-Mar-1995 ->
</head>

<body>
<h1>Symbol support in Arena mathematics</h1>

Arena can represent symbols which are available in the
 adobe symbol font. These symbols must be encoded in HTML
 using the entity reference notation.

Below are the tables which list the entity names and
 their appearance.

<hr>

<h2>Greek symbols</h2>

<table border>
<th>Entity name<th>Appearance<th>Entity
          name<th>Appearance<th>Entity name<th>Appearance
<tr><td>&amp;alpha;<td><math>&alpha;</math><td>&amp;beta;
<td><math>&beta;</math><td>&amp;gamma;<td><math>&gamma;
</math>
<tr><td>&amp;delta;<td><math>&delta;</math><td>&amp;epsi;
<td><math>&epsi;</math><td>&amp;zeta;<td><math>&zeta;
</math>
<tr><td>&amp;eta;<td><math>&eta;</math><td>&amp;theta;
<td><math>&theta;</math><td>&amp;thetav;<td><math>
&thetav;</math>
<tr><td>&amp;iota;<td><math>&iota;</math><td>&amp;kappa;
<td><math>&kappa;</math><td>&amp;lambda;<td><math>
&lambda;</math>
<tr><td>&amp;mu;<td><math>&mu;</math><td>&amp;nu;<td>
<math>&nu;</math><td>&amp;xi;<td><math>&xi;</math>
<tr><td>&amp;pi;<td><math>&pi;</math><td>&amp;piv;<td>
<math>&piv;</math><td>&amp;rho;<td><math>&rho;</math>
<tr><td>&amp;sigma;<td><math>&sigma;</math><td>&amp;
```

(continued)

(continued)

```
    sigmav;<td><math>&sigmav;</math><td>&amp;tau;<td><math>
    &tau;</math>
<tr><td>&amp;upsi;<td><math>&upsi;</math><td>&amp;phi;
<td><math>&phi;</math><td>&amp;phiv;<td><math>&phiv;
</math>
<tr><td>&amp;chi;<td><math>&chi;</math><td>&amp;psi;<td>
<math>&psi;</math><td>&amp;omega;<td><math>&omega;</math>
<tr><td>&amp;Gamma;<td><math>&Gamma;</math><td>&amp;
    Delta;<td><math>&Delta;</math><td>&amp;Theta;<td><math>
    &Theta;</math>
<tr><td>&amp;Lambda;<td><math>&Lambda;</math><td>&amp;Xi;
    <td><math>&Xi;</math><td>&amp;Pi;<td><math>&Pi;</math>
<tr><td>&amp;Sigma;<td><math>&Sigma;</math><td>&amp;Upsi;
<td><math>&Upsi;</math><td>&amp;Phi;<td><math>&Phi;
</math>
<tr><td>&amp;Psi;<td><math>&Psi;</math><td>&amp;Omega;
<td><math>&Omega;</math>
</table>

<hr>

<h2>Mathematical operators</h2>
<table border>
<th>Entity name<th>Appearance<th>Entity
name<th>Appearance<th>Entity name<th>Appearance
<tr><td>&amp;perp;<td><math>&perp;</math><td>&amp;plusmn;
<td><math>&plusmn;</math><td>&amp;or;<td><math>&or;
</math>
<tr><td>&amp;and;<td><math>&and;</math><td>&amp;le;<td>
<math>&le;</math><td>&amp;ge;<td><math>&ge;</math>
<tr><td>&amp;equiv;<td><math>&equiv;</math><td>&amp;ap;
<td><math>&ap;</math><td>&amp;ne;<td><math>&ne;</math>
<tr><td>&amp;sub;<td><math>&sub;</math><td>&amp;sube;<td>
<math>&sube;</math><td>&amp;sup;<td><math>&sup;</math>
<tr><td>&amp;supe;<td><math>&supe;</math><td>&amp;isin;
<td><math>&isin;</math><td>&amp;larr;<td><math>&larr;
</math>
<tr><td>&amp;rarr;<td><math>&rarr;</math><td>&amp;uarr;
<td><math>&uarr;</math><td>&amp;darr;<td><math>&darr;
```

```
</math>
<tr><td>&amp;harr;<td><math>&harr;</math><td>&amp;lArr;
<td><math>&lArr;</math><td>&amp;rArr;<td><math>&rArr;
</math>
<tr><td>&amp;uArr;<td><math>&uArr;</math><td>&amp;dArr;
<td><math>&dArr;</math><td>&amp;iff;<td><math>&iff;
</math>
<tr><td>&amp;forall;<td><math>&forall;</math><td>&amp;
exist;<td><math>&exist;</math><td>&amp;inf;<td><math>
&inf;</math>
<tr><td>&amp;nabla;<td><math>&nabla;</math>
</table>
<address><a href="contents.html">Next Slide</a></address>
</body>
</html>
```

Ramming Math down Their Throats

Even though the nifty HTML 3.0 math tags aren't supported by mainstream browsers (yet), you can still present mathematical equations on HTML pages. The following suggestions tell you how to do just that:

- ✔ First, you can render most mathematical equations using `<PRE>` . . . `</PRE>` tags and the standard ASCII character set. For example, Figure 10-4 shows a screen shot from the draft specification about the `<BOX>` tag.

- ✔ Second, you can draw or render your mathematical equations using a graphics program, or TeX or LaTeX, and capture the output to a GIF file. Then you can use it as an inline image and drop it into your Web page.

- ✔ Third, some GUI word processors, including Microsoft Word, can render mathematical equations. You can capture these renderings to a GIF or save the file as PDF, PS, or other supported plugin formats for Web viewing.

Even though mathematical HTML tags aren't supported by any of the mainstream browsers as yet, all of them promise to include support once the W3C team establishes a math DTD. Until then, you just have to keep your equations to yourself! In the meantime, we'll be stylin' in the next chapter, where we tackle the subject of Web style sheets.

m) /2</math> for (n + m) /2. For more complicated fractions you can use the BOX element with the OVER tag, as in:

$$\frac{1}{x + y} \qquad \{1\text{<over>}x + y\}$$

Figure 10-4:
Examples of
<PRE> text-
formatted
math
equations.

$$\frac{x - y}{1 + \dfrac{a - b}{a + b}} \qquad \{x - y\text{<over>}1 + \{a - b\text{<over>}a + b\}\}$$

Use the ATOP tag when you want to place one thing above another, but without the dividing.

Figure 10-4:
Examples of
<PRE> text-
formatted
math
equations.

Chapter 11

For HTML, Style Is Its Own Reward!

● ●

In This Chapter

▶ Examining styles and style sheets

▶ Understanding external style sheets versus internal style attributes

▶ Cascading style sheets manage complex relationships

▶ Dissecting a style sheet

▶ Following the style sheet trend

● ●

*S*tyle sheets are one of the most exciting new additions to HTML and the Web. Style sheets allow Web authors to specify layout and design elements — such as fonts, colors, and indentation depths — for an entire Web site. No longer can whim-configured (or misconfigured) browsers mangle the display of style-dependent Web documents.

A style sheet's specifications combine with readers' personal style settings to make sure that HTML documents display "properly." Note that it's important to understand that *properly* is defined by the document's creator, not its viewer—if you don't believe me, just ask any artist how he feels about his work.

 Before you dive into this chapter expecting to find out how to create and use your own style sheets with your Web site, you need to know one thing — they're not ready yet! Style sheets are still being developed and tested by the W3C. They have not yet been released for public consumption. This chapter presents the ideas, a few underlying theories, and some proposed syntax for style sheets. If you want more information, you'll need to go online (We tell you where to look—never fear).

Of Styles and Style Sheets

If you've had any experience with desktop publishing, you should be familiar with the concept of a *style sheet* or *template*. If not, the idea isn't that complicated, so bear with us (if you're a member of the cognoscenti on this subject, feel free to skip ahead to the next section, entitled "Deep Background Investigation Reveals . . .").

A style sheet defines design and layout information for a document. Commonly, style sheets also specify the fonts, colors, indentation, kerning, leading, margins, and even page dimensions for their associated documents.

In the publishing world, style sheets are indispensable. Style sheets enable numerous people to work on large projects. All participants can work at their own systems, independently of other project team members. When the pieces of the project are brought together, the final product derives its consistent look and feel (or design and layout, if you prefer the "typographically correct" language) because a common template (what style sheets are often called in the print industry) ensured a shared definition of the overall document.

This consistency is a highly desirable characteristic of final products for both print and electronic (online) document formats. The World Wide Web Consortium (W3C) has therefore made a gallant effort to incorporate the consistency of print to the Web by introducing style sheets. With the use of Web style sheets, an entire Web site can look the same on every platform and within every browser that supports style sheets. For Web authors who want to provide a consistent reading experience, this promises to be a vast improvement over the current state of affairs.

Deep Background Investigation Reveals...

As you're no doubt aware, HTML is both a subset and a superset of SGML. If you don't know what this means, take a quick look online at

```
http://www.w3.org/pub/WWW/MarkUp/
```

Scroll down to the SGML link in the Related Resources section (or read the introductory chapters from our previous book, *HTML For Dummies,* 2nd Edition). The Document Type Definitions (DTDs) that define how HTML functions are written using a Backus-Naur Format (BNF) grammar notation. For more information, please visit the following URL:

```
http://cuiwww.unige.ch/db-research/Enseignement/analyseinfo/
              AboutBNF.html
```

These original DTDs were designed to keep HTML within the structure and limitations of SGML. But recently, HTML's DTDs have been modified to allow non-SGML functionality. For many standards-obedient programmers and designers, this is a violation of proper programming and design. For those simply interested in expanding HTML's capabilities, it has come as a breath of fresh air (and functionality).

A second issue that arises out of proprietary non-SGML-legal HTML extensions is browser envy. Since Netscape introduced its proprietary extensions in 1994, other browser vendors — such as Microsoft and NCSA — have introduced gimmicks and flashy additions to their own browsers. All this effort has been expended in hopes that if a browser is the only one able to correctly display a Web document — which happens to use those proprietary extensions — the consumer base will flock to that browser. Although this conflict has spawned some exciting and eye-catching HTML extensions, it has caused more harm than good. Incompatible HTML dialects, stifled competition, and narrow-minded browser development is just some of the fallout from this battle.

Web-based style sheets offer a promising solution to this situation. Style sheets allow the proper separation of a document's structure and content from its form and appearance. With the implementation of style sheets, HTML can return to handling document structure and content (and get back to being proper SGML); style sheets can handle a document's form and appearance.

This separation should allow both authors and readers to influence the presentation of documents without sacrificing platform and device independence. It should also lessen the need to add new HTML tags, both proprietary and standard, to provide ever more sophisticated layout and appearance controls. Every possible layout or design element of a document can be uniquely defined by an attached — that is, *linked* — style sheet. This should reduce the pressure to add tags and controls directly to HTML, when such capability will be available through another avenue.

What is DSSSL and DSSSL-Lite?

Document Style Semantics and Specification Language (DSSSL) is a long and complicated label for the language used to define SGML style sheets. DSSSL can be used with any SGML document without modifications to the DTD. DSSSL was originally designed to define style parameters for print, but can be applied to online presentations as well.

DSSSL Online or *DSSSL-Lite* is a subset of the full DSSSL standard that specifies formatting requirements for online SGML browsers and readers. DSSSL is a complex and somewhat unfriendly language, which makes constructing quality SGML style sheets both long and arduous. For this reason, DSSSL has had only a limited impact on the Web, primarily among that small fraction of the online publishing community that is already SGML-literate.

For an in-depth and highly technical discussion of DSSSL, please consult the final DSSSL standards draft document. You'll find it at

```
http://occam.sjf.novell.com:8080/dsssl/dsssl96
```

Other DSSSL and DSSSL-Lite information is available from the W3C Web Style Sheet page at

`http://www.w3.org/pub/WWW/Style/`

Wait, Didn't HTML 3.0 Handle Styles?

Well, yes and no. HTML 3.0 (as it used to be called before the DTD was split up into component parts; we call it "the HTML standard formerly known as 3.0" elsewhere in this book, with tongue planted firmly in cheek) incorporated some useful tags and attributes that suit themselves well to styles. This functionality, however, has been neither adopted nor supported by most Web browsers, including the "big boys" of the browser world — namely, Netscape Navigator and Microsoft Internet Explorer.

You may recall reading about <STYLE>, <DIV>, and <SPAN> tags, and the nearly ubiquitous ID and CLASS attributes within most post-2.0 HTML tag definitions. It's not clear whether these tags were intended to deliver style sheet functionality without taking advantage of full-blown style sheets or not. But these tags do lend themselves to a newly adopted style sheet scheme named Cascading Style Sheets (CSS) quite nicely (which we discuss later in this chapter).

The only things that really aren't clear at this point are the specifics. When it comes to the details about how these tags and related attributes are to be used, or the exact requirements of their syntax and the qualifiers and parameters they will accept, those elements are still under construction at the W3C (and in the labs of its corporate partners and sponsors).

So, What's New?

The limited DSSSL applications on the Web revealed an area of Web programming and design that had not previously been addressed within the Web's standards-setting community. Web style sheets eliminate the problem of non-SGML compliant extensions and simultaneously overcome HTML's presentation limitations. The only difficulty has been in creating a style sheet implementation that is easy to understand and use, yet compatible across multiple platforms. Because this is a stiff challenge, it shouldn't be too surprising that a workable solution took a while to put together.

But in a March 5, 1996, press release, the following companies: Adobe Systems, America Online, CompuServe, Eastman Kodak, Grif, Hewlett-Packard, IBM

Corporation, Matra Hachette, Microsoft, NCSA, Netscape Communications, Oracle, O'Reilly & Associates, Reed-Elsevier, SoftQuad, and Spyglass all agreed to participate in furthering the development and implementation of the approach known as Cascading Style Sheets (CSS). For a copy of this press release, visit this URL:

```
http://www.w3.org/hypertext/WWW/Style/960305_News.html
```

CSS defines a simple style sheet mechanism that allows both authors and readers to associate styles with HTML documents. The CSS language is human-readable and -writable, and uses common desktop publishing terminology to describe styles and to define style-related information.

The latest information about Cascading Style Sheets, as conceptualized and drafted by Håkon Lie, the primary author of the current draft standard, is available at

```
http://www.w3.org/pub/WWW/Style/css/.
```

In this document, you will also find extensive examples and suggested syntax for the final CSS scheme, which is still under construction.

Cascading Style Sheets

Because the CSS standard is still in development, expect some further changes before the standard is finalized. Rather than delve into the details in the current draft, we discuss a few of its key concepts that are unlikely to change, to give you an appreciation of its design and capabilities.

One of CSS's most fundamental features is its assumption that multiple, interlinked style sheets can cascade. That is, authors can attach preferred style sheets to a Web document, yet readers can associate their own personal style sheets to the same documents, which may correct for human or technological handicaps. Thus, a print-handicapped reader could override an author's type distinctions between 10 and 12 point sizes, accommodating that reader's need for a point size no smaller than 40. Likewise, local limitations on resolution or display area might override an author's layout and type style selections.

Basically, CSS contains a set of rules to resolve style conflicts that arise from applying multiple style sheets to the same document. Because conflicts are bound to arise, some method of resolution is essential to proper behavior when the content of a document is rendered on a user's machine.

The specifics of these rules are still in flux, but they depend on the assignment of a numeric weight to represent the relative importance of each style item. This is accomplished by assigning a value between 1 and 100 for a particular style element when it's referenced in a style sheet; to prevent users' preferences from being completely overridden by a document's author, authors are strongly encouraged never to set their weights as high as 100; this leaves the door open for users to override settings at will, which is especially helpful for visually handicapped users who may require all characters to be at least 36 point, or who may demand special text-to-speech settings. After all referenced style sheets and their alterations are loaded into memory, conflicts are resolved by applying the definition with the greatest weight and ignoring all others.

For example, assume that a document's author creates a style for a level-one heading, <H1>, so that it uses the color red and assigns it a weight of 75 percent. Further assume that the reader has defined a style for <H1>, colored blue with a weight of 55 percent. In that case, a CSS-enabled browser will use the author's style definition because it has the greater weight.

You can incorporate CSS into a Web document using one or more of four methods. The following code fragment illustrates all four of these methods:

```
<HEAD>
  <TITLE>title</TITLE>
  <LINK REL=STYLESHEET TYPE="text/css"
    HREF="http://www.style.org/cool" TITLE="Cool">
  <STYLE TYPE="text/css">
    @import "http://www.style.org/basic"
    H1 { color: blue }
  </STYLE>
</HEAD>
<BODY>
  <H1>Headline is blue</H1>
  <P STYLE="color: green">While the paragraph is green.
</BODY>
```

Here you can see all four CSS implementation methods:

- ✔ Using the <LINK> tag to link an external style sheet (line 3 of the preceding listing)
- ✔ Using <STYLE> inside the <HEAD> section (lines 5 through 8)
- ✔ Importing a style sheet using the CSS @import notation (line 6)
- ✔ Using the STYLE attribute in an element inside the <BODY> section (line 12)

Other benefits of the CSS implementation of style sheets include the following:

✔ **Grouping:**

Multiple style elements or definitions can be grouped together, as follows:

```
H1 {font-size: 12pt; line-height: 14pt; font-family:
      helvetica}
```

✔ **Inheritance:**

Any nested tags inherit the style sheet definitions assigned to the parent tag, unless the same elements are explicitly redefined.

For example, in the HTML line

```
<H1>The headline <EM>is</EM> important!</H1>
```

if <H1> is defined to display in red, then the text enclosed by <EM> will also display in red, unless <EM> is specifically defined to use another color.

✔ **Alternative Selectors:**

Post-2.0 HTML includes both CLASS and ID attributes for most HTML tags. These can be used to define subsets or alternative sets of tags defined by a style sheet. For example

```
<HEAD>
 <TITLE>Title</TITLE>
 <STYLE TYPE="text/css">
   H1.punk { color: #00FF00 }
 </STYLE>
</HEAD>
<BODY>
<H1>Not green</H1>
 <H1 CLASS=punk>Way too green</H1>
</BODY>
```

✔ **Context-Sensitive Selectors:**

CSS also supports context-based style definition. This is best described using an example:

```
<STYLE>
 UL UL LI    { font-size: small }
 UL UL UL LI { font-size: x-small }
</STYLE>
```

Following this notation, the second and third nested unnumbered lists (<UL>) will use increasingly smaller font sizes.

✔ **Comments:**

Comments may be added inside a style sheet using the common C language syntax: /* comment */.

Anatomy of a Style Sheet

The February 20, 1996 draft of the CSS standards includes a sample style sheet in Appendix A. We include it here for your perusal (and, we hope, for your edification).

```
BODY {
    margin: 1em;
    font-family: serif;
    background: white;
    color: black;
    border-color: black;     /* used by the HR element */
}

H1, H2, H3, H4, H5, H6, P, UL, OL, DIR, MENU, DIV,
DT, DD, ADDRESS, BLOCKQUOTE, PRE, BR, HR
{ display: block }

B, STRONG, I, EM, CITE, VAR, TT, CODE, KBD, SAMP,
IMG, SPAN
{ display: inline }

LI { display: list-item }

H1, H2, H3, H4 { margin-top: 1em; margin-bottom: 1em }
H5, H6 { margin-top: 1em }
H1, H2, H4, H6 { font-weight: bold }
H3, H5 { font-style: italic }

H1 { font-size: xx-large; align: center }
H2 { font-size: x-large }
H3 { font-size: large }
```

```
B, STRONG { font-weight: bold }
I, CITE, EM, VAR, ADDRESS, BLOCKQUOTE { font-style: italic }
PRE, TT, CODE, KBD, SAMP { font-family: monospace }

PRE { white-space: pre }

ADDRESS { margin-left: 3em }
BLOCKQUOTE { margin-left: 3em; margin-right: 3em }

UL, DIR { list-style: disc }
OL { list-style: decimal }
MENU { margin: 0 0 }
LI { margin-left: 3em }

DT { margin-bottom: 0 }
DD { margin-top: 0; margin-left: 5em }

HR { border-style: single none none none }

A:link { color: red }          /* unvisited link */
A:visited { color: dark-red }  /* visited links */
A:active { color: orange }     /* active links */

/* setting the anchor border around IMG elements
   requires context-sensitive selectors */

A:link IMG {
  border-color: red;
  border-style: single;
  border-width: 2px
}
A:visited IMG {
  border-color: red;
  border-style: single;
  border-width: 2px
}
A:active IMG {
  border-color: red;
  border-style: single;
  border-width: 2px
}
```

As you can see, the syntax and terminology used by CSS is not too difficult to understand. After CSS has been standardized and implemented, you shouldn't have too much trouble designing and creating your own style sheets.

If you want a bit more information about the syntax of this example CSS style sheet, please visit the latest draft of the CSS standards proposal at this URL:

```
http://www.w3.org/pub/WWW/Style/css/.
```

It's also not unreasonable to expect that after the standard is finalized, enterprising software vendors will build tools to assist in the construction of style sheets from scratch and in the creation of style sheets based on analysis of word processing or page-layout templates or documents. We look forward to their arrival because they will help to make everybody's jobs a bit easier.

Style's Got Pros and Cons

The CSS standard includes some amazing features and capabilities, most of which will mean little to you until you see them in action. In Figure 11-1 you can take a peek at a sample screen shot from a presentation given by Håkon W. Lie in March of 1996.

Not every aspect of CSS is perfect, but to incline you further toward a positive outlook on style sheets, here are a few more benefits of CSS for you to consider (then we'll bring you back to earth as we cover its drawbacks):

- Style sheets can be turned on and off by the viewer.
- Nonstandard tags such as FONT, CENTER, and BLINK are replaced by style element definitions.
- Most of the complicated presentation markup is removed or hidden within the style sheet, rather than embedded in the document, resulting in cleaner HTML markup.
- Both authors and readers have the freedom to create new, previously impossible Web layouts.

new toys
- small–caps

SMALL-CAPS
- blink
- background images
- drop-caps, big initials

*D*rop it!
- color gradients

Figure 11-1:
This sample Web page, based on CSS, shows some of its more interesting characteristics.

Before you get too excited, though, we feel compelled to point out that CSS lacks a few items that you may consider important:

- **No pixel-level controls.** The complexity of programming pixel level layout would violate CSS's design goals to be simple and easy to use.

- **No absolute style enforcement.** The reader of a page has the option to turn off styles or use a style sheet with higher weights. The author does not have absolute control over the display of his or her creation on another's system.

- **No multiple columns or overlapping frames.** Styles cannot be used to define overlapping <FRAME>s, or to assign the number of columns in a <TABLE> layout. In other words, such definitions must still be hard-coded in the HTML document itself, and cannot be tweaked in a style sheet.

- **No query language.** There's no way to figure out what a style looks or acts like by asking for a definition from some kind of all-knowing style sheet facility — the experimental method is the only way to get that information.

A Bit of Speculation

Before we let you go, here are a few more stylish things that might interest you. The goal (or pipe dream) of the W3C is to create a platform-independent method to control the appearance of a Web (or SGML) document. With CSS, the W3C has taken a large step in that direction, but other issues must be considered while establishing such a new standard.

✔ Some parties have voiced considerable interest in creating a public style sheet server, where standard, general-use style sheets could be housed. The notion is that this practice would encourage users to use widely accepted and broadly compatible style sheets. Although creating a core set of style sheets as a basis for most Web creations is a good idea, forced conformity is what provoked the HTML extension war in the first place. Also, the load placed on a "world wide style sheet server" would be overwhelming, even with lots of mirrors — further diminishing the free bandwidth available on the Internet.

✔ A second issue that's often discussed is the extra lag or transfer time associated with long or complex style sheets. It's not hard to imagine a style sheet (<LINK>ed or included in the <HEAD>) running 50K or more, especially if the author is "layout happy." Although restraint should be practiced, using common style sheets or the same style sheet over an entire Web site shouldn't significantly increase the time needed to transfer and view Web pages. After a <LINK>ed or @imported style sheet is cached, it can be quickly recalled whenever it's needed in another document.

✔ A third and extremely important issue is media-specific style sheets. Most Web content is designed for presentation through a graphical browser viewed by people on a computer monitor. The influences of the Web are quickly expanding beyond pixel-based displays, however. Print, fax, Braille, audio, and other publication media must also be considered for Web content presentation.

Ideas for implementing media-specific style sheets include on-the-fly style cascading by viewing clients, standardized formats available on Web servers, and native browser support for alternate media types. This is an area of style sheet standardization that is sure to attract a lot of attention in upcoming months. Stay tuned for further details.

Suffice it to say that CSS has already made a significant impact on the Web publishing world, even before a final standard has been produced. If you stay tuned to your favorite Web company or Internet news service, you'll be able to keep abreast of the latest advancements and implementations in style sheets.

Chapter 12

Jumping outside HTML's Boundaries

● ●

In This Chapter

▶ The myriad benefits of `<EMBED>`

▶ Using `<EMBED>` markup

▶ Examples of `<EMBED>` use

● ●

A great deal of the Web's explosive appeal has been caused by its graphical capacities. The only tag available in HTML 2.0 to represent images, however, is the `<IMG>` tag, which has lots of limitations.

An arbitrary restriction to image media is one of the `<IMG>` tag's major deficiencies, as is its singleton status (meaning that it doesn't employ a closing `</IMG>` tag). So, Netscape created the `<EMBED>` tag in an attempt to pick up the `<IMG>` tag's slack. `<EMBED>` supports Director film strips (`DIR` files) as well as QuickTime movies and VRML worlds. Netscape hopes to see this tag eventually incorporated into some official HTML standard.

What `<EMBED>` *does*

The `<EMBED>` tag describes plugins in HTML pages in much the same way that the `<IMG>` tag describes images. It lets you embed different kinds of documents of varying data types into HTML documents by showing the browser where special content should appear. When a capable browser (such as Netscape 2.0) encounters the `<EMBED>` tag, it knows that the material requires a plugin and it will load whatever plugin is indicated by the file's extension and its corresponding MIME type.

The `<EMBED>` tag also behaves like the `<IMG>` tag in terms of static graphic placement on a Web page, especially when it's used in conjunction with Netscape's `<IMG>` tag extensions — namely, WIDTH and HEIGHT. `<EMBED>` can take arbitrary attributes. Like the `<IMG>` tag, the `<EMBED>` tag can be placed inside other HTML tags, such as tables.

Advantages of `<EMBED>`

Because `<EMBED>` doesn't restrict itself to a limited class of media handlers or types, it allows portable compound document markup, as well as the modular design of user agents. Proposed embedding extensions such as APPLET and FIG are more restrictive than `<EMBED>`, especially because extensible user agents are becoming the norm. Unlike those other two tags, `<EMBED>` doesn't constrain you to any particular set of specialized functions.

Because `<EMBED>` is a container element, it also offers rich alternative text with links and images. `<EMBED>`'s container element provides excellent extensibility as well, and encourages structured enhancement of SGML content models rather than dependence on the proliferation of attributes for individual tags. The backward compatibility between `<EMBED>` and `<IMG>` is also a strong feature, as this example demonstrates:

```
<EMBED SRC="movie.mpg">
<IMG SRC="movie.001.jpg"> <!— first frame —>
</EMBED>
```

Even if a user agent doesn't know to react to the `<EMBED>` tag or doesn't have a video MPEG handler, the movie's initial frame will still show.

From the point of view of compound document architecture, `<EMBED>` is useful because it

✔ Conditionally creates a presentation resource, as a subordinate in the presentation hierarchy below the presentation of whatever HTML entity contains the `<EMBED>` element.

✔ Declares a link for which the tail anchor's target implicitly uses the newly created presentation resource. This creates a direct mechanism to instruct the browser where to find the resource and how to display it.

The World Wide Web Consortium's proposal to include `<EMBED>` in HTML 3.0 argues that `<EMBED>` is sufficiently "broad and intuitive" to denote a generic embedding element. It also states that `<EMBED>` has the potential to reduce implementation-dependent markup. This makes `<EMBED>` very attractive to multimedia content developers.

<EMBED> *changes from Netscape 1.1 to Netscape 2.0*

When you encounter a Web page that contains an HTML tag that your browser can't identify, its standard behavior is to ignore the unknown or unrecognized tag. This guarantees that HTML's future improvements won't obligate you to pick up new browser software. It also insulates you from outright mistakes in HTML documents (which happens from time to time, as your own authoring experience may prove).

This behavior is problematic, however, when an HTML tag has changed its meaning since a prior release. In fact, this is the case with Netscape Navigator 1.1 and <EMBED>. When Netscape 1.1 sees an <EMBED> tag, it thinks that this tag specifies an OLE link that supports the Windows 3.1 Object Linking and Embedding model. So, if you're using Netscape 1.1 (for whatever obscure reason), you'll get a broken icon wherever this tag appears in a document.

Netscape 2.0 remedies this problem, however. Netscape 2.0 recognizes that <EMBED> is telling it about a plugin and related content for that plugin to use. We expect that other browsers will include this functionality in the near future as well (perhaps even by the time you read this chapter).

HTML <EMBED> *Markup*

The <EMBED> link is activated as soon as an HTML entity's parent presentation is made; in English, this means that once the document where the <EMBED> tag occurs is displayed, the browser follows the link to the embedded resource. If that link somehow fails or the embedded content can't be created, then the <EMBED>.BODY element's content must be rendered instead of the <EMBED> element itself.

Netscape's initial use of <EMBED> was as an empty element, not as a container. Although this results in some forward-compatibility problems, the content model for <EMBED>.BODY permits error recovery to occur after the first paragraph break, as long as the </EMBED> closing tag is omitted.

In Netscape's initial implementation, arbitrary attributes are also used to pass parameters. You can use a combination such as the following for compatibility in the meantime (but be aware that it's not legal SGML!):

```
<EMBED SRC="sample.app" ALT="simple alt text" FOO="3"
   BAR=9>
<PARAM NAME="foo" VALUE=3> <PARAM NAME="bar" VALUE=9>
</EMBED>
```

Because the options that each plugin supports will vary, the syntax for the `<EMBED>` tag must also vary somewhat, depending on the plugin's requirements, behavior, and content.

`<EMBED>` takes three default attributes across the board, however; we cover these in the next section.

`<EMBED>`*'s attributes*

Because the options that each plugin supports will vary, the syntax for the `<EMBED>` tag must also vary according to the plugin employed. This allows particular input requirements for parameters as well as plugin behavior and content, to condition how the content will be displayed.

For information on particular plugins, you should investigate their individual characteristics. A good place to start is the Netscape plugins page, which you can find at

```
http://www.netscape.com/comprod/products/navigator
            /version_2.0/plugins/plugin_download.html
```

`<EMBED>` takes three default attributes:

✔ SRC

```
SRC=<URL>
```

SRC specifies the source document's URL.

✔ WIDTH

```
WIDTH=<size in pixels>
```

This attribute specifies the embedded document's width in pixels. You can scale the document according to these specifications.

✔ HEIGHT

```
HEIGHT=<size in pixels>
```

This attribute specifies the embedded document's height in pixels. You can scale the document according to these specifications.

<EMBED>*'s other attributes*

In addition to these three default attributes, <EMBED> can contain optional parameters, as follows (remember, this isn't an exhaustive list):

```
PARAMETER_NAME=<PARAMETER_VALUE>
```

These parameters can be sent to the plugin that handles the embedded data type. Parameters are specific to each plugin and no limit exists on how many parameters can be passed into a plugin. Here are some examples of parameters:

```
CONTROLS=FALSE
PLAY_LOOP=TRUE
```

Some additional <EMBED> attributes include the following:

```
PARAMS; TITLE, URN, REL, REV; ACCEPT, ACCEPT-CHARSET
ACCEPT-ENCODING; ALIGN, HSPACE, VSPACE, FLOWTO
```

<NOEMBED>

If you want to be loved by the masses, use Netscape's <NOEMBED> tag. Using <NOEMBED> lets you include HTML statements that will appear only in browsers that do not support plugins. Using <NOEMBED> is a nice thing to do, because it lets you create HTML pages that are enhanced for browsers that support plugins, but that also work for browsers that don't support them.

If Navigator 2.0 encounters a <NOEMBED> tag, it ignores everything from that point until it reaches the </NOEMBED> tag. Most other browsers will ignore both the <NOEMBED> and </NOEMBED> and execute the HTML contained between the two tags. See the upcoming section on Shockwave for an example of how <NOEMBED> can be used as a savvy workaround.

Here's <NOEMBED>'s syntax:

```
<NOEMBED> HTML to be ignored </NOEMBED>
```

And here's an example (HTML for both a plugin and a helper application):

```
<EMBED SRC="sample1.rpm" WIDTH="250" HEIGHT="150">
<NOEMBED> <A SRC="sample1.ram">Play the audio!
</A></NOEMBED>
```

For all the details on the `<EMBED>` tag, try the Netscape Search engine, available through this URL:

```
http://home.mcom.com/
```

When we wrote this chapter, Netscape's `<EMBED>` documentation was located at this URL (but things change fast at the Netscape site, so don't be too surprised if this doesn't work when you try it):

```
http://www.netscape.com/assist/net_sites/embed_tag.html
```

Mapping `<APPLET>` *to* `<EMBED>`

You can map the `<APPLET>` element associated with Java to `<EMBED>` with just a couple of essential name changes:

- ✓ Change `<APPLET>` to `<EMBED>`
- ✓ Change `NAME` to `ID`
- ✓ Prefix `CODE` with `CODEBASE`, so it becomes `SRC`

  `CODEBASE` can be deduced from the process of the embedding API that passes the retrieval URL (the `SRC`) to the media handler. Because its function is to let you enhance HTML pages for browsers that lack plugins, you don't need to use it!

If this discussion didn't make much sense, look at a few examples. These should illustrate what I've been discussing and give you something more concrete to cement your understanding.

General examples of `<EMBED>` *tag markup*

Here, we show you a couple of illustrations based on a popular video animation format (`MOV`), and on an even more popular interactive game.

```
<!— Example 1: sizing a window for video playback —>
<EMBED SRC="CSMovie.mov" WIDTH="150" HEIGHT="250"
    CONTROLS="TRUE">
<!— Example 2: sizing a window for game playing —>
<EMBED SRC="DoomGame.ids" WIDTH="400" HEIGHT="300"
    SPEED="SLOW" LEVEL="12">
```

Specific examples of <EMBED> *tag markup*

In each of the sections that follow, we explore the syntax for some of the most popular plugins. These include Macromedia's Shockwave for Director, RealAudio, and ShowMovie.

Shockwave for Director

Here's the standard <EMBED> syntax for Shockwave Director movies (you can find out more about Shockwave in Chapter 15):

```
<EMBED WIDTH="x" HEIGHT="y" SRC="myfile">
<EMBED SRC="path/filename.ext" WIDTH="n" HEIGHT="n"
    TEXTFOCUS="focus">
```

To use the <EMBED> tag to plant a Shockwave for Director movie on an HTML page, substitute the stage height in pixels for "y", the stage width in pixels for "x", and the filename or URL in quotation marks after SRC.

A super Shockwave workaround

At this point, you may need to use a few workarounds to successfully play Shockwave content. A particular workaround, courtesy of the Macromedia development staff, tailors itself to whatever kind of browser it encounters. (We get to the actual workaround soon!)

For Shockwave- and Java-enabled browsers, Macromedia's workaround for Netscape 2.0 does the following:

  ✔ Reveals the <EMBED> tag so that a Shockwave movie appears if the plugin is loaded; a broken icon appears if the plugin isn't loaded.

  ✔ Hides the <NOEMBED> block so that the "consolation HTML" shown to nonenabled browsers will not appear.

If you're using a browser other than Netscape 2.0 — that is, one that cannot handle Shockwave and Java plugins — this workaround allows your users to skip the "broken graphic" icon they would otherwise see whenever they encounter Shockwave content. In this case, the workaround works its magic like this:

  ✔ It hides the <EMBED> tag so that a Shockwave movie can't appear.

  ✔ It reveals the <NOEMBED> block so that the consolation HTML appears instead.

This workaround hides the <EMBED> tag inside a short routine written in *JavaScript,* a programming language built into Navigator 2.0. Because JavaScript routines are hidden inside the HTML comment tags <!– and –>, and only Navigator 2.0 understands JavaScript, any other browser thinks that the <EMBED> tag is just a comment, and therefore ignores it.

Okay, enough explanation already! Here's the workaround:

```
<SCRIPT LANGUAGE="JavaScript">
<!- Hide this script from non-Navigator 2.0 browsers.
document.write( '<EMBED WIDTH="x" HEIGHT="y"
   SRC="myfile">' );
<!- Done hiding from non-Navigator 2.0 browsers. ->
</SCRIPT>
```

Don't remove the comments within the tags; they are necessary for the script's proper functioning.

If you want to display an image or text in place of the "shocked" Director movie on browsers other than Netscape 2.0, use <NOEMBED>, like this:

```
<SCRIPT LANGUAGE="JavaScript">
<!- Hide this script from non-Navigator 2.0 browsers.
document.write( '<EMBED WIDTH="165" HEIGHT="145"
            SRC="mymovie.dcr">
<!- Done hiding from non-Navigator 2.0 browsers. ->
</SCRIPT>
<NOEMBED>
<IMG WIDTH=50 HEIGHT=85 SRC="mystill.jpg">
</NOEMBED>
```

If a user visits your site running a Netscape 2.0 browser, when it encounters this markup, it will execute the JavaScript routine. With the Shockwave plugin installed, the movie that we call `mymovie.dcr` in the HTML code above will play. If that user doesn't have the plugin, the browser displays a broken icon.

When a browser other than Netscape 2.0 encounters this script, its first reaction will be to ignore the JavaScript routine because it thinks it's only a comment. When it comes across `<NOEMBED>`, it will ignore that, too. The browser will, however, ultimately display `mystill.jpg` because it doesn't know that it's supposed to skip over anything between `<NOEMBED>` and `</NOEMBED>`. Tricky, huh?

To see how Shockwave uses this workaround, view the HTML source that surrounds any of Macromedia's movies at the Shockwave Movie Lab:

```
http://www.macromedia.com/Tools/Shockwave/sdc/Dev
            /movielab.html
```

RealAudio

Although many options exist that you can use with Progressive Networks's RealAudio and the `<EMBED>` tag, the basic tag for RealAudio contains only the three following attributes:

```
<EMBED SRC=source_URL WIDTH=width_value HEIGHT=height_value>
```

The `SRC` attribute specifies the RealAudio file's URL, whereas the `HEIGHT` and `WIDTH` attributes specify the embedded component's size. URLs for plugins use the `RPM` extension rather than the normal `RAM` extension — this avoids backward compatibility conflicts with the RealAudio Player.

Before your Web browser can correctly identify `RPM` files, you (or your system administrator) must configure the associated MIME type. Except for this extension, files with an `RPM` extension are identical to `RAM` files.

Here's an example:

```
<EMBED SRC="sample1.rpm" WIDTH="300" HEIGHT="134">
```

That example would produce the following:

```
<SRC="sample1.rpm" WIDTH="300" HEIGHT="134">
```

For more information about the RealAudio plugin, please visit Progressive Networks's Web site at

```
http://www.realaudio.com/
```

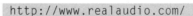

ViewMovie

There is a peculiarity that's produced in Netscape 2.0, owing to the peculiar nature of QuickTime movies (and particularly the QuickTime movie controller). That is, the `HEIGHT` property specified in the tag must be the height of the movie itself plus 16. Sound bizarre? It may be, but it accounts for the size of the movie controller. So, if you want to place a 320x220 movie on your page, you use this markup:

```
<EMBED SRC="mymovie.mov" WIDTH="320" HEIGHT="236">
```

As of ViewMovie version 1.0a6, however, if you hide the controller without a badge, you can indicate the movie's real size (using a badge can show the controller if it's hidden). In that case, the preceding markup looks like this:

```
<EMBED SRC="mymovie.mov" WIDTH="320" HEIGHT="220"
    CONTROLLER="FALSE">
```

You should name these movies with the MOV extension because that is specified by the plugin to identify files as the video/quicktime MIME type. If your server is configured differently (that is, if it specifies that QuickTime files with the extension .qt take thevideo/quicktime MIME type), you can use it as well.

These are the attributes that ViewMovie Version 1.0a10 supports within the <EMBED> tag:

```
AUTOPLAY
CONTROLLER
HREFABS
ISMAP
KEEPASPECTRATIO
LOOP
PLAYEVERYFRAME
PLAYRATE
PLUGINSPAGE
PLUGINSPAGE
QUALITY
VOLUME
```

You can get more information about <EMBED> and ViewMovie at the ViewMovie info page:

```
http://www.well.com/~ivanski/viewmovie
              /viewmovie_info.html
```

Getting underneath <EMBED>

<EMBED> is a tag that enhances the Web's potential for representing graphics and other high-impact information. It lifts restrictions that you'd encounter with the <IMG> tag, or with specific tags such as APPLET. Why? Because it tells your browser that some sort of plugin is required without needing to specify exactly what that plugin's functions might be.

Instead, <EMBED> allows the file extension and corresponding MIME type to take care of that work. Although Netscape 2.0 is the only browser that currently knows how to deal with the <EMBED> tag, given its benefits, other browsers are sure to incorporate it soon.

Chapter 13
Marvelous HTML Miscellany

●●

In This Chapter
▶ Adding special effects to your `<BODY>`
▶ Colorizing your Web site
▶ Enhancing image use with the `<FIG>` tag
▶ Exploiting undocumented tricks of the HTML trade
▶ Developing your characters with the `<FONT>` tag
▶ Surfing for further enlightenment

●●

*I*f you think that you have seen all there is to see in HTML, you're wrong! New tags, new layouts, new multimedia types, new plugins, and new food groups appear almost daily on the Web.

In this chapter, we take a look at a few miscellaneous HTML things that we think are pretty cool. We do try to tell you the origins of most of these new gadgets, but because everyone is trying to adopt all the flashy and potent tags, it can be difficult to say who does and doesn't support what. So, always be sure to test your creations on multiple browsers and platforms before going public — it's the only sure way to avoid unnecessary embarrassment.

Making Decisions about Your `<BODY>`

Just when you think it's safe to use the `<BODY>` tag, new and improved ways to add vitality and flair to your documents will rear their ugly heads. As you probably know, the `<BODY>` tag set surrounds the information that appears in a browser display window. But this innocuous little tag has acquired some powerful attributes recently. Read on to see what's creeping into this once-meek container's bag of tricks.

Backgrounds

The addition of the BACKGROUND="URL" attribute tiles a graphic to create a background for pages as they're displayed by your browser, behind the text and other inline media. This little jewel was introduced by Netscape and has been incorporated into "the tag set formerly known as HTML 3.0." We're sure that you have seen this attribute at work at hundreds of Web sites, but just in case, Figure 13-1 shows a sample page with a background image.

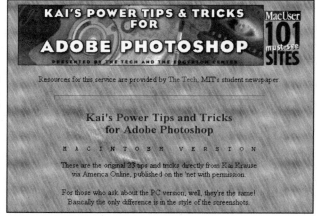

Figure 13-1:
The KPT
Tips and
Tricks Web
site uses a
nice
background
image.

Visit the Kai's Power Tips and Tricks page at

```
http://the-tech.mit.edu/KPT/KPT.html
```

The BACKGROUND attribute is used as follows:

```
<BODY BACKGROUND="path/filename.gif">
```

Most Web authors use small tile-like graphics that appear as a seamless pattern when used as a background, as shown in Figure 13-1. But you need not limit yourself to small graphics; in fact, if your graphic is wide enough (larger than a standard browser display width of 620 to 1,000 pixels), you can create other interesting effects.

For example, David Siegel's Top Five Award page, shown in Figure 13-2, uses a background image to give a two-toned effect to the site. Visit it at the following URL:

```
http://www.highfive.com/
```

Figure 13-2:
David Siegel's Top Five Award page is an example of a large background image.

We could take pages and pages to explain how to create graphics and how to balance your colors, but we'll leave those discoveries up to you. To get some good ideas, however, take the time to look at some interesting sights at these sites:

✔ The Background Sampler:

```
http://home.netscape.com/assist/net_sites/bg/
        backgrounds.html
```

✔ Julianne's Background Textures:

```
http://www.sfsu.edu/~jtolson/textures/textures.htm
```

✔ Pattern Land:

```
http://www.netcreations.com/patternland/index.html
```

Watermarks

Microsoft just can't leave well enough alone when it comes to backgrounds, either. It added a secondary attribute for use with background images. The use of the BGPROPERTIES=FIXED attribute with BACKGROUND causes the image not to scroll but rather to remain fixed in the display window. Microsoft calls it a *watermark* (we call it having too much time and money to spend). This attribute works only in Microsoft's Internet Explorer (a bit obvious, huh?). If you want to give it a try, here's the syntax:

```
<BODY BACKGROUND="path/filename.gif" BGPROPERTIES=FIXED>
```

Text color

Colorizing your Web site has never been easier, with five <BODY> tag attributes introduced by Netscape. These five attributes are as follows:

- ✔ BGCOLOR defines a single color for the background of the browser display area (this replaces the default gray that you tune out because you've seen it everywhere).
- ✔ TEXT defines a color for non-hyperlinked text.
- ✔ LINK defines a color for unvisited hyperlinks.
- ✔ VLINK defines a color for a visited link.
- ✔ ALINK defines a color for a link as you click on it.

You can select the color for any of these attributes in one of two ways: numeric (hex) RGB codes or predefined color names.

RGB (Red Green Blue) notation is used in many graphical images. *Hexadecimal*, or hex, is a numbering method that uses 16 digits rather than the 10 digits used in our common decimal system. These hex digits include decimal 0 – 9, plus the letters a (10), b (11), c (12), d (13), e (14), and f (15); in hex the number 10 equals 16 (or $1*16^1 + 0*16^0$).

By using two hex digits, you can specify a number between 0 (00) and 255 (ff) or any value in between, such as 138 (8a).

The use of three two-digit hex numbers allows you to specify one of 16.7 million (256^3 or 16,777,216) colors from the 24-bit color palette. So, the hex number #0000ff is blue, #00ff00 is green, and #ff0000 is red. By mixing the levels of red, green, and blue, you can create any color you want.

If you need help locating a color, visit one of these sites:

- ✔ Mediarama's Color Page Builder:

    http://www.echonyc.com/~xixax/Mediarama/hex.html

- ✔ ColorMaker:

    http://www.missouri.edu/~c588349/colormaker.html

- ✔ LiveScript Hex/Decimal Color Converter:

    http://durandal.res.cmu.edu/~john/colorcalc.html

Predefined color names constitute the 16 colors hard-coded into your browser. The names for these currently supported colors are as follows:

Black	White	Green	Maroon
Olive	Navy	Purple	Gray
Red	Yellow	Blue	Teal
Lime	Aqua	Fuchsia	Silver

Note: Capitalization is optional for both hex RGB codes and color names. For some browsers, the pound symbol (#) before the hex RGB code is required; on others, it's not — so use it anyway. For a good example of a color picking application to help you set RGB codes, visit the site shown in Figure 13-3 at `http://www.missouri.edu/~c588349/colormaker.html`.

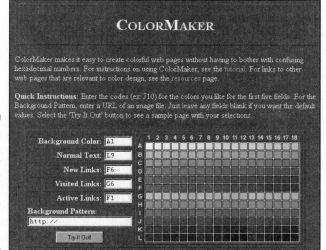

Figure 13-3:
The ColorMaker site shows an example of color usage on a Web site.

Using RGB attributes or color names is pretty simple, as these examples should illustrate:

```
<BODY BGCOLOR="#FFFFFF" TEXT="#330099" LINK="#FF0000"
    VLINK="#66FF00" ALINK="#FF00FF">
```

or

```
<BODY BGCOLOR="white" TEXT="blue" LINK="red"
    VLINK="lime"> ALINK="teal"
```

Margins

Microsoft has added even more small green men to the browser Cold War with the LEFTMARGIN="n" and TOPMARGIN="n" <BODY> attributes. These little guys specify the width of a margin used on the left or top of a browser display window. The value of "n" can be any positive integer (go look it up if you've forgotten your Algebra I). Using zero for "n" causes the information to display flush with the edge of the window. The syntax for these attributes is as follows:

```
<BODY LEFTMARGIN="60" TOPMARGIN="0">
```

The Fabulous Figure and Related Tags

In the tag set formerly known as HTML 3.0, a new set of image and graphic control tags were introduced. Although these tags have yet to be adopted and supported by any popular browsers (just like math and style sheets), getting to know them before they start appearing everywhere may give you the edge you've always wanted. (If that last sentence got you a bit excited, you need to get out more!)

The tag we're talking about in this case is the figure tag (<FIG>). This tag is designed to improve upon the image tag (<IMG>). Obviously, because it isn't in use yet, we really can't make a judgment call right now. But suffice it to say that although <FIG> offers functionality that <IMG> lacks, that doesn't necessarily mean that <FIG> is better.

The figure tag was proposed with three image display operations in mind: basic images, client-side image maps, and overlays.

Like the <IMG> tag, <FIG> can display an inline image. But <FIG> offers the capability to add <CAPTION> and <CREDIT> entities to label an image and indicate its source. You may be thinking that you can do this with the <IMG> tag, but <FIG> offers this capability within its own tag set. See the following for an example:

```
<FIG SRC="texas.jpeg">
  <CAPTION>Aerial view of the state of Texas</CAPTION>
  <CREDIT>Maps-R-Us, Inc.</CREDIT>
</FIG>
```

Before Netscape invented a true client-side image map, the <FIG> tag offered HTML its best hope for this functionality. As shown in the following example, areas of an image can be mapped, labeled, and made into hyperlinks:

```
<FIG SRC="menu.gif">
 <H1>XYZ Company</H1>
 <P>Select One:
 <UL>
  <LI><A HREF="files.html" SHAPE="rect
   30,200,60,16">Download Software</A>
  <LI><A HREF="about.html" SHAPE="rect
   100,200,50,16">About XYZ</A>
  <LI><A HREF="email.html" SHAPE="rect
   160,200,30,16">Contact</A>
  <LI><A HREF="products.html" SHAPE="rect
   200,200,50,16">Products</A>
  <LI><A HREF="links.html" SHAPE="rect
   260,200,80,16">Our Clients</A>
 </UL>
</FIG>
```

The final capability of the <FIG> tag is to overlay images to produce a single complex display, similar to transparency overlays on a printed map.

```
<FIG SRC="newyork.jpeg">
 <OVERLAY SRC="roads.gif">
 <OVERLAY SRC="subway_tunnels.gif">
 <OVERLAY SRC="phone_lines.gif">
 <OVERLAY SRC="electric_cables.gif">
</FIG>
```

In this section, we've discussed the <FIG> tag, many of its attributes, and some of the companion tags used within a figure tag set. But don't rush out and implement these features into your own pages just yet. The information in this section was taken from the HTML 3.0 Draft Specification from March of 1995, which has long since expired. You'll need to watch the W3C (see "Getting Vertigo?" at the end of this chapter) to keep up with figure tag standardization and support.

Exploiting Undocumented Tricks

Quite a few undocumented features exist in Netscape, Microsoft Internet Explorer, and even within HTML itself. They are well-hidden, however, so even our best efforts couldn't uncover more than just a few. Instead of keeping them all to ourselves, in the following sections we give you the lowdown on what we found.

Animation for the rest of us

A wonderful feature of the GIF89a format has finally been exploited—*GIF animation* has come to the layperson. Even though the GIF specification has been around since 1989, few have discovered or employed the hidden features of this slick image format. With a few simple tools (available on the Internet), you can create animations for your Web pages without CGIs, server pushes, movies, Java, or even Shockwave.

For a detailed tutorial, a gallery of animation, and links to shareware to create your own animated GIFs, visit the CyberNet International GIF89a-based Animation Information page at the following URL:

```
http://www.reiworld.com/royalef/gifanim.htm
```

Creating an animated GIF is not difficult; however, you do need to be fairly adept at using graphics utilities. Here's our quick-and-dirty three-step process: First, create each frame of the animation. Second, create an animation GIF using a special GIF utility. Third, add the image to a Web document using the normal <IMG> tag and attributes, and then test. That's about all there is to it!

All this simplicity leaves a lot of room for some really serious screw-ups. You need to watch out for things such as image transparency, color depth, image size, frame positioning, and maybe a few other things specific to your GIF animation utility. As with anything else that you don't understand fully, please read the manual. Or rather, download one of the utilities suggested in the preceding URL, and then read its documentation.

We would like to show you a picture of an animated GIF, but making images move on printed paper is too difficult even for us. So, go check it out on the Web.

Double vision

Many professional Web sites are moving toward large, graphically enhanced pages. These pages take an enormous amount of time to download over a modem. That's why some of the more user-friendly and insightful Web designers have begun to use double images for their more serious graphics.

Here's what the double image technique entails: Make a low-definition black-and-white (or 16-color) version of an image and display this first, followed by its large, detailed equivalent (as shown in Dylan Green's Starting Windows 95 at http://www.wam.umd.edu/~dylan/windows95.html, Figure 13-4).

The low-resolution image loads quickly, giving users the option of sticking around for the four-star feature or going on about their business. We think it's a worthwhile technique, especially if you have graphics bigger than 25K that you want to display.

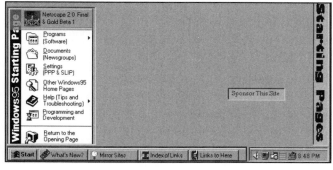

Figure 13-4: A LOWSRC/ SRC site captured while loading.

If you want to add this dandy little feature to your Web site, you'll need to proceed through the following steps:

1. **Make a copy of your high-resolution detailed image (be sure to use the final version!).**

   You should give it an easy-to-recognize name, or just add "low" to the filename before the extension (for instance, rename the low-resolution version of menu.gif to menulow.gif).

2. **Use a graphics utility to reduce the low-res image's color depth to mono/binary/1-bit color (like, black and white, dude!).**

   Be sure to save the file after you're satisfied with the results.

3. **Edit the HTML document where the original image was loaded. Add the** LOWRES="filename" **attribute to the** <IMG> **tag.**

   For example:

   ```
   <IMG LOWRES="graphics/menulow.gif"
      SRC="graphics/menu.gif">
   ```

4. **Save your HTML document and test it.**

   If you test it on a local hard drive, you will barely be able to see the LOWRES image blink as the full-blown image replaces it. You'll need to test this on a real Web server over the Internet to see this feature's true benefit.

Internal images

Netscape has nine built-in images that you can use within your Web pages. Often, these images are used when displaying Gopher or FTP information, but with the following markup, you can use them wherever you want.

```
<IMG SRC="INTERNAL-GOPHER-BINARY">
<IMG SRC="INTERNAL-GOPHER-INDEX">
<IMG SRC="INTERNAL-GOPHER-IMAGE">
<IMG SRC="INTERNAL-GOPHER-MENU">
<IMG SRC="INTERNAL-GOPHER-MOVIE">
<IMG SRC="INTERNAL-GOPHER-SOUND">
<IMG SRC="INTERNAL-GOPHER-TEXT">
<IMG SRC="INTERNAL-GOPHER-TELNET">
<IMG SRC="INTERNAL-GOPHER-UNKNOWN">
```

We used these <IMG> tags to create the images shown in Figure 13-5.

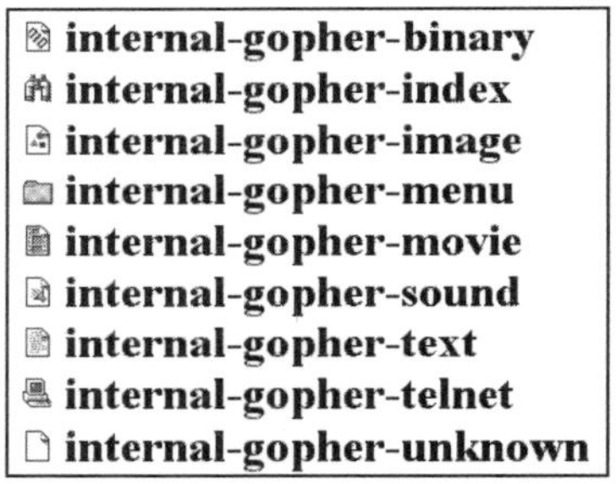

Figure 13-5:
These are the nine internal images of Netscape.

```
🖾 internal-gopher-binary
🏠 internal-gopher-index
🔼 internal-gopher-image
🗀 internal-gopher-menu
📄 internal-gopher-movie
🔉 internal-gopher-sound
🖹 internal-gopher-text
🖳 internal-gopher-telnet
📄 internal-gopher-unknown
```

Scrollin', scrollin', scrollin' . . .

If you want to be a bit cocky and show off a working, but illegal, title animation, try this one. By including multiple <TITLE> tags in your <HEAD>, you can scroll a title onto a page's title bar.

```
<TITLE>H</TITLE>
<TITLE>HO</TITLE>
<TITLE>HOM</TITLE>
<TITLE>HOME</TITLE>
<TITLE>HOMEP</TITLE>
<TITLE>HOMEPA</TITLE>
<TITLE>HOMEPAG</TITLE>
<TITLE>HOMEPAGE</TITLE>
```

Don't get too excited about this, though — this page will never pass the "HTML validation" test. It might even make some browsers puke, so it's more a curiosity than anything else.

Forcing a new browser

One nifty side effect of the frame wave that's sweeping the Web world is the Netscape TARGET attribute. If you're using frames, you should be familiar with this tag; if not, go read Chapter 9.

You can cause a new browser window to pop up when a user clicks on a hyperlink by using the TARGET attribute (illegally). This can be quite irritating if used inappropriately or too often.

We highly recommend — no, make that *insist* — that you use this markup only infrequently. Don't use it when you define a link to an external site and want to keep your site loaded in a viewer's browser (that means that your site needs to be extremely important). Opening multiple browser windows on a client's computer not only angers the user but makes you a prime candidate for the bottom five percent on the "favorite Web sites" lists so beloved by many users.

Okay, we've made it clear that you shouldn't overuse this technique. With that point firmly implanted in your back (sorry about the blood and the hole in your shirt), we'll show you how to do it:

```
<A HREF="http://www.lanw.com" TARGET="_BLANK">
   Cool Site</A>
```

Usually, when a resource appears in the context of a frame, it is indicated by a link through the TARGET attribute to make it appear in the targeted frame or window. But when the named target window doesn't exist, Netscape creates one for you — usually by opening a new browser window.

Use this illegal technique sparingly if at all, or risk the ire of your users!

Advanced Font Controls

For all you anal-retentive control freaks, Netscape and Microsoft (without overt cooperation) have added a whole new area to HTML for you to manage — namely, fonts.

`<FONT>`*ification*

The Netscape `<FONT>` tag may be used wherever you want to alter the font from the norm. With the right attributes, you can alter point size, color, and even text style within a `<FONT>` . . . `</FONT>` tag pair. Like all physical tags (yeah, `<FONT>` is a physical tag because it alters the way that text is physically displayed), you need to use it sparingly. Emphasis and de-emphasis lose their effect when overused (remember that boy who cried "wolf").

The first attribute introduced by Netscape is `SIZE="+/-n"`, which increases or decreases a font's point size. The value of `"n"` can be a number between one and seven, but can be added or subtracted (hence the + and − symbols) from the default or standard font size of the marked text.

The second attribute is `COLOR="#rrggbb/colorname"`. This attribute alters the color of the demarcated text. Who originated this tag is in dispute, because both of the big boys list it as one of their creations (who really cares, anyway?). If you need help with the hex RGB numbers or the legal color names, go back to the "Text color" subsection earlier in this chapter.

The third and final added attribute is `FACE=="name [,name2] [,name3]"`, originated by Microsoft. Using this attribute alters the font style for the selected text. If the system that displays the Web document has the first font installed, that font will be used. If the first font isn't present, the system tries to use the second or third alternates that you define. If none of the values of `FACE` is present on the client system, the browser ignores this attribute.

A possible syntax for this tag follows:

```
<FONT SIZE=+3 COLOR="#0000ff" FACE="Arial, Courier,
   Times Roman">A silly little example</FONT>
```

Four inches is how many points?

Netscape added another font manipulation tag to be used in conjunction with the `<FONT>` tag. This tag, `<BASEFONT SIZE="n">`, alters the base font size for all text that follows it. The value of `"n"` can be a number between one and seven, and the default is three. You can use the `<FONT SIZE="+/-n">` tag to further alter text size. Print-handicapped users find this especially helpful because it lets them display the kind of big characters they can read without requiring an additional plugin or helper application.

The big, the small, and the others

The tags formerly known as HTML 3.0 also introduced a few new physical tags to manipulate the display of text. You must use all these tags in pairs to begin and end the text alteration. These new tags are as follows:

- ✔ `<BIG>` — Specifies that the enclosed text should be displayed using a big font.
- ✔ `<SMALL>` — Specifies that the enclosed text should be displayed using a small font.
- ✔ `<SUB>` — Specifies that the enclosed text should be displayed as a subscript, using a smaller font.
- ✔ `<SUP>` — Specifies that the enclosed text should be displayed as a superscript, using a smaller font.

Getting Vertigo?

If you still have your head screwed on straight and want even more HTML playthings, we haven't left you without a good wave. Grab your board and surf to these sources of late-breaking information. You'll need to be cunning and a bit persistent to locate new and exciting sources, but we're certain that the time you spend will be greatly rewarded.

- ✔ Microsoft's Internet Explorer Page:

    `http://www.microsoft.com/ie/msie.htm`

- ✔ Netscape's Home Page:

    `http://www.netscape.com`

- ✔ NCSA's Mosaic Home Page:

    `http://www.ncsa.uiuc.edu/SDG/Software/Mosaic/`

- ✔ The World Wide Web Consortium:

    `http://www.w3.org/pub/WWW/`

The Web is sufficiently dynamic that, as long as you keep looking for new HTML tricks, tags, and capabilities, you'll probably keep finding them. As for me, it's time to move beyond HTML as we surf into Part III, where we tackle some really cool Web extension technologies.

Part III

Beyond HTML: Cool Web Extensions

The 5th Wave
By Rich Tennant

The embarrassment of Laptop Static Cling

In this part . . .

Part III introduces some wild and wonderful Web extension technologies, beginning with a discussion of helper applications and plugins in Chapter 14. Each of the next four chapters covers a different technology. In Chapter 15, we tackle Macromedia's animated Shockwave for Director and its related Afterburner tool. Next, Chapter 16 presents the Virtual Reality Modeling Language (VRML) that you can use to create complete, three-dimensional virtual worlds for Web access. Following the discussion of VRML comes Chapter 17, where we jump into Sun Microsystems' exciting Java programming language and explore its potential uses on the Web. Finally, we conclude Part III with Chapter 18, a discussion of several of the various text display engines available for use on the Web.

Chapter 14

Adding Animation, 3-D Worlds, and Dynamic Behavior

*U*nless you've been hiding under a rock lately, you've probably heard about all kinds of technologies to extend the Web's capabilities. Today, you can find Web extensions for everything from audio to video, with quite a few points in between. And if the buzz in the developer community is any indication of what's coming, these extensions are just the tip of a pretty major iceberg!

In this chapter, we begin our survey of Web extensions with a discussion of what's currently available. From there, we dip into some of the underlying terminology and technology. We conclude our survey by discussing the pros and cons of extensions that aren't available to all users, including how to design them into your Web pages and how to steer your audience through (or around) them. This survey is intended to prepare you for the next four chapters, which cover a variety of Web extensions in much greater detail.

If Your Browser Can't See It, Is It Really There?

Before we launch into a discussion of Web extensions, we'd like to remind you of a basic aspect of Web browser behavior. Please remember that the convention is for browsers to ignore markup that they can't recognize. In other words, some browsers cheerfully pass over certain Web extensions because they are unable to recognize the extensions and, therefore, are blissfully ignorant of their existence.

Throughout this part of the book, you can see how this browser behavior (that is, ignoring unrecognized extensions) is exploited by Web authors who develop content by using those extensions that rely in part on specialized HTML markup. You find out some clever techniques to deliver one set of materials to users whose browsers can handle special extensions and another set to those whose browsers can't.

We encourage you to provide alternate materials to your users whenever possible. This extra effort ensures that you always reach the broadest audience — if only to evangelize them to adopt the new software and technologies necessary to appreciate your other work! But more importantly, this approach recognizes that not all users bring the same capabilities to the Web and doesn't try to discriminate between those who have the latest — and greatest — Web tools and those who don't.

We advocate the following: Don't alienate part of your audience; always provide alternate materials whenever you use an extension or some other advanced HTML feature. The choice is entirely up to you, but we think that reaching out to those users who can't immediately appreciate your stunning multimedia work or your cool applications is as important as catering to those who can!

Beyond HTML . . .

As Web browsers and related technologies continue to evolve, HTML appears less and less able to handle the requirements for display and interaction that new capabilities so often foster and demand. That's why we tackle two of the most important Web extension technologies in the sections that follow: *helper applications* and *plugins*. Read on to learn how these tools can open your browser up to a whole new world of functionality!

Assisting the browser: helper applications

A long tradition on the Web supports the linking of so-called *helper applications* to certain file types. These file types are usually identified by their extensions (for example, MOV for animated movie files and WAV for wave table audio files) or by their associated MIME types (especially when more than one extension applies to a single MIME type, as is the case with multiple Shockwave extensions you'll find on the Web). The approach to identifying those files that need helper applications works like this:

✔ When a URL points to a resource that a user has selected, the browser requests that source to be delivered.

✔ The server returns the selected information with a header that indicates the MIME type for the resource. You can view this as a form of "explicit labeling" since the server tells the browser exactly what's going on.

✔ The browser looks up the MIME type in a built-in associations table. Through this table, the browser determines whether it can handle that data itself or whether it must involve another application. You can view this as a form of "implicit labeling" since the file extension is used to tell the browser how to handle incoming data.

When the browser requires another application to deliver a selected resource, that application is considered to be *helping* the browser. And thereby, you get the name *helper application*. One unfortunate side effect of running a helper application, however, is that a program other than a Web browser takes control of your display. After the users finish with the materials delivered by a helper application, they must exit that application and explicitly return to the browser to pick up where they left off.

Hooking up with plugins

As technologies go, the helper application method is workable and not terribly inconvenient. But with the release of Netscape Navigator 2.0, Netscape introduced a more tightly integrated way to extend the browser's functionality without forcing it to surrender control to another application. This technology is called a *plugin,* and it works the way its name suggests: Instead of relinquishing control to an external application, a plugin permits third parties to write programs that extend the browser's functionality directly, while maintaining the same familiar interface and behavior.

The plugin architecture is also quite intelligent: While plugins may be installed at any time (or even preconfigured with a browser in some cases), they're not actually loaded into your computer's memory until materials that require the plugin's attention arrive at the browser. This feature lets users add an arbitrary number of plugins to their browsers without causing the browsers to become bloated memory hogs.

For those of you familiar with the Macintosh, Netscape plugins work very much like the operating system extensions called *INITs* that show up as icons when the Macintosh system is booting up. In much the same way, Netscape's Help subsystem provides an "About Plugins" document that you can peruse at any time to see which plugins are installed.

When Netscape relinquishes control to a plugin, that plugin does its thing within the same overall framework as the native browser.

This framework enables users to interact with content and Web extension technologies without necessarily knowing that the browser is no longer running the onscreen display. Even when a plugin is active, though, the browser maintains overall control of the interface and information delivery. An added benefit suggests that an infinite number of content types and resources is theoretically available through the same window. That's why most other Web browser vendors are investigating plugin technology, if they're not already implementing plugin support.

This is the bottom line: A Web browser no longer needs to be conceived of as, more or less, an HTML rendering service. The addition of plugin technology opens the door to all kinds of built-in services and lifts the barriers to functionality that HTML has been unable to support (for example, to support 3-D rendering or animated screen displays). Although this phenomenon introduces a certain amount of disparity among Web user communities (along the lines of those who have certain plugins versus those who lack them), plugin technology promises to add significant new and useful capabilities to the overall Web environment. That's another reason why developers are pursuing this technology so avidly.

What's in Store for Your Web Pages?

Assuming that you've got a properly enabled browser, the answer to the question posed by the section heading is "Almost anything." Because plugins are usually available by download over the Internet and include their own installation programs, adding a plugin is as easy as

1. **Grabbing a file.**

2. **Unpacking the file's contents.**

3. **Running the proper installation program.**

This simple sequence of steps puts all kinds of interesting capabilities within your reach. Today, you can find about a dozen Netscape plugins and/or helper applications that support technologies that range from Adobe's Portable Document Format (PDF) and its Amber reader to Paper Software's Live 3D plugin for VRML. The list of available extension technologies includes all of the topics that we discuss in the next four chapters — namely, Shockwave for Director, VRML, Java, and a variety of document display engines.

For a list of Netscape plugins, visit the Netscape home page at

```
http://home.netscape.com
```

From there, select the `Netscape Search` icon from the image map at the bottom of the page and use *plugin* as your search term. You should find a variety of background and information documents on this subject including

```
http://www.netscape.com/comprod/products/navigator
              /version_2.0/plugins/plugin_download.html
```

At this URL, you find a list of all the plugins currently available for Netscape Navigator 2.0. (The list may change as Netscape introduces new versions of Navigator, so be sure to use the search engine to find the latest and greatest information.)

With the right set of plugins in place, you can use your browser to view fascinating multimedia animations, watch a variety of video formats, listen to high-fidelity audio, and more. One word of warning, however: The more complex or richer the data you seek to display, the bigger the underlying files typically are. If you're upping the ante on what you view, you'll be waiting longer for the results!

The Hottest Plugins...

A quick trip to the plugin list mentioned earlier shows you that we don't cover all plugins in this book. Instead, we choose four categories that have generated the most buzz (and have seen the most use until now). We cover these in detail in the next four chapters, and you can expect to learn more about:

- **Macromedia's Shockwave for Director:** A plugin that permits Director content to be delivered over the Web. Because Director is the tool of choice for game, CD-ROM, and interactive multimedia developers, the use of this plugin opens the Web up to a great deal of interesting content. Shockwave is an excellent tool for delivering new multimedia content; we cover this plugin in Chapter 15.

- **The Virtual Reality Modeling Language (VRML):** A full-fledged computer programming language designed for the creation and navigation of fully-realized three-dimensional graphical spaces called *virtual worlds*. Many pundits believe this kind of interface and data presentation technology represents a major step from current two-dimensional GUI interfaces to something much more intuitive and realistic. We cover VRML in Chapter 16.

- **Java:** An object-oriented programming language from Sun Microsystems. Java includes the capacity to run applications on a wide variety of computers from a single set of source code. Further, Java can deliver small programs, called *applets,* to Web users on demand. Users can execute these applets on their local workstations. Not only does Java deliver client-based program execution to Web users, it also provides a technique to extend browser functionality on the fly! Of the four examples we look at, this one has generated the most buzz; we cover Java in Chapter 17.

- **Text display engines:** These tools enable page designers to deliver full-blown documents via the Web; that is, they give the designers complete control over graphics, page layout, and typography. For delivery of high-quality materials for printing (or electronic viewing of the same information), many organizations find the use of text engines to be a useful augmentation to the more generic capabilities of HTML. We examine several text engines in Chapter 18.

In the upcoming chapters, we explain what's involved in using plugin technologies in your Web pages. We tell you how they work, where to get them, and how to incorporate them effectively in your Web sites.

The Perils of Incompatibility

Okay, so we sound like a broken record. But remember that not everyone in your audience is going to be able to appreciate the work you put into content that requires a plugin. That's why we suggest alternatives where possible; we describe site and page design techniques that permit you to educate your less fortunate users about the benefits of plugins and point them at the resources they could use to remedy their deficiencies (if they're so inclined and circumstances permit).

The most important thing to remember about the Web is that content rules. Where plugins are concerned, this rule has two profound implications:

- Provide multiple alternatives.

  Wherever possible, don't deliver critical content only in a plugin-dependent form. Having content with this dependency prevents those members of your audience who don't have the plugin from accessing your content — and the more important the content, the more important to deliver an alternate form.

✔ Provide ample warnings.

If your site includes plugin-dependent content, warn users on your home page and provide end-arounds on the pages that feature such content. The initial warning lets users know what to expect, and the end-arounds provide a graceful way for disadvantaged users to skip what they can't really view properly anyway.

Both techniques demonstrate a degree of concern for your entire user base. Providing alternatives and warnings shows the users that you care and provides them with pointers for dealing with plugin-dependent materials.

Designing for Extended Capability

Even those users who do have the right plugins won't always appreciate your enhanced content, unless you follow some basic rules of design and delivery. The following list gives our top four recommendations for including plugin-based content on your pages:

✔ **Small is beautiful:** Whether you're delivering audio, video, multimedia, or pancakes, bigger files take longer, and users hate to wait!

✔ **Give users a choice:** Don't force your users to download materials if they don't want to. When you have bigger files, giving the users control over whether they want to see them is increasingly important. Tell the users how big the files are and let them click a link if they want to download!

✔ **Use plugin content sparingly:** Animation, video, and other dynamic formats have a lot of appeal, especially for Web authors in search of excitement. Always ask yourself, "Is this material really necessary?" before using a plugin. When you're convinced (that the material is necessary), ask your beta testers, too. If the beta testers find the material questionable or useless, other users probably will, too.

✔ **The download alternative:** If you can find a way to let users download materials for display offline, give them that option. Users may not want to wait for the download for immediate viewing; offering a self-contained alternative reaches a broader audience and lets everyone keep surfing while the file downloads in the background.

If you follow these four basic rules, you get the most benefit from your plugin-based content. You may be tempted to stray from the rules because this stuff is so much fun, but remember that your main function is to deliver quality content to your audience!

Serving the Audience

In some cases, you can assume that your audience is homogeneous — like on an organizational intranet where policy dictates that everyone uses the same advanced browser. If you're offering Web pages in this environment, you can use plugin-based content with a bit more abandon than if you're serving the general public. But even then, the four principles mentioned in the preceding section still apply.

If you're dealing with the general public, you never know who's likely to visit your Web site. Because the primary goal of having a Web site is to communicate with all your visitors, you want to do as much as you can to avoid excluding anyone. If you keep this simple suggestion in mind, you can design your site to serve everyone with similar, if not identical, materials.

Trends in Web Extension Technology

As we mentioned at the beginning of this chapter, the dozen or so plugins currently available represent only the tip of a sizable iceberg. Our investigations have turned up at least another dozen planned plugins or plugins somewhere in the development process, for capabilities that range from database access, to local system and desktop management, to a variety of stunning visualization and idea-mapping tools.

Although we don't know exactly which plugins will see the light of day, we feel safe in saying that the number and capability of browser plugins are on the way up. As usual, your best source of information in this area is the Web itself: Stay tuned to your browser vendor's "What's New" and news pages so that you find out what's going on as new plugins are released.

While we explore more mature and exciting plugins in the upcoming chapters, remember that we've by no means seen it all. Plugin technology should keep the Web an exciting place to be for some time to come!

Chapter 15
A Shockwave in Full Motion!

• •

In This Chapter

▶ Defining Shockwave for Director

▶ Understanding Shockwave's underpinnings

▶ Installing and using Shockwave technology

▶ Configuring your Web server for Shockwave

▶ Using Shockwave content in your Web pages

▶ Designing effective "shocked" pages

▶ Finding the top Shockwave resources online

• •

*S*hockwave for Director is a new technology that's paving the way for the Web to become a truly interactive, multimedia-oriented arena for information exchange. Shockwave possesses the unprecedented capacity to convert a multimedia creation into an Internet-ready work without using a programming language. The implications of this feature are significant — the feature enables thousands of multimedia professionals to convert content, previously viewable only in CD-ROM format, into Internet-ready material. Shockwave can change the fundamental look and feel of the Web.

With Shockwave's capabilities, text-based and static Web documents can become dynamic multimedia works that incorporate any type of data. We want you to recognize that Shockwave is not a new authoring environment for the Internet, but instead a technology that enables you to convert existing multimedia titles into an Internet-accessible format (that is, ready for inclusion in your Web pages!). All in all, Shockwave's groundbreaking technology is appealing because it is accessible, impressive, Web-savvy, and, best of all, *free* (as long as you have a licensed copy of Macromedia Director, that is).

A Shockwave Overview

Shockwave for Director is not a monolith: it's actually a collection of capabilities, all of which must be present at one time or another, in order to make Director movies available over the Internet. In fact, there are three ingredients that are essential to creating and delivering Shockwave content:

✓ A working copy of Macromedia Director is necessary to create the content that will ultimately be transformed into its Shockwave (or "shocked") equivalent.

✓ The content developer must also obtain a copy of the Macromedia AfterBurner software, which transforms and compresses native Director movie files into another more compact form better-suited for Internet delivery.

✓ Users must have a Shockwave-enabled browser that is able to accommodate and play back Shockwave content. Currently, the only browser that meets these criteria is Netscape Navigator 2.0 once the Shockwave plugin is installed.

With these ingredients in place, authors can create Shockwave content, and users can appreciate their efforts.

Shockwave was developed by Macromedia, a cutting-edge multimedia company that is virtually unchallenged in the realm of digital arts and multimedia software tools. Macromedia's most important contribution to the multimedia field is Macromedia Director, which is considered to be the industry's preeminent software for authoring and animating multimedia. Not coincidentally, Shockwave supports only Director materials, which are used by over a quarter million multimedia professionals. Because such a large percentage of the multimedia industry already uses Director as a primary authoring tool, we believe that Shockwave's chances of success are excellent.

A few words about Macromedia Director

In the realm of authoring tools, Director is considered to be quite powerful. For example, Director is relatively platform-independent, which makes it pragmatic for the Internet's multiplatform demands. But please understand that Director is a large and complex program, which doesn't mean that learning Director is impossible, just that you may need years to fully appreciate all its capabilities. You can check out IDG Books' upcoming *Macromedia Director 5 For Dummies* for more information.

Director's creators based the program on a theater metaphor; its main components are a *Stage,* a *Cast,* and a *Score.* The Cast is where you store items for your project (the metaphorical actors, as it were, which could be anything from titles to animate for your credits, to graphical shapes or figures, or even sound files, that you could manipulate upon the stage), and the Score is used to control what Cast members do on the Stage. The Stage itself is, of course, the arena where the multimedia is played out for the audience, your viewers.

Macromedia developed Director with accessibility in mind, but this attribute doesn't prevent Director from offering excellent expandability. The two features that make Director impressively expandable are *Lingo*, its scripting language, and *Xobjects* — external, custom files that you can program to extend the program's built-in functionality.

Doing the Lingo limbo

Lingo is a scripting language that can be used in conjunction with Shockwave when you observe certain limitations (because Shockwave currently fails to support *linked media* — basically, multimedia files that embed calls to other multimedia files within themselves — it's illegal to use any of the many Lingo commands that create media linkages). You certainly can create multimedia Web content with Shockwave without ever using Lingo, but you should consider using Lingo if you want more complete control over your Shockwave content (or if you enjoy working with complex programming).

If you're already accustomed to working with Lingo before Shockwave hit the scene, be aware that certain Lingo commands were modified to work with Shockwave. Also, you may have to remove some Lingo commands from files that you'd like to convert to Shockwave (this is particularly true for those commands that interlink media files or resources, because Shockwave currently does not support linked media files).

Shockwave's bright future

To further ensure Shockwave's success, Macromedia has formed partnerships with some of the most pivotal companies in the computer industry including Netscape, Microsoft, Silicon Graphics, and NaviSoft. By agreeing to integrate Shockwave technology into their Web browsers, these companies have greatly increased Shockwave's chances of survival in the ephemeral Internet arena.

Macromedia's development of Shockwave brings dramatic new possibilities for high-powered multimedia to the Web. Before Shockwave technology was available, you needed to learn a programming language such as VRML or Java to create multimedia effects; however, Macromedia developed Shockwave specifically for individuals who are more interested in the creative end of multimedia than its programming aspect. The fact that Java requires its users to be familiar with an object-oriented syntax (such as C++) burdens it with an intense learning curve. Shockwave's learning curve is light by comparison, as is Director's.

Interestingly, Macromedia does not view Java as a technology that competes with Shockwave, but as a technology that compliments Shockwave's capabilities. Recognizing that Java's commendable system-level language can serve as a base for network-based applications and multimedia tools, Macromedia licensed Java and plans to integrate these two technologies. Future versions of Director and Authorware (another Macromedia multimedia authoring product that represents a usable subset of Director's capabilities) will feature Java applet playback.

In addition, Macromedia seeks to create a new *continuous publishing tool* by combining Shockwave and Java. This combination is intended for Web authors looking for high-bandwidth, cutting-edge multimedia (continuous publishing means that any changes to source materials are automatically propagated to consumers over the Internet). Shockwave may ultimately act as a front-end to Java-based, custom Internet applications.

Shockwave is an industry darling for another reason as well — Macromedia did not release Shockwave in an alpha or beta form, but instead, as a completely developed package. In addition, its developers actually delivered Shockwave on time. Although its growth as a product isn't yet complete — Macromedia is still working on extensions and enhancements — Shockwave hit the market in a relatively stable form and has enjoyed heavy use since its introduction in December 1995.

What you need to use Shockwave

Obviously, the first thing you need to run Shockwave is a computer. In addition to this key component, you need the following:

- Macromedia Director
- Afterburner
- A Web browser that supports the Shockwave plugin
- A Web server that delivers your multimedia content
- The necessary information to configure your Web server for Shockwave
- A working knowledge of HTML

Our prior discussion of Macromedia Director should help you understand the program's role; we discuss Afterburner and the intricacies of Web server configurations later in this chapter. Currently, the only Web browser capable of handling the Shockwave plugin is the 2.0(+) version of Netscape. However, we expect the compatible browser list to expand soon to include Microsoft Internet Explorer, NaviSoft NaviPress, and Silicon Graphics Web Force (and perhaps even others by the time you read this book).

Installing and Using Afterburner

Afterburner is one of Shockwave's three essential components (the other two are Director and the Shockwave plugin). Afterburner's role in the Shockwave continuum is to enable you to play, over the Internet, movies that you've created with Director. The feature works like this:

- ✔ Director saves documents in a format called a Film Strip.

- ✔ Afterburner takes the Film Strip files, denoted by a DIR suffix, and converts them into DCR files. During the conversion process, Afterburner analyzes the files and applies the compression technologies that are most efficient for compression.

- ✔ Through this process, Director files become ready to be embedded into HTML documents and, therefore, become playable at Shockwave-enabled Web sites. The DCR file extension always tells you that the file was converted with Afterburner.

Afterburner's *post-processor* technology can take a film strip created with Director and compress it significantly — the average file shrinks 60 percent. This compression doesn't affect the quality or the look of the film strip at all; the file becomes more manageable for transport over the Internet. A file that begins at 4MB can potentially be reduced to a transport size of 100K after conversion with Afterburner. Because Afterburner has the ability to apply compression schemes that are tailored to each element's specific media type, files compressed with Afterburner are sometimes smaller than the original GIF images that they may include!

Afterburner's compression technology is extremely beneficial for Internet users with 9.6 Kbps or 14.4 Kbps modems, because delivering high-quality compressed files is so much faster. This allows developers to build larger, more complex files, yet still share them even with modem-based users. Animation appears at around 8 Kbps for these users, so decreasing file size by at least half makes a tremendous difference. Ultimately, Afterburner's high-quality compression makes accessing a graphic-intensive Web site much more efficient and enjoyable.

At the present time, Afterburner can't compress audio files; therefore, you should keep audio materials relatively small (ideally, no more than 20 – 30 percent of a Director movie file's size). We expect Macromedia to license (soon) one of the several options coming available for audio compression (perhaps even by the time you read this), so this limitation shouldn't persist for too long.

Running Afterburner on a Macintosh

To run Afterburner on a Macintosh, you need to meet the following minimum system requirements:

- ✔ 2MB (or more) of free hard disk space
- ✔ Macintosh computer with 68030, 68040, or PPC processor
- ✔ 640 by 480 display with 256 colors
- ✔ 8MB (or more) RAM memory
- ✔ Macintosh OS System 7.5 or later

Installing Afterburner on a Macintosh

We show you the basic instructions for installing Afterburner on a Macintosh in the following list. Although new versions of Afterburner include new sets of instructions, this list still explains the installation process and demonstrates how easily you can install and use the software.

1. **Download the most recent version of Afterburner.**

   You can get the most recent version from

   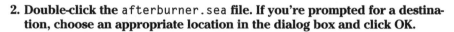

   ```
   http://www.macromedia.com.
   ```

2. **Double-click the** `afterburner.sea` **file. If you're prompted for a destination, choose an appropriate location in the dialog box and click OK.**

   The Afterburner file is uncompressed onto your hard drive.

3. **In the resulting folder you find the Afterburner drag-and-drop compressor and an** `Xtras` **subfolder.**

4. **To initiate compression, drag and drop any completed Director Film Strips onto the Afterburner icon.**

Running Afterburner for Windows

To run Afterburner on a Windows machine, you need to meet the following minimum system requirements:

- ✔ IBM-compatible PC
- ✔ Intel 80386 processor running at speed of 25 MHz or greater (80486/66 or better recommended)
- ✔ VGA or better graphics resolution

- 8MB RAM
- 5MB free disk space
- Microsoft Windows 3.1 or later
- Microsoft DOS 6.0 or later

Installing Afterburner on a Windows machine

We show you the basic instructions for installing Afterburner on a PC running Microsoft Windows in the following list. Although new versions of Afterburner include new sets of instructions, this list still explains the installation process and demonstrates how easily you can install and use the software.

1. **Download the most recent version of the Afterburner software.**

   You can get the most recent version from

   `http://www.macromedia.com`

2. **Move** `AFTBURN.EXE` **from the File Manager into an empty directory on your hard drive. Double-click** `AFTBURN.EXE`.

   The file unZIPs and deposits several files, including `SETUP.EXE`, in the current directory.

3. **Double-click** `SETUP.EXE` **to install Afterburner.**

   This launches a standard Windows Setup program which will ask for install directory and deal with previous versions, if any are present. Then, the program will copy all the necessary files and make necessary environment changes to make it work.

4. **Drag completed Director Film Strips onto the Afterburner icon for compression.**

Implementing Afterburner

The following are the four basic steps to using Afterburner:

1. **Create a movie using Macromedia Director.**

2. **Test the movie on your local computer system and on any other platforms available.**

3. **Use Afterburner to post-process the movie title.**

   That is, create a compressed file by dragging and dropping your movie file's icon onto the Afterburner icon. This creates a file with the DCR extension alongside the original one with the DIR extension.

4. **Put the compressed file on an HTTP server that has been properly configured to deal with Shockwave materials.**

When you process a Director file with Afterburner, the resulting DCR file is said to be *burned*. After you burn a file, remember that you can't use it as a regular Director Film Strip.

If you're creating any kind of content with Macromedia Director, always save a copy of your work as a film strip (a DIR file). The DIR format is the only format that can be reopened and reedited after its initial creation. If you want to leave the door open for future changes, always make sure that you keep a film strip version of your work available — on your main system, on removable media, or on a floppy disk.

Configuring Your Web Server for Shockwave

In order to share your brilliant Shockwave creations with the Internet community, you must post those creations on a Web server. You won't find many servers today that aren't capable of being configured to handle Shockwave files — operating systems such as UNIX, Windows NT, MacOS, or OS/2, all have the ability to handle Shockwave. Many variables affect the process of posting your Shockwave content to a Web server (such as connection type, server/client software, and server hardware), and as a result, giving exact directions for Web server configuration is difficult. Our goal in this section is to give you a general overview of the important Web server considerations that you must address to make a server "Shockwave-enabled."

The type of Web server you select depends on your specific needs. Obviously, having the slickest, speediest connectivity is ideal, but the price of such technology can often be prohibitive (and many people find that issues of cost are the most crucial). If you have the time, the money, and the technical knowledge to house your Web sites on your own server, you need to decide what kind of connection can be most effective. If having your own Web server isn't feasible, you can pay an *Internet Service Provider* (ISP) to post your content on its server. For a more in-depth discussion of Web server issues, see Chapter 2 in this book.

Shockwave configuration for specific Web servers

The process of configuring your Web server for Shockwave consists primarily of telling the server what needs to be done with Shockwave content and then placing that content onto the server. Because HTTP (Hypertext Transfer Protocol) has an intelligent design and can incorporate new types of media, configuring a server to handle Shockwave is not an enormously difficult task.

Although configuration specifics vary among Web servers, you need to remember that you use three pieces of fundamental data when configuring Shockwave for all HTTP servers:

- ✔ MIME type: application
- ✔ Sub Type: x-director
- ✔ Extensions: DCR, DIR, DXR

Shockwave and MIME

MIME (Multipurpose Internet Mail Extensions) formats are a key ingredient for transmission of Web documents between client and server and vice-versa. As an HTTP-based standard, MIME is responsible for facilitating Web server configuration for new types of media. All HTTP-based media handling and identification are founded on this standard, and through MIME information, requesting software (like an e-mail package or, more likely, a Web browser in this case) knows how to process incoming data.

All HTML image files and documents on the Web are identified by their MIME types. When you are on the Web and you request a document from a server, the server responds by sending both the pages contents and the MIME header, which contains information about the data type for each element that composes the page. This header is called *Content-type*. In order to properly display the page, your Web browser must receive the MIME information telling it that the page is an HTML document. If you request an image file from a server, the MIME header similarly identifies the data as JPEGs or GIFs.

Just as HTML files need unique Content-type headers (which look like this: `Content-type: text/html`), and image files need header values (`Content-type: image/gif`), Shockwave files need their own MIME type in order to function on the Internet. The Shockwave MIME type is as follows:

```
Content-type: application/x-director
```

In the preceding header, application is the document's type, and x-director is the primary subtype. The x- before director indicates that the data type is external and requires the help of another application for successful delivery. In this case, the helper application is the Shockwave plugin.

After your Shockwave files have their proper MIME types assigned, make sure that the server knows how to recognize Shockwave content and provide the correct MIME type when a browser requests that information. Although too many types of Web servers exist for us to give configuration examples for them all, the examples of specific server configurations in the following sections give you an idea of the general structure and activities involved.

Shockwave configuration for NCSA httpd

The NCSA's UNIX Web server system, *httpd,* accounts for a large portion of the servers on the Web and provides a good example of how to configure your server. NCSA httpd identifies MIME file types by mapping between MIME types and file extensions. This method enables files sporting an html extension to be identified as text/html while setting the correct Content-type header values. This mapping takes place in a file named mime.types, which lives in the conf directory, found under the server's root directory.

Each line in this file begins with a type/subtype pair and has a comma-delineated list of extensions after spaces or a tab. In HTML, the entry would appear like this:

```
text/html html htm
```

In order to add support for a Shockwave movie, simply add this line to the mime.types file:

```
application/x-director dcr dir dxr
```

DIR is the extension for Director Film Strip files, DCR is the extension for Shockwave-compressed Director files, and DXR isn't currently used by Shockwave — but may eventually be used for adjusting file content. This configuration isn't case-sensitive, so files with extensions like *dcr, DcR, DCR,* and other variations are all equally legal.

Shockwave configuration for tenants

If you have *tenant* status on a server that's running NCSA httpd (tenant status means that you pay for space on the server, but don't control the machine), we doubt that you have direct access to the `mime.types` file. However, even if you don't have administrator access, you can still add support for Shockwave through one of two approaches.

✔ The first method for adding Shockwave support is by asking your server's system administrator to make the changes outlined in the preceding section.

✔ The second method is more hands-on but is only viable with the NCSA server and its offspring (such as Apache): Go to the directory that houses your Shockwave files and add support for the MIME type directly through an access control file. Check to see whether a file of this type already exists (or ask your system administrator). The filename varies from server type to server type, but the default name for NCSA httpd and its derivatives is `.htaccess`.

No matter what kind of naming convention your server uses, you must create an access control file in the directory where your Shockwave DCR files reside. In addition, you must add directives to allow you to map from file suffixes to the correct MIME type, and set the necessary privileges to make these settings world-readable. With default naming in a UNIX system, you can create an access control file by typing

```
cat>.htaccess
```

followed by these directives for httpd:

```
AddType application/x-director dcr
AddType application/x-director dir
AddType application/x-director dxr
```

Then type ^D (press Ctrl+D) to end input into the file. After creating this file, you also need to set the file's permissions to let the server software read the `.htaccess` file (or its equivalent on other Web servers) whenever the server looks for one of your Shockwave files in the directory. You can perform this action in UNIX with the following command line:

```
chmod 644 .htaccess
```

Shockwave configuration for W3C httpd

W3C httpd, formerly called CERN httpd, is the most frequently used UNIX server after NCSA httpd. W3C httpd puts all server directives in a single configuration file, which takes the default path /etc/httpd.conf. Add the following lines to incorporate Shockwave support:

```
AddType .dcr application/x-director 8bit
AddType .dxr application/x-director 8bit
AddType .dir application/x-director 8bit
```

The W3C httpd syntax differs somewhat from NCSA httpd and can only process one extension per line. In addition, the syntax specifies the encoding type (8bit) and reverses the order of listing the MIME type and file extension. You must use the keyword AddType at the beginning of the line to identify the MIME directive, because the W3C httpd configuration file includes every kind of server directive allowed.

Because all the system configuration information is in one place in this file, the chance that you get to make any changes is even more unlikely, unless you're the system administrator. Therefore, be prepared to share this configuration information with your WebMaster or the system administrator charged with control over your Web server.

Shockwave configuration for Quarterdeck's WebSTAR

WebSTAR offers a CGI-based remote administration package that performs some necessary configuration functions on your behalf. The most complete method of performing administrative functions in WebSTAR is to employ the adminstration package, called WebSTAR Admin, that comes with WebSTAR. WebSTAR Admin enables you to use a graphical interface for most common server administration tasks. The Macintosh version of WebSTAR Admin uses a complex Macintosh interface that controls servers running on your machine or on other machines accessible through AppleTalk.

Do the following to configure the Macintosh version of WebSTAR for Shockwave:

1. **Launch the WebSTAR Admin application.**

2. **Select your server in the dialog box that appears.**

   Your server has to be running locally or must be accessible via the network in order for this to work.

3. **Choose Configure⇨Suffix Mapping from the menu.**

   The Suffix Mapping dialog box appears.

4. **Fill out the Suffix Mapping dialog box.**

   This is where you create the collection of file associations between extensions and file type, just as in the MIME extension files discussed earlier in the chapter.

5. **Click the Add button and then click the Update button to complete the configuration settings.**

6. **Repeat these steps for the** DIR **and** DXR **suffixes.**

   Repeat steps 4 and 5 to add all of the file extensions and application associations you think you'll need.

Today, a version of WebSTAR is available for Windows NT. Because of interface differences, the menu names and sequence of instructions are a little different, but otherwise, both versions behave in much the same way.

Shockwave configuration for Netscape Netsite

Netscape's Netsite is the most popular commercially available Web server. Netscape currently offers versions of Netsite for Windows NT and UNIX platforms. The mime.type file for Netsite is similar to the one found on the NCSA server, but its syntax is somewhat different. Netsite's entry for Shockwave support is the following:

```
type=application/x-director exts=dcr,dir,dxr
```

Although Netsite's administration package comes with a Web interface for server configuration, you can't add support for new MIME types through that interface. You have to edit the mime.type file the old-fashioned way, using an ASCII text editor and your own common sense.

Placing Shockwave Files on Your Server

After you've configured your server to deal with Shockwave, the next step is to upload your Web site's Shockwave content. If your Web server is connected to the development machines through your LAN, you can post your content just as you would copy any other normal file over the network.

If, however, your machines are linked to a UNIX server through a PPP or ISDN connection, uploading your content onto your Web server is slightly more complicated. You need to use FTP (File Transfer Protocol) or a similar program to collect and upload your files. FTP is available in a variety of freeware, shareware, and commercial versions, so getting a copy of FTP shouldn't be too problematic.

However, the process of uploading your Shockwave files might be rather slow if you don't have a speedy connection to your server. You may want to construct an archive of the content you've created, compress it, and then upload it during the hours you're normally sleeping. Another idea is to break your archive into smaller parts before you upload it. This piecemeal upload allows you to transfer files in manageable chunks, and if anything goes wrong while you're transferring the data, you won't have to resend the entire collection.

If you transfer files across platforms — for example, from Macintosh or PC to UNIX — keep in mind that not all compression standards work on all platforms. Utilities to create and handle *tar* and *Z* formats are available for Macintosh, UNIX, and Windows platforms, so they're a good overall choice. No matter what compression technique you choose, you must have all the software you need on both sending and receiving sides to ensure that you can work with your files before and after you've transferred them.

Using Shockwave Materials in Your Web Pages

Before you can deliver your Shockwave masterpieces to any users, you'll have to embed your Shockwave files within valid HTML code. You can accomplish this embedding through a number of approaches, which we cover for you now.

Netscape has introduced yet another proprietary HTML tag to support Director movies, as well as QuickTime movies and VRML worlds. The presence of this tag, <EMBED>, tells Netscape Navigator that the material associated with the tag requires a plugin. The embedded file's extension and the MIME type to which the file corresponds determine the type of plugin that Netscape (or any other plugin enabled Web browser) loads.

Because the options that each plugin supports can vary, the syntax for the <EMBED> tag varies according to the actual plugin that's referenced, and depends on the plugin's particular content. However, the standard <EMBED> tag for Shockwave Director movies looks like this:

```
<EMBED SRC="path/filename.ext" WIDTH="n" HEIGHT="n"
    TEXTFOCUS="focus">
```

The URL for this example is specified through the SRC option; this URL may be local, remote, relative, or absolute. The file's extension is usually DCR, to indicate that the file has been *burned* with Afterburner compression, although the Shockwave plugin loads if the browser notices DIR or DXR file extensions as well. The WIDTH and HEIGHT options determine the dimensions (in pixels) for your project's display window.

Remember to verify that the Stage size you've chosen for your Director movie corresponds to the desired height and width, because if it finds a discrepancy, Netscape may position the image in a potentially inartistic fashion.

The final attribute, TEXTFOCUS, is optional. This attribute controls Shockwave Director content by indicating how the Director plugin should react to keyboard input from the user. This attribute has three possible values: onMouse, the default value, indicates that the plugin may accept keyboard input after the user clicks at any place in the movie. The second value, onStart, enables the plugin to accept input from the keyboard as soon as the movie begins to play. Using the final value, never, ensures that the plugin cheerfully ignores any keyboard activity.

The <EMBED> tag behaves similarly to the <IMG> tag in terms of static graphic placement on a Web page, especially when used in conjunction with Netscape's <IMG> attribute extensions, WIDTH and HEIGHT. As you can the <IMG> tag, you can place the <EMBED> tag inside other HTML markup such as table tags (<TABLE>...<TR><TD>content here</TD></TR></TABLE>). If your project requires precise positioning control, you may want to think about wrapping your movie inside a table, where you have greater control over its position and layout.

Internet Do's and Don'ts for Designing Shockwave Materials

The following suggestions are intended to help you use Shockwave as effectively as possible. Because Shockwave technology is progressing quickly, not all of these recommendations may be necessary in the future. To stay current on this technology, be sure to visit the Macromedia Web site at:

```
http://www.macromedia.com
```

Many of these tips relate to reducing file size. If you remember that the majority of Internet users cruise cyperspace at the helm of a 14.4 Kbps modem, it should be easy to understand why they aren't interested in spending the time it takes to download gargantuan movies. The amount of download time a user is willing to invest is often determined by the value of the file — most people are not as eager to download a semi-superfluous animated banner as they are to download something more personally rewarding, such as a game. This leads us to two specific size-related warnings:

- ✔ If you must include large files, warn users how big they are, and attach them via hyperlinks to your pages so they can choose whether or not to download those files.

- ✔ Whether files are large or small, make triply sure that they're important to your content, and that your beta testers agree that they add to the value of your site.

Failure to heed either warning will lead to audience defections to sites more sensitive to their users' needs — and limitations!

DO:

- ✔ DO make your images as small as possible. Big is not better when you're talking about download time.

- ✔ DO keep your target audience in mind. Think of what entices and intrigues the people who may view your Shockwave movies.

- ✔ DO rescale your images after you've imported them into Director. By doing so, you can make them appear larger or smaller while saving valuable file space.

- ✔ DO test your work on multiple machines, especially on a Macintosh if you're on a PC, and vice-versa.

- ✔ DO avoid shading your artwork. Flat colors are more effective, because the computer treats each gradation as a separate color, and this treatment slows the ease and speed of a download.

- ✔ DO create backgrounds with tiling (this tip is for color Macintosh users only, because creating backgrounds with tiling requires QuickDraw). Tiling is an effective, undemanding way to imbue your movies with custom backgrounds.

- ✔ DO use Ink Effects within Director. Employing this technique can save significant amounts of memory in the Cast (Director's "storage area" for elements that you use in your movies) while providing you access to many complex looks.

✔ DO use the Text tool in Director instead of rendering or saving bitmapped text. Using the program's Text tool makes your Shockwave movie sizes more manageable because Director won't save each pixel for the text image (as with bitmapped text); Director saves only the information that defines the text.

✔ DO think carefully about the fonts you use. Computers substitute other fonts when the selected one isn't available. If you're concerned about achieving specific effects through fonts, choose standard ones.

✔ DO lower sampling rates to reduce audio file sizes. The sampling rate that gives the best sound is 22.050 kHz. Although going below this sampling rate is technically possible, dropping to 11.025 kHz causes sound distortion on Windows machines.

✔ DO indicate to your users whenever they must activate the Shockwave movies you include on your pages. The most effective way to tell your users about a movie is through an attention-grabbing graphic or notice that appears in their browser early, while your page is loading.

✔ DO position your content within the boundaries of an average Web browser window — playing your movies on the invisible edge of a browser window is useless. Test your pages with a 14- or 15-inch monitor.

✔ DO think about including a top-level *Welcome* that displays only text and graphics. It should warn users about special content — like Shockwave — and inform them about file sizes and potential download delays. Users with slower modems appreciate information about file sizes and the type of content you offer.

DON'T:

✔ DON'T think of Shockwave as a general-purpose programming language — it isn't. Coupled with Director, Shockwave gives you great animation and interactivity possibilities, but having these features doesn't mean that Shockwave has the breadth of a general-purpose programming language such as Java or VRML.

✔ DON'T forget to allot enough space for sound files. Because Afterburner can't compress audio files, they occupy the same amount of space in a burned file (a 40 kilobyte sound file adds 40 kilobytes to the final size of your Shockwave movie). Good audio can really enhance your Shockwave movie; so we recommend you devote 20 to 30 percent of your project's size to audio.

✔ DON'T let your Shockwave movies overpower your page's content. Yes, Shockwave *is* exciting and fun to play with, but the movies at your site shouldn't overwhelm your viewers or be superfluous or irrelevant.

✔ DON'T make your total page sizes too enormous. You don't need to get carried away and put twelve Shockwave movies on a single page. Although the chosen few with T3 connections might stay around long enough to be impressed, the time commitment for loading such a page may repel many other users.

✔ DON'T forget that some users out there are still using non-Shockwave-enabled browsers. Check out your page to see how it looks if it loads minus your fantastic movies. Think about providing alternate ways to view your work (for example, a download page with equivalent Director Projector files that a user can view on any Macintosh or Windows PC).

The bottom line for creating Shockwave presentations is to make effective use of the technology. Be sure that the movies add to your pages, without imposing unnecessary delays on your users or penalizing those users who don't have high-speed Internet access.

Some Great Shockwave Resources

The ultimate Shockwave resource online is, not surprisingly, the Macromedia Web site, located at www.macromedia.com. This site features an extensive list of complementary services and products for Shockwave and also contains answers to specific questions about using the application.

Within the Macromedia Web site, you find additional pages that contain interesting materials; the following is a list of particularly compelling or informative pages:

✔ The Epicenter and Vanguard galleries pages:

```
http://www.macromedia.com/Tools/Shockwave/Vanguard/
          epicenter.html
```

✔ Macromedia's QuickMarks page:

```
http://www.macromedia.com/quickmarks.html
```

✔ Macromedia's Movie Lab page:

```
http://www.macromedia.com/Tools/Shockwave/sdc/Dev/
          index2.htm
```

When you're designing content for the Web, keeping your knowledge fresh about how people view your site is a good idea. The following site supplies current information about how people are navigating through the Web:

```
http://emporium.turnpike.net/J/jc/public_html/stats.html
```

One of the premier sites for investigating Shockwave technology is the one created by the Apple Austin Training group at

```
http://selfpaced.info.apple.com/.
```

The Apple Austin Training group site uses Shockwave in a practical manner, which sets the site apart from many other Shockwave-crazed Web pages.

Another quality Web page featuring Shockwave is DreamLight Multimedia's page at

```
http://www.dreamlight.com/dreamlt/gallery/pumpkin.htm.
```

These next two are also interesting sites for following Shockwave links:

```
http://www.teleport.com/~arcana/shockwave/
http://silver.nbnet.nb.ca:8080/
```

For detailed information on Shockwave, refer to *The 60-Minute Guide to Shockwave for Director*, by William H. Hurley III, W. Preston Gregg, and Sebastian Hassinger, IDG Books Worldwide, Inc., 1996.

One of the things that Macromedia most hopes to see in Shockwave's future is the use of linked media over the Internet (which Shockwave's first release doesn't support). Macromedia also hopes that future versions of Shockwave will be able to support QuickTime (this support is currently unavailable due to the lack of support for linked media). The development of support for QuickTime would be especially nice because Netscape 2.0 has a QuickTime plugin. Perhaps future versions of Shockwave may also decipher the mysterious DCR extension.

Chapter 16

Virtual Worlds with VRML

● ●

In This Chapter

▶ Defining VRML

▶ Delving into VRML's fascinating past

▶ Creating thrilling VRML content

▶ Configuring your Web server for VRML

▶ Using VRML-enabled Web browsers

▶ Designing VRML

▶ Finding the top VRML resources online

● ●

A VRML Overview

VRML (pronounced *vermul*) is the acronym for Virtual Reality Modeling Language. VRML is an object-oriented programming language that renders scenes modeled in 3-D graphics. HTML (HyperText Markup Language) challenges our ideas of how text is represented — VRML does the same for space. By bringing the possibility of 3-D representation to the Web, VRML literally adds a whole new dimension to the Web experience and promotes a more interactive future.

VRML's debut on the Internet scene pushes the Web toward a more realistic appearance by allowing information to be structured with everyday symbols. Instead of telling your users to follow the third link of a home page and the fourth link after that, VRML's advent enables you to give instructions such as, "Go into the site's living room and open the red door on your left."

VRML was developed not only to push the Web toward a more human-oriented *synesthetic* structure, but also to give normal, nonprogramming folks the chance to create virtual spaces without having to learn a complex programming language. Supporters hope that VRML becomes a standard language for interactive Web documents. Some pundits argue, however, that VRML hasn't lived up to its hype and assert that VRML is not as accessible as it claims to be because a powerful computer is nearly mandatory to run VRML successfully. We see merits to both sides of this discussion and cover issues related to this debate in the following sections.

VRML's brilliant history

When it officially hit the market in April 1995, VRML had barely been in the works for a year. In May 1994, Mark Pesce, a developer interested in bringing a virtual reality interface to the Web, attended the first World Wide Web conference in Geneva, Switzerland, and presented a paper entitled "Cyberspace." That presentation set VRML's creation in motion.

Pesce, whose views about making the Web a more sensual, human place mark him as a sort of *cyber-visionary,* was working with another developer, Tony Parisi, to manufacture a language capable of rendering 3-D on the Web. By the time the first WWW conference rolled around, the pair had succeeded in creating an interface called *Labyrinth* (`http://www.well.com/user/caferace/labyrinth.gif`) that did just that.

Their presentation was a tremendous success and turned other industry professionals on to the power of the 3-D space metaphor for the Web. The presentation also led to an agreement that developers should adopt a single, unified programming language — leading to the creation of VRML. In fact, numerous conference participants elected to lend their contributions to the project and put together a working group on the spot!

In the spirit of true Net collaboration, Pesce set up a mailing list as a forum to support VRML's initial development. You can find the archives of the discussions that took place there at

`http://vrml.wired.com/`

and this group's goals at

`http://www.gold.net/oneday/render/index.html`

The response to the topic was fast and furious, and the forum witnessed a great deal of excited debate over what an initial VRML requirements document should contain.

Pesce moderated the discussion generated via the mailing list personally. He was convinced that VRML would be most effective if it were not a totally new language, but rather a modification of established programming metaphors that people were already comfortable with. The group decided that an ideal language would be accessible, analogous to HTML, and capable of expressing everything that a professional 3-D designer's heart could desire.

Mailing list members debated the merits of several existing languages, each with its obligatory acronym, including the following:

- Object-Oriented Graphics Language (OOGL) for the World Wide Web
- Cyberspace Description Format (CDF)
- Manchester Scene Description Language (MSDL)
- A File Format for the Interchange of Virtual Worlds (ffivw)
- Multitasking Extensible Messaging Environment (MEME)

You can find the drafts and/or overviews of these languages online if you're interested in seeing what didn't translate into *virtual success*:

- Object-Oriented Graphics Language for the World Wide Web:

```
http://www.geom.umn.edu/software/geomview/docs
            ooglman.html
```

- Cyberspace Description Format:

```
http://vrml.wired.com/proposals/cdf/cdf.html
```

- Manchester Scene Description Language:

```
ftp://ftp.mcc.ac.uk/pub/cgu/MSDL
```

- A File Format for the Interchange of Virtual Worlds:

```
http://vrml.wired.com/proposals.ffivw.html
```

- Multitasking Extensible Messaging Environment:

```
http://vrml.wired.com/proposals.meme.html
```

And the winner was . . .

The language ultimately selected for VRML development was Open Inventor, an object-oriented 3-D tool kit from Silicon Graphics, Inc. (SGI). The set of programming libraries for Open Inventor enables users to control objects like trackballs, cubes, polygons, materials, cameras, and text.

Open Inventor emerged as the preferred choice for several reasons. One important reason was its ASCII-based language that enables Open Inventor to work seamlessly with HTML. Other winning points included its professional-level quality, its expandability, and its previous debugging through commercial testing and implementation.

Pesce requested that the language be placed in the public domain, which was a heady demand. SGI eventually complied even though this action means that the company no longer *owns* Open Inventor in the traditional sense. This generous action allows anyone to build upon Open Inventor without having to worry about paying royalties or being sued.

Tony Parisi and Gavin Bell, one of Open Inventor's chief creators, presented VRML 1.0 at the second World Wide Web conference in November 1994. The presentation was a successful, standing-room-only event that alerted much of the industry to VRML's exciting potential. The ball kept rolling — QvLib, a *quick* VRML parser, appeared within a few months, and the WebSpace and WorldView browsers came along soon thereafter. News of VRML hit the mainstream media in April 1995, and the hype (aided by SGI's $2.2 billion marketing engine) was thick enough to make *Newsweek* give VRML its own cover.

VRML and HTML: What's the difference?

In case you're wondering about the exact differences between VRML and HTML, the following few pointers may help you out:

✔ HTML deals with text and was designed as a common text delivery system for the Web. VRML was designed for a parallel function (a common delivery system for the Web), but in terms of visual and graphic presentations instead of primarily textual data.

✔ VRML and HTML work similarly, except that a VRML document represents a 3-D backdrop, while HTML can only display text and graphics in 2-D.

✔ VRML and HTML are definitely neither mutually exclusive nor in competition — in fact, you could say that HTML space *lives* within the grander confines of VRML space.

✔ Although HTML is relatively easy to do by hand, doing VRML by hand is much harder. The reason for this difference in difficulty is pretty clear when you think about it: HTML uses text to make a textual document, but VRML uses text and numbers to produce graphical objects. Consequently, using authoring tools has always been the norm for VRML (but not for HTML).

So, what's VRML good for?

VRML's potential still outstrips its current accomplishments. By early 1996, VRML's primary claim to fame was its ability to portray 3-D spaces and objects. Yet, the future potential for interactivity, complex navigation, and other types of advanced functionality is emerging. The following are just a few examples of the possibilities VRML could enable:

✔ **Medical and scientific research:** Check out NCSA's server (`ftp://ftp.ncsa.uiuc.edu`) for examples of scientific research displayed in VRML format.

By using VRML, researchers can implement many experiments that can't be visualized or performed in real life. The possibilities presented by VRML as a teaching tool are very exciting: Students who can't deal with the idea of dissecting a real animal appreciate the option of cutting into VRML's 3-D models (instead of the real thing).

✔ **Online conferencing:** The possibility of virtual meetings with clients who are thousands of miles away has excited businesses for years. Telecommunication companies are developing *virtual phone booths* that can use VRML for public networking.

✔ **Virtual shopping:** As roads become more crowded and many people find their lives becoming that way, too, the idea of virtual shopping becomes ever more attractive. VRML applications could enable you to examine objects from all angles and, at the same time, provide a wealth of instantly accessible product information.

✔ **Real estate and architecture:** VRML's future in the areas of real estate and architecture is great, because building on land (or land covered by concrete) is a lot more expensive than building on-screen. With VRML, builders can get a look and a feel for their proposed edifices. They can implement custom-building choices quickly and painlessly, and they have lots of room for experimentation and adjustment.

✔ **Entertainment:** The possibilities are endless in the entertainment realm. VR (virtual reality) games and interactive movies are two areas under intense development, and online gambling is already making a killing on the Web. Check out the Virtual Vegas site at

```
http://www.virtualvegas.com/
```

✔ Many die-hard MOOers and MUCKers (and other denizens of virtual realities habituated by acronymophiles) find that VRML versions of fantasy land are a little cheesy right now, but these lands are quickly becoming more believable. *Virtual communities,* such as the one at `http://www.cybertown.com/`, make interesting use of VRML as well.

VRML's characteristics as a language

In technical terms, VRML is an object-oriented programming language that provides methods to group three-dimensional graphical objects. VRML's objects are called *nodes*. These nodes, which can contain practically any type of information, can have offspring, called *children,* which represent modifications to the parent node. Nodes may also be reused through *instancing,* which allows new nodes to inherit an original node's attributes and is ideal because it enables programmers to reuse code fragments efficiently. It also means that display is faster, because another instance of a node simply repositions its descriptive data elsewhere on the display, without needing to create an additional copy in memory.

Unlike most object-oriented languages, VRML's individual components aren't nonlinear or randomly organized. Instead, its source file resides in a *scene graph,* a hierarchical file that indicates the order in which nodes must be parsed. Every entry in a VRML scene graph is classified as a node object. Because scene graphs give programmers control over the order of a scene's rendering, they also imbue VRML with ideal precision and control.

Nodes

Nodes are divided into three classes in VRML 1.0: shape, property, and group. The only way that an object can appear in a scene is through the use of a shape node. On the other hand, property nodes control lighting and material and determine how an object is drawn within a scene. Group nodes are responsible for organizing and enveloping nodes through *containment.* When a node has children or other objects (such as surfaces, textures, light sources, and so on) contained within its parent node, the node is classified as a group node.

The following is a basic definition statement for a node:

```
[DEF objectname] objecttype { [fields] [children]}
```

Only the type declaration and the curly braces are required for the definition to work — including the fields, name, and children is optional. Use DEF only if you're specifying a name for a node.

Nodes have a great flexibility in their design specifications, and likewise, node characteristics are rather loose. A node's properties include the following:

- **Fields:** Fields are variables with parameters, and they describe a node's characteristics (such as color, size, or rotation). A node may contain zero or more fields.

- **Object type:** VRML 1.0 has 36 types of nodes; these nodes can be either actual shapes or influences that affect the way the shapes are drawn (such as an angle rotation or a light source).

- **Name:** Naming is optional because a node can work without a name. However, naming makes a node more flexible and powerful, because knowing a node's name enables you to manipulate the object at will.

As is recommended, you can use one of two nodes in VRML as the foundation for VRML worlds that work with a variety of platforms. LOD, the level-of-detail node, is one, and the other is WWWInline.

These two nodes work well together, especially because they facilitate *lazy loading* (also called *on-demand loading*), which lets the VRML browser decide at what level of detail to load objects and when to load them. When you're loading an object *lazily,* you see an empty box with the object's dimensions before you see the object. Lazy loading is a nice feature because the user can start navigating through a VRML world before all objects are completely loaded — which can be a big deal if you're dealing with hundreds of objects.

Field types

Rendering objects in 3-D requires a variety of mathematical operations that, in turn, demands many data types. VRML's 16 field types are selected from the 42 types inventoried by Open Inventor and fall into two categories: single-value and multiple-value.

Single-value field types can be images, Booleans, vectors, or numbers (integers or real). You can discern single-value fields by their *SF* prefix — multiple-value fields are trickily prefixed by *MF*. Single-value field types can actually consist of an arbitrary number of individual parameters (which makes them seem rather undeserving of their name). But the classification comes from the fact that, unlike multiple-value field types, single-value field types can describe or act upon only a single object or property. Through the use of field types, you have the power to describe practically any kind of 3-D object.

Creating VRML Content

In his book, *VRML — Browsing and Building Cyberspace,* (New Riders Publishing, 1995) VRML guru Mark Pesce gives his list of seven steps to creating effective VRML. We cover these seven steps in the seven sections that follow.

Conception

Pesce identifies *conception* as the step that may take the longest, especially if you're attempting to create worlds that aren't grounded in reality as we know it. This is the step that gives you the room to imagine, to fantasize, to consider artistic ideas.

Planning

After the dreamtime of the conception stage has ended, you can move into the more realistic stage of *planning*. At this point, you should create a physical plan of your project and consider questions of finance, time, and execution. If you're creating a project at the professional level, this stage is the time to investigate applications, such as Autodesk 3-D Studio or Walkthrough Pro, that could ameliorate your work.

Design

How you *design* a project is highly dependent on how you conceive it. Do you see your creation as architecture, art, public space, or something else? If you're modeling a building, you'd probably create a series of surfaces to represent walls, ceilings, and floors, with cutouts for windows and doors. You'd add further objects to represent fixtures, furniture, carpets, and other elements within the spaces you define. In other words, your approach is to recreate the characteristics of a building or room and to populate that room with representative objects that a user would expect to find within that space.

Sampling

Sampling is the process by which you convert real-world objects into cyberspace equivalents. You can handle this process by creating texture maps from actual drawings and wrapping them around idealized or artificial 3-D objects, or you can make 3-D scans of real objects and use the scans as your framework.

Construction

Finally — *construction* is the stage where you get to start building something. In this stage, the focus is on tools, and we hope, by this point, that you know which tools are best for your project.

Make sure that the tools you've selected are appropriate by running a test with a simple model. If you experience conversion problems, note the problems and attempt to find *workarounds*. Because many VRML tools are in early or beta versions, the construction step is often messy — but hey, that's part of the game!

Testing

You can never *test* too much, especially because VRML is such a new technology and people approach your creation from many different platforms and viewpoints. Try as many different browsers and platforms as you can: Start locally and then expand across the Web.

Publishing

Ah, the final glory! When you have your creation in optimum shape, the time is right to *publish* or perish. The initial publication is a test in itself because you find out how people viewing at different connection speeds respond.

Your job as a Web developer isn't over just because you've published your pages — now you get to respond to people's feedback and make adjustments accordingly.

Creation tools for your VRML world

VRML creation tools come in two basic types. Object creation tools, such as Caligari trueSpace, are the first type. They give you a sculpture studio of sorts in which you can design arbitrary objects. The second type of tools, space creation tools, such as Virtual Home Space Builder, are ideal if you're interested in the construction and layout of VRML spaces. These two types of construction tools are far from competitors — in fact, creating an object (with an object creation tool) and then putting it in a space (with a space creation tool) is often useful.

Virtual Home Space Builder

One of the easiest ways to create VRML content is with an entry-level VRML authoring tool, such as Virtual Home Space Builder (VHSB) from Paragraph International. As the name indicates, VHSB was created to enable you to make your own space, which you do by clicking and dragging. The VHSB interface is colorful and easy to use; these features makes VHSB ideal for first-time VRML users with programming anxiety.

If you have questions about any interface feature of VHSB, holding the mouse over the feature delivers a pop-up blurb of explanatory text. Although VHSB is limited in the 3-D items that it offers and handles, the tradeoff between simplicity and ease of use is worthwhile (especially if you're experimenting or exploring, instead of doing professional-quality work).

One of VHSB's nicest features is its Walk View window, which gives a you a real-time rendering of the world you're creating. In the Walk View window, you get a fairly accurate idea of how your world looks to a VRML browser. The Walk View window has nifty buttons, such as a magnifying glass, which (surprisingly) magnifies your work, and crosshairs, which shift an image's perspective to head-on.

You can download a free beta version of VHSB at

```
http://www.paragraph.com/vhsb/freestuff/
```

Virtus Walkthrough Pro

Walkthrough Pro is another authoring tool that provides an interface for building 3-D worlds. James Cameron, director of the movie *The Abyss,* found this tool to be very useful when he was making his movie — he used Walkthrough Pro (actually, an earlier version) to view movie sets in cyberspace before he spent the time and money to build them.

Walkthrough Pro, which works on both Macintosh and Windows platforms, is a more complex and professional tool than VHSB and, consequently, has a steeper learning curve. With Walkthrough Pro, you can create QuickTime movies and Windows AVI movies. You can also make texture-mapped scenes by using textures from the hundreds of choices found in its library or any textures that are scanned in or imported from clip art libraries. Walkthrough Pro has a great selection of furniture with which you can decorate your space, as shown in Figure 16-1.

Installing and Using VRML-Enabled Browsers

In early 1996, you could find almost a dozen Web browsers compatible with a Macintosh (if the system had a 68000-based processor or better) or a Windows-based PC (Windows 95, NT, or 3.1). Unfortunately for most people, the best VRML browsers available were designed for UNIX platforms, particularly for SGI machines. However, the current progress in browser product development should change this situation.

In general, VRML browsers serve as helper applications for standard HTML browsers. A few stand-alone browsers don't require assistance from other applications to display VRML files. But if you're going to look at anything other

Figure 16-1:
An example of furniture objects from the Walkthrough Pro selection.

than VRML content, you want to use such browsers as helper applications, because those same browsers pick up only the VRML portions of Web documents when you use them alone. With Netscape's 2.0 release, VRML plugins also became big news. WIRL (short for Web Interactive Reality Layer) is regarded as one of the best and brightest of the plugins. Through the inline extensions architecture of WIRL, Web users experience fully interactive virtual reality on the Web, as shown in Figure 16-2. That's why we think the plugin approach is the right way to go: They're available when you need them and get out of the way when you don't!

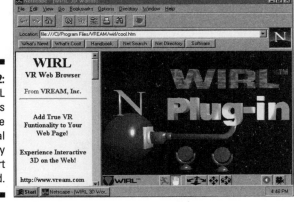

Figure 16-2:
The WIRL plugin offers some of the best virtual reality support around.

Check the list of Web sites at the end of this chapter for links to sites that discuss other new VRML plugins.

Stand-Alone Browsers for PCs

The following entries discuss some of the stand-alone VRML browsers available for PC users.

WorldView from InterVista

WorldView is the only browser that currently works with every one of the Windows platforms. Hypothetically, WorldView should work with a 14.4 modem and a standard PC, because part of its goal is to provide a browser for people running only modest hardware. The minimum processor that you can use is a 50 MHz 80486, loaded with at least 8MB of RAM. (Having 12MB of RAM is more realistic if you use Windows 3.1 or 3.11; and if you use Windows 95, you need at least 16MB to achieve success.) For more information, visit the following URL:

```
http://www.intervista.com/
```

WebSpace for Windows

WebSpace for Windows comes from the fertile breeding ground of SGI, the creators of the Open Inventor rendering language. If you're interested in running WebSpace, you need at least the following hardware:

- A 66 MHz 80486 processor (although a 90 MHz Pentium is preferable)
- 8MB to 16MB RAM
- A 256-color SVGA display system (or better, preferably)

For more information on WebSpace for Windows, visit the following URL:

```
http://webspace.sgi.com/
```

Helper Applications for Standard HTML Browsers

The following browsers work only as helper applications within standard HTML browsers, such as Netscape Navigator or Mosaic. Whenever possible, make sure that you're running the most recent version of the browser as well as the most recent version of the corresponding plugin.

VRWeb for Windows

VRWeb for Windows was developed by three power players: NCSA (the National Center for Supercomputing Applications), the Gopher development team from the University of Minnesota, and IICM (the Institute for Information Processing and Computer-Supported New Media). Because all these organizations are non-profit, this browser is available as freeware at the following location:

```
http://www.iicm.tu-graz.ac.at/Cvrweb
```

Configuring Your X Browser for VRML

Your first priority in the VRML arena is to make sure that your Web browser knows what to do with VRML files when they arrive. To do so, modify the Preferences settings (or whatever configuration utility it uses; if you're in doubt check out its Help utility with the term "MIME" or "MIME types" — it should tell you what you have to do to add support for a new MIME type) so that your browser is able to handle a new MIME type (in this case, x-world/x-vrml). In addition, let your browser know what default extension to use for VRML files. WRL is the extension most commonly used for VRML files, but VRML is used as the extension on occasion.

Instead of changing the defaults stored in your home directory, changing the browser's defaults is a better idea. (In Netscape, you make this change by altering the .usr/local/lib/netscape/.mime.types file, not by changing your personal ~/.mime.types file.)

To get the MIME types file configured properly after you've successfully integrated your VRML helper application, do the following:

✔ Edit your .mime.types file by adding the following line:

```
x-world/x-vrml       wrl
```

✔ Edit your .mailcap by adding the following line:

```
x-world/x-vrml;      /install_directory/vrweb    %s;
```

If these changes don't work, you may need to talk to your system administrator to make system-wide VRML-enabling changes, especially if you don't have *root privileges* (this is a level of file access that lets you change basic system definitions; for security and control reasons, it's not a common end-user privilege).

Configuring Your Windows Browser for VRML

To successfully run a browser such as VRWeb on your PC, you need

✔ At least a 66 MHz 80486 processor
✔ A minimum of 12MB RAM

✔ A 256-color SVGA display, video card, and driver

✔ Win32s — if you're using Windows 3.1; it is downloadable at

`ftp://ftp.outer.net/pub/mswindows/win32s.zip`

If you want to use Mosaic or Netscape to integrate with your browser, you must define a new MIME type within your Web browser. If you're doing this with VRWeb and Netscape, try the following:

1. **Choose Options⇨Preferences.**

2. **Select Helper Application from the pull-down menu.**

3. **Click the New Type button.**

4. **In the Configure New MIME Type dialog box, enter** x-world **for MIME type and** x-vrml **for MIME subtype.**

5. **Enter** WRL **for the Extensions field.**

6. **Click Launch Application in the Action selection box.**

7. **Select pathToVRWeb\vrw_win.exe for the application.**

8. **Close the dialog box and continue on with your work.**

Configuring Your Macintosh Browser for VRML

The first functional VRML browser for the Mac is called Whurlwind. Whurlwind is a helper application, not a stand-alone VRML browser; and you can configure Mosaic or Netscape to integrate with Whurlwind, as described in the preceding section. We think that you may want to take this one suggestion: Push your memory allocation up to 4,000K while you're using Whurlwind (because of its heavy graphical requirements).

The only VRML browser in general release for 68K Macintoshes is Virtus Voyager. This browser also offers a version for Power Macintoshes (which is much faster than Whurlwind) and a version for Windows 95.

ExpressVR is the first Macintosh VRML plugin for Netscape 2.0. You can find ExpressVR at:

`http://www.pond.com/~ribit/ExpressVR`

Configuring Your Web Server for VRML

Adding VRML to existing Web sites is easy because the addition doesn't require any change in the way servers operate. The essential thing to tell your Web server is that VRML documents take the extension. WRL and a MIME type of x-world/x-vrml. After it has this information, your server can detect VRML documents and let your browser know whenever a VRML document is on its way.

To prepare your Web server for your VRML masterpiece, analyzing the VRML files you've created so that you can give the administrator an idea of what's in store is crucial. If you've created a gargantuan world, the administrator may need to distribute your world across several servers or reorganize it to decrease the burden on any individual server.

Related VRML object files should be identified (usually because they occur in the same scene or are "nearby" — as in "the other side of a doorway") and placed on different hosts if possible. This helps to ensure optimum performance. If the processing load associated with delivering large numbers of objects isn't spread out, server loads may be inconsistent. In its most extreme case, this can sometimes cause a *cascade effect* — where a call to one object results in an immediate call to another object, and so on — that could overload one of your servers and cause all your users to lose touch with your virtual reality!

Because *object inlining* use — that is, where objects are rendered within the framework of a particular scene graph — is heavy in VRML, we recommend that you use professional VRML publishing tools to conduct an analysis of any document set. Then you can use the results of this analysis to give the site administrator any publishing recommendations that are offered by these tools. Even though some VRML publishing tools are still in development, you can also adapt Web server analysis tools (available on the Web) for use in VRML publishing.

Design Do's and Don'ts for VRML

Do

✔ DO make your graphics as small as possible — 100–200K is ideal. VRML's precision is sometimes counterproductive because the language can describe an object's mathematical qualities so accurately that the object is impossible to handle.

✔ DO keep your target audience in mind. Think of what may entice and intrigue the people who view your VRML site.

✔ DO check the following site for cutting-edge information about VRML and troubleshooting help:

```
http://www.tcp.ca/gsb/VRML/vrml-news.htm
```

✔ DO use GZIP. The VRML community has consensually agreed that you should compress VRML 1.0 files by using the GZIP algorithm. Using GZIP can reduce your file sizes by up to 80 percent — and GZIP is free! Try it, you'll like it.

✔ DO view your work on multiple platforms; for example, view your work on a Mac if you use a PC and vice versa.

✔ DO think about how your page may look to non-VRML users. Then check the page with a non-VRML-capable browser to see!

✔ DO test your page more than once! Try the following for more information on testing:

```
http://www-dsed.llnl.gov/documents/tests/vrml.html
```

✔ DO use LOD (level-of-detail) or WWWInline as the foundation for creating VRML worlds. Using one of these two nodes increases your odds of making sure that your creation works with a variety of platforms.

Don't

✔ DON'T think seriously about coding your VRML creation by hand. Coding VRML by hand is much, much harder than coding HTML by hand. Coding VRML manually is advisable only as a learning experience — or if you've got hundreds of hours to spend.

✔ DON'T forget to test your page from all angles. Make sure that the page loads every time and that it runs at an acceptable speed (even with less-than-killer equipment). Failure to test can mean site failure!

The Top Ten VRML Resources

Check out these resources for more information on VRML.

- *VRML — Browsing and Building Cyberspace,* by Mark Pesce, New Riders Publishing, 1995. This interesting book covers not only the history and scope of VRML, but also Pesce's visionary ideas about VRML and the Web.

- *60 Minute Guide to VRML,* by Sebastian Hassinger and Mike Erwin, IDG Books Worldwide, Inc., 1995. This work is divided into three sections that each take about an hour to read. In addition to being accessible, the guide includes a good list of VRML links.

- The VRML FAQ:

  ```
  http://www.oki.com/vrml/VRML_FAQ.html
  ```

- WAXWeb is regarded as one of the most successful and interesting VRML forays. This site's highly interactive page includes VRML objects and scenes, as well as HTML-formatted text, video images, and a MOO (MUD, Object-Oriented). Its creator, David Blair, sees WAX as a post-modern, *meta-fiction* site that pushes the boundaries of linear narrative.

  ```
  http://bug.village.virginia.edu/
  ```

- Arc Gallery, one of the most developed VRML sites, lets you wander around a furnished, multilevel building:

  ```
  http://vrml.arc.org/gallery95/index2.html
  ```

- Multimedia Gulch is San Francisco's foray into virtualhood:

  ```
  http://www.hyperion.com/planet9/vrsoma.htm
  ```

- The VRML software repository:

  ```
  http://www.sdsc.edu/SDSC/Partners/vrml/
         repos_software.html
  ```

- The following site contains good links, information on VRML, and specific system software:

  ```
  http://www.well.com/www/caferace/vrml.html
  ```

✔ If you're having trouble keeping up with the latest and greatest in VRML software and documentation, this cutting-edge VRML library can help out:

```
http://cedar.cic.net/~rtilmann/mm/vrml.htm
```

✔ The following is another hip VRML site:

```
http://www.sony.co.jp/TechnoGarage/VRML_sample.html
```

Chapter 17

Jumpin' with the Java Jive!

● ●

In This Chapter

▶ Looking at a Java Overview

▶ Creating content with Java and JavaScript

▶ Installing and using Java-enabled browsers

▶ Java-fying your Web pages

▶ Programming do's and don'ts in Java

▶ Finding top Java resources online

● ●

*I*n the words of Sun Microsystems, Inc., Java's developer, Java is "a simple, object-oriented, distributed, interpreted, robust, secure, architecture-neutral, portable, high-performance, multithreaded, and dynamic language."

Those of you who aren't walking dictionaries can read on for an explanation of the product that those terms describe. In it's own perverse way, this statement is incredibly accurate, although completely overcome by jargon!

A Java Overview

"Way cool. Stratospheric. White hot. Sizzling."

The Web community describes Java with these words. What's so great about this object-oriented language with the funny name? Its multimedia capacities, for one thing. Many people see Java as the most exciting avenue for bringing interactivity to the Web.

The unique features that Java offers, in combination with browsers such as Netscape and Mosaic, bring to the Web a form of real-time multimedia interactivity that has previously been available only from CD-ROMs. Instead of just following hyperlinks, you get information in the form of moving pictures, audio, and video when you surf the Net with a Java-friendly browser. If you're looking for hotel information online, Java lets you walk through rooms on-screen to decide which one piques your fancy. You can plan stock or other financial portfolios with completely live data. And online shopping could change dramatically.

Java's specific features include the following:

- ✔ Cartoon-style animation
- ✔ Music that plays in the background while the user loads the Web page
- ✔ Inline sounds that play in real time while the user loads the Web page
- ✔ Real-time video
- ✔ Multiplayer interactive games

We've heard Java's potential impact compared to the advent of the spreadsheet for PCs or the development of Mosaic, the first Web browser. Java's future is regarded brightly in areas as diverse as electronic commerce, software distribution, and gaming. And as a bonus, Java is one of the most secure and virus-resistant languages ever created.

What makes Java different?

Java's applets (small Java programs that you can include in HTML documents) are Java's most radical and brilliant creation. Applets greet you at Java-enhanced sites. Instead of viewing a table of contents at a Web site, you may encounter an applet showing a talking head that smiles, laughs, blinks its eyes, and tells you what the site contains. As long as you're using a browser that incorporates Java, having the specific software to run an applet isn't necessary — the applet is automatically picked up by the Java environment in your browser and run from your desktop.

This last feature is what sets Java apart from other languages. With a standard Web browser, you can't use a new content type (such as a special image format or game protocol) until the browser is updated to include that new type.

In stark contrast, Java compatibility is a feature that any browser is able to implement. Java sends the browser the requested content and the program needed to view it. Another bonus for you Web authors is that you no longer have to wait until a browser implements support for certain file types to use these types on your Web sites — instead, you can write the code yourself (in Java) and send your file to any user who requests it!

One of Java's most stellar features is its platform independence. A Java application can run on any platform and requires only that a single copy of the master version of that application be stored in a controlled location (on a Web server somewhere on the Internet). This process is truly revolutionary because it transforms the Net into a software distribution system and changes your Web browser into a platform capable of running an infinite variety of software.

Therefore, when you request a Java application over the Internet, the application runs on your local machine — without having to consider what type of hardware or software you use. This omniplatform capacity is a boon for system administrators as well because they need to worry about revising and controlling access to only one copy of the code. A Java-capable user can take advantage of applets from anywhere and everywhere.

Yet even among developers, Java's real power hasn't been fully realized. Professional developers can exploit Java's thundering power by creating tool kits that sit on top of raw Java. In turn, these tool kits should enable users to create powerful applications that are customized to their needs.

About those terms . . .

Now that we helped you recover from the original Java gibberish that we quoted in the first sentence of this chapter — and (we hope) have you just a little excited about the potential — we want to explain *those terms*. Remember, we said that Java is "a simple, object-oriented, distributed, interpreted, robust, secure, architecture-neutral, portable, high-performance, multithreaded, and dynamic language." In the interests of clarity, the following sections tell you what that *really* means.

Simple

Programmers call Java both *simple* and *elegant*. Java syntax eliminates the unnecessary and esoteric elements that plagued C++. Many people think that Java is going to replace C++ as the programming language of choice.

Object-oriented

Every Java class is directly or indirectly descended from the Object class — the grandfather of all Java's classes. (*Class* refers to a method for defining a set of related objects that can inherit or share certain characteristics.) Likewise, everything in Java is required to be an object, unlike in C++. Only the most basic, primitive operations and data types (such as `int`, `while`, `for`, and so on) in Java operate at the subobject level. In Java-speak, every class *extends* directly or indirectly from the Object class and, thereby, makes Java *object-oriented*.

Distributed

From its inception, developers designed Java to be run over a network (to be distributed). Consequently, Java features well-developed, inherent HTTP and TCP/IP capabilities. COBRA-style Interface Definition Language bindings may soon grace Java; in programmer-speak, this means that Java programs may soon have the ability to invoke remote procedures over a network from server-based objects. And in something closer to English, this means that Java programs may be able to request remote services across the network, with some reasonable expectation that the requests will be fulfilled.

Interpreted

Java's unique, hard-core compiler converts any Java source code into a machine-independent format. This advanced conversion enables the source to run on any computer that is equipped with the Java Virtual Machine (a special platform-specific program that implements a Java run-time system, allowing the machine to interpret Java code).

The *bytecodes,* which result from the conversion, are the key to Java's impressive application portability. Although this portability is a groundbreaking feature, Java isn't completely different from other programming languages. That is, programmers who are well-versed in the Java source language write the application code and save it in files with a JAVA extension. These files, or programs, are then translated into a format that enables your computer to run them.

Robust

Java is considered *robust* because its design completely eliminates pointer manipulation from the language (pointers are names or locations of specific memory addresses and are often used by programmers to play games with memory allocation and data access, both of which can be fraught with peril). Eliminating this element removes a big source of run-time errors. Although pointer abstraction in languages such as C and C++ can benefit seasoned programmers, it can cause memory leaks and other obscure run-time errors.

Another of Java's winning features is its garbage collection mechanism that remembers to deallocate memory in Java. After an object is *thrown away* in the Java run-time environment (that is, after it's been used and is no longer needed in a program), other objects can reclaim and reuse the memory vacated by the thrown-away object.

Secure

Java is *secure* because it is a client-side technology. Java programs are, in effect, downloaded from the host machine to your client machine by using conventional Web server transports (such as HTTP). Java has safety precautions in place to prevent viruses from reaching your machine — before running any applet, the Java run-time system looks at incoming Java bytecodes to make sure that the program code is safe. Any code that is not safe is unequivocally rejected. Although this feature may be the safest thing going, that very distinction can attract renegades who revel in code-cracking, so don't count on 100 percent safety. Still, Java's security should only improve as the language matures.

Architecture-neutral and portable

Java's byte-ordering issues (that is, the order in which it interprets bytes in memory when handling numbers and values) are largely negligible. Also, its bytecodes operate independently of any underlying architecture (the *architecture-neutral* feature means that it doesn't depend on hardware support to represent data). In addition, Java's character sets are Unicode-based for internationally *portable* applications. By the time you read this, the portable Java run-time system may be available on a variety of systems, including Windows 95 and Windows NT, Solaris, HP/UX, SunOS 4.1.3, AIX, OS/2, and Digital UNIX (OSF/1). This means that the same program can run on all these operating systems (and their associated hardware) without requiring any modification!

High performance

To call Java a *high-performance* language may be slightly premature, because Java code seems to run 20-30 times slower for CPU-intensive programs. The promise of high performance is definitely apparent, though. Sun Microsystems, Inc. is committed to making Java's on-the-fly performance rival that of native C or C++ applications. This situation may occur once Java's current compiler, which resembles a more conventional C or C++ compiler, is converted to a just-in-time class compiler. The converted compiler will be able to provide more dynamic run-time support for Java's unique abilities.

Multithreaded

Multithreaded means that Java can run multiple subtasks (the threads) within the context of a single large application. Multithreading usually ameliorates interactive performance. Java is capable of creating threads and is inherently multithreaded; that is, Java has certain threads (such as the garbage collection system for reallocating memory) that run in low-priority mode.

Java borrowed the idea of the synchronized keyword from Mesa programming language and Xerox's Cedar environment. When code is wrapped with the synchronized keyword, the objects and methods it contains may only be accessed by one object at a time. In other words, use of the synchronized keyword makes any associated code single-threaded only, rather than inherently multi-threaded (the normal Java default).

Dynamic

Java lets you patch applications *dynamically*, so (unlike patching in C++) you have to worry much less about recompilation. Because releasing a perfect piece of software is rare, making adjustments to your application at some point is practically inevitable. Java makes these adjustments much easier by deferring lots of its linkage manipulation until run-time, which basically eliminates C++'s superclass problems.

That's it for the gibberish, but aren't you glad we told you all about Java? If you can simply appreciate the incredible thought and effort that's gone into Java's design and development, we've succeeded in delivering the right message!

Java's history: from seedling to coffee bean

Java came out of the fertile breeding grounds of Sun Microsystems, Inc. The growing process began when a disgruntled employee, Patrick Naughton, told Sun's chief Scott McNealy that he was leaving Sun to go to NeXT Computer, Inc., because NeXT was doing more interesting work. McNealy asked Naughton to tell him (McNealy) what he (Naughton) thought was wrong with Sun before leaving.

The list of suggestions that Naughton created was well-received by Sun executives, who gave him, along with some select coworkers, carte blanche to pursue new research projects. The team code-named themselves *Green* and set to work on developing the fundaments of what would eventually become Java. They initially thought the key to success lay in the area of consumer electronics (such as interactive TV) — finally in 1994, after a series of disappointments, they realized that the Web was Java's ideal medium.

In the early days, the development team's metaphors were more organic than caffeinated: Not only was the team named *Green* — but the language that emerged into Java was named *Oak* (because James Gosling, its creator, gazed upon an oak tree from his office). But by 1995, Oak was renamed *Java*, and Naughton had written Java's interpreter for a Web browser called *HotJava*.

In May of the same year, Sun formally announced Java and HotJava at the SunWorld '95 exposition. Netscape, always interested in cutting-edge technology, simultaneously announced its intention to license Java for use in its version 2.0 browser. Netscape was Java's first commercial client. The buzz was thick from this time on, because Java's potential to turn the Web on its ear (and garner lots of profit) was obvious. Sun agreed to make Java and HotJava available free of charge, banking on the idea of making money by licensing the programs for commercial use.

Licensees must pass conformance tests in order to license Java and receive branding from Sun Microsystems, Inc. The purpose of this testing is to ensure that applets work on all branded products. Current Java license owners (besides Netscape) include Macromedia, Inc., Spyglass, Sybase, Symantec, Mitsubishi Electronics, IBM, Microsoft, and Adobe.

Even with such illustrious licensees, it's still early to tell whether Sun will ever make loads of money from Java (although Java's reputation has already increased the price of Sun stock). One thing is sure — Sun's plan to make Java an essential programming language and a crucial part of the Web has already worked.

The 1995 release of JavaScript, a more accessible Java language that nonprogrammers can use, also increases Java's market power. Microsoft's postponement of the release of Internet Studio in February 1996 gives Java even more time to become ubiquitous before Microsoft tries to capture the market on such technology. (Internet Studio was formerly named *Blackbird* and is basically a browser that was first predicted to rival HotJava, but now is supposed to revolutionize Web content creation and management.)

This site contains a timeline of Java's evolution:

`http://ils.unc.edu/blaze/java/javahist.html`

Java's learning curve

As far as developers are concerned, Java's learning curve is minimal because its syntax is so close to that of C++. However, for mere mortals uninitiated into the complex wonders of C or C++, Java is a complicated — and largely unnecessary — language to learn.

Unlike HTML, Java wasn't designed to be particularly accessible, and you don't really need to learn Java just to write for the Web. Writing in Java can be compared to the more complicated and professional realm of creating CGI (Common Gateway Interface) programs. The *lite* version of Java, called *JavaScript,* is much more viable than Java for most HTML authors to learn and work with. Sun Microsystems, Inc. has also voiced its intentions to develop tool kits for nonprogrammers.

So, the bottom line is: Nonprogrammers don't need to worry about learning Java to enjoy its benefits. The only thing you need to experience Java's full-bodied flavor is a Java-enabled Web browser (such as a recent version of Netscape or Internet Explorer) that lets you install a Java plugin, which delivers Java's run-time interpreter. For those of you who are interested in programming in Java or JavaScript, read on for the exciting details.

Java versus C++ — the differences

Java features the following:

- ✓ **Single inheritance:** Keeps object relationships simple and easy to follow
- ✓ **Garbage collection:** Reclaims available memory and lets Java applications run more efficiently
- ✓ **Native multithreading:** Lets Java applications "divide and conquer" processing tasks, which also improves efficiency

C++ features these elements:

- ✓ **A preprocessor:** Lets programmers work with useful abstractions, without building them directly into the language
- ✓ **Operator overloading:** Lets programmers play all kinds of tricks with variables and memory; while risky, this technique can provide substantial power when properly applied
- ✓ **Header files:** Lets programmers invoke standard collections of type definitions, variables, and library elements
- ✓ **Pointers:** Lets subroutines and modules move addresses around, rather than values, which can speed up program behavior
- ✓ **Multiple inheritance:** Lets programmers combine aspects of existing objects at will; while often confusing, it's also incredibly powerful

Creating Java and JavaScript Content

For nonprogrammers, creating Java content isn't nearly as easy as creating Web page content with HTML. But if Java's seductive programming power is too appealing for this information to daunt your interest, we suggest that you do some research before plunging into programming.

The following URL takes you to the Java Message Board, where you can ask questions and read about other people's experiences with the language:

```
http://porthos.phoenixat.com/~warreng/WWWBoard/wwwboard.html
```

Sun Microystems, Inc., has a site that features helpful Java tutorials, and covers topics such as writing Java programs, writing applets, creating a user interface, and much more:

```
http://java.sun.com:80/tutorial/index.html
```

Another excellent way to learn Java is to look at Java source code wherever you can. Study and mimic examples of Java that you find on the Web — imitation is not only the highest form of flattery, but also a great way to learn.

Unfortunately, Java source isn't as easy to come by as HTML: You can't simply hit a View Source button in your browser and instantly immerse yourself in Java code. (That's because applets move as bytecodes across the Internet, not as source code.) To look at Java source code, you need to find the Java-related newsgroups (like comp.lang.java) and mailing lists, or surf the Web and grab all the source code you can find. But don't despair — you can find plenty of Java source code out there!

About Java programming . . .

You can use any word processing program or editor to create and edit a Java program, as long as the tool you use can save files in ASCII format. Just remember: All Java programs must be saved in a file ending with the *java* extension.

Before you run your Java program, you must compile it with the Java compiler, usually a program named *javac*. The compiler is responsible for translating Java source code into Java *bytecodes,* an intermediate form of code that's been converted from a set of Java language statements to a set of machine instructions.

The bytecode doesn't go the final step of adopting a machine language that corresponds to a specific operating system and computer — the Java run-time environment fills in that step. The process for completing this final step is Java's key to platform independence and the reason that we call Java both *interpreted* and *compiled*. After you've compiled your program, though, you're ready to roll. If you encounter any problems with compilation or interpretation of Java code, the following site's troubleshooting tips should quiet your woes:

```
http://sunsite.unc.edu/javafaq/
```

Say "Hello World" with Java: creating a Java program

Starting programming tutorials with the simple "Hello World" program has been customary since Kernighan and Ritchie released their first edition of *The C Programming Language* (Prentice-Hall, 1978). This program, which prints the string Hello World to the screen, doesn't teach a great deal of programming but does demonstrate the mechanics of writing code and constructing a simple program.

Before you start, make a directory or folder called JAVAHTML and create a subdirectory or subfolder called CLASSES within that directory. (Calling the first directory JAVAHTML is not actually required, but you do need to call the subdirectory CLASSES.)

The code that we show next is the "Hello World" application written in Java. To run the application, type the following lines into a text file and save the file with the name HelloWorld.java in the JAVAHTML directory.

```
class HelloWorld {
public static void main (String args[]) {
System.out.println("Hello World!");
}
}
```

Compile this program by typing javac HelloWorld.java at the command prompt (make sure that you're in the JAVAHTML directory).

If, for some reason, this program doesn't work, check out the following trouble-shooting tips:

- ✔ Did you include the semicolon (;) after System.out.println("Hello World!")?
- ✔ Did you remember the closing bracket?
- ✔ Did you type everything exactly as it appears in the preceding code lines? Precise capitalization is essential because Java is case-sensitive.

The compiler places the executable output in a file named HelloWorld.class in the JAVAHTML directory after the program is successfully compiled. At this point, you can run the program simply by typing java HelloWorld at the command prompt. The program (hypothetically) responds by printing Hello World! on the screen.

Programming with JavaScript

JavaScript isn't the same as Java, although the two are closely related. Created as a joint venture between Netscape and Sun, JavaScript has been monikered as *Java-lite* (it was called *Mocha* during development — getting tired of the coffee metaphors yet? Keep reading).

We describe JavaScript as a compact, object-based scripting language used to develop client and server applications. What can it do for you? Well, JavaScript provides a faster and more accessible means (than does Java) to incorporate applets and small programs into your Web site. JavaScript is frequently regarded as Java's decaf version, which isn't wholly accurate, because JavaScript addresses a different market niche.

Dynamically typed languages (which permit type definitions to be added at will) that are less complex and more compact than Java, such as dBASE and HyperTalk, are considered to be JavaScript's predecessors. They, like JavaScript, appeal to a wider audience than does a highly specialized language like Java. Their accessibility can be attributed to certain qualities: easier syntax; specialized, built-in functionality; and minimal requirements for object creation and use.

JavaScript was explicitly developed for use in the context of Netscape 2.0, where it provides a solution for client-side APIs (Application Program Interfaces). With this client-side API, JavaScript addresses the nuisances of static Web text. When JavaScript statements are embedded in a Netscape HTML page, they have the beneficial capacity to recognize and react to mouse clicks, page navigation, and <FORM> input. Although it lacks Java's strong type-checking and static typing mechanisms, JavaScript still supports the majority of Java's basic control flow constructs and expression syntax.

When you're working with JavaScript, you don't have to use (or know anything about) classes. Instead, you acquire finished script components from a JavaScript resource (perhaps from a commercial product, or an online collection of such materials) that expose high-level properties (like *color* or *visible*) susceptible to scripting controls. This allows you to set these properties to achieve whatever effects you desire in your Web document. JavaScript may offer the next best thing to writing code, and for many Web authors, its capabilities make the difference between including advanced functionality in their pages and being left out!

Differences between Java and JavaScript

JavaScripts may run more slowly than Java applets. This difference in speed happens because JavaScript interprets each line separately, while Java applets' code is immediately executable by the Java run-time environment within the browser. JavaScript doesn't possess all the object-oriented features that Java has; in JavaScript, you can define objects but not object classes.

JavaScript also lacks Java's object inheritance. Neither of these omissions is too significant for the average JavaScript user, because the shorter scripts that are typically created with JavaScript don't generally have the same reuse requirements that objects in Java may have. In general, this means that JavaScript writers must content themselves with such predefined objects and attributes as are available. And they miss the richness and flexibility that full-blown Java provides, especially when it comes to recasting or tweaking objects for added functionality. But since JavaScript has been created to reduce complexity and speed development, anyone who shares these concerns will be better served by working with Java directly, rather than by using JavaScript.

Because developers created JavaScript specifically to allow HTML writers to support different HTML tags and to enable elements to interact with each other, input from one HTML form can influence HTML information inside another HTML page. In addition, JavaScript may change the text of the HTML page where it resides. By contrast, authentic Java applets don't usually interact with HTML or change the text on a Web page. Instead, Java applets limit themselves to a specific region of a page that's reserved for their exclusive use (much like a separate display frame).

Also, JavaScript can quickly deliver interactive Web forms more efficiently than can Java. JavaScript enables you to handle error-checking with built-in, event-handling mechanisms that are conveniently based upon user interaction with the Web form.

The following lists should help to elucidate some key differences between Java and JavaScript. The first list describes Java characteristics:

- Java code is compiled on a server before it's executed on the client.
- Java applets are distinct from HTML.
- Java has strong typing requirements, which means that the program code must declare variable data types.
- Java applets consist of object classes with inheritance.
- Java has static binding, which means that its object references must exist when the Java code is compiled.

The following list describes JavaScript characteristics:

- ✔ JavaScript is interpreted, not compiled, by the client.
- ✔ JavaScript code is both integrated and embedded in HTML.
- ✔ JavaScript has loose typing, which means that the JavaScript code need not declare variable data types.
- ✔ Although JavaScript code uses built-in objects, it doesn't have classes or complete object-orientation.
- ✔ JavaScript has dynamic binding, which means that its object references are checked at run time.

Viewing source code is a good way to figure out how to use JavaScript, just as this same tactic is useful when you're trying to learn Java. The following is an example of JavaScript code:

```
<HTML>
<HEAD>
<TITLE>My First JavaScript Page</TITLE>
<SCRIPT LANGUAGE="Javascript">

<!-
document.write("This text should appear before the body
 of the HTML page.<P>");
// ->

</SCRIPT>
</HEAD>
<BODY>
<H3> Check out my first JavaScript Web page! </H3>
</BODY>
</HTML>
```

Finding and Using Java-enabled Browsers

You need several components to use Java:

- ✔ A Web browser that can run Java applets — HotJava, Netscape 2.0 or later, or Internet Explorer 2.0 or later
- ✔ A Java compiler that turns Java source code into bytecodes
- ✔ A Java interpreter to run Java programs

✔ A text editor, preferably a programming-oriented tool, such as BBEdit or Brief

✔ A suitable operating system (Windows 95 or Windows NT, Mac/OS 7.5 or better, many flavors of UNIX)

The following components are nice to have for your Java adventure, but they're not crucial:

✔ A Java debugger

✔ A Java class browser

✔ A Java-capable visual development environment

✔ Java documentation, either online information, or any of the many books now available on this subject

You can find elements of these components, along with detailed instructions for their use, at the Sun Microsystems, Inc., page:

```
http://java.sun.com/
```

Before Java's technology emerged, the Web was confined to static pages filled with only images and text. However, now that Java's on the scene, you not only have the same features as a CD-ROM — animation, multimedia, and instant interactivity — but when you're plugged into a network and you're using Java, you also have live data, communication, and instant updates. Java, working in tandem with the Web, is a heady idea for anyone who realizes the full possibilities of the technology.

To get the full impact of souped-up Java pages, HotJava is still an ideal browser. Despite the incorporation of Java into other Web browsers, you can do other things with HotJava (such as viewing applets written in Alpha3) that you can't do with other browsers.

This flexibility shouldn't be too surprising, because HotJava, like Java, was developed at Sun Microsystems, Inc. In early 1996, HotJava wasn't available for Macintosh or Windows 3.1 computers, but Sun keeps promising that this situation may change any day. However, the Roaster software from Natural Intelligence can run most Java applets on a Macintosh. You can find Roaster at this URL:

```
http://www.natural.com/
```

HotJava is available for many other types of machines, especially for computers at the high-powered end of the market. You can download HotJava at Sun's site:

```
http://sunsite.unc.edu/java/
```

After you download, you see that HotJava runs pretty much like any other Web browser. Its interface is similar: HotJava has buttons, a toolbar, a hotlist, and a history list. Unlike a conventional browser, however, HotJava is based on Java, not on HTML. Because Java is an object-oriented language, providing interactive experiences is much easier for HotJava than for its HTML-based predecessors. Because HotJava can download applets to your client computer, you don't have to worry about having special software to run animation or manipulate graphics. If you need a certain application to show the applet, HotJava simply brings that application to your desktop.

Some of HotJava's nifty features

The following list outlines some of HotJava's nifty features:

- ✔ HotJava can perform delayed image and applet loading. You can choose to load images *lazily* so that they load only when you click on them. This lazy loading can be a big time saver.

- ✔ HotJava supports most Netscape extensions including all Netscape HTML extensions to the <IMG> and <HR> tags, except LEFT and RIGHT.

- ✔ HotJava is multithreaded, which means that it can fetch multiple images at once. This feature also enables you to start browsing immediately, while HotJava is fetching images, because another thread to manage user interaction is also available.

- ✔ HotJava supports all the major Internet transfer protocols: ftp, HTTP, news (NNTP), mailto:, and gopher.

- ✔ Applets provide a great deal of network security because they're not permitted to write or change your files in any way. (You *can* allow applets to make a change if you want, by altering your HOTJAVA_WRITE_PATH.) By choosing Options⇨Security from the menu in HotJava, you can also put restrictions on the capabilities of incoming content.

HotJava's drawbacks

At this time, HotJava is a high-end technology because it isn't available for two of the most popular platforms, Windows 3.*x* and the Macintosh. We've heard arguments that HotJava is *elitist* because Java is such a complicated language to learn and, therefore, only computer professionals and die-hard buffs are actually interested in its capabilities. JavaScript has deflated that argument to some extent. Nevertheless, JavaScript's CPU, RAM, and disk space requirements can be somewhat daunting, so this program is by no means perfect, either.

Referencing Java Materials in Your Web Pages

Incorporating Java materials into your Web pages can endow them with a whole new look and feel, as well as new potential. By using applets, you can actually walk your viewers through a sequence that you'd like them to see.

The following list gives you tips for effective use of Java applets in your pages:

- ✔ Read about Java before you start trying to program with it. You can find a number of helpful resources on the Web and a number of books on Java as well.

- ✔ Surf to see what's going on in Java programming. The list at the end of this chapter provides URLs for a number of interesting Java sites.

- ✔ Select an applet that you would like to emulate. GAMELAN, at `http://www.gamelan.com/`, is a directory that offers lots of sample applets. Study the HTML code from the applets page and consult the code as you create your applet's parameters.

- ✔ Access an applet. You can't use applets in your pages unless you have the ability to access them! You have two paths of access: remote call and local compilation.

- ✔ Do some experimenting with `call` commands and figure out what HTML tag calls the applet for use on your pages. Directories called `CLASSES` are the repositories for all compiled applets.

To invoke a Java applet from inside an HTML document, use Sun's HTML extension tag, `<APP>`. The following code shows the general syntax for utilizing the `<APP>` element:

```
<APP
CLASS="class name"
SRC="URL"
ALIGN="alignment"
HEIGHT="height in pixels"
WIDTH="width in pixels"
APPLET_SPECIFIC_ATTRIBUTES="values"
...>
```

In order to preserve their security, applets can't do certain things. The following list tells you some of the things that applets can't do:

✔ Applets can't make network connections to any host except the one where they originated.

✔ Applets can't read every system property.

✔ Applets can't define native methods or load libraries.

✔ Applets can't read or write files on the host that runs them.

If you stop to think about these restrictions, most are aimed at preventing applets from violating system security or data integrity, primarily to discourage hackers from trying to use Java's normal behavior (of moving code from one system to another) for their own malefic purposes.

Design Do's and Don'ts for Java Materials

Do the following things when you design Web page elements with Java:

✔ DO make sure that your applet stops running when it's off-screen. If the browser is iconified (minimized) or displaying a page other than the one containing the applet, the applet generally shouldn't be running — doing so drains CPU resources. It's okay for your applet to run off-screen only if your applet code doesn't explicitly launch any threads.

✔ DO implement the stop() method if your applet code launches any threads (or have a really good explanation for not implementing the stop() method). The stop() method can halt and destroy the threads you've launched by setting them to null. For example:

```
public synchronized void stop() {
   if (refresh != null) {
      public synchronized void stop() {
      refresh.stop();
      refresh = null;
```

✔ DO give your users a way to stop the applet's behavior, especially when the applet does something that is potentially annoying, like playing sounds (think of all those people secretly surfing at work!).

One way to stop an applet's behavior is to implement the mouseDown() method (in an applet that normally doesn't respond to mouse clicks) so that clicking the mouse suspends or resumes the thread. The following code shows one approach to using the mouseDown() method:

```
boolean threadSuspended = false; //an instance variable
public boolean mouseDown(Event e, int x, int y) {
if (threadSuspended) {
  myThread.resume();
} else {
  myThread.suspend();
}
threadSuspended = !threadSuspended;
return true;
}
```

Don't do the following things when you design Web page elements with Java:

- ✔ DON'T forget to remove or disable debugging output. Debugging output (which is usually created with System.out.println()) may be useful to you, but it can be annoying or confusing to users. If you want to give your users textual feedback, try doing so in the status area at the bottom of the window or inside the applet's display area.

- ✔ DON'T forget to end the source URL in your CLASSES directory with a slash.

Lots of other do's and don'ts exist for doing Java right. Read on for some excellent resources on this topic.

Top Java Resources

Not surprisingly, Sun Microsystems, Inc. has an excellent collection of Java resources at java.sun.com/. In addition to that page, the following Web resources contain helpful and interesting information about Java:

- ✔ The Java Message Board is a Web page full of questions and discussions about Java:

  ```
  http://porthos.phoenixat.com/~warreng/WWWBoard
             /wwwboard.html
  ```

- ✔ Gamelan is an excellent listing of Java Applets:

  ```
  http://www.gamelan.com/
  ```

- ✔ John December's page features an impressive collection of Java information:

  ```
  http://www.rpi.edu/~decemj/works/java/info.html
  ```

✔ Obtain a list of Java's bugs at the Java Developer's Kit 1.0 known bugs site:

```
http://java.sun.com/JDK-1.0/knownbugs.html
```

✔ This page contains useful information about Java, as well as downloads and links:

```
http://sunsite.sut.ac.jp/java/
```

✔ The Java Authoring Guide covers a range of information on JavaScript:

```
http://home.netscape.com/eng/mozilla/2.0/handbook
            /javascript/index.html
```

✔ The FAQ (Frequently Asked Questions) for JavaScript:

```
http://www.his.com/~smithers/freq/beta/jsfaq.html
```

✔ A great page of Java links:

```
http://www.nebulex.com/URN/devel.html
```

✔ Sun's helpful Java tutorials cover topics such as writing Java programs, writing applets, creating a user interface, and many more:

```
http://java.sun.com:80/tutorial/index.html
```

✔ Cafe au Lait is a superlative resource listing:

```
http://sunsite.unc.edu/javafaq/
```

✔ If you have compiler or interpreter problems, this next site is full of troubleshooting tips to help out:

```
http://java.sun.com/tutorial/troubleshooting
            /index.html
```

✔ IDG's JavaWorld page is one of the most extensive Java resources on the Web:

```
http://www.javaworld.com/cgi-bin/w3com/start?JW+main
```

Java's Future

The fact that Java can automatically improve the quality of Web applications is not a given. Without vision, Java's cool applets alone can't push Web users into a higher realm of surf-nirvana. However, Java's potential is undeniable and its possibilities in terms of multimedia and interactivity are staggering. If used well by developers, undoubtedly Java can succeed in permanently enriching the Web.

Java is not without its rivals — Microsoft does not relinquish such rich territory easily, and the company's postponement of the release of Internet Studio indicates that Microsoft may be scrambling to develop similar groundbreaking technology. In addition, the fact that UNIX developers at AT&T Bell Labs are working on a rival version of Java was revealed in February 1996. The project, code-named *Inferno,* was considered important enough for these developers to table development on UNIX's successor, Plan 9. Bell's beef with Java is that the program is too large and too restrictive for a variety of machines.

Whether development continues with Java or a similar technology, you can't deny the growth and progress that Java has stimulated for the Web. Plus, Java is the world's greatest excuse for lame, caffeine-inspired puns! In the next chapter, we leave the jive behind, though, and move into the highly-formatted modalities delivered by text-handling technologies like Envoy, Acrobat, and Common Ground.

Chapter 18

Controlling Web Text to the nth Degree

*T*he advent of the Web brought an entirely new set of ideas about how text should be created and viewed. Although the Web has changed ideas of how to organize text and graphics electronically, some documents remain best rendered in a traditional, paper-oriented layout.

This chapter explains the programs that give you the best of both worlds — portable document programs. Portable document technology enables you to combine the benefits of traditional, dead-tree publishing with those of online publishing by reproducing your documents on the Web just as they look on paper. These programs give you the opportunity to go beyond traditional formats of document exchange: paper, ASCII text-only, or native-file format (with all the required fonts and graphics for which recipients must have the same application).

Through portable document programs, you have the power to represent complex documents consistently and to control their layout rigorously; HTML can't give such guarantees. For example, HTML has major problems dealing with columnar text, and precise character positioning (*kerning*) and line-spacing (*leading*) are beyond its current capabilities.

Because documents created with portable document software are completely portable, you can downloaded, share, and view these documents on different computer operating systems — without worrying about platform issues. Corporations appreciate the power of these programs versus the capabilities of HTML. With portable document technology, businesses can convert complex documents (containing a variety of text formats and intense graphics) into Web documents that have a more conventional, professional appearance.

The *digital paper* option (offered by portable document technology) encourages offices to become less reliant on paper transmissions and thereby reduces clutter and useless filing. The environmental considerations of such technology mustn't go unnoticed, either — if you don't have to print some documents, that causes less paper and ink waste and creates fewer recycling concerns.

The cross-platform communication capability of portable document technology represents another useful feature for companies whose employees work on multiple operating systems. With a program of this type, you can seamlessly transport documents among a variety of operating systems and never worry about losing formatting or style.

A Portable Document Overview

Text engines are the tools responsible for converting your original document into a Web-ready one. PDF (Portable Document Format) from Adobe Systems, Inc., and Digital Paper from Common Ground are examples of text engines. Platform-independent by nature, these tools employ technology that reproduces the fonts, graphics, colors, and styles of your original document. These programs are based on powerful languages (PDF is based on PostScript), and they use technology that offers cross-platform support for font substitution instead of font reformatting.

How do text engines work?

Text engines may seem simply to take a screen shot of your document and reproduce it as a bitmapped image — but that's not the way the process works. Instead, text engines capture ASCII characters along with information about a document's graphics, layout, and fonts. The format information encompasses a document's visual appearance as well as additional style controls that are only possible in an electronic representation. Because the engine stores text and graphics in vector format, such stored information basically works like a scaleable image of a page.

This process makes documents much more compact than bitmapped images. After you save a file in a format such as PDF, you can't usually edit it, because that file captures a document's final form. Acrobat Exchange does enable you to add annotations to PDF files, however, and a plugin for Adobe Illustrator enables Illustrator to open a PDF file and perform minor editing on single pages. Several applications have plans for supporting the editing of PDF documents in future releases; these applications include Adobe Illustrator, PageMaker, and FreeHand.

Who can use this portable stuff, anyway?

People in a variety of professions and interest groups make use of portable document technologies:

- Graphic designers working with a variety of text, layout, and graphical content
- Coworkers using different operating systems but collaborating on a single document or document set
- Collaborators who need to exchange documents that can't be adequately represented in HTML, ASCII, or RTF
- People who are interested in experimenting with Web content and style issues
- People who aren't interested in experimentation, but who want things on the computer to look and act like they do on paper

Benefits

The following list highlights some benefits of using a text engine:

- Because you download an entire document with a text engine, after your download is complete, your access to intradocument information is faster than with a Web document.
- Controlling exactly how your document looks online is hard. Using a portable document program ensures that your document is going to look (online) as it does on paper.
- The cross-platform capabilities of this technology greatly facilitate information exchange.
- You have no need to fax or overnight-mail long, complicated documents.
- No matter what printer you use, a document printed in PDF maintains your format, even when the receiving computer doesn't have any of the fonts used to create the document.

- Portable documents promote efficiency. You can save money and time by online manipulation of content that you would previously have printed out. Also, the structure of portable document programs enables efficient viewing and navigation, including hypertext linking and indexed searching.

- The potential distribution of an online document is much greater than that of its paper counterpart.

- Although their contents can be copied to other applications, portable documents can't be modified or altered. This feature permits group markup and edits without risking document file corruption.

- With the addition of hyperlinks, portable document programs enable you to "open" your document to a new realm of information.

- The text engines often compress your files, so the converted document ends up being smaller than the original.

- Most of the portable document programs, including Acrobat, Common Ground, and Envoy, have versions available free online.

Drawbacks

We feel that we also must mention the drawbacks to portable document technology:

- Even though the viewing software is free, you still need the software before you can see the portable documents it supports. The software can also be limited by your computer's power.

- Download times are often longer for portable documents than for Web documents with inline images.

- When you're using a Web browser, you have the option of stopping your transmission part-way through. A portable document is like a word processing document — that is, the document is either open or not open.

- Portable documents are forcing new technology (HTML) to conform to old standards by making a digital medium behave exactly like paper. For some this is a drawback, but for others, an advantage!

Creating (or Using) Special Text Formats

When you want to put a document that contains complex graphics, typefaces, and page layouts on the Web, your best bet is often a portable document program. In the days before portable documents existed, the process of laying out and formatting complex documents was time consuming (and often unrewarding). Even when a computer publisher spent hours setting up such documents, the time invested didn't guarantee that viewers would be able to view a document's electronic counterpart exactly as intended. ASCII was accepted as a standard method to transmit text between platforms; although ASCII is still widely accepted, it is also cumbersome.

As the Web's influence upon the business world grew, Web-friendly companies recognized a need to transmit documents that would ensure consistent document viewing for viewers inside and outside the organization. Portable document technology was developed to meet this need — to provide the assurance that information transmitted electronically is as loyal to its creator's intentions as is information on paper. Programs such as Adobe Acrobat and Digital Paper are examples of the type of technology that attempts to marry the two formats.

Using portable document technology brings many of the same benefits that paper does. For example, you can attach electronic sticky notes to papers that can stay with the document for years (no need to worry about the glue drying up!). Portable document technology reproduces your font, format, color, and style choices exactly because the person who views your documents uses the same software that you used to create them.

In addition to featuring some of paper's positive traits, portable documents also contain some of the Web's positive side. Portable documents can have hyperlinks to other locations within themselves or outside to a Web site. This capacity really pushes a document's structure from text's linear limitations to hypertext's grand possibilities.

Adobe Acrobat and PDF

PDF, the text engine used by Adobe Acrobat, was first introduced in 1992. The program was intended to create a new document standard to share document information electronically, and the plan worked — PDF is regarded as the industry standard. Acrobat 2.1 is available for Macintosh, Windows, HP-UX, SunOS, and Solaris; Acrobat Reader 1.0 is available for DOS and IRIX.

PDF files are created by Adobe Acrobat Programs, which are actually a bundle of programs that work in cooperation with each other. If you're only interested in viewing content created with Acrobat, no monetary investment is necessary — you can download Acrobat Reader from the Web (the next section contains additional downloading information). Adobe Systems, Inc., gives its official characterization of Acrobat Reader as the program that "enables corporate and commercial publishers to electronically distribute finished documents to large audiences." Acrobat Reader is a read-only program; that is, you can't save anything by using that software.

If you want to create content by using an Acrobat program, you need Acrobat Exchange, the "general-purpose electronic document solution." For Windows and Macintosh platforms, Acrobat Exchange works in conjunction with PDF Writer, a printer driver installed with the program. By using these together, you can create PDF files for virtually any document.

If you have a UNIX or DOS platform, you can't use PDF Writer — you need Acrobat Distiller instead. The distiller creates PDF documents from practically any documents that have been saved as PostScript language files. When you're trying to reproduce 24-bit images, high-quality EPS artwork, or documents that exploit features sported only by PostScript printers (like blends), Distiller is the program to use. You can install Acrobat Distiller as a personal application for your computer or as a shared application for a network server.

Minimum system requirements for Acrobat

The minimum system requirements for using Acrobat on the Macintosh platform are as follows:

- ✔ Macintosh computer with 68020 CPU or greater
- ✔ Apple System Software 7.0 or later
- ✔ 2MB application RAM for Acrobat Exchange or Acrobat Reader
- ✔ 4.5MB application RAM for Acrobat Exchange or Acrobat Reader on Power Macintosh
- ✔ 6MB application RAM for Acrobat Distiller or Catalog
- ✔ 8MB application RAM for Acrobat Distiller on Power Macintosh
- ✔ Adobe Type Manager (this is included and can be installed privately)

The minimum system requirements for using Acrobat on the Windows platform are the following:

- ✔ 386- or 486-based personal computer
- ✔ Microsoft Windows 3.1, Windows 95, Windows NT 3.5 or later
- ✔ 4MB RAM for Acrobat Exchange or Acrobat Reader (which don't run in Windows Standard Mode)
- ✔ 8MB RAM for Acrobat Distiller and Acrobat Catalog

The minimum system requirements for using Acrobat on the UNIX/Sun platform are these:

- ✔ Sun SPARCstation workstation
- ✔ SunOS version 4.1.3 (Solaris 1.1) or Solaris 2.3 or later

- ✔ OpenWindows (3.0 or later) or Motif (1.2.3 or later); windowing environments used with Acrobat Exchange or Acrobat Reader

- ✔ 32MB RAM

- ✔ 8MB hard disk space for Acrobat Reader

- ✔ 20MB hard disk space for Acrobat Exchange

- ✔ 12MB hard disk space for Acrobat Distiller

The minimum system requirements for using Acrobat on the UNIX/HP platform are as follows:

- ✔ HP Series 9000 workstation, model 700 or higher

- ✔ HPVUE desktop environment

- ✔ 32MB RAM

- ✔ 6MB hard disk space for Acrobat Reader

- ✔ 14MB hard disk space for Acrobat Exchange

The minimum system requirements for using Acrobat on the DOS platform are the following:

- ✔ 386- or 486-based personal computer

- ✔ DOS version 3.3 or greater

- ✔ 2MB RAM (4MB is recommended)

- ✔ 5MB free hard disk space

Viewing one page at a time with Acrobat's Amber

Amber, due for release in 1996, is the newest program by Adobe Systems, Inc., in the Acrobat line. Amber provides a new way to optimize PDF files for delivery on the Internet or online services. With Amber, you view the document one page at a time instead of waiting for the whole PDF file to download. This feature eliminates one of PDF's least-appealing characteristics — namely, downloading the entire document before you can see it.

Amber makes the viewing process much more Web-oriented and transparently integrates with your Web browser's navigation functions (such as Go Forward). Amber offers a progressive display of the PDF file; that is, you see the text first, then the images, and then the embedded fonts.

In order to view one page at a time, you need the following:

- ✔ The Amber Reader (available at the Adobe Web site)
- ✔ A Web server (such as Netscape 2.0) that can deliver PDF files, one page at a time, to the Amber Reader
- ✔ Web links that connect your PDF files to other Web content
- ✔ PDF-optimized files that offer maximum file compression and progressive display

Envoy and Tumbleweed

Envoy is a program that Novell designed to address problems of electronic document distribution. Key attributes of Envoy include online viewing, transmission, flexible navigation, efficient searching, printing, and annotation.

In contrast to Acrobat, which grew from Adobe PostScript printing language, Novell designed Envoy from scratch. Envoy works with WordPerfect and boasts the most compact overall file sizes of all portable document programs. Its system requirements are fairly low — Envoy generally requires less memory than Acrobat. For example, as the Windows 95 Netscape plugin, Envoy requires 1.2MB of RAM, while Acrobat takes 2.5MB.

Envoy also features a link builder and an outline builder, two features that Acrobat lacks, and it supports conversion with other portable document formats. Envoy also claims to have the only complete set of annotation tools in its class — you can make comments on your portable documents with a variety of fun tools, including sticky notes, highlighter pens, hypertext links, and bookmarks.

The capacity to maintain the author's name and style that Envoy offers is also a unique feature. In addition, after you distribute a document for feedback, Envoy enables you to import annotations from other documents and users, which is obviously a critical feature for collaboration. All you need to view documents created with Envoy is the Envoy viewer, which is available free at

    http://wp.novell.com/elecpub/edv.htm

You can also order a copy of the Envoy Viewer for Windows on disk by telephone (800-444-6022). In this format, the software costs $9.00 (the price includes shipping and handling). The online format is available for Macintoshes only.

Envoy 1.0a system requirements

To use Envoy on a Macintosh platform, you need the following:

- ✔ A Macintosh computer with 68020 or greater CPU to run the Envoy Viewer and the Envoy Publisher; MacPlus or above to run the Envoy Viewer only
- ✔ Apple System Software 7.0.1 or later to run the Envoy Viewer and Envoy Publisher; System 6.0.5 for the Envoy Viewer only
- ✔ 900K RAM
- ✔ 1MB hard disk space

To use Envoy on a Windows platform, you need

- ✔ A personal computer with 386 or greater processor
- ✔ 1MB – 2MB hard disk space
- ✔ 500K RAM
- ✔ A graphics card and monitor with VGA (or higher) resolution
- ✔ Windows 3.1 or later
- ✔ A mouse

Differences between Envoy (and similar programs) and HTML

Like any other text engine, Envoy behaves differently than HTML. Here are some of the most significant differences:

- ✔ An Envoy document preserves your formatting exactly the way you want it, regardless of the platform or Web browser. HTML, on the other hand, always conforms to the browser's capabilities and "personality settings."
- ✔ An Envoy document enables you to embed fonts directly into the document, so the font that you've selected is automatically the one that appears. Because HTML supports only select fonts, if you want to use special fonts, you usually need to convert your text into bitmaps.
- ✔ HTML doesn't support scaleable vector graphics; Envoy does. In HTML you're limited to depicting all your graphical material as large bitmaps. A scaleable bitmap can size itself to maintain its proportions on the display area, so it occupies the same portion of a page, no matter whether the on-screen display area is large or small.
- ✔ Your graphically rich files are usually smaller in Envoy than in HTML because the bitmaps that HTML uses produce large files. Surprisingly, this means that some documents will display faster through an Envoy reader than through a Web browser!

Common Ground and digital paper

Common Ground (CG) works on a basic computer with 80386 processor and 4MB RAM. Common Ground incorporates Search, Copy, Paste, and Move commands. OLE support enables you to incorporate e-mail and database documents into compound transportable Common Ground documents. With the CG Save As command, you can save CG documents to common word processing applications for editing and still keep your page breaks and line breaks.

UNIX and DOS versions of Common Ground are upcoming. You can download a free Common Ground mini-viewer for Macintosh, Power Macintosh, and Windows at

```
http://www.teknovation.com/cgindex.html
```

Common Ground configuration for your Web browser

Here are the basics of how to configure most Web browsers to support Common Ground documents:

- MIME type: application/common ground (add this definition to your MIME types file)
- Viewer: Common Ground viewer for the platform you're using
- File extension (optional): dp
- File Type (Macintosh): CGDC

External Text-Handlers and Plugins

Using a plugin with portable documents allows you to view stand-alone documents and documents embedded in HTML pages by using the Web browser. Plugins facilitate creating and following links containing URLs in portable documents, and plugins are widely available for Macintosh and Windows.

Take advantage of plugins to view portable documents. Envoy has a plugin with Netscape Navigator 2.0, and Acrobat has a plugin called Weblink that comes bundled with Acrobat Version 2.1 or is available for downloading at

```
http://www.adobe.com/Acrobat/Plug-Ins/
```

Installing text handlers is not too complicated — the main work is generally downloading and decompressing the file. The following information gives you a look at how to go about installing Adobe Acrobat 2.1.

The download site for Adobe Acrobat software is

```
http://w1000.mv.us.adobe.com/Acrobat/readstep.html
```

If you want to download Adobe software but are having trouble connecting to their Web site, you can order a "sampler CD" that costs $9.95 (this price covers shipping and handling) and contains Adobe Acrobat Reader 2.1 for Windows, Macintosh, SunOS, Solaris, HP-UX, and the Acrobat Reader 1.0 for Silicon Graphics IRIX and DOS. Call 800-272-3623 to order and ask for part number 0397-1492.

Configuring helper applications

Most Web browsers use a *preferences* file similar to the one that Netscape employs. This type of preference file enables users to add new helper applications to their external viewer tables.

Follow these steps for the set of standard configurations for Netscape:

1. **Choose Options⇨Preferences from the main menu.**
2. **Select Helper Applications from the pop-up menu at the top of the resulting dialog box.**
3. **Type** application **in the MIME type text box and** PDF **in the MIME sub-type text box; then click OK.**
4. **Select the new entry in the scrolling list — the entry should say** application/pdf.
5. **Click the Browse button.**
6. **Select the appropriate Viewer from the dialog box that lists the files on your hard drive and click OK.**
7. **Choose File Type⇨Text from the pop-up menu in the middle-right of the dialog box.**
8. **Type** PDF **in the Extensions text box.**
9. **Click the Launch Application radio button under Action.**
10. **Click OK.**

Configuring Adobe Acrobat

The following information takes you through configuring your system for Adobe Acrobat for platforms that don't have plugins. The instructions should give you a general idea about configuration for other programs as well.

Sun SPARC and HP

Acrobat Reader 2.1 is available for SunOS 4.1.3 or 4.1.4, Solaris 2.3 and 2.4, or HP-UX 9.03 and later. To install Acrobat Reader on these systems, simply download the appropriate *.tar* file from `http://w1000.mv.us.adobe.com/Acrobat/readstep.html`; then *untar* the file and read the INSTGUID.TXT for installation steps.

Silicon Graphics

You can find two duplicate versions of the archive for Silicon Graphics computers. One version is compressed with GNU *gzip,* and the other is a regular UNIX *tar* file. Because the gzipped version is smaller, you can probably download this version more quickly (from `http://w1000.mv.us.adobe.com/Acrobat/readstep.html`). Select the gzipped version if your Web browser is configured to handle gzipped data. If not, try using the Save Next Link As or Save to Disk commands in your Web browser and then unpack the file.

After reading the current README file for information about the application, take a look at the INSTGUID.TXT file for installation information. Following this process brings you to the online Reader Electronic End User License Agreement.

You use the Software Manager to install the application with these steps:

1. **Create a directory for the product.**

   Don't forget that for the Software Manager to work, the directory that's receiving the *untarred* files must have read and executed permissions for everyone. The following example uses *acroread* as the new directory name:

   ```
   mkdir acroread; chmod a+rx acroread; cd acroread.
   ```

2. **Download the Adobe Acrobat installation package from the Web or through FTP (the address is at the beginning of this section).**

   If you're using FTP, select the binary mode because the package contains binary data.

3. **Decompress the file's contents and extract the contents from the archive with the following command:**

   ```
   gunzip < IRIXR.TAR.gz | tar -xvfBp -
   ```

4. **Start the Software Manager and point to the location where you've *untarred* your components. You can now proceed with the installation process.**

AIX 4.1.3 and above

You can also obtain versions of the software for IBM's AIX UNIX implementation. One version is compressed with GNU *gzip,* and the other is a regular UNIX *tar* file. Because the gzipped version is smaller, you can probably download this version more quickly (from `http://w1000.mv.us.adobe.com/Acrobat/readstep.html`). Select the gzipped version if your Web browser is configured to handle gzipped data. If not, try using the Save Next Link As or Save to Disk commands in your Web browser and then unpack the file.

1. **Create a suitable directory for the Acrobat product.**

   For example, with *acroread* as your directory name, execute the following commands:

   ```
   mkdir acroread
   cd acroread
   ```

2. **Retrieve the Acrobat Reader installation package from a Web site or with FTP (the address is at the beginning of this section).**

   If you're using FTP, select the binary mode because the package contains binary data. Acrobat Reader provides two packages:

   AIXReader.TAR.Z — the compressed *tar*

   fileAIXReader.TAR.gz — the GNU zipped file

3. **Decompress the contents and extract the contents from the archive.**

   If you're using the compressed TAR file, type

   ```
   zcat AIXReader.TAR.Z | tar -xvf -
   ```

4. **Run the INSTALL script that's provided in the extracted file contents.**

   You may have to obtain root-level system access to run this script successfully. If it doesn't work, contact your system administrator.

Acrobat 1.0 for DOS

Only the 1.0 version of Acrobat is available for DOS; you'll find it at `http://w1000.mv.us.adobe.com/Acrobat/readstep.html`. Install this version as follows:

1. **Download and run ACRODOS.EXE.**

   When you do this, acrodos.exe unpacks into your current directory.

2. **Run INSTALL.EXE. After you've accepted the license agreement, you can configure and install Acrobat 1.0 for DOS.**

   You may need to use the Save Next Link As or Save to Disk functions of your Web browser to make this installation work.

Configuration for Special Text Formats

You may need to configure your Web server if you want to distribute portable document programs. These next sections tell you how to configure a variety of popular servers for the Adobe PDF documents — if you're working with other servers, this information gives you a general idea about configuration. Servers need to know certain things about handling portable documents such as:

- How to identify PDF documents on your server (".pdf" extension)
- What the PDF MIME type is (application/pdf)
- How to treat a PF data stream (binary data)

NCSA HTTPd (Version 1.3)

The PDF MIME type must be defined in the `ServerRoot/conf/mime.types` file. The entry should read as follows:

```
application/pdf   pdf
```

Place the `PDFmid.gif` file in the `ServerRoot/icons/` directory if you want to use the PDF icon in server-generated directory listings. Also add an entry similar to the next line in your `ServerRoot/conf/srm.conf` file:

```
AddIcon/icons/PDFmid.gif .pdf .PDF
```

You can add a short text description after PDF files in server-generated directory listings by tacking on two entries to your `ServerRoot/conf/srm.conf` file:

```
AddDescription "PDF document" .pdf
AddDescription "PDF document" .PDF
```

WebStar

WebStar is preconfigured to serve PDF files to the Web. The file `MacHTTP.config` contains the mappings for suffix file types.

CERN HTTPd 3.0

To your configuration file in `server_root/config/`, add the following line:

```
AddType .pdf  application/pdf 8bit 1.0
```

If you want to provide a PDF icon in server-generated directory listings, place the `pdficon.gif` **GIF** file in the `server_root/icons/` directory and add this line to your configuration file in `server_root/config/`:

```
AddIcon /icons/pdficon.gif PDF application/pdf
```

Using Special Text Formats in Your Web Pages

The following information tells you how to publish Web pages in the Envoy format. Envoy works similarly to the other portable document programs, so these instructions should give you a general idea of how to publish in this format.

- ✔ Convert your existing documents into the Envoy format.
- ✔ Print your document through the Envoy printer driver from any application (the printer driver is included in Envoy from Novell and from Tumbleweed Publishing Essentials).
- ✔ Use the Tumbleweed Publisher for batch publishing of documents into Envoy and direct conversion from complex file types such as PostScript and Acrobat PDF. The Tumbleweed Publisher is included in Tumbleweed Publishing Essentials.
- ✔ If necessary, organize your documents by using the tools provided by Tumbleweed Publishing Essentials.
- ✔ Create a full-text index.
- ✔ Make cross-document hypertext links.
- ✔ Make an outline to facilitate navigation.
- ✔ Make your Envoy file available for viewing. You can use the following tools for viewing:

  - The Envoy viewer (free online) at:

    ```
    http://wp.novell.com/elecpub/edv.htm
    ```
  - Web browser plugins (Netscape Navigator offers one).
  - Your very own Envoy viewer, customized with the Envoy SDK (Software Developer's Kit).

Use the following basic syntax to embed Envoy documents in your HTML Web pages:

```
<EMBED SRC="file.evy" WIDTH="320" HEIGHT="200">
```

The following keywords are specific to the embedded Envoy documents (the default value is italicized):

- ✔ Set TOOLBAR to *false* if you don't want to show the Envoy toolbar.

  ```
  TOOLBAR="true"|"false"
  ```

- ✔ Set SCROLLABLE to *false* if you don't want to show a scrollbar.

  ```
  SCROLLABLE="true"|"false"
  ```

- ✔ Set SHOWPAGE to the page number of the desired page.

  ```
  SHOWPAGE="pagenumber"
  ```

- ✔ Select how you want the Envoy page to be fitted to the HTML embedded rectangle.

  ```
  ZOOM="fitwidth"|"fitheight"|"fitpage"
  ```

Design Do's for Special Text Formats

The following list applies to most special text formats:

- ✔ DO make sure that your document is easy to read. This issue is especially important when you're dealing with documents that you've replicated from their original paper versions. Determine whether the fonts are still the correct size for the on-screen medium. Set the size of your documents by assuming that your viewers use 14-inch displays.

- ✔ DO think seriously about whether reproducing your document's paper image is the most effective way to present it. Sometimes a straight Web document can be much more impressive than an image of a paper document.

- ✔ DO use the MS-DOS file-naming convention. Many network and e-mail programs truncate long filenames, so this eight-character filename followed by a three-character extension is the safest way to go. Using this file-naming convention ensures that PDF files retain the PDF extension as they're transferred among computers.

The Top Special-Text-Format Resources

We selected the following Web resources for their wealth of information on text format issues and tools:

- ✔ This amazing maze game, called *mazeworld,* is an example of how PRF can be used creatively:

  ```
  http://www.ep.cs.nott.ac.uk:80/~pns/mazeworld/
  ```

- ✔ A list of cool PDF sites:

  ```
  http://w1000.mv.us.adobe.com/Acrobat/PDFsites.html
  ```

- ✔ A fine resource for Adobe Acrobat:

  ```
  http://w1000.mv.us.adobe.com/Acrobat/acroweb.html
  ```

- ✔ A deluxe list of Tumbleweed partner sites:

  ```
  http://www.twcorp.com/related.htm
  ```

- ✔ *Access* magazine is an example of the power of PDF (but beware — this magazine is 99 pages long and the PDF document is 2.5MB):

  ```
  http://www.internex/net/access/
  ```

- ✔ Developer and SDK (Software Developer's Kit) information for Acrobat is available at either of the following URLs:

  ```
  http://www.adobe.com/Support/ADA.html
  ftp.adobe.com.
  ```

- ✔ This next Web page offers current articles and reports on Envoy and other portable document programs:

  ```
  http://www.twcorp.com/pressall.htm
  ```

- ✔ Novell's Envoy page contains a wealth of information:

  ```
  http://wp.novell.com/busapps/elecpub/tocepub.htm
  ```

The Final Word on Portable Document Technology

Even though its popularity is a recent phenomenon, the Web has already had an irrevocable impact on the way people view text and documents. The Web's hypertext orientation and user empowerment have altered Web users' reactions to documents and text presented in a conventional, paper-oriented fashion. As the limitations of paper documents (in terms of environmental resources and physical storage space) become increasingly apparent, we need to reevaluate the way we use printed documents.

Many people have become accustomed to hypertext's speedy links to unlimited volumes of information at their fingertips, and they miss this quality in paper documents. By attempting to unite the conveniences of hypertext with paper's charms, portable document technology gives the paper document the opportunity to survive in the 21st century. The benefits of portable document technology in terms of collaboration are easy to recognize, and the barriers among computing platforms that this technology eliminates are of paramount importance.

Instead of displacing or competing with HTML, portable document technology enriches it. Benefits of portable document technology that we classify as HTML compliments include the following:

- ✔ Document-level security features
- ✔ Print-ready documents
- ✔ Compressed, cross-platform files
- ✔ Cross-document search capability
- ✔ Ease of authoring
- ✔ Design control and integrated graphics

Portable document technology enables you to combine the Internet's infrastructure with the comfort of the desktop and, by doing so, gives the paper document a chance to make a transition into cyberspace. In the next part of the book, we change focus to look at how to extend and expand your use of the Web in general. That is, we provide shortcuts and tips galore about how to apply what you've (hopefully) learned from this book!

Part IV
Shortcuts and Tips Galore

The 5th Wave   By Rich Tennant

Re'al Pro'gram·mers

Real Programmers curse a lot, but only at inanimate objects.

In this part . . .

Part IV provides a traditional . . .*For Dummies* conclusion to this book, as we review the highlights of the preceding parts in quick, whimsical — and, we hope, useful — restatements of key concepts, principles, and approaches. In Chapter 19, we cover the top maintenance do's and don'ts, which you want to follow as you build and maintain a Web site. In Chapter 20, we cover the highlights of using advanced HTML markup and techniques including some key points on how to serve the part of the audience that may otherwise not be able to appreciate your work. Finally, in Chapter 21, we conclude the book with a refreshing rehash of the key Web extension technologies and their most appropriate uses.

Chapter 19
Maintenance Tips and Tricks

• •

• •

*B*uilding a Web site isn't anywhere near as hard as living with it afterwards. Sure, there's a great deal to learn about HTML and setting up a Web site, but it's exciting to build something and call it your own.

Just don't ever forget that the real work begins as soon as you open your Web site to the public. Sure enough, your users will find things that you've over-looked. Or they'll ask you questions that force you to recognize that you may have left some important things out. You may even begin to understand that your materials need reworking, because not even you can remember some of the points that you were trying to get across!

Don't despair: You've simply entered the "maintenance zone." It's where most of the time and dollars spent on computing-related activities and products goes (some 70 percent of the overall costs of software and systems occur during maintenance, after implementation is complete, according to the experts). That's why it should be no surprise that you'll be spending a lot of time in the zone (along with everybody else in the business).

In this chapter, we take you through some maintenance-related do's and don'ts that should help you survive — and perhaps even enjoy — this process. Just don't say that we didn't warn you.

For Maintenance, Routine Is Everything

The reason that the words *regular* and *maintenance* occur together so often in discussions of the subject is because irregular maintenance is only slightly preferable to none whatsoever. The whole key to running a shipshape Web site is to plan to work on it regularly and then to carry out those plans as scheduled.

Even though the contents of a Web site aren't as perishable as what's in your refrigerator, the two environments have a great deal in common. This is best explained as follows: Leave either one of them alone long enough and both will contain things that are way less than appetizing and which resemble the kinds of science experiments that the government doesn't want you to know about.

That's why setting aside a significant chunk of time — usually half a day or more at some regular interval — to devote exclusively to your Web site is absolutely imperative. Even if you use this time only to look for comparable sites on the Web and compare your stuff to other stuff, it will be time well spent. You are more likely to find yourself looking at things and saying, "Boy, does this need to be renovated!" than you are to find yourself mooning about like the Maytag repairman.

Automating whatever parts of the maintenance routine that you can is also a wonderful idea. UNIX includes a built-in scheduling utility called cron; most of the other operating systems support one form of scheduling utility or another. If you set up an automated process to assist you with maintenance, here are some of the things that it can do:

- ✔ Send you e-mail to remind you when it's time to perform maintenance tasks.
- ✔ Tell the Web server to run various maintenance utilities, such as a link checker, a validation service, and other tools that can do their thing without intimate human interaction.
- ✔ Remind outside reviewers, content authors, or other contributors to revisit your Web site and send you their feedback, all via e-mail.

In the final analysis, it's not so much what you do, maintenance-wise, that matters; it's the fact that you do it seriously and regularly, just like a real job!

Remembering the Content

While you're keeping your Web site clean and polished, don't ever forget the real reason that people will visit: It's the content, silly! The value and significance of content varies with the subject matter — for example, a recipe for quesadillas will be as good next year as it is today, but the directions to your office must be changed every time you move. That's why staying on top of the content and adjusting it as your users and circumstances demand are essential.

Force yourself to look at as much of your site as you can during each regularly scheduled maintenance period. If it's too big to cover completely each time, schedule a regular rotation through its components. You will be surprised how many times you can look at something before you find all the boo-boos, typos, gotchas, and other signs of human involvement.

Inviting others to read their way through your site on a regular basis is also a good idea. Make it an assignment for new employees; beg your regular customers to visit and share their feedback; give prizes or rewards for finding bugs or mistakes; try to get other "interested parties" involved, at least to read things germane to their interests or that reflect a common business focus. The more people check out the content, the more feedback you'll be able to elicit from them, by hook or by crook!

Keeping Track of Dates

As you review the content in your documents, check out the footers each time you pass by. You should always include a "last revision date" marker on each page so that you can tell at a glance how long it has been since a page has been touched. By itself, checking the date can deliver a powerful wake-up call, as in, "Has it really been since last *summer* that we updated this page?"

On the other hand, if you're feeling especially productive, you can write a short program or *grep* script (grep stands for "general regular expression parser" and is a powerful UNIX tool that may be used to read and recognize patterns that occur within text files) to find the update line in each .HTM or .HTML file on your site and append it to the filename. Then you can scan this list to look for especially old or suspicious dates.

Of course, the success of this technique depends on you having the discipline to update the date information each time that you change anything in an HTML document. If the date is wrong, it won't do you any good to look at it.

Avoiding (or Mitigating) Browser Dependencies

Because not even your humble authors have been able to avoid the fatal allure of proprietary Web extensions, markup, and widgets, we certainly can't demand that you avoid these potential pitfalls, either. But if you do use proprietary markup, you'll need to keep a regular eye on how that markup changes over time. You'll also need to be ready to deal with obsolete or deprecated HTML (*deprecated HTML* is HTML that's fallen out of favor and is seldom used, but has not yet been declared "obsolete" by the IETF or W3C) as it changes.

Make this consideration a part of your regular maintenance routine. Keep tabs on the "What's New" pages and specifications documents at your favorite browser's (or browsers') Web site(s). Stay abreast of what's new and changing. Then, when the rug starts slipping out from under your feet, you will be able to stay upright and shift out the old while shifting in the new. If you keep yourself informed, you've already won half the battle.

Evolution Beats Revolution Every Time

As your site changes over time, you may occasionally suffer from the temptation to shuck the old version and replace it completely with something new. Although a radical Web-ectomy is sometimes required, it's not the treatment for ennui, either.

The best course of action is to let your site evolve with changing times and demands. Integrating a series of small changes into your regular maintenance routine is a great deal easier than a wholesale replacement. Your users will also find it easier to digest a step-wise set of changes than a complete and sudden makeover.

The Beauty of a Test Web

Because change is inevitable, you can do more than expect it to happen to your Web site. You can also plan for change and set up your environment to make coping with its effects easier. One of the best things that you can do for yourself is to create a "test Web" that mirrors your production Web site but contains those portions that have been changed.

Of test and production computing facilities

For Information Systems (IS) and data processing professionals, the distinction between test and production facilities is too well-known to make reading this sidebar worth your while. If you know what this means, skip ahead to the next section. If not, here's what this distinction means:

- A *test facility* is private, restricted to authorized personnel only, and is used when testing and debugging new computing facilities or capabilities. In the case of a "test Web site," this refers to a password- or port-controlled Web site that's not publicized and used only prior to unleashing its contents to the world at large.

- A *production facility* is public, available to all (authorized) users, and provides day-in, day-out services as part of an organization's overall information systems offerings. In the case of a "production Web site," this refers to those URLs that front for any Web sites that are made generally available, whether only within your organization, or to the entire Internet.

In general, it's considered a good idea to develop and debug new or changed materials in a test environment before putting them into use in a production environment. Where the Web is concerned, this means using a "test Web site" until such materials are ready for prime time, and then carefully transferring them to the production version of that Web site after you're convinced that they're accurate, correct, and meet your audience's requirements. Be sure to test your production Web site thoroughly whenever you add materials from your test Web site; whenever things change is also when they're most likely to manifest problems.

By exposing this separate Web site with its own URL to a select cadre of alpha and beta testers, you can shake all the bugs out and smooth off the rough edges before opening a new set of pages to the public. When you decide that the materials are ready, you can copy them over to your production Web site, perform a quick test to make sure that all the graphics and links are working, and declare victory.

This approach goes double for a complete facelift on your Web site; it becomes increasingly more important to test your materials as the volume of change increases. Because a complete facelift involves maximum change, it should get maximal testing, too.

If It Changes, Test It (Again)

When it comes to testing, be sure to make that activity part of the maintenance routine. Every time something changes, even if you just go into a file to correct a typo, be sure to check your work. You never know when an accidental keystroke (or a glitch in a file-save routine) might introduce more changes than you think should be present.

The only way to be sure that your changes affect neither more nor less of your materials than you want them to is to check them thoroughly and completely. So, be sure to check and double-check the impact of change, no matter how trivial and slight. Because the little things are prone to catching us all in the end, don't let them catch you unaware.

Overcoming Inertia Takes Constant Vigilance

Because the roots of the Web lie deep in the physics community, we decided to close this section on maintenance with a physical metaphor. Physicists spend a lot of time dealing with inertia, which they like to define as the tendency of objects to keep heading in the direction that they are already going or to remain at rest when they are not going anywhere.

In human terms, inertia is the tendency to leave things alone that haven't been touched for a while. When it comes to a Web site, the tendency is to revel in its completion (or recent update) and to leave it alone after that. Don't let this happen to your site; make sure that you plan your next visit and schedule those activities so essential to keeping your content fresh and interesting. Check those links; revisit that material; look at revision dates; in short, stay on top of it so that it doesn't wind up on top of you!

Chapter 20

Advanced HTML Tips and Shortcuts

● ●

In This Chapter

▶ Building accessible Web sites

▶ Making sure of Internet delivery

▶ Leaving choices for your users

▶ <TABLE>-ing alternative

▶ Finding <FRAME> replacements

▶ Avoiding <MATH> dependencies

▶ Knowing when to split

▶ Mentioning multiple miscellany

▶ Adding value for value

● ●

*W*e hope that one of the many things this book demonstrates is that plenty of new HTML markup exists to contend with — and use — in your Web documents. Although the temptation to rush right out and start using the heck out of advanced HTML might be nearly irresistible, we remind you that not everyone benefits from those efforts.

Don't Forget the "Other Guys"

Even though a large portion of your viewing audience may be using Netscape or some other advanced browsers already (some 65–75 percent, depending on whose statistics you believe), not everybody has access to that browser and its advanced capabilities. It's the old problem of the "haves" versus the "have-nots" in its Webified form: If two-thirds to three-quarters of your viewers can see and appreciate advanced HTML, that also means that one-quarter to one-third of them can neither see nor appreciate it. This leads to the inevitable question: "Which audience should you cater to, the haves or the have-nots?"

Unless you're working on an in-house Web site where organizational policy dictates an advanced browser, we think that the answer to this question should be "Both!" In other words, when you build pages that exploit advanced functionality, it's important to provide an alternative view.

The "quick and dirty" approach to this is to create static, text-only alternatives to advanced markup. We cover this idea in detail in many of the sections that follow. For now, consider the needs of those of your users who aren't able to render — or benefit from — advanced markup. We strongly suggest that you provide an alternative for such users.

In the broadest of terms, here's how you might accomplish such a goal:

✔ On those pages that use advanced markup, place a hyperlink to a text-only alternative version near the top of the page. It should read something like this:

```
The following page uses HTML &lt;TABLE&gt;s and
associated tags. Unless you're sure that your browser can
display this material properly, please view our
<A HREF="ta-page.html">text-only version</A>instead.
```

✔ If your entire site is liberally sprinkled with advanced markup throughout, you may want to apprise users when they enter your home page.

Many sites now advertise themselves as "Netscape friendly" or as requiring Netscape 2.0 or greater. We don't necessarily advocate this approach, but it's best to be up front about it for the benefit of those users who might elect to pass on a visit rather than contend with strange on-screen displays.

✔ Another alternative to warning off those users ill-equipped to appreciate your advanced markup is to provide a more context-sensitive site implementation. Some designers ask users to identify their browsers upon entry (or read a combination of CGI environment variables) to determine what kinds of information a viewer can handle.

Then they will generate the right kind of Web pages on the fly for those viewers. That way, properly equipped visitors will see pages that include advanced markup; others will see text-only equivalents that won't strain their browser's capabilities.

This approach is much more work for the WebMaster and content authors but does the best job of accommodating a broad and diverse audience. For an excellent discussion of this technique, see the Spring 1996 issue of *Web Developer* magazine for a story by Glenn Fleishman entitled "Environmental Awareness," pp. 21–25.

We remind you that there is a portion of the user base that may not really "view" your pages at all. These are print-handicapped individuals who may have to use a Braille printer or text-to-speech translation to access the information on your Web site. Although this is a small portion of the overall audience, to be sure, it's an important component whose special needs must be anticipated in order to be served. These needs also help to explain why ALT text is so important for graphics, because it provides information about what is showing for those incapable of otherwise appreciating graphics content.

Multiple Means of Delivery

In much the same vein as our preceding request that you anticipate some of your users' more special needs, it's a good idea to remember that not all users have built-in e-mail access within their Web browsers, and that, for some, http-based file transfer isn't always practical. The list continues, but the principle remains the same: Give them another way to accomplish what the built-in functionality provides.

For e-mail, this means including an explicit e-mail address, preferably at the footer on each page, so that users can reach you by e-mail even if they can't use a mailto: URL. For file transfer, this means providing access to download files through an alternate FTP site and perhaps providing documentation on how to order file delivery from FTP sites via e-mail. There's an excellent program by Paul Vixie called ftpmail that can provide this service; for more information, please visit this URL:

```
http://www.acad.bg/beginner/ftpmail.html
```

Whatever your delivery or communications needs, there is usually at least one alternative method available. If you use a search engine to help you locate information on such topics, you'll probably be able to point your users at alternative software, explanations (such as the ftpmail document referenced in the preceding URL), and other useful information as well.

Let the Users Choose

Throughout this book, we have suggested that whenever special content or large amounts of data appear on your Web site, you should give your users fair warning and a way to steer around potential difficulties or download delays. We remind you that this is always a good idea, whether it applies to advanced HTML or to large graphics or multimedia data sources on your pages.

Here's a short list of summarized suggestions for you to ponder:

- ✔ Warn your readers when you're about to used advanced HTML. Point them at alternative representations (even if it's just a .TXT file with statically-formatted text) and give them a way to jump around this material.

- ✔ Warn your readers when something big and time-consuming is about to occur; this applies equally to long documents, big graphics, Shockwave or multimedia content, or whatever. It's often a good idea to build a thumb-nail or miniature version of the material and present it as a hyperlink to the real — and big — version.

Those users who want to see the "real thing" can choose to download it. If they do it by choice, they can't complain when it takes half an hour to see an image. If you force them to download something huge, they will blame you instead!

The best approach can be summed up as "Always leave your users a way out." If you don't, they will simply jump out of your site, never to return.

‹TABLE› *Alternatives*

HTML tables are wonderful and convenient tools. Yet, anyone who's using less than a state-of-the-art browser can't appreciate them. Worse yet, viewing table information in such a browser can be completely unintelligible. For an example of what we mean, compare the text-only version of a file download table rendered by the character mode browser, Lynx, shown in Figure 20-1 to its nicely laid-out equivalent rendered by Netscape Navigator in Figure 20-2. A reader would have to be quite astute to recognize the paragraph in mid-screen in the first figure as representing the same information as the second figure!

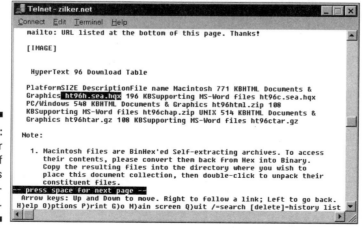

Figure 20-1:
The tabular nature of data gets lost in a text-only display.

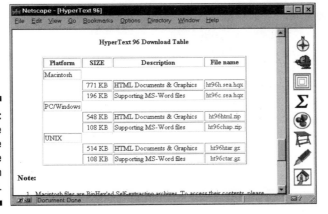

Figure 20-2:
Netscape
gives the
table its true
realization
on-screen.

This helps to show why a text-only alternative is critical. But when it comes to building such alternatives, especially using the <PRE> text tag, you might be able to use a few tips:

- ✔ Enter all text in columnar format first. Be sure to use a monospaced font (not a proportional one). Make sure that everything lines up as you want it to.

- ✔ Edit the text within the <PRE>. . .</PRE> block and insert all HTML markup, without adding extra spaces. This maintains a columnar format.

- ✔ Another alternative: Create a simple text file in which no HTML is required. Users can then either download or view this information through their browser, depending on how it's configured.

As an illustration of the first approach, compare the HTML markup in the following code section to its on-screen display, shown in Figure 20-3.

```
<HTML>
<HEAD>
<TITLE>Testing &lt;PRE&gt;</TITLE>
</HEAD>
<BODY>
<PRE>
<B>Column 1    Column2    Column3</B>
    Entry1,1    Entry1,2    Entry1,3
    Entry2,1    Entry2,2    Entry2,3
<A HREF="#end">Link1</A>         Entry3,2    Entry3,3
</PRE>
</BODY>
</HTML>
```

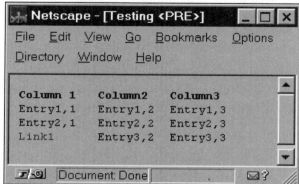

Figure 20-3:
The inclusion of HTML markup within <PRE> text makes it look unaligned until you see it displayed.

<FRAME> *Alternatives*

Unfortunately, repetition is the only alternative to the use of the frame-related tags. You can either build alternative pages altogether and steer your "frame-disadvantaged" users (that is, those users whose browsers don't support frame markup) at them explicitly, or you can use the <NOFRAME>. . .</NOFRAME> markup to provide an alternative directly within the same pages where you use <FRAME> and <FRAMESET> markup.

Either way, you'll have to set some kind of limit on the number of lines within the unframed materials that you want to display between navigation bars or equivalent static structures within an HTML document. You can use this technique to replace such things as a navigation frame or a company logo and attribution information. In our own designs, we have made a conscious decision that users would never have to scroll more than one screen up or down to get to a navigation bar and have built our pages accordingly. This seems to work pretty well. But it's a matter of choice, so you can follow your own instincts.

When it comes to a side-by-side frame-up (such as the one that Netscape uses for its online documentation, with a table of contents on the left and details on the right), the only reasonable alternative is make the table of contents a navigation bar item and to make it easy to jump back and forth between the table of contents and related detail documents. It's nowhere near as convenient as jumping between two simultaneously visible frames on-screen, but this approach has the same effect and works acceptably.

<MATH> *Alternatives*

The primary alternative to using <MATH> markup within your documents is to build a representation of the equations and other materials that you need in some other environment. Perhaps you would create this in a word processing, page layout, or typesetting program that can render mathematical notation. Next, you would capture the mathematical copy as a screen shot or PostScript image, convert it to a .GIF, and use the <IMG SRC="URL"> technique to position it on your page. Until HTML supports explicit mathematical notation, this kind of workaround will remain your best bet.

Knowing When to Split

By now, you may have received the impression that we think you should build your Web sites in pairs: One for advanced browsers that can handle all the bells and whistles of advanced HTML, and another for the more vanilla capabilities represented by HTML 2.0. This isn't necessarily the case, appearances to the contrary notwithstanding.

We actually advocate a document-by-document approach in which everyone who visits the site shares at least some common information. Only those documents that incorporate advanced markup need to be available in alternate forms; others can serve both audiences equally well. That's why you should approach the design of each document with a fresh pair of eyes, ready to decide whether your communication needs call for multiple versions of the same information or whether a single, vanilla version will do for everybody.

As you approach this decision, here are some questions that you will want to answer:

- ✔ What's your overall design structure? Does it demand advanced markup? (Some sites are built entirely around HTML tables and graphics and perforce must include complete alternatives; others require only selective alternates.)

- ✔ Why does the document on which you're working need advanced markup? Improved accessibility or intelligibility are valid reasons; advanced markup for the heck of it is not!

- ✔ What benefits does advanced markup deliver? Improved navigation, easier access to documents, and quicker selection of relevant materials are the best benefits you can get; the "gee whiz" factor gets lame after a while. . . .

Always try to get a feel for how much of your audience will be unable to appreciate your advanced efforts before you take on the extra work involved. If you're providing benefits to more than half your user population, go for it; if not, you may want to reconsider.

Managing Miscellany

Some aspects of advanced or proprietary HTML can show up on your pages without affecting the portion of your audience that must remain indifferent to it. We're talking about such things as background images or colors.

As long as you make your images take on transparent backgrounds, users won't necessarily care that they're missing an embossed 3-D bas-relief of your company's logo as a background. But if you forget and use a colored background, it may look a little funky for some user who has selected her favorite shade of fuchsia only to have her sense of tasteful color completely overwhelmed by your choice of a glaring puce.

Although the many little oddments and markup widgets that you could employ without unduly discommoding your "disadvantaged users" are simply too numerous to mention, we can provide a sure-fire technique to make sure that they don't become too onerous. Make sure to use some older and less capable browsers when you begin your page testing: With luck, you and your testers will be able to winnow out the less appealing aspects of your documents before the public ever sees them.

Adding Value for Value

As we close this chapter, we want to jump back from markup details and return to the content that gives your Web site its reason to exist. There's nothing wrong with using advanced HTML markup on your Web site as long as it adds to that site's capability to deliver and communicate its content.

When you add functionality or capability to your site, especially by adopting cutting-edge or proprietary markup to your documents, make sure that it enhances the content. You never want anything to detract from the content. As long as you add value for your audience, you will be respected and rewarded for your efforts. But if you obfuscate the content or alienate your users, you can expect to lose their respect, if not their support (and their continued referrals and visits).

In the next chapter, we move beyond HTML markup to the extensions and plugins that can add visual excitement and dynamism to your Web site. Stay tuned for some tips on how to carry this off with grace and wit!

Chapter 21

Extenuations for Extensions

In This Chapter

- ▶ Warning! Strange stuff ahead . . .
- ▶ Shelling into Shockwave
- ▶ Visualizing VRML Worlds
- ▶ Jumping into (or around) Java
- ▶ Mastering the mechanics of text
- ▶ Getting there from here
- ▶ Finding the latest resources
- ▶ Maximizing impact and interest

*T*he proliferation of added capability for advanced browsers has been nothing short of amazing. In the recent past, we've seen Netscape and other leading vendors either deliver or promise support for a list of technologies that range from advanced document presentation (Adobe Acrobat and its Portable Document Format, or PDF) to three-dimensional worldscapes (VRML).

A recent visit to Netscape's plugins page at

```
http://www.netscape.com/comprod/products/navigator
            /version_2.0/plugins/plugin_download.html
```

shows more than a dozen plugins in commercial release. We're aware of another dozen or more in beta test or under development for release sometime in 1996.

What does all this added capability mean to average users? Well, if those average users are running Netscape 2.*x* (or higher) or some other advanced browser, it means that they can add significant functionality to their desktops simply by downloading and installing the appropriate software. On the other hand, if those users don't have an advanced browser, it doesn't amount to a hill of beans!

That's why our most telling point in this chapter is to remind you that you absolutely cannot reach your broadest audience through content that depends on a plugin . . . at least, not today. This will probably change in the future, but for now, we strongly suggest that you refrain from delivering critical content through plugin-based material unless you have no other choice.

Thus, if your business is multimedia, you're probably safe in assuming that your audience will use a related plugin such as Shockwave. But if you're simply trying to add spice to conventional text or images, you want to provide an alternate form for materials delivered through a plugin. Think of it as an extension of the "alternate form discussion" from the preceding chapter if you like, but it's important not to withhold important content from anyone who visits your site, even if someone's browser can't handle what you've got to offer. We discuss the particulars in the sections that follow.

Warning! Strange Stuff Ahead

First, you want to include some scaffolding around plugin-based materials on your Web pages whenever you use them. The information on your Web site should include, but not be limited to, the following elements:

✔ A warning that certain browsers might be useful (or required) to get the best results from your site. This should include pointers to a download site for the "right browser," where appropriate. See Figure 21-1 for an example of this genre.

Figure 21-1:
The HyperText 96 Class Materials include a "Netscape only" warning right on the home page!

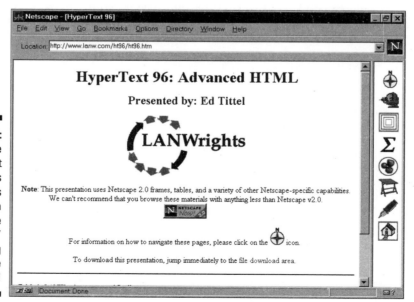

✔ A similar warning before any plugin-specific materials, with a download site for the necessary plug wherever possible. For some kinds of materials, additional supplementary materials may also make sense.

For example, Shockwave content can be supplemented by an appropriate Macromedia Director Projector file. This lets users download a self-running demonstration, as long as they're using either a Macintosh running Systems 7.*x,* or a PC running Windows 3.*x* or higher.

✔ Whenever it's reasonable to expect that your audience may be unfamiliar or inexperienced with your plugin(s) of choice, providing pointers to basic introductions and other resources is also a nice touch. This will help those users who are motivated or curious enough to want to learn more about your choice(s) of supplementary technologies.

In short, if you make it easy for users who may want to try out your plugin-based materials to obtain the building blocks they need, you will not only pique their interest but add to their bag of tricks. This can help improve your image and your visitation rates.

Shelling into Shockwave

In Chapter 15, we provide a thorough review of Shockwave technology, its constituent components, and the basics of its use. If you've succumbed to its allure or are thinking about adding "shocked" materials to your site, you'll want to follow our advice from the earlier section — namely:

✔ Warn your users that your pages contain Shockwave content on your home page.

✔ State browser and plugin requirements, and provide pointers to one or both sets of software.

✔ Include a pointer to an "About Shockwave" page, where you give its broad outlines and capabilities, and provide pointers to examples and tutorials.

✔ Discuss the "Director Projector" alternative to "shocked" content and provide alternative downloads for those users who aren't Shockwave-enabled.

With this kind of approach, you'll be sure to alienate as little as possible that portion of your audience that isn't ready to deal with Shockwave. Because you demonstrate ample concern for your users' plight, and show them a path to overcome their lack of Shockwave capability, you also show them that you care.

As for Shockwave content itself, our advice is more pointed:

✔ Given that most users must download via modem, keep your content as compact as possible. When files are large, provide ample warning, and give users a choice whether to download or not (this is another good reason for the Projector alternative, even for users with properly equipped browsers).

✔ Make sure that you use the Shockwave TEXTFOCUS attribute for the <EMBED> tag appropriately. If in doubt, try it on your beta testers and find out what they think!

✔ Use Shockwave content appropriately. Not everything benefits from this kind of treatment.

✔ Always test your work on multiple machines, especially the "other" platform (on a Mac if you've developed your Director materials on a PC, and vice versa).

✔ Use the Text tool whenever possible instead of importing bitmapped text; this helps keep movies small and manageable, too.

✔ Always provide instructions if users must interact with your Shockwave content. Use an icon or some consistent signpost with which they can find instructions, and tell them what this means in advance. Then, use the signpost wherever appropriate so that they can get help when they need it.

If you follow these simple guidelines, you stand a good chance of pleasing your site's visitors. Otherwise, ignore them at your peril!

Visualizing the Virtual with VRML

VRML's introduction to the Web pushes it toward a more realistic appearance. By allowing information to be structured and organized using everyday signs and symbols, it promises to extend the Web's capabilities while making the virtual world as familiar as the everyday one.

For developers, the biggest secret to using VRML is in the tools. It's no accident that the most powerful and best-developed VRML toolsets have been developed for high-end workstations such as the Silicon Graphics IRIS machines. This is one of those cases when the costs of entry are high but the benefits of up-front spending can pay off in increased productivity and in the quality of the resulting final products. This requires some careful balancing between budget constraints and your natural desires to produce the best possible content.

For users, the requirements are similar to those of other plugins — namely, the right browser and the right supplementary software. Here again, you want to point your users at those materials and provide the explanatory information as well. VRML puts pretty serious demands on bandwidth and on user platforms, as well as on developers, so you also want to warn your users about the size of your materials and about basic processing requirements.

For details on VRML design do's and don't's, as well as the very best resources on VRML online, we suggest that you check out the final pages of Chapter 16. You'll find this information, and more, waiting for you to bring your materials to (virtual) life!

Jumping into Java

Java is such a hot new topic on the Web right now that we have to shrink a little from the task of reducing it to its quintessence (like instant coffee?). Suffice it to say that you'll find ample sources of information online — so ample, in fact, that your biggest chore will be identifying the "good stuff" and separating it from the dross.

Beyond requiring you to master the details of an object-oriented programming language and a whole new set of HTML markup, Java also requires a new mindset. The best way to learn is to prowl the Web looking for good (and bad) examples of this technology. If you emulate the good examples and try to avoid the techniques or mistakes that mar the bad ones, you will probably do just fine.

As with the other plugin technologies mentioned in this chapter, be sure to flag your use of Java on your pages. Provide pointers to appropriate browsers, plug-ins, and explanatory materials. Build alternate pages, or use the <NOEMBED> tags to provide equivalent information to the less technically-priviledged side of your audience (or at least a blow-by-blow description so that your users know what they're missing).

When it comes to including Java materials, some of the best tips for effective use of applets in your pages are as follows:

- ✔ Learn as much as you can about Java or JavaScript before trying to use this new technology. The more you know, the better your product.

- ✔ Prowl the Web to find out about the latest Java trends, tools, tips, and techniques. Check the list at the end of Chapter 17 for a good set of "getting started" resources.

✔ Start by picking applets that you want to emulate; try to build them yourself by studying sample code and by making your emulation as much like the original as possible. The important thing here is not verisimilitude, though; it's understanding what makes Java tick!

✔ Learn and master the Java toolset: Obtain and use a compiler and a debugger; locate and use other useful tools. Stay tuned to the `comp.lang.java` newsgroup and other Java programmers' hangouts.

✔ Test the Java classes and commands systematically. Many features and functions within the Java environment are poorly documented, if they're documented at all; the only way to be sure how a component behaves is by trying its possibilities.

✔ Learn how to use the `<EMBED>` and `<APP>` tags and how to provide alternate content on your pages.

If you can become familiar with the Java development environment and keep track of what others are doing to use it, you will be able to add some super functionality to your Web site. As with CGI programs, don't feel compelled to reinvent the wheel every time you need an applet; be sure to cruise the Web to see what's already available for your use.

Be sure to revisit the final pages of Chapter 17 for more information about Java do's and don't's, and for a list of online Java-related resources.

Mastering the Mechanics of Text

When it comes to delivering additional text materials through your pages, your natural inclination may be to turn to some kind of advanced text reader. Although this can be advantageous to you and your readers, don't overlook some other obvious options, either — namely, common word processing or page layout files, or even plain text materials.

Again, heed our general advice about plugins, and advertise the presence of your text engine of choice along with download and background information pointers. Just be sure that your materials lend themselves to this kind of delivery and representation. Don't rely on your own good opinion, either — the only way to be sure is to aggressively solicit (and respond to) your beta testers' feedback in this area.

Concerning selecting a text viewing engine, Adobe's Acrobat technology and its Amber reader enjoy the biggest user share right now. But other technologies, such as Envoy and Common Ground, have also garnered appreciative audiences.

The best way to decide which one to use is to poll your user base for strong preferences, and then to weigh the costs of the distillation and delivery tools versus the benefits they deliver. Don't necessarily settle for the cheapest option; be sure to let user accessibility and convenience guide your decisions as well.

In many cases, you may even have to support multiple formats to reach the broadest possible audience. When that happens, be sure to settle on a base format, and build programs to generate the other formats that you support from that base. Concentrate your maintenance efforts on that master copy and let your software do the rest. That way, the human (that is, fallible) element will be reduced as much as possible.

For more information about using special text formats in your Web pages and about related resources and information, consult the concluding pages of Chapter 18 in this book.

Effective Augmentation

Given the plethora of plugins for Netscape (soon to be showing up on other browsers everywhere) it's probably just a matter of time before some kind of augmentation appears on your own Web pages. As long as you use this capability wisely and don't neglect the legions of users who may not be able to exploit your plugin(s) immediately, you should do well with whatever extensions you erect around your HTML documents.

The important thing is to stay focused on *content*. This means using plugins where they add to or enhance content, and eschewing them otherwise. Although the temptation to play may be nearly overwhelming, remember that delivering the content is the ultimate goal. Among other things, this also means taking the time to provide alternate forms of data that depend on plugins, instead of leaving the less advantaged part of your audience out. The more important the content is, the more crucial it is to make it available to everyone, plugged in or not. If you follow this suggestion, you will be able to grow your user base — and perhaps even persuade those users to upgrade their capabilities to match yours!

Glossary

.DCR — File extension for a Director film strip that's been converted from its original format by using Afterburner; the file is destined for Web delivery.

.DIR — File extension for an original, editable Macromedia Director file.

.SEA (Abbreviation for Self-Extracting Archive) — File extension for a self-extracting version of the most popular Macintosh file compression format, StuffIt (.SIT).

.SIT (Abbreviation for StuffIT archive) — File extension for the native StuffIt Macintosh compressed file format.

absolute — When used to modify pathnames or URLs, absolute means a full and complete specification (as opposed to a relative one). See *relative.*

Acrobat — A viewing program (helper application) from Adobe Systems; Acrobat is used for the portable document format (PDF) text display system. See *Amber.*

Afterburner — File compression software, used in conjunction with Shockwave from Macromedia, to compress native Director film strips for delivery over the Internet; compression is usually by 60 percent or more.

agent — Any of a class of software programs capable of interacting with network or Internet resources on another user's behalf.

alternative selectors — In HTML, alternative selectors refers to tag attributes that serve a similar function. For example, the functions of the CLASS and STYLE attributes can overlap.

Amber — The Netscape plugin version of Acrobat that allows you to view PDF files within Netscape.

anchor — In HTML, an anchor is a tagged text or graphic element that acts as a link to another location inside or outside a given Web document. Alternatively, it may be a location in a document that acts as the destination for an incoming link. The latter definition is most commonly used in this book.

animation — A computerized process of creating moving images by rapidly advancing from one still image to the next.

anonymous ftp — A type of Internet file access that relies on the File Transfer Protocol (ftp) service, where any user can typically access a file collection by logging in as *anonymous* and supplying his or her e-mail address as a password.

AppleScript — The scripting language for the Macintosh operating system, AppleScript is used to build Common Gateway Interface (CGI) programs for Macintosh-based Web servers.

ASCII (American Standard Code for Information Interchange) — A coding method used to represent standard alphabetic, numeric, and other keyboard characters in computer-readable, binary format.

attribute — In HTML tags, an attribute is a named characteristic of an associated tag. Attributes may be required or optional. Depending on the tag and the attribute, some attributes take values (if so, the syntax is ATTRIBUTE="value").

authoring software — In the context of HTML, authoring software refers to programs that understand HTML tags and their placement. Some authoring programs can even enforce HTML syntax; others can convert from word processing or document formatting programs to HTML formats.

authoring tool — See *authoring software.*

back end — The server-side of client/server structure is called the back end because this part of the processing is usually handled by programs running in obscurity on the server, out of sight (and mind) for most users. See also *front end.*

bandwidth — Technically, bandwidth is the range of electrical frequencies that a device can handle; more often, bandwidth is a measure of a communications technology's carrying capacity.

Basic — (Beginner's All-purpose Symbolic Instruction Code) A programming language, Basic (also called *BASIC*) is easy to learn and use. The most popular implementation of the language is QuickBasic from Microsoft Corporation.

beta test — The phase of software testing where a program or system is turned over to a select group of users outside the development organization for use in more or less real-life situations.

BIOS — (Basic Input/Output System) A basic driver software for a PC, the BIOS permits component devices to communicate with one another.

bitmapped — A graphic image that's represented as a matrix of binary on-off values, usually by conversion from some other graphics format.

body — The body is one of the main identifiable structures of any HTML document and is usually trapped between the <HEAD> information and the footer information.

bookmark — Most Web browsers include a facility for building a list of URLs that users want to keep for future reference. In its browser, Netscape calls such references *bookmarks.*

Boolean — Computer shorthand for logical operations, like those defined to combine or compare values (AND, OR, NOR, NOT, NAND, and so on).

broken graphic icon — A standard icon that appears within a browser when an <IMG> or other graphics tag is encountered, but the associated image file cannot be located or displayed.

browser — A Web access program that can request HTML documents from Web servers and render such documents on a user's display device. See also *client.*

BSD — (Berkeley Software Distribution) A flavor of UNIX that was particularly important in the late '70s and '80s when most of the enhancements and add-ons to UNIX appeared first in the BSD version (like TCP/IP).

bugs — Small verminous creatures that sometimes show up in software in the form of major or minor errors, mistakes, and gotchas. Bugs got their name from insects that, having been attracted to the glow of the filament in a tube, were found in antiquated tube-based computers of the late '50s and early '60s.

burn — To convert a file from its original uncompressed Macromedia format to a compressed Shockwave format using the Afterburner software.

bytecode — The intermediate, semi-compiled form of Java code created by the Java compiler *javac.*

C — A programming language developed at AT&T Bell Laboratories, C remains the implementation language for UNIX and the UNIX programmer's language of choice.

Cascading Style Sheets — (CSS) The latest W3C-sponsored specification for HTML document style sheets, which describe formatting and layout rules and conventions.

case sensitive — Means that the case of the letters used in computer input is significant. For example, HTML tags can be input in any mixture of upper- and lowercase (HTML tags are not case sensitive), but because HTML character entities (like É) are case sensitive, these entities must be reproduced exactly.

cast — In Macromedia Director, the cast is the collection of objects, which may be graphics, sounds, animations, or other data, that appears on the main display area.

CD-ROM — (Compact Disc – Read-Only Memory) A computer-readable version of the audio CD; CD-ROMs can contain up to 650MB of data, making them the distribution media of choice for many of today's large (some would even say *bloated*) programs and systems.

CERN — (Centre European Researche Nucleare) The Center for High-Energy Physics in Geneva, Switzerland; the birthplace of the World Wide Web.

change log — A record of changes made to elements within a Web site including files, text entries, graphical objects, and so on. The change log is used to keep track of changes and enhancements during the maintenance process.

character entity — A way of reproducing strange and wonderful characters within HTML, character entities take the form &string; where the ampersand (&) and semicolon (;) are mandatory metacharacters, and string names the character to be reproduced in the browser. Because character entities are case sensitive, the string between the ampersand and the semicolon must be reproduced exactly.

character mode — When referring to Web browsers, character mode (also called text mode) means that such browsers can reproduce text data only. Character-mode browsers cannot produce graphics directly without the assistance of a helper application.

chatterbots — In chat rooms and other interactive environments on the Web, these software agents provide help, give advice, and explain local conditions.

clickable map — A graphic in an HTML file that has had a pixel coordinate map file created for it. This map file enables regions of the graphic to point to specific URLs for graphically-oriented Web navigation.

client — The end-user side of the client/server arrangement, client typically refers to a consumer of network services. A Web browser is, therefore, a client program that talks to Web servers.

client/server — A model for computing that divides computing into two separate roles that are usually connected by a network: The client works on the end-user side of the connection and manages user interaction and display (input and output, and related processing), while the server works elsewhere on the network and manages data-intensive or shared processing activities (like serving up the collections of documents and programs that a Web server typically manages).

Common Gateway Interface (CGI) — The specification governing how Web browsers can communicate with and request services from Web servers; CGI is also the format and syntax for passing information from browsers to servers via forms or document-based queries in HTML.

Common Ground — A portable document format used to create input to one kind of text display engine available via the Web.

compiler — A special computer program that takes human-readable source code from some programming or scripting language and turns the code into a computer-readable binary equivalent.

computing platform — A way of referring to the kind of computer someone is using; this term encompasses both hardware (the type of machine, processor, and so on) and software (the operating system and applications) in use.

connections per minute — On a Web server, one of the most important capabilities is the simultaneous handling of user requests. The rate of this capability is measured in connections per minute, or the number of user requests that a server can handle simultaneously over the course of 60 seconds.

content — For HTML, content is its *raison d'etre;* although form is important, content is why users access Web documents and why they keep coming back for more.

content-type — A MIME convention for identifying the type of data being transported over a network for delivery to any of a set of programs, including e-mail readers and Web browsers.

convention — An agreed-upon set of rules and approaches that enables varying systems to communicate with one another and work together.

conversion program — In general, a program that converts one type of format to another; in the context of the Web, conversion program refers to a program that reads a native word processor or page layout file format and converts it to a corresponding HTML layout.

CPU — (Central Processing Unit) The master circuitry or chip that provides the brains of a typical computer.

cron — A UNIX utility that permits programs to be scheduled to run at specified times or at regular intervals. The *cron* utility is useful for handling automated maintenance tasks.

CSU/DSU (Channel Service Unit/Data Service Unit) — A special translating piece of hardware, found between a network and a digital telephone line, that translates data between the two formats. CSU/DSU is most commonly used to attach a network router to a T1 or other digital telephone line.

daemon — A special type of program (usually in the UNIX world) that runs constantly in the background, ready to handle certain types of network service requests. E-mail, http, and other Internet services depend on daemons to handle user service requests.

default — In general computer-speak, a default is a selection that's made automatically in a program, instruction, and so on when no selections are made explicitly. For HTML, the default is the value assigned to an attribute when you don't supply one.

desktop — (desktop machine) The computer that a user typically has on his or her desktop; desktop is a synonym for end-user computer or computer.

dial-up — A connection to the Internet (or some other remote computer or network) that is made by dialing up an access telephone number.

Director (Macromedia Director) — A large, complex software program used to create animated multimedia presentations on either a Macintosh or a PC. Director provides multimedia content for delivery via Shockwave technology.

directory path — The device and directory names needed to locate a particular file in any given file system; for HTML, UNIX-style directory paths usually apply.

directory structure — The underlying file container structure that describes the hierarchical organization of most computer file systems.

DNS (Domain Name Server) — *See* **domain names.**

document headings — The class of HTML tags that we generically refer to as <H*>, document headings enable Web page authors to insert headings of various sizes and weights (levels 1 through 6) to add structure to their documents' contents. As structural elements, headings identify the beginning of a new concept or idea within a document.

document root — On a Web server, the document root is the base directory where HTML files and other components for any particular Web site are located or where the directories containing these components are ultimately attached.

document structure — For HTML, document structure refers to the methods used to organize and navigate within HTML documents or related collections of documents.

document — The basic unit of HTML information, a document refers to the entire contents of any single HTML file. Because this concept doesn't always correspond to normal notions of a document, we refer to what could formally be called *HTML documents* more or less interchangeably with *Web pages,* which is how such documents are rendered by browsers for display.

document transfer rate — For Web servers, this rate refers to the speed at which pages can be delivered to users in response to their document requests (usually measured in documents per minute).

document-based queries — One of two methods of passing information from a browser to a Web server, document-based queries are designed to pass short strings of information to the server by using the METHOD="GET" HTTP method of delivery. This method is typically used for search requests or other short lookup operations.

domain names — The names used on the Internet as part of a distributed database system for translating computer names into physical addresses and vice versa.

DOS (Disk Operating System) — The underlying control program used to make most Intel-based PCs run. MS-DOS, from Microsoft Corporation, is the most widely used implementation of DOS and provides the scaffolding atop which the equally widely used Microsoft Windows software runs. See also *operating system.*

download — To transfer a file from a server to a user across a network or the Internet.

DSSSL (Document Style Semantics and Specification Language) — An early contender for HTML standardization, this is a formal language used to define SGML style sheets. By unanimous agreement, this language was found too complex and difficult for Web use.

DSSSL-Lite — A svelte subset of DSSSL, this style sheet language was considered for adoption as an HTML standard, but it, too, was judged too complex and difficult for ordinary mortals.

DTD (Document Type Definition) — A formal SGML specification for a document, a DTD lays out the structural elements and markup definitions that can then be used to create instances of documents.

dumb terminal — A display device with attached keyboard that relies on the intelligence of another computer to drive its display and interpret its keyboard inputs. Such devices were the norm in the heyday of the mainframe and minicomputer and are still widely used for reservation systems, point of sale, and other special-use applications.

electronic commerce — The exchange of money for goods or services via an electronic medium; many companies expect electronic commerce to do away with mail order and telephone order shopping by the end of the century.

e-mail — An abbreviation for electronic mail, e-mail is the preferred method for exchanging information between users on the Internet (and other networked systems).

encoded information — A way of wrapping computer data in a special envelope to ship it across a network, encoded information refers to data-manipulation techniques that change data formats and layouts to make them less sensitive to the rigors of electronic transit. Generally, recipients (of encoded information) must decode the encoded information before using it.

entity — See *character entity.*

Envoy — A portable document format and reader created by Novell for delivery and viewing of formatted documents over the Internet.

EPS (Encapsulated PostScript) — A special form of PostScript that includes all external references within the file to make it self-containing and ready to render in any environment.

error message — Information delivered by a program to a user, usually to inform the user that things haven't worked properly, if at all. Error messages are an ill-appreciated art form and contain some of the funniest and most opaque language we've ever seen (also, the most tragic for their unfortunate recipients).

error-checking — A collection of software utilities that systematically checks input or data for errors. An error-checking utility can respond to any condition for which it includes a pro-grammed response.

Ethernet — The most common local-area networking technology in use today, Ethernet was developed at about the same time (and by many of the same people and institutions) as the Internet.

event-handling mechanism — A built-in software facility that permits a program to respond to conditions or circumstances as they occur.

external reference — A resource that is stored somewhere other than where a Web document or program is located.

FAQ (Frequently Asked Questions) — Usenet newsgroups, mailing list groups, and other affiliations of like-minded individuals on the Internet usually designate a more senior member of their band to assemble and publish a list of frequently asked questions (and their answers), in an often futile effort to keep from answering them quite as frequently.

file dependencies — Contents of one file that depend on the contents of some other file (so that the containing file depends on the contained file).

file extension — In DOS, file extension refers to the 3-letter part of a filename after the period. For UNIX, Macintosh, and other file systems, file extension refers to the string after the right-most period in a filename. File extensions are used to label files as to type, origin, and possible use.

File Transfer Protocol — See *FTP*.

flame — Used as a verb ("He got flamed."), it means to be the recipient of a particularly hostile or nasty e-mail message; as a noun ("That was a real flame."), it refers to such a message.

flamewar — What happens when two or more individuals start exchanging hostile or nasty e-mail messages; this exchange is viewed by some as an art form and is best observed on Usenet or other newsgroups (where the `alt.flame...` or `alt.bitch` newsgroups are good places to browse for examples).

font manipulation — In the display of a Web document, font manipulation refers to increasing or decreasing the default font size, typeface, and style based on HTML extensions or style sheet settings.

footer — The concluding part of an HTML document, the footer should contain contact, version, date, and attribution information to help identify a document and its authors.

forms — In HTML, forms are built on special markup that enables browsers to solicit data from users and then deliver that data to specially designated input-handling programs on a Web server. Briefly, forms provide a mechanism to enable users to interact with servers on the Web.

front end — In the client/server model, the front end part refers to the client side, where the user views and interacts with information from a server; for the Web, browsers provide the front end that communicates with Web servers on the back end. See also *back end.*

FTP (sometimes ftp; File Transfer Protocol) — An Internet file transfer service based on the TCP/IP protocols, FTP provides a way to copy files to and from FTP servers elsewhere on a network.

full-text indexing — The ability to search on any string that occurs within a text file, full-text indexing enables you to search a collection of HTML or other documents by keyword, string, or substring.

fuzzy logic — A way of matching terms or keywords (for search purposes) that finds terms or patterns that are *somewhat* like the terms supplied to drive the search, as well as exact matches.

garbage collection — The ability to reclaim and reuse computer memory that has been allocated within a program, after the variables or data structures that used that memory are no longer needed.

gateway — A type of computer program that knows how to connect two or more different kinds of networks, how to translate information from one network's format to the other's, and vice versa. Common types of gateways include e-mail, database, and communications.

GIF (Graphics Information File) — GIF is one of a set of commonly used graphics formats within Web documents. GIF is commonly used because of its compressed format and compact nature.

global renaming — On a Web site, global renaming refers to the capacity to change a name in one place and have a software tool make equivalent changes to any other occurrences (of that same name) throughout the entire site. Global renaming is very useful when moving a site or changing existing content and references.

GNU free software license — A software license promulgated by the Free Software Foundation that permits royalty-free distribution of software, as long as all source code is included with the distribution package and all changes to the original are clearly marked and attributed to their authors.

Gopher — A program/protocol developed at the University of Minnesota, Gopher provides for unified, menu-driven presentation of a variety of Internet services, including WAIS, telnet, and FTP.

Graphical User Interface — See *GUI*.

graphics — In HTML documents, graphics are files that belong to one of a restricted family of types (usually GIF or JPEG) that are referenced via URLs for inline display on Web pages.

Graphics Information File — See *GIF*.

grep — An abbreviation for general regular expression parser, *grep* is a standard UNIX program that looks for patterns in files and reports on their occurrences. The *grep* program handles a wide range of patterns, including so-called regular expressions which can use substitutions and wild cards to provide powerful search-and-replace operations within files.

group — In VRML, a group is a named collection of nodes that acts as a single object within a virtual world.

GUI (Graphical User Interface, pronounced *gooey*) — GUIs are what make graphical Web browsers possible; they create a visually-oriented interface that makes users' interaction with computerized information easier.

Gzip — A popular file compression technology, used largely among the UNIX community, Gzip is freely available through any of the countless GNU licensees.

HDTV (High Definition TeleVision) — An emerging, fully digital, high-resolution form of video data that should become the next prevailing broadcast TV standard.

header files — In the Web world, these files contain information that identifies incoming data by MIME type (and subtype, where applicable).

heading — For HTML, a heading is a markup tag used to add document structure. The term is sometimes used to refer to the initial portion of an HTML document between the `<HEAD>` . . . `</HEAD>` tags, where titles and context definitions are commonly supplied.

helper applications — Today, browsers can display multiple graphics files (and other kinds of data); sometimes, browsers must pass particular files — for example, motion picture or sound files — over to other applications that know how to render the data they contain. Such programs are called helper applications, because they help the browser deliver Web information to users.

hierarchical filing system — A typical computer file system, where directories are organized in a hierarchical organization (one directory acts as the root, with a tree of other directories sprouting from it).

hierarchical structure — A way of organizing Web pages by using links that make some pages subordinate to others. See *tree structure(d)* for another description of this kind of organization.

history list — Each time a user accesses the Web, his or her browser normally keeps a list of all the URLs visited during that session; this list is called a history list and provides the user with a handy way to jump back to any page that he or she has already visited while online. History lists normally disappear when the user exits the browser program.

Host — An Internet-connected computer that supports one or more of the standard services, including Web access, e-mail, file transfer, and more.

HotJava — The Java-enabled Web browser from Sun Microsystems, which is written in the Java programming language.

hotlist — A Web page that consists of a series of links to other pages, usually annotated with information about what's available on that link. Hotlists act like switchboards to content information and are usually organized around a particular topic or area of interest.

HTML (HyperText Markup Language) — The SGML-derived markup language used to create Web pages. Not quite a programming language, HTML nevertheless provides a rich lexicon and syntax for designing and creating useful hypertext documents for the Web.

http or **HTTP** (Hypertext Transfer Protocol) — The Internet protocol used to manage communication between Web clients (browsers) and servers.

httpd (http daemon) — The name of the collection of programs that runs on a Web server to provide Web services. In UNIX-speak, a daemon is a program that runs all the time and listens for service requests of a particular type; thus, an *httpd* is a program that runs continually on a Web server, ready to field and handle Web service requests.

hyperlink — A shorthand term for hypertext link. See also *hypertext link.*

hypermedia — Any of a variety of computer media — including text, graphics, video, sound, and so on — available through hypertext links on the Web.

hypertext — A method of organizing text, graphics, and other data for computer use that lets individual data elements point to one another; hypertext is a nonlinear method of organizing information (especially text).

hypertext link — In HTML, a hypertext link is defined by special markup that creates a user-selectable document element that, when selected, can change the user's focus from one document (or part of a document) to another.

IETF (Internet Engineering Task Force) — The official standards organization (a suborganization of the Internet Architecture Board, or IAB) that governs all TCP/IP and other Internet-related standards.

image map — A synonym for clickable image, image map refers to an overlaid collection of pixel coordinates for a graphic. This image map can be used to locate the region of a Web page graphic that a user selects by clicking the mouse. The map location, in turn, is used to select a related hypertext link for further Web navigation.

inheritance — In the object-oriented programming world, inheritance defines a relationship among objects in a hierarchy, where objects that are subordinate to other objects acquire attributes and characteristics because of that relationship. By inheritance, subordinate objects automatically include information defined for their parents in the hierarchy.

INIT — On the Macintosh, a program that runs during the computer's initialization phase to augment or modify the basic operating system's behavior or characteristics.

ink effects — Within Macromedia Director, text-based colorization or animation effects are generically referred to by this term.

input-handling program — For Web services, a program that runs on a Web server and is designated by the ACTION attribute of an HTML <FORM> tag. The job of the input-handling programs is to field, interpret, and respond to user input from a browser. The program typically custom-builds an HTML document in response to some user request.

interleaved — For graphical images on the Web, interleaved describes the manner of the image's initial display. An interleaved image displays on-screen in increasing levels of detail instead of from the top down. The levels of detail appear as individual lines of pixels separated by a constant interval during the display. This process gives interleaved images the appearance of being drawn in slices.

intermediate code — A way of representing a computer program in a form that's somewhere between human-readable source code and machine-readable binary executable code. Java bytecode is a form of intermediate code, ready to be converted into a binary executable form at the user's workstation through the agency of the Java runtime system.

internal link — A hyperlink on a Web site that links to a resource on the same site (or in some cases, within the same document).

Internaut — Someone who travels using the Internet (like *Astronaut* or *Argonaut*).

Internet — A worldwide collection of networks that began with technology and equipment funded by the U.S. Department of Defense in the 1970s that today links users in nearly every known country, who speak nearly every known language.

Internet Studio — A planned Microsoft software product (formerly code-named *Blackbird*) that will include Web document authoring, management, and maintenance utilities.

InterNIC (Internet Network Information Center) — The Internet agency that handles IP address allocation and domain name registration facilities.

IP — (Internet Protocol) IP is the specific networking protocol of the same name used to tie computers together over the Internet; IP is also used as a synonym for the whole TCP/IP protocol suite. See also *TCP/IP*.

IP address — A unique numeric address for a particular machine or physical interface on the Internet (or any other TCP/IP-based network); an IP address consists of four decimal octets separated by periods (such as, 108.28.36.51).

IPnG (IP Next Generation, or IPv6) — An emerging replacement standard for TCP/IP that will broaden the address space for IP from its current ceiling of available addresses.

ISDN (Integrated Services Digital Network) — An emerging digital technology for telecommunications that offers higher bandwidth and better signal quality than old-fashioned analog telephone lines. It is not yet available in many parts of the U.S. or in the rest of the world.

ISO (International Standards Organization) — The granddaddy of standards organizations worldwide, the ISO is a body made of standards bodies from countries all over the place. Most important communications and computing standards — like the telecommunications and character code standards mentioned in this book — are the subject of ISO standards.

Java — A specialized object-oriented programming language designed for creation of platform-independent, network deliverable, client-side applications. Some Java applications may be invoked within Web documents to add dynamic, ongoing behavior.

JavaScript — A scripting language that draws on underlying Java classes and objects to provide a simplified method to include dynamic behavior within Web documents.

JPEG or **JPG** (Joint Photographic Experts' Group) — An industry association that defined a particularly compressible format for image storage that is designed for dealing with complex color still images (like photographs). Files stored in this format usually take the extension JPEG (except on DOS or Windows machines, which use the three-character JPG equivalent). Today, JPEG is emerging as the graphics format standard of choice for use on the WWW.

Kbps (Kilobits per second) — A measure of communications speeds, in units of 2^{10} bits per second (2^{10} = 1,024, which is just about 1,000 and explains the quasi-metric K notation).

kerning — In typography, kerning refers to the relationships between characters as they appear on a document, including spacing and relative positioning.

KISS (Keep It Simple, Stupid!) — A self-descriptive philosophy that's supposed to remind us to "eschew obfuscation," except it's easier to understand!

LAN (Local Area Network) — Typically, one of a variety of communications technologies used to link computers together in a single building, business, or campus environment.

LaTeX — A specialized version of Donald Knuth's TeX typesetting program, LaTeX includes templates and definitions for creating book-length manuscripts.

layout element — In an HTML document, a layout element is a paragraph, list, graphic, horizontal rule, heading, or some other document component whose placement on a page contributes to its overall look and feel.

leading — In typography, leading refers to the amount of space between lines of text (pronounced properly, rhymes with "bedding").

linear text — Shorthand for old-fashioned documents that work like this book does: by placing one page after the other, ad infinitum in a straight line. Even though such books have indexes, pointers, cross-references, and other attempts to add linkages, users must apply these linkages manually (rather than by clicking your mouse).

Lingo — A scripting language used within Macromedia Director to create and automate animation and other repetitive or time-based behavior in a multimedia presentation.

link — For HTML, a link is a pointer in one part of a document that can transport users to another part of the same document or to another document entirely. This capability puts the *hyper* into hypertext. In other words, a link is a one-to-one relationship/association between two concepts or ideas, similar to cognition (the brain has triggers such as smell, sight, sound that cause a link to be followed to a similar concept or reaction).

link map — Within a Web site, a directed graph that shows the links between and among constituent documents.

linked media files — In the multimedia world, linked media files refer to multimedia content files that include references to other files within themselves. Shockwave for Director does not currently support such files for Internet-based delivery.

list element — An item in an HTML list structure tagged with the `<LI>` (list item) tag.

list tags — HTML tags for a variety of list styles, including ordered lists `<OL>`, unordered lists `<UL>`, menus `<MENU>`, glossary lists `<DL>`, or directory lists `<DIR>`.

listserv — An Internet e-mail handling program, typically UNIX-based, that provides mechanisms to let users manage, contribute and subscribe to, and exit from named mailing lists that distribute messages to all subscribed members daily. A common mechanism for delivering information to interested parties on the Internet, this program is how the HTML working group communicates amongst its members.

Local Area Network — See *LAN.*

LOD (Level of Detail) — The name of a specific root node in the VRML environment, this node often acts as the basis upon which entire virtual worlds are constructed.

log files — On a Web server, log files accumulate data about errors, data access, and user activity that may later be analyzed and perused to determine site behavior, solve problems, and improve document relationships and designs.

logical markup — Refers to any of a number of HTML character-handling tags that exist to provide emphasis or to indicate that a particular kind of device or action is involved.

Lynx — A widely used UNIX-based character-mode Web browser.

Macromedia Director — See *Director.*

maintenance — The process of regularly inspecting, testing, and updating the contents of Web pages; also, an attitude that such activities are both inevitable and advisable.

majordomo — A set of Perl programs that automate the operation of multiple mailing lists, including moderated and unmoderated mailing lists and routine handling of subscribe/ unsubscribe operations.

map file — A set of pixel coordinates on a graphic image that correspond to the boundaries of regions that users might select when using the graphic for Web navigation. This map file must be created by using a graphics program to determine regions and their boundaries, and then stored on the Web server that provides the coordinate translation and URL selection services.

markup — A way of embedding special characters (metacharacters) within a text file to instruct a computer program how to handle the contents of the file itself.

markup language — A formal set of special characters and related capabilities used to define a specific method for handling the display of files that include markup; HTML is a markup language that is an application of SGML and is used to design and create Web pages.

Mbps (Megabits per second) — A measure of communications speeds, in units of 2^{20} bits per second (2^{20} = 1,048,576 which is just about 1,000,000 and explains the quasi-metric M notation).

metacharacter — A specific character within a text file that signals the need for special handling; in HTML the angle brackets ($<$ $>$), ampersand ($\&$), pound sign ($\#$), and semicolon ($;$) can all function as metacharacters.

method — In object-oriented programming, a method defines a legal operation or transformation associated with a particular object. For HTML, a method refers to one of several types of data delivery associated with communicating `<FORM>` input from a user to a Web server.

MIME (Multipurpose Internet Mail Extensions) — http communications of Web information over the Internet rely on a special variant of MIME formats to convey Web documents and related files between servers and users, and vice versa.

mis-matched tags — In HTML, mis-matched tags refer to opening a marked segment of text with one tag, and attempting to close it with an invalid or incorrect closing tag (for example, `<H1>This is wrong!</H2>`).

modem (acronym for **mod**ulator/**dem**odulator) — A piece of hardware that converts between the analog forms for voice and data used in the telephone system and the digital forms for data used in computers. In other words, a modem lets your computer communicate by using the telephone system.

MOO (MUD, Object-Oriented) — A particular implementation of a MUD, MOOs are built to be flexible and extensible, rather than bounded and static, like ordinary MUDs. See also *MUD.*

Mosaic — A powerful graphical Web browser originally developed at NCSA, now widely licensed and used for a variety of commercial browser implementations.

MPEG or **MPG** (Motion Picture Experts' Group) — A highly compressed format designed for use in moving pictures or other multiframe-per-second media (like video). MPEG can not only provide tremendous compression (up to 200 to 1), but it also updates only elements that have changed on-screen from one frame to the next. This feature makes the MPEG format extraordinarily efficient as well — MPEG is the common file extension to denote files using this format and MPG is the three-letter equivalent on DOS and Windows systems (which can't handle four-letter file extensions).

MPPP (Multilink Point-to-Point Protocol) — An Internet protocol that allows simultaneous use of multiple physical connections between one computer and another to aggregate their combined bandwidth and create a larger virtual link between the two machines.

MUCK (Multi-User Consensual Knowledge-base) — A user-extendible, multiuser adventure game.

MUD (Multi-User Dungeon) — A text-based virtual world where multiple users can collaborate and compete within an orchestrated fantasy environment.

multimedia — A method of combining elements such as text, sound, graphics, and full-motion or animated video within a single compound computer document.

multiple inheritance — Some object oriented programming languages, like C++, support multiple inheritance. In this kind of environment, an object can have multiple parents in the object hierarchy and can inherit characteristics and attributes from all parents.

MVS (Multiple Virtual Storage) — A file system used on IBM mainframes and clones.

Native multithreading — A programming language with a built-in thread-handling mechanism (like Java). Native multithreading enables programs to create and manage multiple execution threads explicitly.

navigate — The process of finding your way around a particular Web site, or the Web in general.

navigation — In the context of the Web, navigation refers to the use of hyperlinks to move within or between HTML documents and other Web-accessible resources.

navigation bar — A way of arranging a series of hypertext links on a single line of a Web page to provide a set of navigation controls for an HTML document or a set of HTML documents.

navigation buttons — Using graphics to provide navigation links; otherwise, a form of navigation bar. See also *navigation bar.*

NCSA (National Center for Supercomputing Applications) — A research unit of the University of Illinois at Urbana, where the original Mosaic implementation was built and where the NCSA *httpd* Web server code is maintained and distributed.

nesting — In computer terms, one structure that occurs within another is said to be nested; in HTML, nesting happens most commonly with list structures which may be freely nested within one another, regardless of type.

netiquette — A networking takeoff on the term *etiquette*, netiquette refers to the written and unwritten rules of behavior on the Internet. When in doubt if an activity is permitted or not, ask first, and then act only if no one objects (check the FAQ for a given area, too — the FAQ often explicitly states the local rules of netiquette for a newsgroup, mailing list, or other group).

network link — The tie that binds a computer to a network; for dial-in Internet users, the network link is usually a telephone link. For directly attached users, this link is whatever kind of technology (Ethernet, token-ring, FDDI, or so on) that is in local use.

node — A basic object within the VRML environment, a node can appear to be an independent graphic within a scene or may be a constituent part of a group node.

numeric entity — A special markup element that reproduces a particular character from the ISO-Latin-1 character set, a numeric entity takes the form &#nnn; where nnn is the 1, 2, or 3-digit numeric code that corresponds to a particular character.

object — The basic element within an object-oriented environment, any single object represents a particular instance of a class of possible objects, where all share a common underlying definition and an associated set of methods.

object type — A named kind of data structure in programming languages, an object's type is the specific data type associated with an object.

object-oriented — A programming methodology that concentrates on the definition of constituent parts of a program and the operations that can be performed upon the parts (called methods).

obsolete elements — Within HTML, obsolete elements are markup codes that are no longer supported within the current HTML specifications.

OCR (Optical Character Recognition) — A class of software that can "read" and interpret image data to convert pictures of text to a best-guess translation into actual textual data.

on-demand connection — A dial-up link to a service provider that is available whenever it's needed (on demand, get it?).

online — A term that indicates that information, activity, or communications are located on, or taking place in, an electronic, networked computing environment (like the Internet). The opposite of online is offline, which is what your computer is as soon as you disconnect from the Internet.

operator overloading — In programming languages (like C or C++) operator overloading refers to the ability to use one type of operator on data that may not belong to that type (for example, to use the + operator to add two strings together).

orphan files — On a Web site, an orphan file is a file that is not referenced by any other file (so you have no way to get to the orphan file, except through its absolute URL).

OS (Operating System) — The underlying control program on a computer that makes the hardware run and supports the execution of one or more applications. DOS, UNIX, and OS/2 are all examples of operating systems.

packet — A basic unit (or package) of data used to describe individual elements of online communications; in other words, data moves across networks (like the Internet) in packets.

pages — The generic term for the HTML documents that Web users view on their browsers.

paragraphs — The basic elements of text within an HTML document, <P> is the markup tag used to indicate a paragraph break in text (the closing </P> tag is currently optional in HTML).

parser — A program that reads text input for the purpose of recognizing and interpreting particular strings. A parser is the first part of a compiler, and reads the source code to recognize language terms and operators, to build a formal representation of the program's contents and structure.

path, pathname — See *directory path*.

PC (personal computer) — Today, PC is used as a generic term to refer to just about any kind of desktop computer; its original definition was as a product name for IBM's 8086-based personal computer, the IBM PC.

PDF (portable document format) — The name of the document format for Acrobat from Adobe Systems, Inc. .PDF is also used as the file extension for files in this particular format.

Perl — A powerful, compact programming language that draws from the capabilities of languages like C, Pascal, and BASIC. Perl is emerging as the language of choice for CGI programs. Its emergence is partly owing to its portability and the many platforms on which it is currently supported and partly owing to its ability to exploit system services in UNIX quickly and easily.

pipe — As used in this book, pipe generally refers to the bandwidth of the connection in use between a user's workstation and the Internet (or the server on the other end of the connection, actually).

pixel (abbreviation for picture element) — A single group of phosphors on a CRT creates a dot of color. When it is considered part of an image being displayed, this dot corresponds to a pixel.

plain text — Usually refers to vanilla ASCII text, as created or viewed in a simple text-editing program.

platform — Synonym for computer.

plugin — A Web browser add-in program that operates under the umbrella of the browser itself, thereby extending the program's overall capabilities (for example, Amber and Shockwave are both Netscape plugins).

pointer — In general, a name or value that points from one location or document to another. In this book, we often use this term to mean a URL that points from one HTML document to another.

port address — TCP/IP-based applications use the concept of a port address to know which program to talk to on the receiving end of a network connection. Because many programs may be running on a computer at one time — including multiple copies of the same program — the port address provides a mechanism to uniquely identify exactly which process the data should be delivered to.

portable document technology — See *PDF*.

PostScript — An Adobe page description language, used as a format for printing and display purposes by many programs and devices.

POTS (Plain Old Telephone System) — The normal analog telephone system, just like the one you probably have at home.

PPP (Point-to-Point Protocol) — A modern, low-overhead serial communications protocol, typically used to interconnect two computers via modem. Most Web browsers require either a PPP or SLIP connection in order to work.

preprocessor — A special program that parses source code or other text to translate embedded strings into (more verbose or complex) final forms before interpretation or compilation occurs.

property — A particular object attribute, or its associated value.

proprietary — A data format, specification, or operation that's defined (and owned) by a company rather than by a standards organization. Proprietary HTML markup is that markup created and used exclusively within certain browsers (like the <CENTER> tag in Netscape, for example).

protocol — A formal, rigidly-defined set of rules and formats that computers use to communicate with one another.

provider — See *service provider*.

publication process — For the Web, the process of gathering, organizing, and delivering information in the form of HTML documents and supporting materials.

QED (Latin abbreviation for *Quod erat demonstrandum*, or "Which was to be demonstrated") — A mathematical organization devoted to promoting effective uses of mathematics and computers, this group is advising the W3C on the final form of HTML mathematics notation.

QuickTime — An Apple-derived multimedia/animation format, QuickTime is used across a broad variety of platforms today.

RAM (Random Access Memory) — The memory used in most computers to store the results of ongoing work and to provide space to store the operating system and applications that are actually running at any given moment.

Random Access Memory — See *RAM.*

RealAudio — The audio helper application, from Progressive Network, which adds audio playback to a variety of Web browsers across multiple platforms.

relational database — A special type of database that organizes individual records into tables, where the columns specify the fields and attributes for all records, and the rows contain individual record instances.

relative — When applied to URLs, relative means that in the absence of the <BASE> tag, the link is relative to the current page's URL in which the link is defined. This makes for shorter, more compact URLs and explains why most local URLs are relative, not absolute. See also *absolute.*

request — In a client/server environment, clients request information to be delivered by a server. When you click a URL, you're implicitly requesting some server to deliver the corresponding HTML document or other resource to your workstation.

rescale — For graphics, rescale means to resize an image while maintaining its original aspect ratio and relative dimensions.

resource — Any HTML document or other item or service available via the Web. Resources are what URLs point to.

response — When a client makes a request in a client/server environment, the server responds with the requested information or with some other kind of response that reports on the request itself (invalid request, data not available, or whatever).

return (short for carriage return) — In text files, a return is what causes the words on a line to end and makes the display pick up at the leftmost location on the display. As used in this book, return means don't hit the Enter or Return key on your keyboard in the middle of a line of HTML markup or a URL specification.

RFC (Request for Comment) — An official IETF standards document.

RGB (Red Green Blue) — The name of a computer-based color representation scheme for graphics displays.

RGB code — A specific numeric value that corresponds to particular values for red, green, and blue components, used to designate particular colors and shades.

robot — A special Web-traveling program that wanders all over the place, following and recording URLs and related titles for future reference (like in search engines).

ROM (Read-Only Memory) — A form of computer memory that allows values to be stored only once; after the data is initially recorded, the computer can only read the contents. ROM is used to supply constant code elements like bootstrap loaders, network addresses, and other more or less unvarying programs or instructions.

root — The base of a directory structure above which no references are legal.

router — A special-purpose piece of internetworking gear that helps to connect networks together, a router is capable of reading the destination address of any network packet. The router can forward the packet to a local recipient if its address resides on any network that the router can reach or on to another router if the packet is destined for delivery to a network that the current router cannot access.

RTF (Rich Text Format) — A platform independent text representation often used as an intermediate format when converting one type of text, word processing, or page layout file into some other form. Also, the file extension for a Rich Text Format file.

sampling rates — For audio, the sampling rate refers to the number of bits used to represent sound information over a particular time interval. The higher the sampling rate, the more true-to-life the corresponding sound information.

scene graph — In VRML, the scene graph defines the ordering and precedence among all the nodes in any virtual world. The earlier a node appears in such a graph, the higher its precedence and the more impact it has on how the scene looks when displayed.

score — In Macromedia Director, the score describes the sequence of events and animation actions that are scheduled to occur as individual frames are played in sequence. The score also describes conditional processing and frame sequence alterations that can occur during playback.

screen — The glowing part on the front of your computer monitor where you see the Web do its thing (and anything else your computer might like to show you).

search engine — A special Web program that can search the contents of a database of available Web pages and other resources to provide information that relates to specific topics or keywords supplied by a user.

search tools — Any of a number of programs that can permit HTML documents to become searchable by using the `<ISINDEX>` tag. This tag informs the browser of the need for a search window and behind-the-scenes indexing and anchoring schemes to let users locate particular sections of or items within a document.

server — A computer on a network whose job is to listen for particular service requests and to respond to those that it knows how to satisfy.

server root — On a Web server, the server root defines the root of that server's programs and documents. This concept is used to define the scope for file access permissions for users and administrators alike.

service provider — An organization that provides individuals or organizations with access to the Internet. Service providers usually offer a variety of communications options for their customers, ranging from analog telephone lines, to a variety of higher-bandwidth leased lines, to ISDN and other digital communications services.

setup — When negotiating a network connection, the phase at the beginning of the communications process is called the *setup*. At this point, protocol details, communication rates and error-handling approaches are worked out, allowing the connection to proceed correctly and reliably thenceforth.

SGML (Standard Generalized Markup Language) — An ISO standard document definition, specification, and creation mechanism that makes platform and display differences across multiple computers irrelevant to the delivery and rendering of documents.

shading — In a graphics environment, shading represents the results of the complex calculations that must occur to depict the effect of light and shadow on three-dimensional graphical objects.

shell — See *UNIX shell.*

Shocked — Used as an adjective, Shocked often indicates that Web materials have been prepared for use with a Shockwave plugin for display.

Shockwave — The Macromedia technology (and plugin) used to create Internet-deliverable Director presentations and to display them within a Web browser.

single inheritance — In object-oriented languages, single inheritance refers to the capacity to inherit attributes and characteristics from only one parent object (as is the case with Java).

singleton — For HTML, a singleton tag has no corresponding closing tag (for example `<P>` and `<BASE>` are both singletons, even though `<P>` takes no attributes, while `<BASE>` does).

SLIP (Serial Line Interface Protocol) — A relatively old-fashioned TCP/IP protocol used to manage telecommunications between a client and a server that treats the phone line as a slow extension to a network.

SMTP (Simple Mail Transfer Protocol) — The underlying protocol and service for Internet-based electronic mail.

spider (Web spider, WebCrawler) — A class of Internet software agents that tirelessly investigate Web pages and their links, while storing information about their travels for inclusion in the databases typically used by search engines.

SSL (Secure Sockets Library) — A Netscape-designed Web commerce programming library, intended to help programmers to easily add secure transactions across the Web.

stage — For Macromedia Director, the stage represents the display window where a presentation ultimately appears during playback.

stdin (UNIX standard input device) — The default source for input in the UNIX environment, stdin is the input source for CGI programs as well.

stdout (UNIX standard output device) — The default recipient for output in the UNIX environment, stdout is the output source for Web browsers and servers as well (including CGI programs).

style sheet — A document that rigorously describes how classes of markup are to be rendered upon HTML document display, including font selections, font styles, leading, kerning, and color schemes.

syntax checker — A program that checks a particular HTML document's markup against the rules that govern HTML's use; a recommended part of the testing regimen for all HTML documents.

syntax — Literally, the formal rules for how to speak, we use syntax in this book to describe the rules that govern how HTML markup looks and behaves within HTML documents. The real syntax definition for HTML comes from the SGML Document Type Definition (DTD).

T1 — A high-speed (1.544 Mbps) digital communications link.

tag — The formal name for an element of HTML markup, usually enclosed in angle brackets (< >).

TCP (Transmission Control Protocol) — The transport layer protocol for the TCP/IP suite, TCP is a reliable, connection-oriented protocol that usually guarantees delivery across a network. See also *TCP/IP.*

TCP/IP (Transmission Control Protocol/Internet Protocol) — The name for the suite of protocols and services used to manage network communications and applications over the Internet.

telnet — The Internet protocol and service that lets you take a smart computer (your own, probably) and make it emulate a dumb terminal over the network. Briefly, telnet is a way of running programs and using capabilities on other computers across the Internet.

template — Literally, a model to imitate, we use the term template in this book to describe the skeleton of a Web page, including the HTML for its heading and footer, and any consistent layout and navigation elements for a page or set of pages.

template-based search — A search that follows a set of values specified within a form.

tenant — A term applied to the WebMasters or administrators who manage a site located on somebody else's Web server (usually an ISP's).

terminal emulation — The process of making a full-fledged, stand-alone computer act like a terminal attached to another computer, terminal emulation is the service that telnet provides across the Internet.

test plan — The series of steps and elements to follow when conducting a formal test of software or other computerized systems; we strongly recommend that you write — and use — a test plan as a part of your Web publication process.

TeX — Donald Knuth's powerful typesetting environment, which pioneered the delivery of comprehensive, practical mathematical typesetting, that defines the foundation on which HTML <MATH> notation is based.

text controls — Any of a number of HTML tags, including both physical and logical markup, text controls provide a method of managing the way that text appears within an HTML document.

text engine — A browser plugin or helper application that can render highly-formatted text and graphics based on a particular and specific format, either for printing or computer display.

text mode — See *character mode.*

throughput — Another measure of communications capability, throughput refers to the amount of data that can be "put through" a connection in a given period of time. Throughput differs from bandwidth in being a measure of actual performance, instead of a theoretical maximum for the medium involved.

thumbnail — A miniature rendering of a graphical image, used as a link to the full-sized version.

tiling — A technique for filling an entire region with graphics data that relies on taking a small area of graphics within that region and repeating it like a set of tiles to cover the area.

title — The text supplied between <TITLE> . . . </TITLE> defines the text that shows up on that page's title bar when displayed; the title is also used as data in many Web search engines.

transparent background — See *transparent GIF.*

transparent GIF — A specially rendered GIF image that takes on the background color selected in a browser capable of handling such GIFs. This makes the graphic blend into the existing color scheme and provides a more professional-looking page.

tree structure(d) — Computer scientists like to depict hierarchies in graphical terms, which makes them look like upside-down trees (a single root at the top, multiple branches below). File systems and genealogies are examples of tree structured organizations that we're all familiar with, but they abound in the computer world. This type of structure also works well for certain Web document sets, especially larger, more complex ones. See also *hierarchical structure.*

unclosed elements — In HTML a marked region of text that's missing a required closing tag (for example <H1>This is wrong).

UNIX shell — The name of the command-line program used to manage user-computer interaction, the shell can also be used to write CGI scripts and other kinds of useful programs for UNIX.

UNIX — The operating system of choice for the Internet community at large and the Web community, too, UNIX offers the broadest range of tools, utilities, and programming libraries for Web server use.

URI (Uniform Resource Identifier) — Any of a class of objects that identify resources available to the Web; both URLs and URNs are examples of URIs.

URL (Uniform Resource Locator) — The primary naming scheme used to identify Web resources, URLs define the protocols to be used, the domain name of the Web server where a resource resides, the port address to be used for communication, and the directory path to access a named Web file or resource.

URL-encoded text — A method for passing information requests and URL specification to Web servers from browsers, URL encoding replaces spaces with plus signs (+) and substitutes special hex codes for a range of otherwise unreproducible characters. This method is used to pass document queries from browsers to servers.

URN (Uniform Resource Name) — A permanent, unchanging name for a Web resource, URNs are seldom used in today's Web environment. They do, however, present a method guaranteed to obtain access to a resource, as soon as the URN can be fully resolved. (A URN can consist of human or organizational contact information, instead of resource location data.)

Usenet — An Internet protocol and service that provides access to a vast array of named newsgroups, where users congregate to exchange information and materials related to specific topics or concerns.

ViewMovie — A Netscape plugin for viewing MOV animation files.

virtual shopping cart — A stateful Web construct that lets users visit multiple Web pages, gathering a set of items that they've selected along the way.

virus — A type of self-replicating program that seeks to distribute itself around a network, or the Internet, for either benign or malign purposes.

VRML (Virtual Reality Modeling Language) — VRML is a fully-fledged computer programming language designed to facilitate creation of complete, three-dimensional, graphical spaces called *virtual worlds*.

wanderer — A synonym for spider or robot, wanderer refers to a class of software agents that prowl the Web, following links and documenting what they find as they go. These programs provide much of the raw material that's organized by search databases, for investigation by search engines.

watermark — A technique for maintaining a fixed background for HTML documents that stays the same, even as foreground materials scroll across the display.

Web — Shorthand for the World Wide Web (or W3), we also use Web in this book to refer to a related, interlinked set of HTML documents.

Web pages — Synonym for HTML documents, we use Web pages in this book to refer to sets of related, interlinked HTML documents, usually produced by a single author or organization.

Web server — A computer, usually on the Internet, that plays host to *httpd* and related Web-service software.

Web server administrator — The individual responsible for the setup, configuration, and maintenance of a Web server.

Web site — An addressed location, usually on the Internet, that provides access to the set of Web pages corresponding to the URL for a given site; thus, a Web site consists of a Web server and a named collection of Web documents, both accessible through a single URL.

Web spider, Web crawler — See *spider.*

Webify — The process of converting a document of any kind into a Web-viewable format, typically by translation into HTML.

white space — The breathing room on a page, white space refers to the parts of a document or display that aren't occupied by text or other visual elements. A certain amount of white space is essential to make documents attractive and readable.

Windows (MS-Windows) — The astonishingly popular (and sometimes frustrating) GUI environment for PCs from Microsoft Corporation, Windows is the GUI of choice for most desktop computer users.

World Wide Web (WWW or W3) — The complete collection of all Web servers available on the Internet, which comes as close to containing the "sum of human knowledge" as anything we've ever seen.

worm — A self-replicating computer program that seeks to visit as many locations on a network as possible. Less of a nuisance than viruses, worms still consume precious network bandwidth and are abhorred for that reason.

WWWInline — Another basic VRML node, WWWInline is often recommended as the root node when constructing a virtual world for Web display.

WYSIWYG (What You See Is What You Get) — A term used to describe text editors or other layout tools (like HTML authoring tools) that attempt to show their users on-screen what final, finished documents will look like.

X Windows — The GUI of choice for UNIX systems, X Windows offers a graphical window, icon, and mouse metaphor similar to (but much more robust and powerful than) Microsoft Windows.

Xobject — Within Macromedia Director, Xobject refers to externally defined data resources, such as sounds, graphics, or animated sequences, for inclusion within a Director film strip. Director support for Xobjects greatly expands the type and quality of materials that can be included within its playback environment.

Index

· ·

• *Symbols & Numbers* •

• *A* •